THE HEATH GOVERNMENT 1970–1974
A Reappraisal

THE HEATH GOVERNMENT 1970–1974

A REAPPRAISAL

Edited by Stuart Ball and Anthony Seldon

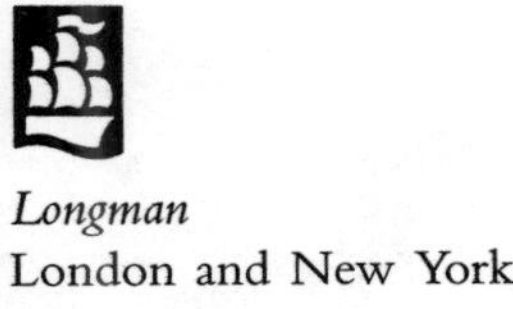

Longman
London and New York

Addison Wesley Longman Group Limited,
Edinburgh Gate
Harlow, Essex CM20 2JE, England
and Associated Companies throughout the world.

Published in the United States of America
by Addison Wesley Longman Publishing, New York

First published 1996

ISBN 0 582 25992 4 CSD
ISBN 0 582 25991 6 PPR

British Library Cataloguing-in-Publication Data

A catalogue record for this book is
available from the British Library

Library of Congress Cataloging-in-Publication Data

Ball, Stuart, 1956–
The Heath government, 1970–1974 : a reappraisal / edited by Stuart Ball and Anthony Seldon.
p. cm.
Includes bibliographical references and index.
ISBN 0–582–25992–4 (CSD). — ISBN 0–582–25991–6 (PPR)
1. Great Britain—Politics and government—1964–1979. 2. Heath, Edward. I. Seldon, Anthony. II. Title.
DA592.B28 1996
941.085′7—dc20 9549157
CIP

Set by 20 in 10/12 Bembo
Produced by Longman Singapore Publishers (Pte) Ltd.
Printed in Singapore

Contents

The Heath Government 1970–1974

Notes on contributors

Paul Arthur is Professor of Politics at the University of Ulster. He is author of *Government and Politics of Northern Ireland* (Longman, 1980, 1984, 1987); *Northern Ireland since 1968* [with K. Jeffery] (Blackwell, 1986) – a new edition will appear early in 1996; *Aspirations and Assertions: Britain, Ireland and the Northern Ireland Problem* (Routledge, forthcoming); 'Reading Violence: Ireland', in D. E. Apter and Bruce Kepferer (eds), *Democracy and Violence* (Macmillan, forthcoming).

Stuart Ball is a Reader in History at the University of Leicester. He is author of *Baldwin and the Conservative Party: The Crisis of 1929–31* (Yale University Press, 1988) and *The Conservative Party and British Politics 1902–51* (Longman, 1995), and editor of *Parliament and Politics in the Age of Baldwin and MacDonald: The Headlam Diaries 1923–35* (The Historians' Press, 1992) and *The Conservative Party since 1945* (Manchester University Press, forthcoming). He has co-edited *Conservative Century: The Conservative Party since 1900* (Oxford University Press, 1994).

Lewis Baston took a First in PPE in 1991 and subsequently became a postgraduate student at Nuffield College, Oxford. He is currently Research Fellow at the Institute of Contemporary British History and is chief researcher on the forthcoming biography of John Major. He is a regular contributor to the political press, including *Parliamentary Brief*.

Vernon Bogdanor is Reader in Government at the University of Oxford and a Fellow and Tutor in Politics at Brasenose College. His many publications include *Devolution* (Oxford University, 1979), *The People and the Party System* (Cambridge University Press, 1981), *Multi-Party Politics and the Constitution* (Cambridge University Press, 1983) and *What is Proportional Representation?* (Martin Robertson, 1984). He has edited *Coalition Government in Western Europe* (Heinemann, 1983), *Liberal Party Politics* (Oxford University Press, 1983), *Representatives of the*

People? (Gower, 1985), and *Constitutions in Democratic Politics* (Policy Studies Institute, 1988); he was also co-editor of *The Age of Affluence 1951–64* (Macmillan, 1970). His latest publications are *The Monarchy and the Constitution* (Oxford University Press, 1995) and *Essays on Politics and the Constitution* (Dartmouth, 1995).

Alec Cairncross was Master of St Peter's College, Oxford until his retiral in 1978. He is the author of numerous books, including *Home and Foreign Investment 1870–1913* (Cambridge University Press, 1953); *Years of Recovery: British Economic Policy 1945–51* (Methuen, 1985); *The British Economy since 1945* (second edition, Blackwell, 1995); *Managing the British Economy in the 1960s* (Macmillan, 1995); *Economic Ideas and Government Policy: Studies in Contemporary History* (Routledge, 1995); and *A Treasury Diary 1964–69* (The Historians' Press, 1995).

Christopher Hill is Montague Burton Professor of International Relations at the London School of Economics and Political Science. He is the author of *Cabinet Decisions in Foreign Policy: The British Experience, October 1938–June 1941* (Cambridge University Press, 1991) and the editor (with Pamela Beshoff) of *Two Worlds of International Relations: Academics, Practitioners and the Trade in Ideas* (Routledge, 1994).

Dennis Kavanagh is Professor in Politics at the University of Liverpool. His most recent publications include *The British General Election of 1992*, with David Butler (Macmillan, 1992), *The Major Effect*, co-edited with Anthony Seldon (Macmillan, 1994), and *Election Campaigning: The New Politics of Marketing* (Blackwell, 1995).

Zig Layton-Henry is Professor of Politics and Director of the ESRC Centre for Research in Ethnic Relations at the University of Warwick. He is author of *The Politics of Race in Britain* (1984) and *The Politics of Immigration* (1992). He is editor of *Conservative Party Politics* (1980), *Conservative Politics in Western Europe* (1982), *Race Government and Politics in Britain* (1986, with Paul Rich) and *The Political Rights of Migrant Workers in Western Europe* (1990).

Christopher Lord is Jean Monnet Chair in European Studies and Senior Lecturer in Politics at the University of Leeds. He is the author of *British Entry to the European Community under the Heath Government of 1970–4* (Dartmouth, 1993) and *Absent at the Creation: Why Britain did not join in the Beginnings of the European Community, 1950–2* (Dartmouth, 1995).

Rodney Lowe is a Reader in Economic and Social History at the University of Bristol. He is the author of *Adjusting to Democracy* (Oxford University Press, 1986), *The Welfare State in Britain since 1945* (Macmillan, 1993) and *The Watershed Years: The Replanning of the Welfare State in Britain, 1957–1964* (Oxford University Press, forthcoming), as well as many articles on twentieth-century welfare policy.

John Ramsden is Professor of Modern History at Queen Mary and Westfield College, University of London. He is the author of three volumes in the Longman History of the Conservative Party, *The Age of Balfour and Baldwin 1902–1940* (1978), *The Age of Churchill and Eden, 1957–1975* (1995), *The Winds of Change: Macmillan to Heath, 1957–1975* (1996), and of *The Making of Conservative Party Policy* (Longman, 1980).

Anthony Seldon is the founding Director of the Institute of Contemporary British History and Deputy Headmaster of St Dunstan's College. He is author of *Churchill's Indian Summer: The Conservative Government 1951–55* (Hodder and Stoughton, 1981); among works he has edited and co-edited are *Ruling Performance: British Governments from Attlee to Thatcher* (Blackwell, 1987), *The Thatcher Effect* (Oxford University Press, 1989), *The Major Effect* (Macmillan, 1994), and *Conservative Century: The Conservative Party since 1900* (Oxford University Press, 1994).

Robert Taylor is the employment editor of the *Financial Times*. He is the author of a number of books on industrial relations and labour markets including *The Fifth Estate: Britain's Unions in the Modern World* (Routledge and Kegan Paul, 1978 and Pan, 1980); *Workers and the New Depression* (Macmillan, 1982); *The Trade Union Question in British Politics since 1945* (Blackwell, 1993) and *The Future of the Trade Unions* (André Deutsch, 1994).

Kevin Theakston is Senior Lecturer in Politics at the University of Leeds. He is author of *Junior Ministers in British Government* (Blackwell, 1987), *The Labour Party and Whitehall* (Routledge, 1992), and *The Civil Service since 1945* (Blackwell and the Institute of Contemporary British History, 1995).

John Young is Professor of Politics at the University of Leicester. His publications include *Britain, France and the Unity of Europe 1945–51*

(Leicester University Press, 1984), *France, the Cold War and the Western Alliance* (Pinter, 1990), *Cold War Europe 1945–1989* (Edward Arnold, 1991), *Britain and Europe Unity, 1945–92* (Macmillan, 1993), and *Winston Churchill's Last Campaign: Britain and Cold War, 1951–5* (Oxford University Press, 1996).

Preface and acknowledgements

As the end of the twentieth century approaches, the importance of the Heath government of 1970–74 as a turning point in postwar British history is becoming ever more apparent. This volume, sponsored by the Institute of Contemporary British History, aims to provide a re-assessment of this crucial but under-studied administration. It explores the conduct and effectiveness of the government in all significant aspects of its domestic and external policies, the extent to which it was forced to adapt to circumstances and change direction, and the political atmosphere in which it operated. The records of government departments will not become available until 2006, and the present volume is based upon other sources (in particular in the Conservative Party archive), contemporary materials, and interviews with persons involved. From these perspectives we believe that a clearer and fuller picture of the Heath government has emerged, illuminating not only the events of the early 1970s but also wider themes and issues in contemporary British history.

The editors wish to thank the Conservative Party for permitting the authors access to papers in the archive at the Bodleian Library for the period 1965–74, and we are especially grateful to Alistair Cooke, Director of the Conservative Political Centre, for his guidance and support. We are much indebted to Martin Maw, the archivist responsible for the Conservative Party papers at the Bodleian, for invaluable guidance through this rich and complex collection, and also to the staff of the Modern Manuscripts Reading Room where the documents are consulted.

We would like to thank the many ministers, MPs, civil servants and Party officers of the period, not all of whom can be named, who kindly gave interviews or assisted the project with advice and information. The 'witness' seminars on the Heath government organised by the Institute of Contemporary British History, and held at the Institute of Historical Research, University of London, were a fruitful source of insight, and we are grateful to all those who attended them and contributed to the discussion. The transcripts of these sessions have been published in the journal of the ICBH, *Contemporary Record*.

David Butler kindly hosted the initial meeting associated with this volume at Nuffield College in February 1994. This was attended by the contributors to the book and by other leading figures in the field, and we are grateful to all those who were present for the many constructive comments voiced on that occasion.

The editors are grateful to the contributors for the care taken in the researching and writing of their chapters, and for their responsiveness to editorial suggestions. We would like to thank Andrew MacLennan of Longman for his cheerful support of the project, and all those at Longman involved in the production of the finished book.

On a personal note, Stuart Ball is grateful for the unstinting support and encouragement of his family, and above all of his wife, Gillian, who has been a tower of strength during the pressures of the last few years. Anthony Seldon wishes to thank his wonderful colleagues at the ICBH, and in particular Peter Catterall, Peter Hennessy and Virginia Preston. Annemarie Weitzel, his secretary, remains a saint, and the toleration and support of his wife Joanna and their three children remain boundless.

Stuart Ball
Anthony Seldon
November 1995

List of abbreviations

ACP	Advisory Committee on Policy
CA	Conservative Association
CAP	Common Agricultural Policy
CBI	Confederation of British Industry
CCO	Conservative Central Office
CPA	Conservative Party Archives, Bodleian Library
CPAG	Child Poverty Action Group
CPRS	Central Policy Review Staff
CRD	Conservative Research Department
CSCE	Conference on Security Cooperation in Europe
CSD	Civil Service Department
DTI	Department of Trade and Industry
DoE	Department of the Environment
EC	European Community
EMU	Economic and Monetary Union
ERDF	European Regional Development Fund
FCO	Foreign and Commonwealth Office
FIS	Family Income Supplement
GDP	Gross Domestic Product
ICBH	Institute of Contemporary British History
IEA	Institute of Economic Affairs
IMF	International Monetary Fund
IRA	Irish Republican Army
LCC	Leader's Consultative Committee
MBFR	Mutual Balanced Force Reductions
NEDC	National Economic Development Council
NIO	Northern Ireland Office
NIRC	National Industrial Relations Court
NU	National Union of Conservative and Unionist Associations
NUM	National Union of Mineworkers
OECD	Organisation for Economic Cooperation and Development
OG	Official Group

OPEC	Organisation of Petroleum-Exporting Countries
PAR	Programme Analysis and Review
PESC	Public Expenditure Systems Control
PSRU	Public Sector Research Unit
RUC	Royal Ulster Constabulary
SC	Steering Committee
TGWU	Transport and General Workers' Union
TUC	Trades Union Congress
UDA	Ulster Defence Association

CHAPTER ONE

The Heath government in history

Anthony Seldon

The Heath government was in office from June 1970 to February 1974 during the main turning point in postwar British history. Five years before it came to power, the Labour government of Harold Wilson set up a Prices and Incomes Board, Tony Crosland's circular on secondary schooling sought to give comprehensive schools a decisive push and kill off grammar schools, and the National Plan was published. In this 'old' world, the state was seen as having a major role as monopoly supplier of many goods and services, trade unions were lauded and powerful, and the pursuit of equality was regarded as a core objective of government. Five years after Heath's government fell from power, Mrs Thatcher was in Downing Street in 1979, and a new world was shortly to unfold where government itself was no longer considered to be benign, priority was given to boosting private provision at the expense of the collective, and a vast expansion of unemployment and even poverty was openly tolerated. The Heath government is intriguing in part because it promoted elements of both the old and the new worlds and was trapped uneasily as one paradigm was beginning to lose its hold, but the other model had yet to secure intellectual credibility or popular backing. The government's predicament moreover was compounded as it was in office at a time of unusual unrest and turbulence, both domestically and internationally. Two events in particular occurred in 1973: the ending of the Bretton Woods system, and the first great oil shock, both having profound and lasting repercussions.

RIVAL INTERPRETATIONS

The government is fascinating also because it has become such a battleground of rival views and interpretations. Historical assessment of Heath's government has been clouded by a number of factors. The government's most decisive and long-lasting initiative was taking Britain into the European Economic Community (EEC). But opinion is sharply divided on whether it was a wise and necessary move, and whether membership benefited Britain. The second difficulty stems from the impact of Thatcherism, the apparent success of which in the 1980s made Heath's government look wrong-headed and indecisive. Third, the government changed course in several areas mid-term; were those switches wise pragmatism, inevitable, or unprincipled weakness? Finally, Heath as Prime Minister was unusually single-minded: was this very personal style of leadership responsible for the apparent inconsistencies and floundering, or did it result in the government achieving as much as it did in very volatile and difficult circumstances? Four main interpretations of the government present themselves.

- The government was a success, implementing most of its manifesto pledges, and showing flexibility in the face of great difficulties (the Heath loyalist view).
- The government was a failure, with its initial right-wing objectives being abandoned in the face of difficulties (the Thatcherite view).
- The government had some initial successes, but failed ultimately as little or nothing was left of its policies in the longer run (the pessimistic view).
- The government achieved some successes, but failed ultimately to achieve fully its objectives because of circumstances beyond its control (the contingencies view).

Each of these views, which are not mutually exclusive, will be considered before an answer is advanced which best fits the historical evidence of the years 1970–74.

A SUCCESSFUL GOVERNMENT

The major case for the government has been left to be made by Sir Edward Heath himself and a very few loyal supporters.[1] Overwhelmingly, the balance of judgement on the government's record has been critical. Even the Conservative Party rapidly disowned it after Heath's defeat as party leader in 1975.[2] Most press and pundit commentary after the February 1974 election defeat was critical of the government's

1. Heath gave a full defence of his policy in his ICBH conference paper on 11 July 1995. Sympathetic memoirs are I. Gilmour, *Dancing with Dogma* (London, 1992) and P. Walker, *Staying Power* (London, 1991). The author wishes to thank John Barnes, Dennis Kavanagh and John Ramsden for their comments on an earlier draft.

2. D. Kavanagh, 'The Heath Government 1970–74', in P. Hennessy and A. Seldon (eds), *Ruling Performance: British Governments from Attlee to Thatcher* (Oxford, 1987), 216.

achievement, as has been subsequent writing, notably works by Jock Bruce-Gardyne, Patrick Cosgrave, Martin Holmes and Lady Thatcher herself.[3] John Campbell's biography published in 1993 has redressed the balance to some extent, arguing that Heath's 'reputation is beginning to be restored'. But Campbell never explains exactly why he believes this to be the case, nor is he particularly clear about where he stands on the government's record.[4]

The loyalist view points to some substantial achievements. Many manifesto pledges were fulfilled, as ministers were quick to observe in both 1974 general elections. The 1970 manifesto, *A Better Tomorrow*, was unusually detailed in its policy commitments, many of which were realised by 1974: entry into the EEC, income tax cuts and tax reform, industrial relations reform, recasting of local housing finance, ending of compulsory comprehensive education, some steps of denationalisation (or privatisation) and greater selectivity in welfare.[5]

Heath himself lays stress on the broad consultation and very careful preparation for office during the period of opposition from 1964–70, the most thorough planning the Party has ever undertaken: 'by the time we came to 1970 we had everything we needed for policy and for the manifesto . . . we knew we could go straight ahead on that basis'.[6] He argues that on matters of social and economic policy, he was firmly in the 'One Nation' centre tradition of former Conservative Prime Ministers Anthony Eden and Harold Macmillan. Rodney Lowe in Chapter 8 finds 'competition with compassion' to be the aims in social policy, an area in which the government was unusually active, as in housing finance, in reorganisation of the National Health Service, and in expansionary policies in education. The Commonwealth Immigration Act of 1971 went some way to reducing tension over a highly volatile area, taking the initiative away from Enoch Powell and the far right, notably the National Front.

In foreign policy, the government placed the European relationship above both that with the Commonwealth and the 'special relationship' with the United States, although Heath enjoyed cordial personal

3. J. Bruce-Gardyne, *Whatever Happened to the Quiet Revolution?* (London, 1974); P. Cosgrave, 'The failure of the Conservative Party, 1945–75', in R.E. Tyrrell, Jr. (ed.), *The Future That Doesn't Work: Social Democracy's Failures in Britain* (New York, 1977), 95–125; M. Holmes, *Political Pressure and Economic Policy, British Government 1970–74* (London, 1982); M. Thatcher, *The Path to Power* (London, 1995).

4. J. Campbell, *Edward Heath: A Biography* (London, 1993), 811; the best recent analysis is in J. Ramsden, *The Winds of Change* (London, 1996), 319–83.

5. Kavanagh, 'Heath Government 1970–74', 222.

6. Author's interview with Sir Edward Heath, 21 February 1995.

relations with Richard Nixon (US President 1969–74).[7] Heath's motivations for achieving what he had failed to do in 1961–63, namely Britain's entry into the EEC, was threefold: avoiding another European war; providing a major stimulus to British industry; and finding an appropriate role for Britain after the empire had been dismantled.[8] John Young below argues that entry into the EEC was 'a great success for the Prime Minister and the most important step for Britain taken by his government'. Moreover he 'seemed to win reasonable terms for British membership'.[9] The Conservative Party was split on the European issue (if only mildly compared to the 1990s), and public support for entry fell below 20 per cent in early 1971.[10] Despite the political difficulties at home of bringing off entry into the EEC, Christopher Hill and Christopher Lord in their chapter argue that Heath should have gone even further with a reappraisal of British foreign policy and re-thinking of overseas aspirations.[11]

Economic policy saw the largest raft of reforms. The Industrial Relations Act of 1971 introduced legislation on industrial relations which Harold Wilson and Barbara Castle had conspicuously failed to achieve in 1969 with their *In Place of Strife*: the 1971 Act was indeed the most dramatic labour legislation to be introduced since 1945. Major reforms to indirect tax (value added tax) and corporation tax were initiated. Some limited measures of privatisation occurred in the cases of Thomas Cook, the travel agent, and the state-owned public houses in Carlisle and in Scotland. But overall economic policy saw little consistency over the life of the government. The death a month after the 1970 general election of Iain Macleod, the powerful and independent-minded Chancellor of the Exchequer, militated against continuity. Douglas Allen, Permanent Secretary at the Treasury, noted 'nearly all the emphasis of Macleod's approach was totally different from what happened within the next two years'.[12] Macleod was an expenditure cutter and non-intervener, whereas government expenditure was to

7. Sir Donald Maitland and Lord Armstrong, evidence in 'The Heath Government' witness seminar, *Contemporary Record*, vol. 9 no. 1 (1995), 208.

8. Armstrong, ibid., 206.

9. John Young, Chapter 11 below, 283.

10. M.A. Young, 'The Heath Government reassessed', *Contemporary Record*, vol. 3, no. 2 (1989), 25.

11. Christopher Hill and Christopher Lord, Chapter 12 below, 312–4.

12. Lord Croham (Douglas Allen), 'The Heath Government' witness seminar (1995), 190. Robert Shepherd reaches a similar conclusion in his biography: 'the loss of the most effective political communicator of his generation – in the Commons, on the conference platform and on television – would have been damaging at any time, but it came when the Tories could ill afford it.' *Iain Macleod: A Biography* (London, 1994), 538.

increase dramatically, and policy toward industry – notably in the Industry Act of 1972 – to become highly interventionist. More significant still was the deterioration of the economic outlook after 1971, with unemployment and inflation both rising swiftly, producing an inevitable reappraisal of policy. This may well have been the more important factor: Macleod might well have been forced by circumstances to behave little differently to his successor Tony Barber.

No premier since Lloyd George has been such an innovator in organisational reform as Heath, or believed in its importance to national regeneration as clearly, according to Peter Hennessy.[13] Institutional reform was indeed the vogue in the 1960s and 1970s, in the US as well as in Europe, with many politicians perhaps naively seeing it as a panacea for stagnant growth and other ills. To Kenneth O. Morgan, Heath's belief in institutional reform and managerialism made him 'resemble not so much a British party politician as a French centre-right technocrat on the pattern of Raymond Barre or Edouard Balladur.'[14] Whitehall departments were reduced in number, and two 'super-departments', Trade and Industry, and Environment, created. The Central Policy Review Staff (or 'Think Tank') was set up; a new management scheme to improve Whitehall efficiency introduced, Programme Analysis and Review (PAR); functions were hived off from departments to executive agencies, such as the Procurement Executive, and unprecedentedly large numbers of outside professionals introduced into Whitehall as political advisers. Both the National Health Service and local government were reformed, the latter by the Local Government Act of 1972.

Finally, the government was innovative over policy to Northern Ireland. In March 1972, Heath, in the face of mounting civil unrest, suspended the Northern Ireland Parliament at Stormont, and instituted direct rule from London. In December 1973, a conference was held at Sunningdale in Berkshire, out of which agreement was reached to establish a Council of Ireland involving all parties, the transfer of power to a new assembly and executive in Belfast, and the end of direct rule from January 1974. This was to prove the boldest initiative on Northern Ireland until the 1990s. The February 1974 general election, however, damaged its prospects for success when 11 out of 12 seats were won by 'Loyalist' critics, and the new power-sharing executive eventually collapsed in May 1974. The century-old Conservative–Unionist alliance was at an end.

Michael A. Young highlights the administration's achievement: 'It

13. P. Hennessy, 'Awaiting Repair', *Times Educational Supplement*, 2 July 1993.
14. K.O. Morgan, 'One of Us', *New Statesman and Society*, 2 July 1993.

was a government that was prepared to tackle tough issues and take difficult decisions. In many respects it was a government ahead of its time.' It did not lack principles or convictions, he argues, but 'it was prepared to sacrifice philosophical consistency for the national interest'.[15] It is not a popular line of argument, but as Campbell has shown, the Heath government is again, in the 1990s, being taken more seriously by academics and commentators.

CRITICS FROM THE RIGHT

'The Heath Government', in the eyes of Martin Holmes, Thatcher loyalist and arch Heath detractor, 'was a disaster for the Conservative party, and for the people of Britain.' Moreover, its only legacy was 'the lessons of failure'.[16] Mrs Thatcher (if not Geoffrey Howe) looked back in disapproval on the government to which she belonged when she wrote her memoirs in the mid-1990s.[17] To her 'the poisoned legacy of our U-turns was that we had no firm principles, let alone much of a record' to show for all the effort during 1970–74.

To those of a Thatcherite or 'new right' persuasion, the government was a failure precisely because it did not adhere to policies which it had initially laid out. Instead it abandoned them progressively after the first eighteen months in office in favour of conciliatory and consensus policies which, it is argued, had been proved such a failure in the years since 1945. To Cosgrave, one of the earliest critics, Heath lost his nerve when conditions became adverse in 1971–72: 'he pondered the spectrum of consensus and, like Mr Macmillan, moved to the left'.[18] There is an echo here in the charge of betrayal made by the Thatcherite right against the Major government in the 1990s.

A key event in the new right interpretation of Heath is the conference of the shadow cabinet that took place at the Selsdon Park Hotel near Croydon, over a weekend in January 1970. At this conference, it is asserted, the shadow cabinet moved to the right, and sounded a tough note at the press conference on law and order. At the general election, new right policies were again articulated, notably reducing government expenditure, reducing tax to provide incentives, adopting a policy of detachment to industry (no further subsidies for lame

15. M.A. Young, 'Heath Government reassessed', 26.

16. M. Holmes, 'The Heath Government reassessed', *Contemporary Record*, vol. 3, no. 2 (1989), 27.

17. Thatcher, *Path to Power*, 240; G. Howe, *Conflict of Loyalty* (London, 1994).

18. Cosgrave, 'Failure of the Conservative Party', 122.

ducks'), no incomes policies, smaller and more effective government, and greater selectivity and direction in welfare spending. Trade unions were to be legislated on, and their power significantly limited. The 1970 manifesto, *A Better Tomorrow*, declared boldly that 'once a decision is taken, once a policy is established, the Prime Minister and his colleagues should have the courage to stick to it'.[19] An obscure undertaking was given in a Conservative Party press release to reduce the rise in prices 'at a stroke'. (There is some evidence for doubting that this much-quoted 'promise' was approved by shadow ministers.)

Once in power, the government – it is alleged – failed to stand by its declared objectives, in contrast to the performance of Mrs Thatcher who not only announced at the 1980 Conservative annual party conference that 'the Lady's not for turning', but stuck to her objectives of confronting trade unions, and reducing direct taxation and government spending when economic conditions turned adverse. No fewer than four U-turns were allegedly executed by the Heath government.[20] Rather than pursuing a policy of privatisation, the opposite occurred when two companies were bailed out of financial difficulty in 1971 and taken into public ownership: Upper Clyde Shipbuilders and Rolls-Royce (though the latter's cars division was immediately privatised again). The following year saw economic reversals when regional policy was reintroduced via the establishment of an Industrial Development Executive, and a vigorous industrial policy in the 1972 Industry Act. The latter was described by the chairman of the Conservative backbench 1922 Committee as 'a Socialist bill by ethic and philosophy'.[21] The third U-turn was the abandonment of the hands-off approach to trade unions of the 1971 Act and the adoption of a concerted approach to bring government, unions and the Confederation of British Industry (CBI) together in tripartite talks, initiated in September 1972. A compulsory prices and incomes policy followed in November 1972, which caused particular upset to some on the right like Bruce-Gardyne, Nicholas Ridley and Ian Gow, who regarded the repudiation of the 1970 'no incomes policy' pledge as a signal betrayal.[22] The final U-turn was the considerable increase in public expenditure in late 1972 and 1973 (after which the government changed tack again in May 1973 and again that December and brought in huge expenditure cuts).

The Thatcherite or new right critics see Heath and the Cabinet as having fallen under the spell of civil servants, particularly at the Cabinet

19. Conservative Party Manifesto 1970, *A Better Tomorrow* (London, 1970).
20. Stuart Ball, Chapter 13 below, 328–30, sees five U-turns.
21. *House of Commons Debates*, 5th series, vol 841, col. 2402, 28 July 1972.
22. Lord Howe, 'The Heath Government' witness seminar, 192.

Office and the Foreign and Commonwealth Office, a 'trap' Mrs Thatcher was careful to avoid after 1979. David Howell, a junior minister under Heath and a new right enthusiast, argues that the reforming and anti-government zeal that had informed Conservative thinking on the civil service prior to 1970 was sabotaged by senior civil servants, infected deeply with a Keynesian dirigiste mentality.[23] Far from the size of government being reduced, the size of the public sector increased by an estimated 400,000 officials. Further evidence of the government's weakness is seen in the calling of five states of emergency (out of a total of only twelve since governments were given this weapon by the Emergency Powers Act of 1920).[24] Jeremy Thorpe, Liberal leader, was prompted to ask in November 1973 in the House of Commons 'whether there had ever been a precedent for a State of Emergency being declared for a threatened ban on overtime'.[25] Douglas Hurd, Heath's close ally and Political Secretary from 1970–74, is marshalled by the new right to provide further evidence of the government's weakness and appeasement: during the 1972 miners' strike, the government – he writes – was 'wandering vainly over [a] battlefield looking for someone to surrender to – and being massacred all the time'.[26]

Failure of the government is further reflected in the eyes of Cosgrave and co. by published statistics: over 23 million days lost to strikes in 1972, the largest number since 1926, the year of the General Strike; a postwar record high level of inflation in the month the government left office, February 1974; a rapid increase in 1971–73 of M3, a broad measure of money supply in the economy; higher annual increases in government expenditures in many departmental areas than even during the 1964–70 Labour government.

Further government actions added to new right ire: despite the 1971 Act, immigration continued to rise significantly, due in large part to a liberal policy on entry to Britain after the expulsion by Idi Amin of Asians from Uganda after August 1972. The government was weak on terrorism, seen in the release from custody of Leila Khaled, the Palestinian hijacker, in 1970, and in negotiations with the Provisional IRA in the search for a settlement in Northern Ireland. The Sunningdale Agreement, never popular with the more hard-line Protestant Unionists, is a further object of oppobrium for compromising Unionism and threatening the position of the Protestants. Finally, the government's

23. Auathor's interview with David Howell, 20 April 1995.

24. Kavanagh, 'Heath Government 1970–74', 227.

25. *House of Commons Debates*, 5th series, vol. 864, col. 263, 13 November 1973.

26. D. Hurd, *An End to Promises* (London, 1979), 103. Cited by Holmes, 'The Heath Government reassessed', 27.

entry into the EEC, and on the terms attained, subsequently improved by both Wilson and Thatcher, is a source of singular hostility from the new right.

Subscribers to this particular view saw defeat at the general election in February 1974 as the inevitable fruit of the U-turns and sacrifice of principle. 'All the great ideas of 1970 had been abandoned', writes Cosgrave of the 1974 general election, 'and Conservatives did not go into battle – as they had done in that election – convinced that they were standing for something different from socialism.'[27] Holmes neatly summarises the judgment from the new right: 'Heath's U-turns led to 27% inflation . . . Heath nationalised more industries than his Labour predecessor whereas Thatcher has successfully privatised; Heath was repeatedly humiliated by the unions while Mrs Thatcher . . . tamed trade union power . . . Heath lost both 1974 elections in contrast to Mrs Thatcher's electoral hat trick'.[28]

LONG-TERM FAILURE

As with the second perspective, this interpretation praises many of the initial objectives, and applauds some of the policies, which anticipated many of the stances both main political parties were progressively to adopt, the Conservatives after 1975, and Labour under successive leaders after 1983. But it still sees the government as ultimately a failure because so few of its policies endured. John Campbell praises the government for anticipating many of the successful innovations of the Thatcher government after 1979, including greater efficiency in government and business, more competition and market discipline, while at the same time deploring the socially divisive way that Mrs Thatcher introduced these policies.[29] According to Dennis Kavanagh, leaving aside entry into the EEC, 'the Heath Government has probably left the least policy legacies of any postwar government' (with the exception of the Home government of 1963–64).[30] It might be added that even EEC entry would not have survived if the only national referendum to have been held in the UK had gone against it in 1975. Also, had Wilson won in 1970, he would almost certainly have continued to work for admittance

27. Cosgrave, 'Failure of the Conservative Party', 123.
28. Holmes, 'Heath Government reassessed', 26.
29. Campbell, *Edward Heath: A Biography,* 810–11. Also 'The Heathman – an interview with John Campbell', *Contemporary Record*, vol. 7, no. 3 (1992), 587–8.
30. Kavanagh, 'Heath Government 1970–74', 233–4.

to the EEC. (De Gaulle, who had blocked his application in 1967–68, had resigned in 1968.)

Supporters of this school observe that the government's organisational reforms were mostly abandoned after 1974. The Department of Trade and Industry (DTI) was partly dismantled in 1973 (when Energy became a separate department in December) and the remainder was broken in three in March 1974. Environment was partly dismembered in 1976, when Transport was hived off. Programme Analysis and Review never lived up to its hopes and was formally abolished in 1979, as was the Central Policy Review Staff in 1983. The health and local government reforms were widely criticised and partly dismantled subsequently. Neither minister directly concerned, Joseph and Walker, had adequately thought through what they were trying to achieve. The Industrial Relations Act was repealed by the incoming Labour government, as was part of the Housing Finance Act. Heath's incomes policy was abandoned, and extension of comprehensive schooling was again, albeit briefly, made compulsory for Local Education Authorities (though the rate of creation of new comprehensives never reached the number which came to fruition under Heath). The Northern Ireland initiative lasted only to the Ulster workers' strike in May 1974. Museum charging, and a host of other policies, did not last even until the government's end in February 1974.

GOOD INTENTIONS, FAIR STRATEGY, HOSTILE ENVIRONMENT

The final interpretation stresses the powerful adverse circumstances faced by the government. But for these factors, Heath's attempt to make the *status quo* work better might have succeeded. Had it done so, Britain today would have had a more social democratic type of state, with closer cooperation between industry, labour and government, and become more of the 'developmental state', as advocated by David Marquand in his *The Unprincipled Society* (1988). Heath's project, according to Keith Middlemas, sought no less than to modernise the British state, and to galvanise industry, hence the establishment of the DTI as a powerhouse to accomplish it. Financial institutions Heath saw as a key to economic success, hence the reforms in 1970–71 in competition and credit control designed to improve the flow of cash from the financial sector into industry. He wanted a new deal with labour, hence the Industrial Relations Act. The whole drive into Europe was similarly forward-looking. To Middlemas, 'Heath's is the first synoptic attempt to rework the postwar settlement in accordance with the original aims.' But as Middlemas also argues, 'at the same time it is backward-looking, because he is trying to make work and revive the original postwar settlement which by the early 1970s may well have been already fatally weak'.[31] Why did the drive, which contained both forward and backward looking elements, become unstuck?

A first constraint was the death of Macleod. Heath was 'terribly shaken'[32] by the news, and 'deeply, personally offended' by the way the media handled it.[33] Robert Armstrong, who was Heath's Principal Private Secretary at Number 10, has noted that 'his loss unbalanced the government for a considerable period of time'.[34] The view of Francis Pym, Heath's Chief Whip, was that 'Iain Macleod was the heaviest heavyweight and he lost his absolutely star performer and one on whom so much of the Cabinet and the party centred.'[35] Terence Higgins, then a Treasury minister, argues that if Macleod had remained alive 'the course of the government would have been quite different'.[36] No government this century indeed has suffered the blow of losing such a crucial player at its outset, but it is wrong to lay so much weight on the role of any one individual at the expense of circumstances, which might well have led him to behave quite differently to expectations.

Second, the government was not popular, seen in losses at by-elections, in which the Liberals were riding high (Sutton and Cheam, Ely and Ripon), mopping up support from middle classes alienated from the government.[37] For much of the time from the end of 1970 until January 1974, Gallup recorded a Labour lead in opinion polls. With the exception of *The Times* and *The Economist*, which Campbell depends on perhaps overmuch, the intellectual and media climate was mostly critical of the government. The *Daily Telegraph* and the *Spectator* were in particular often hostile. There was little time or opportunity to bask in comfort after the 1970 election victory, and scant room for manoeuvre, or ability to pursue and persist with unpopular policies.

The domestic environment was unpromising. Trade unions were at

31. D. Marquand, *The Unprincipled Society* (London, 1988). The Middlemas quotations are taken from a forthcoming *Contemporary Record* interview, based on his new book *Orchestrating Europe, The Informal Politics of the European Union 1973–95*. (London, 1995).

32. Sir Timothy Kitson, 'The Heath Government' witness seminar, 194. Kitson was Heath's Parliamentary Private Secretary.

33. Sir Donald Maitland, 'The Heath Government' witness seminar, 195. Maitland was Chief Press Secretary.

34. Lord Armstrong, ibid., 194. See also the comment of Robert Shepherd in note 12 above.

35. Lord Pym, ibid., 195.

36. Sir Terence Higgins, ibid., 195.

37. Stuart Ball, Chapter 13 below.

the height of their powers, and the ability of union leaders to command obedience from the rank and file at a low. The unions found a way of legally defeating the Industrial Relations Act of 1971, and then when union leaders subsequently asked their members to abide by the terms of the statutory incomes policy, the miners resisted, prompting a crisis that ultimately led to Heath calling the 1974 general election. Industry was sluggish to respond to chiding from government to invest more and to become more competitive. The CBI failed also at the critical point in the tripartite discussions on counter-inflation in early 1974 to support the government line. So the government could not depend on capital any more than on labour. Violence in Northern Ireland was escalating. Student and youth unrest was at a high point, with student extremism being partly informed by industrial and extremist political agitation. The National Front and far left groups such as the Socialist Workers' Party were self-confident. Decimalisation of the currency in February 1971 contributed to a sense of unease, especially among the elderly. The property boom, and distaste for some of its more unsavoury gainers, was a further destabilising factor. Inflation undermined savings and confidence, with retail prices rising by over a third during the life of the government. The rise of unemployment to over one million in January 1972 caused further social unrest, with persistent strikes and states of emergency deepening the malaise. All of these woes were beamed nightly onto the nation's television screens, contributing to a growing belief that the government was not the master of events.

Above all, international developments caused profound difficulties, including the collapse of the dollar and the end of the Bretton Woods system, which ended fixed exchange rates and led to fluctuating currencies. Then in the autumn of 1973, at arguably the worst moment for the government in the midst of negotiations with the National Union of Mineworkers, the Yom Kippur war in the Middle East sparked a quadrupling of oil prices. Raw material price inflation further contributed to blowing the counter-inflation strategy off course in the two years after January 1972, cocoa rose in price by 173 per cent, and zinc by 308 per cent.[38]

It is a supreme irony that this government, the most systematically prepared of any Conservative government since the war according to John Ramsden, and with the innovation of the Central Policy Review Staff to help keep it on track, should have been one of the most bounced off course of any government this century.[39] Ultimately, Heath

38. Cited in M.A. Young, 'Heath Government reassessed', 24.

39. See 'Conservative Party Policy Making' witness seminar, *Contemporary Record*, vol. 3, no. 3 (1990).

chose to be more of a skipper of a yacht, changing course dramatically when confronted by very hostile weather, than a conductor of an orchestra, who persisted with his score regardless of the disasters befalling his musicians and their instruments.

THE VERDICT

All judgement in history is, to some extent, provisional. Some questions – who initiated policy, what it was, when did it occur and where – are easier to answer than why did events happen as they did, and with what effect. For historical judgement to have any value, it must be deeply rooted in the events as they unfolded, and the options which were open at the time.

For these reasons, the Thatcherite critique can be dismissed as ahistorical. It is based upon an exaggeration of the right-wing intent of the government in 1970. As John Campbell has argued, 'the competitive, free-market talk was the opportunism of opposition. It was necessary to state a different sort of rhetoric from the Labour government, which forced Heath and Macleod into talking a more free market language than they meant or intended to act upon'.[40] The confidential records of the Selsdon conference in the Conservative Party Archive reveal only a limited proto-Thatcherite thrust to deliberations.[41] The meeting was intended as a pre-election meeting, for shadow ministers to get to know each other better, review policy options, and consolidate manifesto proposals. Heath and the Shadow Cabinet allowed the conference and subsequent pronouncements to be invested with a right-wing ideological coherence that was neither initially intended nor deserved. The conversations over the two days of the conference were wide-ranging and often contradictory. At one point, Heath slaps down Mrs Thatcher for her advocacy of an independent university. 'I wouldn't trust [the prime mover] for a minute. We have too many universities already.' At another point he advocates the government building houses in Yorkshire and moving workers over from West Cumberland where there were insufficient jobs.[42]

Heath was never a believer in *laissez-faire*, but was a traditional Tory who saw the state as an essential deliverer of economic and social

40. Campbell, 'The Heathman – an interview with John Campbell', 589.

41. Selsdon Park papers, filed in CPA CRD/3/9/92–3 and LCC papers (uncatalogued).

42. Ibid.

policy.[43] Macleod, his most influential lieutenant, although to the right of Heath was firmly in the One Nation centre tradition of the Party. As Hugo Young has argued, the Selsdon Park conference achieved an importance in the thinking and mythology of the new right that was never justified by what took place at it. So while some policies advocated at the 1970 general election, such as the rejection of an incomes policy and tax and spending cuts were more right-wing than offered by the party at any general election since 1945, the motives for the policies were instrumentalism and opportunism, not ideology. The first error of the Thatcherite right is thus to see a clarity and consistency of policy objective in 1970 that was never intended.

Second, there was no alternative and acceptable philosophy available which would have provided the intellectual underpinning for an assault on the prevailing orthodoxy of Keynesianism.[44] Douglas Allen has said that 'up to about 1972 the general body of opinion in the Treasury was Keynesian. From about 1973, we were beginning to think that more attention should be given to the money supply.[45] Geoffrey Howe, who as Chancellor under Mrs Thatcher was responsible for pushing forward the monetarist economic policy, agrees that non-Keynesian thinking had made little headway among ministers and senior civil servants during 1970–74.[46]

Third, Heath lacked the popular, intellectual and media backing for a full frontal assault on Keynesian consensus-type policies, even if he had wanted to do so. As Robert Blake has written, 'The outlook of commentators, economists, intellectuals, journalists – the opinion formers in general . . . was still *dirigiste*. Planning, high public expenditure, high taxation, a rising role for the state, remained the accepted shibboleths . . . There was no serious challenge in intellectual circles to this orthodoxy.' The government was all too aware of the precarious social and economic state of the country in the early 1970s: the Cabinet judged that to abandon Rolls-Royce or Upper Clyde Shipbuilders courted too high economic and social risks. The nosedive of Rolls-Royce – most prestigious of all British companies – had been a particularly shattering and formative experience for Cabinet ministers. By 1979, after the experience of another five years of Labour failing to tame trade unions, or settle long-run problems in the British economy,

43. See D. Butler and M. Pinto-Duschinsky, *The British General Election of 1970* (London, 1971).

44. Author's interview with Lord Armstrong.

45. Lord Croham, 'The Heath Government' witness seminar, 197.

46. Lord Howe, ibid., 197–8; Howe, *Conflict of Loyalty*, 81.

the country had become ready for a qualitatively new set of policy prescriptions.

Finally, and ultimately most telling, the three main architects of the Thatcherite revolution were all present in the Heath Cabinet. Mrs Thatcher in her Conservative Political Centre lecture in October 1968 and Keith Joseph in articles in the *Financial Times* in 1969 advocated new right stances. But, in office, they were among the highest spenders of the government, the former at Education and the latter at Health. The third architect, Geoffrey Howe, readily admits that 'Thatcherite' solutions were not seriously on the agenda from 1970–74. To criticise the Heath government for failing to persist with new right policies during 1970–74 when Thatcher, Joseph and to a lesser extent Howe were in key positions and failed to argue strongly for such policies, is a plain absurdity. Thatcher and Joseph were also two of the least successful departmental ministers in the Cabinet, not the least reason being, as Rodney Lowe shows in Chapter 8, because they failed to make economies and to target spending where most needed.

The positive interpretation (the 'Heath view') is more worthy of serious attention. As the chapters that follow show, the government's policies were often thoughtful, constructive and forward-thinking. Even Heath's much derided industrial policy, as Robert Taylor argues in Chapter 6, set the tone for much of government policy to industry over the next twenty-five years. Paul Arthur in Chapter 10, while not uncritical of Heath's Irish policies, nevertheless credits him for his vision, 'outlining the parameters of the problem before virtually everyone else', and anticipating the Anglo-Irish Agreement of 1985 and the Downing Street Declaration of 1993. But to label the government a major success is over-stating the case. Only three governments have been significant innovators across a broad front this century the Liberal government of 1906–15, the Labour government from 1945–51 and the Conservative government from 1979–90. With the exception of Europe, there were no comparable and enduring innovations from Heath's government. The Asquith government during 1908–15 faced up to severe problems, including a major constitutional crisis, trade-union and suffragette unrest, a deteriorating position in Ireland and a coming European war; arguably, it performed better.

At a lesser scale of achievement, several governments this century have solid records of steady administration and introducing legislation, such as the second Baldwin government of 1924–29 or the Churchill government of 1951–55. Heath's government does not measure up to these. Baldwin's humiliating U-turn over the miners' subsidy in 1925 notwithstanding, he handled the General Strike of 1926 with good sense: both Baldwin and Churchill governments initiated more policies that lasted than Heath's, and gave an impression of competence Heath's never achieved. Roy Jenkins has compared the Heath government in stature to that of Balfour from 1902–05, and the comparison is fair.[47] Both governments introduced important domestic and foreign policies (the Anglo-French Entente of 1904, for example) but encountered severe domestic turbulence. Both governments allowed themselves to be bundled into general elections, which they lost.

The second Labour government of 1929–31 bears an even closer comparison in terms of achievement with that of Heath. Both had dominant Prime Ministers and achieved some successes at home and abroad, but became destabilised by economic forces beyond their immediate control. The Heath government can be placed above the Lloyd George Coalition of 1918–22, and the third Thatcher government of 1987–90. Both possessed some considerable advantages, including a large majority and a clear sense of purpose, not enjoyed by Heath's government, and the latter in particular was conspicuously less successful at meeting expectations.

Comparing governments resembles a parlour game more than a serious historical exercise. Nevertheless, it serves to show that if the Heath government cannot be considered one of the more successful this century, it certainly was far from the worst, as some on the new right allege. Thus, neither of the first two interpretations of the Heath government appears satisfactory. That leaves the 'pessimistic' and the 'contingency' interpretations. In weighing these, resort must be made to a fresh approach.

Evaluating government performance provides severe problems for the historian, and as I have argued elsewhere should take account of at least five dimensions.[48]

- Inheritance. What was the legacy left behind by the outgoing government? What was the government's position immediately on taking office?
- Exogenous factors. Were factors beyond the government's immediate power to control – economic, social, international – generally benign, or malign?
- Parliamentary and electoral factors. This takes into account such factors as how long did the government have in office, what was the size of its majority, and the quality of the opposition?

47. R. Jenkins, 'A Steady Beam of Internationalism', *Daily Telegraph*, 26 June 1993.
48. A. Seldon, 'Assessing Governmental Performance: Britain's Administrations since 1945', unpublished ICBH paper, 1991.

- Foreign governments' experience. How did governments overseas fare during the similar time?
- Legacy. What was the legacy left by the government to its successors?

The Labour inheritance in June 1970 was not unfavourable. Ben Pimlott, Harold Wilson's biographer, might have reason to praise his subject's legacy, but his argument is valid that Heath in 1970 'was given an exceptional opportunity – far greater than that of either Wilson in 1964 or Mrs Thatcher, both of whom took over at times of crisis. In 1970 the economy was in surplus, and offered a rare chance for imaginative reform'.[49] Alec Cairncross in Chapter 5 agrees broadly that in 1970 'in most respects the economy was in a healthy and a stable condition'.[50] The Wilson government's record on the other hand did not provide a giant shadow and a record difficult to emulate or follow. It had tried and failed to bring about British entry into the EEC in 1967 and to introduce legislation on trade unions in 1969. Heath, moreover, benefited from the great fillip of an election victory widely seen as personal: as *The Economist* said 'Only one man has really won this election and that man is Mr Heath'.[51] Heath further enjoyed the support of a loyal and strong team, who admired his abilities, and were to prove quite exceptionally loyal, at least until February 1974.[52] So the balance of evidence on the inheritance, even with a build-up of inflationary pressure and a brashly confident trade-union movement, lay in the government's favour.

In contrast, the balance of exogenous factors ran powerfully against the government. As has been pointed out above, the government suffered from an excessively turbulent period in office. It also lacked a supportive intellectual climate and, more importantly, the benefit of North Sea oil to offset balance of payments difficulties, two boons enjoyed by the Thatcher governments. The public had also not yet seen a decade of trade-union obstructionism which helped turn them against excessive union power. Without the experience of 1970–74, for both Conservative politicians and the electorate, the Thatcher governments would not have made the headway they did in key economic areas. Historians will find how close her government came, even with these advantages, to failure.

Parliamentary factors were mixed. The comparatively small Con-

49. B. Pimlott, 'A Goose that Failed to Lay', *Independent on Sunday*, 4 July 1993.

50. A. Cairncross, Chapter 5 below, 108.

51. Quoted by Kavanagh, 'Heath Government 1970–74', 219.

52. P. Norton, *Conservative Dissidents: Dissent within the Conservative Parliamentary Party 1970–74* (London, 1978), 228–9.

servative overall majority of 30 after the June 1970 general election (the third smallest Conservative majority postwar, after 1951 and 1992) proved to be no great handicap. Seven seats had been lost by 1974, insufficient to threaten the government's majority. Heath was particularly well served by Francis Pym, his Chief Whip, who did much to compensate for the off-hand management of the Parliamentary Party by Heath himself. Philip Norton has argued that the surge in back-bench dissent during 1970–74 owed much to Heath's abrasive and unsympathetic handling of Conservative MPs. The election of Edward Du Cann as chairman of the 1922 Committee in November 1972 provides further evidence of back-bench unrest with Heath's leadership. The Labour Party were not formidable opponents in the House of Commons. Wilson was tired, and initially preoccupied by writing his memoirs on the government of 1964–70. His leadership was under threat from both left and right.[53] As Eric Shaw shows in his new book on Labour since 1945, effectiveness as an opposition party during 1970–74 was also hampered by complex divisions between left and right, and within the centre-right over Labour's stance on British entry into the EC.[54] The comparatively short length of the government's life, three years and eight months, must be weighed, especially considering how many spending commitments are inherited, and how long it takes to make the governmental ocean liner change direction. Roy Jenkins has argued that comparative brevity in office stunted the government's opportunities: 'It is, I believe, impossible . . . to achieve the very [top level] unless they have served at least a cumulative five years.' Had Heath's government indeed seen out its lifespan until June 1975, the U-turns would have seemed less stark, and various initiatives, not least power-sharing in Northern Ireland, have been given longer to bed down. The balance of this third factor runs slightly against the government.

The experience of other governments abroad confirms that the 1970s, in contrast to the 1980s, was not as comfortable a decade for many right of centre parties. Student revolts in the late 1960s and early 1970s were seen in France, Italy and Germany as well as in Britain and the United States. Anti-war movements, racial unrest and assertive trade unions combined in several advanced industrial countries to provide a severe challenge to governments. In France and Italy, right-wing governments were forced onto the defensive but held on to power throughout the 1970s. In the US and UK, the Nixon and Heath

53. P. Ziegler, *Wilson: The Authorised Life* (London, 1995), 355–99.
54. E. Shaw, *The Labour Party since 1945* (Oxford, 1996).

governments collapsed, albeit for very different reasons, after which their respective parties move to the right.

Finally, the legacy bequeathed to Labour in 1974. As many of the chapters below reveal, the 'wipe-out' or 'pessimist' version does not hold up to scrutiny. In many spheres, economic, social, administrative, defence and foreign, important initiatives taken by the Heath government made a lasting impact. The DTI re-emerged in 1979, the Department of the Environment proved far-sighted, 'special advisers' have grown in number, and 'hiving off' returned in the 'Next Steps' under Mrs Thatcher. The explosion of the money supply under Tony Barber, however, stored up great trouble for Labour after 1974.

Ultimately, then, it is the 'contingencies' view which provides the fairest judgement on the Heath government. No government since 1945 has been in office at such an awkward time. Had he been a better, more inspiring communicator to the country and to his own party, Heath might have made more headway even in the unpropitious circumstances. But as it stands, Heath's government cannot be considered a success. Ultimately, it failed to satisfy its own party faithful, and it failed to produce policies in the realms of economic, industrial or social policy which endured or which resolved long-term problems. Nevertheless, to dismiss the government as a failure would be trite, and wrong. The Labour governments of 1964–70 and 1974–79 faced similar difficulties, and fared no better. As Peter Clarke has argued, 'the policies of the Wilson and Heath Governments showed striking similarities', above all 'in the U-turns which they performed'.[55] Arguably, they were operating in a less hostile environment. So the verdict is that the Heath government's initial policies were sound, as were the adaptions to those policies in the U-turns. Another government *might* have succeeded more fully in the early 1970s; one can never know. But praise is still due for the courage, integrity and flexibility shown by Heath and his government after 1970.

On a different plane, the controversial Heath government provides an ideal case study on judgement in history, as the chapters that follow reveal. Ultimately, any verdict on the government will say as much about the political outlook of the judger, their temperament, the time when the judgement was made, and the analytical or conceptual approach adopted. The ambition of this chapter must thus be limited: to clarify, rather than to close, the case on the Heath government.

55. P. Clarke, 'Tales from a Silver Age', *London Review of Books*, 22 July 1993.

CHAPTER TWO

The Prime Minister and the making of policy

John Ramsden

Four general propositions stand out in the historiography of Edward Heath's government: first, that it was to an unusual extent the government that the Prime Minister himself wanted it to be; second, and following closely from that first proposition, it was among the best-prepared of all governments ever to take office in modern Britain; third, it was a government whose policies in the second half of its term ran significantly counter to what it had done in the first two years; and fourth, though such writers as John Campbell have presented a persuasive case in defence of the government's leadership, decision-making and actual policies, it has still attracted little admiration either for the quality of its political judgement or for the presentation of those policies.

HEATH'S LEADERSHIP

'In public and in private, it was a Heath government throughout', thought Butler and Kavanagh, writing in 1974.[1] The style and personality of the Prime Minister was therefore even more than usually central to the government's working, though this can easily be overlooked in view of the still greater dominance achieved by Heath's successor as Tory leader. Even when first elected leader in July 1965, he had been viewed as a strong personality who would exercise considerable authority, but not in very predictable directions. The MPs who elected him can scarcely have forgotten that in all three of the key events that had marked his rise – (as Chief Whip at the time of Suez, as Common Market negotiator in 1962, and as the abolisher of Resale Price Maintenance in 1964 – Heath had demonstrated an inflexible determination and a readiness to override Party views when his own mind was once made

1. D. Butler and D. Kavanagh, *The British General Election of February 1974* (London, 1974), 25.

up. A 1965 editorial in *The Economist*, written or at least approved by Alastair Burnet, one of Heath's strongest supporters in the press, noted that the Conservatives had chosen Heath as the man 'most likely to bullock their way back into power'; but it also pointed out that it was not at all clear what Heath would want to do with power when once he had it. The *Daily Telegraph* reported a senior Tory MP saying that 'we have elected a rough-rider, and it is time to fasten our safety belts'.[2]

Even before he was elected to the leadership, Heath had his hands firmly on the tiller of policy-making. He became the shadow minister responsible for managing the Party's policy review in Sir Alec Douglas-Home's opposition team, and added to this the chairmanship of the Party's Advisory Committee on Policy (the ACP) and of the Conservative Research Department (the CRD), the influential combination of posts that Rab Butler had occupied to such powerful effect since 1946. It was clear from the start that Heath intended to keep personal control of the operation to a greater extent than Butler had done, and during his time as party leader he never allowed any but the most trusted colleagues – Edward Boyle, Reginald Maudling, Anthony Barber and Ian Gilmour – even to deputise for him in any of these roles. Under Heath, no front-bencher acquired the institutional influence over policy-making that he himself had enjoyed under Douglas-Home, or Butler under Churchill and Macmillan. How tight that control was emerged clearly enough from the 1965 leadership contest, when Reginald Maudling had to get Douglas-Home's specific directive to entitle him to see policy papers emanating from Heath's review – though Maudling was actually deputy leader at the time.[3] With the leader's authority added to these existing positions, Heath was unchallengeable in the policy field, at least from within the ordinary Party machinery. When Nicholas Ridley's policy group came up with a programme of privatisation in 1968, an idea that Heath regarded as a political diversion from the real task of modernising the economy, in the words of the then CRD Director, 'Ted Heath just put a veto on it. He wasn't prepared to consider it.'[4]

It is no accident that the only overt challenges to his authority over policy came from men like Angus Maude and Enoch Powell who were

2. J. Campbell, *Edward Heath* (London, 1993), 183–4; A. Roth, *Heath and the Heathmen* (London, 1972), xii; R. Dudley Edwards, *The Pursuit of Reason: The Economist, 1843–1993* (London, 1993), 838.

3. J. Ramsden, *The Making of Conservative Party Policy: the Conservative Research Department since 1929* (London, 1980), 236–7.

4. Institute of Contemporary British History (ICBH) witness seminar, 'Conservative Policy-making, 1964–1970', *Contemporary Record*, vol. 3, no. 3 (1989), 35.

prepared to – and indeed had to – step outside normal Party channels to make their pitch. Neither held office in Heath's government.

PREPARATIONS FOR OFFICE

It was most significant then that Heath ran his opposition for five years explicitly as an opportunity to prepare for office – to a far greater extent than Margaret Thatcher was to do between 1975 and 1979. Martin Burch thought in 1980 that Heath had been 'a classic exponent of the alternative governmental approach to opposition leadership'.[5] The choice of a front-bench team reflected these 'government in exile' priorities, with natural House of Commons raiders like John Boyd-Carpenter (who would have improved the fighting calibre of the Opposition *as* an opposition) relegated to the back benches, and with both senior and junior spokesmen specifically chosen as a means of preparing them to hold office, as for example in the team that Anthony Barber selected to fight the Labour government's Steel Bill in 1967.[6] Portfolios were exchanged from time to time but, when the 1970 election returned the Conservatives to office, fifteen of the seventeen shadow ministers went into the Cabinet (the exceptions being Lord Balniel and Joseph Godber, the second of whom did join the Cabinet in 1972), and in nearly every case took up the posts that they had been shadowing. Where changes were made in 1970, as for example with the decision *not* to make Sir Keith Joseph Secretary of State for Industry, the post which he had shadowed, this almost certainly reflected a policy disagreement with the Leader over the field in question; at Social Services Joseph's policies would be much more in tune with Heath's ideas than they were likely to have been at Industry.

This unflagging insistence on a governmental approach was not entirely popular with the Party's free spirits; it was one reason for Powell's increasing estrangement from Heath, but it was just as unwelcome to Edward Boyle, who complained of being 'expected to remain on parade as though one were nothing but the alternative Government'. Iain Macleod, free in his own front-bench role to indulge in his taste for opposition as well as to prepare for office, seems to have accepted pragmatically that he must go with the flow in Heath's opposition; but on entering the Treasury in 1970 he told his officials that he was now

5. M. Burch, 'Approaches to Leadership in Opposition: Edward Heath and Margaret Thatcher', in Z. Layton-Henry (ed.), *Conservative Party Politics* (London, 1980), 172.

6. A. Alexander and A. Watkins, *The Making of the Prime Minister, 1970* (London, 1970), 98; K. Ovenden, *The Politics of Steel* (London, 1978), 106, 112–13.

starting the job, and not just carrying over from the previous years of policy-making: 'Whatever I may have said in Opposition, I am not interested in Opposition. I am interested in administration.' The annual retreat weekends at which the shadow cabinet discussed strategic policy issues, usually at Swinton Conservative College in North Yorkshire but most famously in the last of the series at the Selsdon Park Hotel in 1970, were characteristically christened 'Chequers weekends', much as Macmillan had used the concept when Heath had first served in Cabinet. James Douglas at the CRD thought in 1966 that 'there is something radically wrong with the way in which the Shadow Cabinet operates. It seems to me that they still go on pretending that they are the Cabinet, discussing the topical questions of the day just as if they had to decide what the Government should do about them'.[7]

This was not entirely fair, for shadow ministers did spend a great deal of time and attention on policies for the future. The policy review that Heath had run for Douglas-Home had already been through its most important phase in the first half of 1965, and the key proposals were published as *Putting Britain Right Ahead* before Heath's first Party Conference as leader. In spring 1965, there were some forty policy groups, each containing a mix of Conservative MPs and outside specialist advisers, most of them chaired by a front-bencher or a junior spokesman, and over the following summer nearly all of their reports were debated by both the shadow cabinet and the ACP. This involved shadow ministers in a mountainous task of reading and a marathon series of meetings on the detail of a policy which they well knew would become relevant only in years to come. It all had to be done so quickly because of the imminence of a second general election after Labour had won so narrowly in 1964.

The Conservative manifesto of 1966, with the characteristically Heathite title *Action Not Words*, contained most of the material published in *Putting Britain Right Ahead* the previous year, and was in effect the core of the programme with which the Conservatives entered government in 1970.[8]

The crucial decisions on industrial relations policy were therefore taken in early 1965, and then steadily refined as the portfolio passed through a succession of hands before it finally rested with Robert Carr. This was intended to be a balanced package of incentives to trades union leaders to encourage participation, and legal requirements to protect the rights of members and employers, something much discussed

7. Alexander and Watkins, *Making of the Prime Minister*, 100; N. Fisher, *Iain Macleod* (London, 1973), 305; Ramsden, *Making of Conservative Party Policy*, 255, 273, 275–6.
8. Ramsden, *Making of Conservative Party Policy*, 240–2, 249–51.

in 1965, when Labour had set up the Donovan Royal Commission for a similar purpose. The later refining of the detail did not allow for any reconsideration of general principles. Heath rather brutally put down Enoch Powell's later attempts to raise such general issues with the observation that it had now been gone into and settled, and he was 'not just going to, at this stage, have it picked to pieces and fought over'. From 1968 onwards such a reconsideration would have been impossible anyway, for the publication by the Party of *Fair Deal at Work* both reinforced the principles already agreed and added a mass of detail to them. Any retreat would have involved a huge loss of face, not least when the Party had extracted so much political capital from Harold Wilson's own climb-down when confronted with trade union power in 1969.[9]

It is notable that, in planning the Selsdon weekend in January 1970, Maudling as Heath's policy deputy decided that this session should now be restricted to the top table of shadow ministers only, and not augmented by junior spokesmen and senior back-benchers as previous years' Swinton weekends had been. The reason for this was that it was felt that policy did not now need to be discussed as such, more that the policies already agreed should be assembled into a programme and integrated into an order of priority. It was on the basis of such Selsdon decisions that the CRD then produced a detailed action plan for the next Tory government's first two years in office which was in due course sent over to Downing Street on the weekend after the election. This 'future legislation exercise' was a complex flow-chart that allocated time periods for White Papers, parliamentary drafting, legislation and implementation for each Bill, so as to maximise the opportunity of getting the programme through quickly – just what a Cabinet Committee and the Cabinet Office would normally do for a government that was *not* in exile. The times allotted for consultation were notably short – hardly surprising when it is remembered that the Party had made up its mind in such detail – and it would prove difficult to change any part of such a carefully dovetailed programme without creating a log-jam somewhere else in the system. On industrial relations policy, this mattered a great deal; the law was changed remarkably quickly after the 1970 election, but the shortness of time allowed for 'consultation' was a political blunder of the first order even if that consultation was not going to change anything.[10]

Writing in 1968, Samuel Brittan thought that

9. Ramsden, *Making of Conservative Party Policy,* 243–5; ICBH witness seminar, *Contemporary Record,* vol. 3, no. 3, 36.

10. Ramsden, *Making of Conservative Party Policy,* 279–83.

> eat no time have [the Opposition's] leaders – with the significant exception of Mr Enoch Powell – seemed at all excited by the opportunity that opposition provides of leading a real debate on public policy. On the contrary the impression they have given is that they have no stomach for the constitutional role of Opposition, that all their hopes and interests are entirely centred on the time when they hope to return to office.

He decided, in a perceptive analogy that was quoted from Albert Einstein, that Heath's Conservative policy statements had been more like themes written by Schubert ('rounded self-contained melodies') than themes by Beethoven (which contained 'motifs that actually work to build up subjects and make possible the drama of coherent development sections'). In 1970, Ferdinand Mount reached very similar conclusions, in arguing that Heath 'has certainly seemed more interested in presenting an image of the Conservatives as a firm alternative government than as a lively forum for ideas. He has sacked the two liveliest minds in the Party, Enoch Powell and Angus Maude.'[11]

There were some exceptions even to the generally detailed approach, for example in education policy which was both internally contentious and not central to Heath's own interest. Here, as Sir William Pile recalled in 1994, Thatcher arrived in office in 1970 'with no great printed document, but with a page from an exercise book with fourteen points she had made up herself'.[12] More often though, the policies were far more detailed, and it was on these that rested the Party's claim to be uniquely prepared for office. In his role as policy impresario, Heath had been constrained in 1965 by the need to do something that was both definitive and quick, and this led to the leap straight into detailed commitments without any real consideration of underlying philosophy. But this problem-solving approach was, anyhow, the one that appealed to his own way of thinking. He told a *Weekend Telegraph* interviewer that the making of policy was merely a matter of 'getting rid of certain nonsenses', and on several other occasions he placed economic growth and the means to achieve it at the top of his personal agenda, with nothing else even approaching it in significance. In his introduction to the 1965 policy statement, Heath observed that 'as I go around the country, I find that people are asking for an entirely fresh approach to the country's problems. They are looking for constructive policies, *how* we do things rather than what needs to be

11. S. Brittan, 'Some thoughts on the Conservative Opposition', *Political Quarterly*, vol. 39 (1968), 145; F. Mount, 'Edward Heath', in T. Stacey and R. St. Oswald (eds), *Here Come the Tories* (London, 1970), 7–18.

12. Sir William Pile, at ICBH witness seminar, February 1994, text published in 'The Heath Government', *Contemporary Record*, vol. 9, no. 1 (1995), 188–219.

done.'[13] This was an unashamedly unphilosophical doctrine that led to a row with Angus Maude and then to Maude's sacking by Heath when he took their disagreement into the public arena with the statement to the *Spectator* that 'a technocratic approach is not enough'. There may have been more than a grain of truth in Powell's 1989 observation (regarding this period) that 'if you showed [Heath] an idea he immediately became angry and would go red in the face'. He presumably got equally angry with Edward du Cann when as Party Chairman he told the ACP in 1966 that Tory policy ought to be about more than just efficiency.[14] Though their relations were by then bad anyway, Du Cann's support in the Party meant that it took time before he could be sacked and replaced by Anthony Barber. Like Powell and Maude, Du Cann never became a Heath Minister. But the comment on Heath's lack of philosophical underpinning became a commonplace; in 1973, Patrick Cosgrave, writing of Heath as 'a Prime Minister with a doubtful future', felt that 'Heath was not himself acute in seeing the dangers of practical contradictions between different elements in his policies'. In 1994, Sir Robert Armstrong, who had been Heath's principal private secretary, suggested that Heath was a natural pragmatist when in office, but that pragmatism had to an extent been forced on him anyway: 'he had a vision of what he wanted to achieve, but I don't know that he would have set it out as a set of principles. A series of things happened and he responded to them, as a matter of necessity.'[15]

Within all this detail, originating from policy review groups for whom had been set few general guidelines and finalised through an ACP and shadow cabinet that were also discouraged from considering basic philosophy, it was difficult to draw the threads together. The CRD thought in March 1965 that the twin themes of a European future and the modernisation of Britain were emerging from group after group, and these ideas clearly excited Heath too, but the policy advisers already worried that so uncompromising a package might be 'too cold and technical to be inspiring'.[16] When the full package was officially unveiled by Heath himself later in the year, he highlighted four themes which were said to make the proposals cohere into a single programme: tax reforms would reward the high-fliers on whom the

13. Roth, *Heath*, 196; J. Ramsden, 'Churchill to Heath', in Lord Butler (ed.), *The Conservatives* (London, 1977), 471.

14. Ramsden, *Making of Conservative Party Policy*, 251; ICBH witness seminar, *Contemporary Record*, vol. 3 no. 3, 36; Advisory Committee on Policy, 6 October 1966, CPA ACP/2/2.

15. P. Cosgrave, 'Heath as Prime Minister', *Political Quarterly* vol. 44 (1973), 435; Lord Armstrong at ICBH witness seminar, February 1994.

16. Ramsden, *Making of Conservative Party Policy*, 247.

prosperity of everyone would depend, there would be an attack on restrictive practices on both sides of industry, there would be selectivity rather than universality in social provision, and Britain would enter Europe. In effect this all came down to the modernisation of British industry and the public sector to allow the country to make the most of the European opportunity, something that Heath himself found inspiring in the extreme, but which the public *en masse*, then as later, resolutely refused to endorse as anything more than an undesirable (if probably unavoidable) necessity. It is not fanciful to argue that for ten years as Tory leader Heath was unwavering in his belief that the twin themes of Europe and modernisation were all that really mattered, or at least that anything else came a long way behind them in importance. The policies and policy-making mechanisms of the Heath government cannot be adequately understood unless this is constantly borne in mind. The huge volume of work done in opposition to prepare for the introduction of VAT, for example, is difficult to understand without the same basic European framework.[17]

DIVISIONS FORESHADOWED

Ian Trethowan has recalled how the 'dangerous hole in the Tory economic policy, the absence of any clear idea how they were going to deal with the inevitable pressure on incomes', was handled by Heath when questioned by friendly journalists:

> Heath (and Macleod too) tended to dismiss such questions rather impatiently by saying that one should look at 'the policies' as a whole, and they would automatically encompass the problem of incomes. Some of us did not see how this would happen and, when the gap in the policies was so cruelly exposed by the first miners' strike and the Government's ignominious defeat, the emperor was seen in this area to have no clothes.

In a curious reversal, the lack of philosophical coherence in the Party's array of new policies was disguised before the 1970 Election by political events from outside. At the Selsdon Conference, Heath's Saturday lunchtime address to the press corps camped on the Hotel doorstep concentrated on law and order (which had not been a major feature of discussions, but which was thought on Macleod's advice to be good for a favourable headline or two) and this misled the press into seeing

17. Ramsden, 'Churchill to Heath', 470–74; Ramsden, *Making of Conservative Party Policy* 246; Campbell, *Edward Heath*, 134.

a lurch to the right and reporting it as such. Harold Wilson then completed the process by coining the phrase 'Selsdon Man' to encapsulate an atavistic new Toryism, so both giving an identity to a package that had so far obstinately failed to acquire one and highlighting policies like trades union reform on which Conservative policy was anyway rather popular. All of this took place only weeks before the start of the 1970 election campaign and so was still fresh in the voters' minds, but it had very little to do with what actually constituted Tory policy. It did though provide a tempting rhetorical stance on which the Party could campaign for votes – and raise expectations in a way that was to prove dangerous.[18]

Nowhere was this more true than in the central area of economic management, not least because the plethora of policy detail in almost every field tended to mask the fact that important strategic issues had hardly been discussed, let alone decided, before Heath became Prime Minister. Heath had been chairman of the Party's Economic Policy Group in 1965 since he had then been shadow Chancellor, but he also kept the position for himself when he became leader. This was mainly because of the need to hold the ring between the mutually incompatible views of Reginald Maudling (the last Tory Chancellor) and Iain Macleod (scheduled to be the next one), most of all on pay policy and the control of inflation. Outside the circle of those with key economic portfolios, Keith Joseph was already beginning to flex his monetarist muscles, sending personal invitations to colleagues in 1967 to come to seminars at Edward Boyle's house, to be addressed by economists of the Chicago school; only the sympathetic and the intellectually curious tended to turn up, and Heath was not to be found in either category.[19] Much detailed policy work was done over five years in the gestation of the tax policies that Barber implemented after 1970, but very little debate ever took place on core economic issues. The extent of the statutory controls introduced in Labour's 1966 wage freeze allowed Conservatives to denounce the policy without ever quite committing themselves against the idea of an incomes policy; in 1968 Heath declared that 'compulsory controls are wrong in principle' but also said in the same speech that 'I am quite prepared for a tough incomes

18. I. Trethowan, *Split Screen* (London, 1984), 138–9; Ramsden, *Making of Conservative Party Policy*, 275–6; D. Butler and M. Pinto-Duschinsky, *The British General Election of 1970* (London, 1971), 129–30.

19. Ramsden, *Making of Conservative Party Policy*, 244; M. Halcrow, *Keith Joseph: a Single Mind* (London, 1989), 37–42; M. Harrington, 'Sir Keith Joseph', in T. Stacey and R. St. Oswald (eds), *Here Come the Tories* (London, 1970), 75–82; information about discussions with economists are in the Boyle papers, Brotherton Library, University of Leeds, MS. 660/23862-6.

policy'.[20] Only early in 1970 do the shadow cabinet really seem to have decided even what to say at the coming election. It was then decided simply as short-term tactics, as Peter Walker's memoirs recount, with Iain Macleod as so often taking the lead on such tactical questions:

> [Macleod] said that . . . we might have to have an incomes policy, but to explain in a manifesto that you might have to do it in certain circumstances was grey. Manifestos had to be black or white. Either we said we were going to have an incomes policy and it would be superb or that we were not going to have one at all. We should say that we were not going to have one and if in a few years we changed our minds we would have to explain there were special circumstances. As far as the manifesto was concerned it should not be blurred. No 'ifs' or 'buts'. Everybody said it was right and so it got into the manifesto.[21]

This sounds all too plausible; the 1970 manifesto promised to 'make curbing inflation the first priority in everything we do', but during the campaign Conservative spokesmen made ever more incautious attacks on Labour's statutory control of incomes as a threat to freedom. Again, this apparently cynical approach is only to be understood in the context of Heath's own conviction that all such matters were no more than tactical means to a more important strategic end, on which he would *not* compromise. One consequence of this silence and ambiguity on a core issue was that the policy on industrial relations had to assume more and more of the burden of the Party's anti-inflation policy, if only so that spokesmen could have *something* definite to say about future policy. It was not well placed for this purpose, for which it had indeed never been designed.[22]

This inheritance, brought into office with them by Heath's ministers in June 1970, was an ominous one, but the problem was magnified by two further factors, the Prime Minister's idea of how a government should behave and his idea of the mandate he had achieved in the process of getting there. The sudden slump in Conservative popularity in the winter of 1969–70, after three years in which the Party had been miles ahead in the opinion polls and won almost every by-election seat to fall vacant, dramatically changed expectations for the general election – indeed brought one about earlier than Wilson needed to call it. Throughout the campaign, Heath was almost alone among Conservatives in continuing to believe (and against all the published evidence) that he was going to win. When on 19 June he moved into

20. Fisher, *Macleod*, 276, 284; *Notes on Current Politics*, 8 April 1968.
21. P. Walker, *Staying Power: an Autobiography* (London, 1991), 52.
22. Brendon Sewill at ICBH witness seminar, *Contemporary Record*, vol. 3, no. 3, 36.

Downing Street, he did so with a firm conviction that he had won a personal victory for the policies and style that he had advocated. If in doing so he underestimated the extent to which Wilson's unpopularity and a slick Conservative campaign had also contributed to the outcome, he was far from alone in doing so; the *Daily Express* cheered the troops with the words, 'Welcome to Mr Heath . . . Let there be no mistake, the Tory victory was attained by the Prime Minister's own guts and leadership.' The National Union Executive was told by its chairman on 23 July that the victory was 'a great personal one for the Prime Minister'. It would have taken an extraordinarily modest man to be unaffected by such accolades.[23]

POLICY-MAKING IN OFFICE, 1970–1972

Encouraged, then, by the conviction that the policies that they had expounded had been explicitly endorsed by the voters, Heath and his ministers embarked in 1970 on the programme that they had planned over the previous five years. In view of the government's historiographical reputation for reversals of policy, in part foisted on it through a Thatcherite re-writing of the past after 1975, it is important to stress just how quickly and how successfully the government did indeed implement the bulk of its manifesto commitments. In fact, in 1972, a climacteric year in which so much did indeed reverse, Heath could still be criticised by a well-informed observer for doing *too much* of what he had promised: Speaker Selwyn Lloyd remarked that 'Ted's difficulties sprang from his working out his policy in detail before taking office. By the time he was in Downing Street, things had changed.'[24]

The Industrial Relations Act may stand both as the prime example of rapid action to implement a manifesto commitment and of the truth of Selwyn Lloyd's observation that things had changed. In July, only a few weeks after taking office, and with Parliament hardly even yet in session, Heath promised 'the Bill before Christmas and the Act on the Statute Book this session'; the huge and complex Bill became law in summer 1971. In explaining the case for the Bill in January 1971, the CRD's *Notes on Current Policy* gave first priority to the 'Conservative mandate for reform', on the grounds that the Party's policies had been declared in detail at the preceeding two elections and that the electorate had returned the Party to power on that basis. (This

23. Butler and Pinto-Duschinsky, *General Election of 1970*, 343–4; National Union, Executive Committee minutes, 23 July 1970.

24. C. King, *The Cecil King Diary, 1970–1974* (London, 1975), 211.

was curious, for if the presentation of the same policy in 1966, when the Party had *lost*, was in any way relevant, it would undermine the idea that the electorate had voted for trades union reform in 1970.) The claim of an explicit mandate was further highlighted in the June issue, entitled 'Conservatives keep their promises'.[25] Against interviewers who probed the dangerous question of whether the trades unions would in fact accept a new law imposed on them without their consent, Heath had always argued that they would respect the will of Parliament once it was clear that statute was backed by an electoral mandate. Despite multifarious evidence to the contrary in 1971 and 1972, he was still arguing much the same in defence of his somewhat different trades union policy in 1974: his government had long wanted to amend the 1971 Industrial Relations Act, but had awaited the opportunity of a general election in order to get a fresh mandate to do so. Heath's use of the idea of the mandate was another area in which the more extreme actions of his successor may tempt us to underestimate both his determination and his success rate.[26]

There was thus a respectable record of policies implemented by the Heath government on the basis of pre-1970 Conservative Party planning, all justified to a greater or lesser extent on the basis of the electoral mandate. The Nuffield Election study of February 1974 decided that action had been taken 'on a large proportion of the specific promises in the Conservative manifesto', and listed entry into the EEC, housing policy, social services, and the machinery of government as representative examples. The problem with this was that where policy coherence had been wholly or partially lacking in pre-election policy planning, there was little that could be done to create unifying themes after the Party took office and proceeded to implement the parts.[27]

A key area to illustrate this would be industrial policy. The 1970 manifesto had proclaimed that 'we regard an effective regional development policy as a vital element in our economic and social strategy', but it also pledged (giving a remarkable hostage to fortune in the process) that 'a Conservative government would not create a body like the Commission for Industry and Manpower with broad and ill-defined powers to interfere in the running of industry on any excuse'.[28] These interventionist-but-not-interventionist ideas had to be implemented in

25. *Notes on Current Politics*, 3 August 1970, 11 January and 14 June 1971.

26. R. Taylor, *The Trade Union Question in British Politics: Government and the Unions since 1945* (Oxford, 1993), 193; Butler and Kavanagh, *General Election of February 1974*, 51, 75.

27. Butler and Kavanagh, *General Election of February 1974*, 10–11.

28. Conservative Central Office, *Daily Notes*, 30 May 1970.

office by a ministerial team whose chief (after the reshuffle following Macleod's death) was a man who had not even been in politics until the election (and whom the Prime Minister now found to be a man who could deal with the detail but not the broader issues of policy), with juniors whose preference for a full-scale retreat from industrial intervention had been overruled by Heath himself in 1968. The Permanent Secretary with the responsibility for making sense of all this, Sir Anthony Part at the DTI, later recalled that he had been given a double instruction by the new Prime Minister, 'the first was "disengage from industry" and the second was "act like Great Britain Limited" ', for both of which contradictory ideas the government had a 'mandate'.[29]

PARTY AND CIVIL SERVICE INPUTS ON POLICY

Much of this was in any event greatly affected by the way in which Heath set about government itself, so that a government with an unusually large injection of Party thinking in 1970 had become a government almost divorced from any Party advice by 1973. As Leader of the Opposition, Heath had been in constant touch with Party advisers, serviced for policy purposes by CRD staff, and – in 1969–70 at least – ready to listen even to the Party's polling and media advisers. Once in office, he became steadily more cut off from Party advice; his Attorney-General Sir Peter Rawlinson has recalled how far after 1970 Heath 'began to show his isolation. His temper shortened, and his touch with the parliamentary party, so sure when he was Chief Whip, began to desert him'.[30] This tendency was no doubt reinforced by the extent to which he became more dominant on his own front bench. Powell had already left the Conservative front bench in 1968, Macleod died in 1970, and Hailsham more or less withdrew from Party affairs on becoming Lord Chancellor. When Maudling resigned in 1972, Heath appointed no successor to him as deputy leader. Sir Alec remained an independent figure at the Foreign Office but rarely intervened in other policy areas. In the second half of the government, then, there was nobody with the experience and political clout to challenge him, nobody left who had been talked of as a potential Party leader in the succession crises of 1963 and 1965.

Macleod's death was clearly the most significant single blow in this

29. ICBH witness seminar, *Contemporary Record*, vol. 3, no. 3, 36; P. Whitehead, *The Writing on the Wall: Britain in the Seventies* (London 1985), 56; interview with Sir Edward Heath.

30. P. Rawlinson, *A Price Too High: an Autobiography* (London, 1989), 181.

context, for it deprived the Heath government both of its best communicator – Robert Carr later called Macleod 'our trumpeter' – and of its best tactical brain.[31] Despite his reputation as a one-nation Tory of unshakeable liberal principles, Macleod had also been for a generation the front-bencher who could most be relied on to force his colleagues into thinking cynically – or at least tactically – in his belief that every policy debate needed a weather eye kept on the relative electoral effects of the policy options under discussion.[32] When in 1972 the Heath Cabinet found itself moving into uncharted waters, it lacked both the facility to explain itself to the Party and the country, and the resolution to think through the electoral politics of policy choices as well as the economics. It was perhaps unavoidable that Macleod's actual successor at the Treasury, Anthony Barber, though a junior Treasury Minister before 1964, initially lacked confidence in handling a brief for which he had not prepared. The Party's carefully thought-out tax reforms could be implemented without too much difficulty, but in the more contentious (and less well prepared) field of economic management, Heath had accidentally acquired a Chancellor who would tend to do as he was told rather than articulating a strong Treasury view, and was being exceptionally careful not to allow the media to detect any difference between them.[33] Since Heath had never served at the Treasury himself – Churchill, Macmillan, Callaghan and Major being the only postwar premiers who have done so – and had, to say the least, a sceptical view of the Treasury's judgement (ever since its lukewarmness on Europe in the early 1960s), this was unfortunate; the Treasury was not always invited to send a ministerial representative to Chequers meetings and when European negotiations were in progress the Treasury team was given a minder from the Cabinet Office.

On public spending, Macleod's instinct to cut expenditure to facilitate tax cuts was replaced by Barber's greater readiness to accept the plans of his spending colleagues, especially when these plans had the backing of the Prime Minister; one way in which Heath did not always see eye to eye with the Treasury was in their insistence on taking a tight view of expenditure and – as he saw it – in underestimating the buoyancy of government income. John Nott, who served under Barber, was quite clear in 1985 that 'the so-called Barber boom was the responsibility of the Prime Minister, Edward Heath', which certainly exaggerates the situation, but articulates a widely-held belief. Since, as John Vaizey has pointed out, Macleod in all his previous ministerial

31. Whitehead, *Writing on the Wall,* 54–5.
32. Ramsden, *Making of Conservative Party Policy,* 202.
33. Campbell, *Edward Heath*, 303; interview with Lord Barber.

posts had become the articulate defender of the department's own policies, Macleod as Chancellor would almost certainly have clashed with Heath on the control of public spending. On many other areas, the Treasury had an unusually small input into the making of policies relating to economic management and public spending.[34]

Once again, Heath's personal dominance mattered so much largely because he had such strong views as to how his government ought to be run. He had come into office determined to offer the country 'a new style of government', 'a quiet revolution' that would change the historic destiny of the British nation. More specifically, he wanted to show the country that government need not be reduced to a series of squalid compromises, pragmatic politicking and unplanned, reactive gestures – which is the way he thought that Britain had been governed by Harold Wilson. If the European context was the critical framework for the substance of policy, then the reaction against Wilson was equally critical in shaping the style and manner in which policy was made. As Douglas Hurd wrote in 1978, for Heath 'the government of Britain was too serious a matter to be carried forward in the style of Mr Harold Wilson'. After only a few months in office, Willie Whitelaw was telling Cecil King that 'unlike Wilson, Ted is deeply interested in governing the country. At times he sees too clearly what has to be done and is reluctant to listen to people who point out the difficulties that will have to be surmounted.'[35]

One symptom of this was the way in which he allowed his life and his office to be run by civil servants rather than by Party people, much as Churchill had tried to do on returning to office in 1951; in much the same way he resisted pleas for the appointment of a Conservative Research Department chairman of Cabinet rank (other than himself) who could feed Party policy ideas into government at the highest level. Heath was the only Tory premier since its creation in 1930 not to have done this. Within months, it was being said that Heath had 'gone native' as Prime Minister, that he now listened far too much to civil service advice, and especially to Sir William Armstrong and Sir Burke Trend, Head of the Home Civil Service and Cabinet Secretary respectively. Even Victor Rothschild, the leader that Heath had appointed to the new 'think tank', did not get as much access as he would have liked, and complained privately that the Prime Minister was 'cocooned'

34. Whitehead, *Writing on the Wall*, 54–5; Lord Croham and Terence Higgins MP at 1994 ICBH witness seminar; interview with Sir Edward Heath; J. Vaizey, 'Iain Macleod', in his *In Breach of Promise* (London, 1983), 54.

35. D. Hurd, *An End to Promises: Sketch of a Government* (London, 1978), 14; King, *King Diary*, 80.

by Armstrong and Trend. Armstrong was openly referred to by the soubriquet 'the Deputy Prime Minister' after Maudling left, and Heath added credence to this view by taking Armstrong with him to the most public of platforms when holding televised press conferences, a level of visibility such as no civil servant had enjoyed since the time of Beveridge and his Report in 1942–43. So central was Armstrong to the process of government that his increasing hysteria about the threat to civilised life posed by the miners *must* have influenced ministerial perceptions; the personal collapse he suffered at a critical moment early in 1974 had a devastating effect on the whole Government and its machinery.[36]

Questioned in 1994, senior civil servants of the period strongly resisted the idea that they and their colleagues had wielded undue influence or that Heath had leaned unduly on their collective advice – but then they would say that, wouldn't they? What is clear enough is that at the time this was *thought* to be the case; his political secretary, Douglas Hurd, minuted Heath in August 1971 to the effect that 'there is a general impression at all levels within the Party that this administration is in fact less politically conscious than its Conservative predecessor'. If this was a specific reference to the team led by Sir Alec Douglas-Home in 1964 then it was a damning indictment, but even if it was a more general reference to 1951–64 then it was still a very critical remark. The criticisms though went deeper even than this. It was already being said at the time, and much more widely since, that Heath himself was (as Norman Shrapnel put it in 1980) nothing 'but a gifted administrator, one of nature's civil servants'. Once again, the civil servants questioned in 1994 denied this fact, but they were arguing against the general perception.[37]

The reason that such matters remain open for debate is that Heath was clearly a man who made up his own mind, usually after soaking up a great deal of advice, but during the process of listening he tended to say little about his own opinions (another rather significant contrast with his successor). His press secretary recalled 'that Ted Heath listened to a very wide range of people and then made up his own mind'; his principal private secretary argued that 'he used to get us all together to talk something through. He would sit down and say nothing for half an hour. And then suddenly he would say "That's enough." He would listen to a talk and then he suddenly would make up his

36. Ramsden, *Making of Conservative Party Policy*, 289; P. Hennessy, *Cabinet* (Oxford, 1986), 74; Whitehead, *Writing on the Wall*, 52; T. Blackstone and W. Plowden, *Inside the Think Tank* (London, 1988), 54.

37. ICBH witness seminar, 1994; Hurd, *End to Promises*, 37–8; N. Shrapnel, *The Seventies* (London, 1980), 92.

mind.'[38] As a result of this habit, the temptation to assume that he was most influenced by those he saw most often was a natural one, even if not necessarily correct. It was therefore significant that the Prime Minister did become more and more isolated from alternative sources of advice. His diary secretary lamented in January 1974 that over the past year he had become 'worried about the trend of entertainment here at Number Ten'. While the Prime Minister had entertained 'a great number of foreign visitors', 'the people of Britain are not getting their fair share of the Prime Minister's time'; of fifty-seven dinners and receptions hosted by Heath in 1973, only nine had involved any British guests from outside Parliament and Whitehall, and only two of these had been in the second (crisis) half of the year; he concluded that Heath now hardly ever heard the views of ordinary British people at all.[39]

The common assumption that Heath was 'a permanent secretary *manqué*', as Peter Hennessy has put it, rested also on the unusual interest that he took in policy detail and in the management of government and administration, which contrasted starkly with the remarkable lack of interest that he took in the more party political arts. This too stemmed largely from work done before 1970. The Party's Public Sector Research Unit under David Howell had made a detailed study of the way in which the Whitehall machinery could be sharpened up and its proposals were largely incorporated into the 1970 White Paper, *A New Style of Government*.[40] Heath's 'new style' was intended to encompass unprecedented strategic thinking about long-term policy objectives, more detailed scrutiny of whether those objectives were being delivered, and tighter management to control the staffing costs of the public sector itself. The 'Programme Analysis and Review' process, intended to achieve the second of these objectives, had little effect, falling an early victim to the territorial warfare between Whitehall departments, while early successes in the third field were not maintained as the government moved into a public expenditure boom and a growth of interventionism in the second half of its term.[41]

However, the strategic thinking intended in the first objective was institutionalised in the creation of the Central Policy Review Staff

38. Sir Donald Maitland and Lord Armstrong at 1994 ICBH witness seminar; interview with Lord Carr of Hadley.

39. Party Chairman's department papers, CPA CCO/20/8/16.

40. Hennessy, *Cabinet*, 74, 75, 78; Ramsden, *Making of Conservative Party Policy*, 256–8; P. Hennessy, *Whitehall* (London, 1989), 235.

41. J. Bruce-Gardyne, *Whatever Happened to the Quiet Revolution*? (London, 1974), 123–5; K. Baker, *The Turbulent Years: My Life in Politics* (London, 1993), 34.

(CPRS), of which Heath made more imaginative use than Wilson, Callaghan or Thatcher in later years. Its first director, Lord Rothschild, was an effective and imaginative choice, and he assembled around him a team of about fifteen clever, free-thinking men and women to pursue the objective of 'rubb[bing] the Government's nose in the future'. Willie Whitelaw explained to the Commons in December 1970 that 'the Central Review Body will merely [sic] enable Ministers to carry out their collective responsibility better by making their decisions more soundly based'.[42] Since Rothschild himself was not a Conservative supporter, and nor were many of his staff, and since the placement of the new CPRS in the Cabinet Office gave its appointees civil service status, their presence did not in any way improve the government's ability to plan for a *Party* election to come, or to pursue the Conservative *Party* programme they had been elected on in 1970. The CRD was initially suspicious of the CPRS on just this ground, but relations improved over time, and senior CRD staff were then invited along with their political masters to the CPRS's major presentations. These were usually done in the relaxed context of a weekend at Chequers, intended to take place twice a year but not in practice held so often – there were three in the forty-three months in which the government held office. Donald Maitland, 'watching the expressions on the faces of the assembled Cabinet Ministers' at the first such session, noticed that they were 'quite astounded. Some of them were hearing, it seemed to me for the first time, that there was something called a "strategy", to which perhaps they were a party and to which they might conform. Lord Hailsham I remember was very disturbed by what went on.'[43]

It is notable though that for a government that was committed both to strategic thinking and (from 1972 at least) also to consensual politics, the Heath government made virtually no use of Royal Commissions as a basis for the development of major policy initiatives, an approach that has been usually (and critically) laid at the door of the Thatcher government. The report of Redcliffe-Maud on Local Government (1969), or of Kilbrandon on the Constitution (1973), both set up by Wilson, had little impact on the Heath government's policies in their fields, and the only Royal Commission that Heath himself set up was on the scarcely central issue of Civil Liability and Compensation (under Lord Pearson, appointed 1973, reported 1978). Heath's attitude had been signalled in advance when he refused to allow the Party even to

42. Blackstone and Plowden, *Inside the Think Tank*, 11.

43. Ramsden, *Making of Conservative Party Policy*, 300–1; Sir Donald Maitland at 1994 ICBH witness seminar.

submit evidence to the Kilbrandon Commission, on the ground that 'we have much more important things to do'.[44]

Ironically, the CPRS was so successful in demonstrating its ability to think laterally and to pull together thoughts from disparate policy areas, that its time was increasingly taken up with thinking through reactively the implications of the short-term crises with which the government was beset from 1972, and so had less time to devote to the longer-term thinking for which it had been created; reviewing the role of the CPRS in 1974, Christopher Pollitt wrote that 'acute short-term economic problems steadily eroded the priority that the Government apparently felt able to give to long-term strategy'. In Party terms, the same broad outcome had been the experience of the CRD ever since its formation in 1930. Rothschild did predict ahead of almost everyone else in Whitehall or Westminster the likelihood of a large hike in the price of oil in the mid-1970s (though even he underestimated the actual size of the increase), and his staff did outline some of the dramatic consequences for Western economies that higher oil prices would generate, but there is little sign that this message had been absorbed by the government before the price explosion itself occurred in 1973.[45]

POLICY-MAKING, 1972–74

It remains to consider the way in which the tilt of government policy towards a more interventionist stance in 1972 was generated, a policy package that had certainly not been planned for by Party teams in opposition. Since Heath at the time, and his defenders since, have denied that there ever was a 'U-turn' in 1972, it may be as well to begin by citing some opinion from the centre of the Party. Robert Blake, never a great critic of Heath, nevetheless concluded in 1976 that

> The [Heath] Cabinet began with the intention of 'getting government off people's backs', but . . . somehow ended with an even larger number of public employees in the non-productive sector than ever before. It began with a determination to abandon lame ducks and avoid all forms of intervention in wage-fixing, but it ended by capitulating to the sit-in at Upper Clyde Shipbuilders and by trying to impose the most complete statutory wage policy ever attempted.[46]

As we have seen, this view credits the government with more policy

44. Douglas Hurd to Michael Fraser, 14 July 1969, CCO/20/8/14.

45. Blackstone and Plowden, *Inside the Think Tank*, 76–7; C. Pollit, 'The Central Policy Review Staff, 1970–1974', *Public Administration*, vol. 52 (1974), 375.

46. Quoted in Halcrow, *Joseph*, 54.

coherence in 1970 than it could fairly claim, and underestimates the continuing commitment to a single strategic policy objective (a competitive Britain fit to enter Europe); it also ignores the fact that even in its first years the Heath government had pursued, in the public sector at least, a quite deliberate 'incomes policy'. Nevertheless, few would now disagree with Blake's broad opinion that a big shift occurred in 1972. Willie Whitelaw, another man who was never an out-and-out critic of Heath, felt able to accept in 1989 that the policies pursued in the second half of the Heath government's life were 'a complete reversal of the declared policies of the 1970 manifesto'.[47]

How did this occur? In the first place, the planning of the policies was taken outside normal departmental channels, and to a quite remarkable extent also behind the backs of some key figures. The tilt of policy that led to the Industry Bill of 1972 was known about by the Secretary of State for Industry, John Davies (but not by his more hawkish juniors, who had to be moved or removed before the policy could be announced); detailed work was done by a special team of civil servants under William Armstrong, with little input from the DTI, the CBI or the Treasury. So secret were these discussions that Tory backbenchers were struck dumb with amazement when the proposals were revealed to the Commons at the end of the 1972 budget debate. What is even more remarkable is that the Chief Secretary of the Treasury, Patrick Jenkin, who was responsible for public expenditure, which would be materially affected by the new proposals, and who had to wind up the debate only a few hours after John Davies made the announcement, had no inkling of the new proposals until he heard the announcement in the House, so far was the Treasury kept in the dark.[48] In the circumstances, Conservatives were not well-placed to respond politically to such jibes as those of Edmund Dell ('our pragmatic Prime Minister, having marched his troops up the hill to *laissez-faire* and disengagement, is marching them down to selective intervention on a massive scale') or Brian Walden (who jubilantly told Kenneth Baker, 'Just wait till we get our hands on clause 12. We are better socialists than you are').[49]

Something similar seems to have happened with the plan for a statutory incomes policy, also generated by a team under Armstrong, reporting directly to Heath, and again with little input from the Treasury, as

47. W. Whitelaw, *The Whitelaw Memoirs* (London, 1989), 125.

48. K. Middlemas, 'The Party, Industry and the City', in A. Seldon and S. Ball (eds), *Conservative Century, the Conservative Party since 1900* (Oxford, 1994), 482; N. Ridley, *My Style of Government: The Thatcher Years* (London, 1991), 4; Whitehead, *Writing on the Wall*, 82; interview with Lord Jenkin of Roding.

49. Whitehead, *Writing on the Wall*, 83; Baker, *Turbulent Years*, 37.

was the case with the plans for increased public spending which was 'whooped up' by the CPRS (according to a Treasury minister). On this second reversal of direction then, as on industrial policy, the buck returned to the door of Number 10. What had made Heath switch course? In part, it may be argued that Heath was simply returning to home base after a foray into unfamiliar territory in 1970–72, for much of Heath Mark II (1972–74) bears a strong family resemblance to Macmillan Mark II (1961–63), and it is no coincidence that Heath's own formative years as a national leader (as opposed to a Party man, which he had been before 1959) were when Macmillan's interest in planning was at its height. On industry, there is some evidence that the rocketing rates of unemployment in 1971, and the shock administered early in 1972 when the total neared a million for the first time since 1947, affected Heath deeply. He was after all a man who had personal experience of the effects of unemployment in the 1930s, something that scarred him for life, much as it had impressed Macmillan as a Teesside MP in the same years, and made Heath into the advocate of economic growth at all costs that he was to be for the whole of his political career.[50] It is difficult, though, to disentangle this abiding priority from the immediate impact in 1972 of Europe. January 1972 was after all both the peak month of unemployment during Heath's premiership *and* the month in which Heath himself signed the Treaty of Accession that took Britain into the EEC. Europe was perceived as both a great opportunity for Britain and a real danger. The modernisation, mobilisation and restructuring of British industry, of which Heath in his 'Heathco' persona had been an advocate for ten years or more, was now an urgent necessity. This is the key explanation both of Heath's ability to drive such a contentious policy through Cabinet and of the relative lack of Party opposition in the Commons; Christopher Chataway, one of the Industry ministers appointed to carry through the 1972 policy, argued in 1994 that

> the driver for it was entry into the [European] Community. The rationale that I remember most strongly being put to me, when I was moved to the Department of Trade and Industry, was that we were now going to be entering the Common Market, were going to be faced with a degree of competition that we hadn't faced before, and this therefore involved much reconstruction, attention to industrial policy. Overall they were not very good policies, but that was actually the principal rationale.[51]

Andrew Roth, usually extremely critical of Heath, conceded in 1972

50. J. Prior, *A Balance of Power* (London, 1986), 74; Campbell, *Heath*, 13, 99–100
51. Lord Croham and Sir Christopher Chataway, at 1994 ICBH witness seminar.

that 'people outside [Westminster] may think it scandalous that a government should jettison in its second year principles thought essential and distinctive in its first year. But the target has always been the same, to enter the EEC with the economy at full stretch.'[52]

On incomes policy, Heath's personal position is harder to divine, since this was not so clearly an issue that related directly to his central vision of a European future for Britain. Here it does seem that the rhetoric of 1970 was always at odds with the reality of his underlying views. Within a few months of Heath's taking office, the TUC leaders were invited to talks at Number Ten, as indeed Conservative frontbenchers had kept in touch with them in opposition before 1970, and it was only the entirely unanticipated ferocity of the battles over the 1971 Industrial Relations Act and the 1972 miners' strike that created the impression of a government bent on confrontation. As soon as the miners were back at work, Heath determined that 'we must find a more sensible way of settling our differences'.[53] From that point on, Heath was as Prime Minister a tireless advocate of a partnership or corporatist approach to running the economy, again a stance that derived from his experiences in office before 1964. The talks of summer 1972 between government, CBI and TUC were directly descended from the initiatives that had led to the National Economic Development Council and the National Incomes Commission under Macmillan. Few have argued that the government was other than open-minded in these tripartite talks (though it is only fair to add that previous government policies had done much to sour the relations that now had to be sweetened), or that Heath was anything other than generous in his readiness to accommodate the trade unions' ideas. Only when those talks broke down in November, and could not be productively restarted during 1973, and when inflation reached such dangerous levels even before oil price rises came on stream (again something for which government policy was partly to blame), did Heath turn to the imposition of controls. The recognition that the government itself must take the responsibility for action if it could not find partners in an agreed programme was an illustration of Heath's sternly Peelite view of the responsibilities of office-holding. Back in 1970, the historian Esmond Wright, who had the mixed pleasure of losing his own seat in the Commons when the Party won office, had made that comparison. Heath and Peel were 'both self-made men attuned to urbanism and industrialism, owing little to predecessors or to the selection processes

52. Roth, *Heath*, xvi.
53. Whitehead, *Writing on the Wall*, 89.

of the Establishment; both putting devotion to State and Crown before Party . . . men interested less in the acquisition of power than in putting it to use; administrators first, politicians second, myth-makers least of all'. This was a comparison full of insights but – perhaps permissibly in the euphoric mood of 1970 – Wright did not go on to remind his readers of the fate Peel himself had suffered as a result of taking this view of the relative importance of government and party. It was a warning of which Heath might well have taken note.[54]

In taking such draconian powers over prices and incomes, Heath can only have been encouraged by the desperate analysis of the country's future that was all too common in Whitehall circles in the years 1972 to 1975. Brendon Sewill, a policy adviser at the Treasury, has recalled how far panic set in during 1972; the analogy was widely used in Whitehall of civil breakdown producing something akin to the effects of a minor nuclear attack – loss of power supplies, food supplies, sewerage, effective government, and law and order. In 1975, reflecting on all of this and with the added experience of the Heath government's own traumatic final days to draw on, Heath's friend Alastair Burnet was asking in his Conservative Political Centre lecture, 'Is Britain governable?'[55] To a great extent, Heath after 1972 was straining every fibre to discount just such fears and questions, to prove indeed that Britain *was* governable by demonstrating the success of his government at whatever Party political price had to be paid for it. In the Cabinet, as Jim Prior has recorded, few ministers with busy lives to lead in their own policy fields felt well enough informed to challenge the Prime Minister and his Chancellor on such matters as the rescuing of Rolls Royce (where the government's legal obligations were in any event a strong reinforcement of the case for intervention), and from then on the new policies rolled forward logically, in the pursuit of overall objectives with which they agreed anyhow. By mid-1973, they were in any case an exhausted team of men whose battering in the previous two years had left some at least even more unwilling to think about anything outside their own portfolios.[56] If indeed some had grave doubts, as was reported of Margaret Thatcher even at the time, and if some ministers voted for the Industry policy while feeling 'as resentful of the Bill as those who were voting against it', as Geoffrey Howe has put it, then such doubts were never carried to the point of resignation, the only tactic available to dissenting ministers

54. E. Wright, 'The Future of the Conservative Party', *Political Quarterly*, vol. 41 (1970), 387.

55. B. Sewill and R. Harris, *British Economic Policy, 1970–74: a view from the inside* (London, 1975), 50; A. Burnet, *Is Britain Governable?* (London, 1975).

56. Prior, *Balance of Power*, 75; Lord Howe at 1994 ICBH witness seminar.

that can be effective across so fundamental a policy divide. It was much the same lower down; William Deedes noted in 1973, of 'deflationists' like Enoch Powell, that 'whether or not in the eyes of the electorate they have made a convincing argument of it, they have provided no serious obstacle to the government having its way on expansion'. In Powell's case, he was by then heading for resignation from the Party altogether, but it is significant here that Powell (but few others) rejected the European concept that lay at the heart of government policy as well as the symptoms of interventionism that Europe encouraged.[57]

PARTY AND GOVERNMENT IN 1973–74

It is now clear enough that the Party response in 1972 and 1973 contained enough in the way of negative reaction to the tilt of policy to warn off a Party leader more receptive to his followers' views; a real divide was emerging by the summer of 1973, even before the oil crisis doubled the stakes and set off the chain of events that led to an early election and the government's defeat at the polls. The chairman of the 1922 Committee, Sir Harry Legge-Bourke, was among those who verbally opposed the 1972 Industry Act as a 'socialist' measure, but then voted for it because it was seen merely as a temporary expedient justified by the high level of unemployment; he was effectively putting the government on notice of an intending dissent in the near future, as did many of his colleagues.[58] When Sir Harry retired from his post, he was replaced in November 1972 by Edward du Cann, whose election was an even clearer warning to Heath. Du Cann was a personal foe of Heath's from years earlier, and was an open critic of the government when elected, as were a high proportion of those elected by Tory MPs to the Executive of the 1922 Committee. To this must be added the election of critics of interventionism to nearly all the key offices in relevant back-bench committees. Too much should not be made of this last point, for with a hundred MPs in office, there was a dearth of qualified applicants for such posts, but it was nevertheless another deliberate warning shot across the government's bows.[59] Outside Parliament, regular motions passed by constituency associations, the views of the National Union Executive (whose chairman was, along with Du

57. Lord Howe at 1994 ICBH witness seminar; W. Deedes, 'Conflicts within the Conservative Party', *Political Quarterly*, vol. 44 (1973), 391.

58. P. Norton, *Conservative Dissidents: Dissent within the Parliamentary Conservative Party 1970–1974* (London, 1978), 95–7.

59. Campbell, *Edward Heath*, 482–3.

Cann, another unrelenting critic from the inside of the government's policy from 1972), and debates at the ACP, all highlighted a degree of disaffection far worse than that faced by Macmillan in 1962–63, and anticipated the state of Party warfare that would arise after February 1974. None of this indicates that a Party rebellion was *going* to happen, for had the Heath Cabinet surmounted the 1973 crisis and run to a full term, seeking re-election only in mid-1975 after getting its policies back on course, then much of the Party disaffection would no doubt have withered away. But the government's refusal to take serious notice of the unprecedented Party discontent at the time, and to shape its policies accordingly, suggests that front bench and Party supporters would hardly have fought the next election in the state of policy harmony that prevailed in 1970, however long the contest was delayed.[60]

By the summer of 1973, those with their ears to the ground and their eyes open could see that the divorce between the Party's policy priorities and the government's was becoming a dangerous one. Reviewing the Heath government for the *Political Quarterly* in summer 1973 – that is after the 'U-turn' of 1972 but before the oil crisis and the second miners' strike – Patrick Cosgrave thought that 'the debate is not yet closed; if Heath succeeds, he will have a memorial far less distinct, and different from, that visualised for him by his admirers in 1970, but a substantial one nonetheless. If he fails, he will be reviled, and politics in Britain will take turns none can foresee.'[61] When Heath did indeed 'fail', in the sense of losing the February 1974 election, Cosgrave in his *Spectator* column became one of his most persistent critics, and one of the earliest promoters of Margaret Thatcher as a replacement leader. In the same issue, Julian Critchley, a Heath admirer who was to jump ship in 1974–75 precisely because of Heath's failure to stay on terms with Tory voters, argued that.

> the state of the Tory Party following on defeat at the next election does not bear thinking about. In the 'civil war' that could ensue, the Conservative Party as we know it could be obliged to fight for its survival . . . It is impossible to forecast the result; the party establishment might survive, and the Conservatives survive as a party of the centre, but were the ideologues to win, we could become the party of the aggrieved motorist.[62]

60. I demonstrate this in the final volume of the Longman History of the Conservative Party, J. Ramsden, *Winds of Change: Macmillan to Heath, 1957–1975* (London, 1996).

61. P. Cosgrave, 'Heath as Prime Minister', *Political Quarterly*, vol. 44 (1973), 435.

62. J. Critchley, 'Strains and stresses within the Conservative Party', *Political Quarterly*, vol. 44 (1973), 401; J. Critchley, *A Bag of Boiled Sweets: An Autobiography* (London, 1994), 142.

It is notable that even before its terminal crisis, prophets of the Party's position after the Heath government had decided that the Prime Minister, his personal policy line and the future of the Party were all inextricably bound up together.

CHAPTER THREE

Number 10 under Edward Heath

Lewis Baston and Anthony Seldon

Edward Heath ran his government in part in conscious reaction to the management of his immediate predecessor, Harold Wilson. Such a reaction is certainly evident in Heath's Number 10. A combination of an office and a home, Number 10's operation is a blend of the most traditional and apolitical parts of the British state with the idiosyncratic personal and political tastes of its occupants. It is ironic that this key office has received virtually no scholarly study from political scientists or historians.[1] This gap is all the more significant because of the fluid way that Number 10 operates: jobs, offices and individuals come and go, yet terms of reference or job descriptions are scant. This chapter aims to survey the key individuals in office in Number 10 under Edward Heath, to describe their roles and to assess their relative importance.

PREPARING FOR POWER

During opposition in the 1960s the Conservatives re-examined most aspects of policy and administration. Perhaps strangely, the body at the heart of government, Number 10, was not examined in detail after Heath became party leader in 1965, although the machinery of government in general was subject to intensive study. Attention was given primarily to the management structures within the Whitehall departments and the reorganisation of ministries.[2] The Public Sector Research Unit ceased to function after the general election in 1970.[3] There was to be no more institutionalised party thinking about structures in Whitehall after 1970.

David Howell wrote a long paper for the Machinery of Government

1. See for example G.W. Jones, 'The Prime Minister's Aides', Hull Paper in Politics, No. 6 (1980). Dennis Kavanagh and Anthony Seldon are currently working on an Economic and Social Research Council-funded project and book on Number 10 1970–95.

2. See Kevin Theakston, Chapter 4 below.

3. *Sunday Telegraph* 9/8/70, filed in Conservative Party Archive (CPA), CRD 3/14/10.

Group in 1970[4] called 'A New Style of Government', in which the principles and proposals of the reshaping of Whitehall were discussed. Great detail was brought to bear on the management systems and definitions of output of the departments, leading to the adoption of the Programme Analysis and Review (PAR) system after 1970. The only mention of the central institutions of Downing Street was in the proposal for an increase in the staff attached to the Prime Minister and the Cabinet, and the inclusion of a 'high powered analytical capability' at central level with a particular role in overseeing the budget. Earlier in this research project Mark Schreiber wrote that Dame Evelyn Sharp (Permanent Secretary at the Ministry of Housing and Local Government, 1955–66) had advised him of several deficiencies in Whitehall, including the fact that 'there is a serious lack of advice available to the Prime Minister'.[5]

Occasional ruminations were heard from Heath advisers about the establishment of something akin to a Prime Minister's Department. Similar ideas had been toyed with in the highest reaches of the civil service. William Armstrong, Head of the Home Civil Service (1968–74), had a dream of splitting the role of Cabinet Secretary and taking over and developing what he called 'the Prime Minister's Chief of Staff' role as the nucleus of a prime ministerial department.[6] The context for such ideas was in the reform of the Executive Branch of the United States government leading to the establishment of the Office of Management and Budget in 1970 and the increased importance of White House advisers under President Nixon. Interest was also high among British administrative circles about the work of the Chancellor's Secretariat in the Federal Republic of Germany.[7]

HEATH'S LIFE AT NUMBER 10

As British government lacks a transition period, Prime Ministers arrive at Number 10 in a flurry of packing cases, often while the previous occupant is still in the process of departing. From 19 June 1970 to 4 March 1974, Heath used Number 10 as an office and a town house, but also as a social base and showcase for his tastes more than any other Prime Minister before or since.[8] His personal space extended downstairs

4. Howell paper, CRD/3/14/4.
5. Schreiber memorandum 30 April 1968, CRD/3/14/4.
6. Authors' interview with Lord Hunt, 6 June 1995.
7. Authors' interview with David Howell, 20 April 1995.
8. Heath describes some of this activity in his book on music.

from the residential flat on the second floor into an upstairs drawing room where he would relax and play his piano. The internal appearance of Number 10 changed considerably during Heath's tenure. Marcia Falkender, familiar with the house as Political Secretary to Harold Wilson in 1964–70 and again 1974–76, commented that in March 1974 'the first thing that struck me was the number of changes that had been made inside the house'.[9] The Cabinet Room had been restyled in a lighter and more modern taste throughout. Heath replaced replica portraits with eighteenth- and early nineteenth-century portraits, and also introduced some French Impressionist paintings and light pastoral scenes on the walls. His campaign against dry rot may have proved more successful than his attempt to arrest Britain's economic decay, but still left a few patches for Wilson when he returned in 1974. Office arrangements and usage of State Rooms faced periodic upheaval as the renovators roamed the building. Marcia Falkender, on balance, approved of the changes, 'there had been a general modernisation, an improvement of the building's facilities, and considerable refurbishment'. The changes to the design of Number 10 were an aspect of Heath's personality and sense of command; the internal changes in the Wilson era were minimal.[10] The cultural profile of Number 10 was also enhanced by Heath's periodic musical evenings, at which celebrated musicians would perform.

The Cabinet Room and flat at Number 10 became on Heath's insistence a smoke-free workplace and home. Harold Wilson's pipe and cigar smoke was dispelled by the austere clean air ordinance of Edward Heath. Some members of his Cabinet found Heath's no-smoking diktat an ordeal, like Maudling who would spend the last period of cabinet meetings toying with a cigar, and others who would light up in the toilets.[11]

Heath's daily routine showed that he was capable of resisting the incursions of the job into normal human life. He was not obsessed by his newspaper coverage; he would read one or two first editions at 11 p.m. and read most newspapers over breakfast after waking up at about 7.45 a.m., late for a Prime Minister. He did not have the press pre-digested and edited for him, as was Mrs Thatcher's practice. Robert Armstrong, Principal Private Secretary, Douglas Hurd, Political Secretary, and Donald Maitland, Press Secretary, would go up to the flat to see him most mornings to discuss the day's business. Heath wanted to listen to firm recommendations.[12] He would then work on boxes

9. Lady Falkender, *Downing Street in Perspective* (London, 1982), 104.
10. Falkender 104–107; John Campbell, *Edward Heath* (London, 1993), 292–4.
11. Authors' interview with Henry James, 6 June 1995.
12. Authors' interview with Sir Donald Maitland, 19 April 1995.

upstairs until the first meeting of the day, normally at 10 or 10.30 a.m. for Cabinet or a cabinet committee. On Tuesdays and Thursdays he would eat a tray lunch with Maitland, Hurd, Christopher Roberts from the Private Office and Timothy Kitson, Parliamentary Private Secretary – occasionally joined by Michael Wolff – while preparing for Question Time. Until dinner time he would have meetings or work in the Cabinet Room, and he would try to go swimming at about 6 or 7 p.m., at either the RAC Club in Pall Mall or the Grosvenor House Hotel. He tended then to go to the sitting room upstairs on the first floor, saw little television in the evening, and would tend to go to bed at around midnight. 'As well as trying to organise a Government properly, I ought to organise my own life properly, and that is why I deliberately take recreation', he told a reporter in 1972.[13] He worked hard, but compared to the workaholism of Mrs Thatcher, with her three to four hours sleep a night, and even of John Major, with his six to seven hours, he had a more measured lifestyle.

Pressures on Heath's time, as on that of any Prime Minister, were formidable. All non-media requests for meetings and engagements went first to the Diary Secretary in the Private Office (journalist requests went first to the Press Secretary). Liaison would then take place between Heath, Private Office and political staff to see who would secure a meeting, and for how long. Requests from foreign dignitaries would be limited usually to Heads of Government and Foreign Ministers. Heath's staff also tried to keep slots available for others who requested time with him, like businessmen. Regular weekly meetings, usually on Friday morning, took place with the Cabinet Secretary, planning and reviewing business.[14]

Heath was very keen on relaxing during the weekend. As Robert Armstrong, his Principal Private Secretary, said, 'he would leave Number 10 on Friday afternoon either to go to Chequers or down to Cowes; he would not be seen again until Sunday evening'. He would not take boxes when on the boat, and regarded that as wholly leisure time. He enjoyed going to Chequers, the country residence of the Prime Minister in Buckinghamshire, and felt more at home there than James Callaghan or John Major. At Chequers he would entertain and seek conversation with people who interested him or who he felt had something to contribute to political discussion.[15]

Perhaps curiously, for a Prime Minister who so loved the house at

13. *Evening Standard*, 25 May 1972, interview with Robert Carvel and Charles Wintour.

14. Authors' interview with Lord Armstrong, 21 April 1995.

15. Ibid.

Number 10, he did not want to show off to the media more of his power base in Downing Street. He did not, for example, attempt the 'Rose Garden' strategy – which Harold Wilson had followed in 1970 – when the February 1974 election came. He made little use of the trappings of office to show off his aura of power and went out on the road a great deal, to the subsequent regret of his publicity advisers.[16]

Below the Prime Minister were his three most powerful advisers – Armstrong, Hurd and Maitland. The demarcation between the three was informal but entirely clear. Materials from Hurd were given to Heath in a special box, different in colour from the regular government business. 'A very important feature of the Heath administration was the clear division between the permanent and the Conservative Party staff. Heath was absolutely determined that this would be the case', Maitland insisted.[17]

THE PLEASURES AND PAINS OF WORKING FOR EDWARD HEATH

Working for Edward Heath was a unique experience, relished by many if not all. His enigmatic character meant that few people felt that they could totally comprehend him, and his insistence on hard facts and concrete recommendations was a cause of mutual incomprehension when he encountered more traditional civil servants, such as Burke Trend, Cabinet Secretary, with their Socratic means of eliciting decisions.[18]

Number 10 was suffused with Heath's brand of sharp, oblique wit during his government. Douglas Hurd comments that 'it did not take the form of verbal fireworks, let alone a string of jokes. The outrageous statement in a deadpan voice, the sardonic question, the long quizzical silence – these were all difficult for a newcomer to handle'.[19] Colleagues who could share this, such as Donald Maitland, flourished; others like Barbara Hosking, a junior Press Office figure, who could cope with it found themselves given more importance than their positions might have entailed.[20] Others were lost in the slipstream. To most, there was a sense that if you couldn't laugh, you would have to cry.

Heath's silences performed an important function, congruent with

16. David Butler interview (confidential), 28 March 1974.
17. Maitland interview.
18. Hunt interview.
19. D. Hurd, *An End to Promises* (London, 1979), 137.
20. Authors' interview with Barbara Hosking, 11 April 1995.

his approach to taking decisions. As Henry James, the Press Secretary, recalled:

> He was always a great listener. He would ask a question, you would answer but he would rarely show any reaction. His silences drew you out further than you originally intended. It was his way of making one think out loud. You would find in a subsequent discussion that he had been listening and your points would come up. . . . He would rarely join in arguments over policy questions, he would listen and then make a clear cut decision.[21]

Heath was good at taking advice, and listening to recommendations; indeed, he would become angry and impatient if someone was bringing him questions or problems without having a clear recommendation about what to do on the issue. He would ask – sometimes bully – staff into telling him their advice.[22]

To junior staff, Heath was always a rather remote figure, likened by one to an Easter Island statue.[23] He retained some of the awe that accrues to his position of power, even among people who worked quite closely for him. Harold Wilson had known the names of all the staff, all the secretaries and cleaners. John Major is given to wandering the corridors and popping in unannounced to have a quick word with his staff. Edward Heath was 'terribly aloof. It was a year before he knew my name', recalled one former civil servant.[24]

Heath would occasionally engage in what one takes to be self-parody about his lack of human understanding for his staff; for instance, on learning that he had called an officer away from his wedding anniversary he sniffed and said, 'You're well out of that'.[25] He would have no compunction about whisking people away from family and garden on weekends to come in to work. Such demands are not unusual in the pressured life at the heart of government service, but even in that world Heath gathered a reputation as a demanding boss. Uninitiated civil servants would occasionally take literally his gruff instructions to get straight to work and not bother with eating lunch.[26] Decoding Heath was an art, which most acquired with time.

21. James interview.
22. Maitland interview; Hosking interview.
23. Private information.
24. Hosking interview.
25. James interview.
26. Hunt interview.

THE POLITICAL OFFICE

Douglas Hurd took over from Marcia Williams as Political Secretary, a party job regularised by Wilson in 1964. Hurd was a former diplomat (from 1952–66) and committed European who joined Edward Heath's Private Office in 1968 after a spell in the Conservative Research Department. It was assumed by all sides that he would join Number 10 in some capacity if the Conservatives won the general election, and he was peremptorily given the title 'Political Secretary' on the day after the result. The remit of the Political Secretary, like many jobs at Number 10, was not clearcut; on taking office, Douglas Hurd admits, 'I had no idea what a Political Secretary was or what he did. Nor was there anyone I could ask'.[27] His experience perfectly endorses our initial statement about the fluidity of roles in Number 10. Marcia Williams had carved out a specific role for herself, and part of the idea of Heath's new broom image was to avoid having a Marcia figure; 'the one point made clear to me about my new duties was that I was expected to carry them out in quite a different way to Mrs Williams'.[28] The perception in the Heath camp was of frequent turf wars between the Political Secretary and both the Press Office and the Private Office in 1964–70, and there was a determination to prevent such problems from recurring under Heath. By all accounts this aim was realised throughout 1970–74, though the credit must be due more to the diplomacy and emollience of Hurd, Maitland and Armstrong than to any diktats on the subject from Heath. There was general agreement on policy questions, particularly over Europe, between the three offices. On questions where different perspectives appeared – such as incomes policy and Northern Ireland – long, rational (almost 'Socratic') discussions took place.[29]

The job of Political Secretary was larger and more powerful than it has become at some points since, notably in Mrs Thatcher's latter years. Its importance during 1970–74 is partly a reflection of the personal value of Douglas Hurd to Heath, and partly that the Policy Unit, created by Wilson in 1974 with Bernard Donoughue as its first head, took over some of the work formerly done by the Political Secretary. Hurd had unrestricted access to the Prime Minister and extensive rights to information (including classified papers) and would attend many important ministerial meetings with the Prime Minister. Hurd's office

27. Hurd, *End to Promises*, 27.
28. Letter from Lord Bridges to authors, 14 August 1995.
29. Hurd, *End to Promises*, 28.

was also a clearing house for political gossip and chat for ministers going in and out of the Cabinet Room.[30]

The job of Political Secretary, which had been conceived as a way of keeping the Prime Minister in touch with the party, became increasingly concerned with crisis management. The years 1970–74 were a particularly turbulent period, seeing one unrelated crisis after another, though the pace of matters requiring the attention of Number 10 is usually frenetic. Douglas Hurd found himself skipping erratically from one issue to another:

> Suddenly an issue would take the centre of the stage for a day or two. During that short time I would know where each of the characters stood. I would go to their meetings, listen to their private talk, maybe draft a speech or notes for a broadcast. Then the issue would disappear from my sight as suddenly as it had come.[31]

The political direction provided by the Political Secretary was, reflects Hurd, 'crowded out by the sheer pressure of events',[32] while civil service advice outweighed it. Hurd's position as neither a career civil servant nor a member of Parliament meant that his access to the worlds of Whitehall and Westminster was less than he thought desirable. Though the diplomatic calendar was not as crowded in the early 1970s as it has become since, the Political Secretary played a considerable role in accompanying the Prime Minister on foreign trips.

The structure of the system of ministerial 'special advisers' was beginning to emerge during the Heath government. Special advisers were drawn from party ranks, or from business, and were short-term appointments to give the minister political and policy advice. Part of Hurd's duties, in which he was assisted by Wolff, was to find these political advisers for ministers, particularly in Trade and Industry and Health and Social Security; Brendon Sewill, one such adviser, was already ensconced in the Treasury.[33] In the dying months of the administration Douglas Hurd attempted, as if in response to a perception of lack of strategic direction, to bring the developing network of special advisers together to share problems and give a common purpose. But this initiative did not have the time or the propitious circumstances to succeed. The same can be said about the expansion of the Political Office with the recruitment of William Waldegrave in late 1973: 'I

30. Hurd, *End to Promises*, 34–5.
31. Hurd, *End to Promises*, 51.
32. Ibid., 33.
33. Authors' interview with Brendon Sewill, 20 April 1995.

came in quite explicitly as Douglas Hurd's successor . . . I had my own room. I was supposed to have a year's training.'[34]

Tim Kitson, MP for Richmond in Yorkshire from 1959 to 1983, was appointed Edward Heath's Parliamentary Private Secretary after the 1970 election. This was a surprising choice; Kitson was not known as a political ally or personal friend of Heath and had roots on the centre right of the party; he had voted for Reginald Maudling in the 1965 leadership election. But it was felt that he would be able to build bridges with the right, as well as more generally to the parliamentary party.[35] After an awkward first few weeks, he and Heath hit it off on a personal level and he became one of Heath's most loyal friends. Kitson worked from the second-floor office, opposite the door to the PM's flat. In Heath's domestic rearrangements he was allocated the portrait of Churchill from outside the Cabinet Room. He also spent a lot of time at the Commons.[36] Kitson became a regular late-night confidant and conversation partner of Heath.

Kitson's job of justifying the ways of Edward Heath to the parliamentary party was not an easy one. Heath was in some ways not interested in 'politics' at all. He was interested in reaching the right, rational, decision. Once he had done so, he regarded anyone who did not agree with him, including Conservative MPs, as obstructive. He had notoriously little time for day-to-day politics, being much more at home in Whitehall than Westminster, and having a Chief Whip's functional attitude to getting the flock through the correct division lobby. The House of Commons environment of rather superficial and transitory personal contact was one in which Heath's brand of humour was not always appreciated and, as his biographer John Campbell shows, he could seem unambiguously rude.[37] There is no doubt that Heath increasingly neglected his backbenchers, and spent insufficient time talking with them and befriending them in the smoking room or tearoom. Mrs Thatcher was fully aware of this deficiency in her predecessor, and set out to avoid the same mistake – but in her last few years she too let this aspect of her job slip. Without Kitson's mediation, the gulf between Heath and his backbenchers would have been deeper still.

Kitson, and his wife Sally, became close to Heath, a relationship that blossomed after the February 1974 general election defeat to the point of them offering Heath the use of their London flat until he could

34. Authors' interview with William Waldegrave, 20 April 1995.
35. Authors' interview with Sir Timothy Kitson, 19 June 1995.
36. Falkender, *Downing Street*, 105.
37. Campbell, *Edward Heath*, 667.

find somewhere else, and accompanying him abroad. In 1975 Kitson was one of the principal organisers of Heath's leadership campaign.

Also attached to the Political Office was Rosemary Bushe, who had handled personal and constituency correspondence for Heath long before he arrived at Number 10.

THE PRESS OFFICE

Donald Maitland, with the new, upgraded title of Chief Press Secretary 1970–73, was a civil servant much to Edward Heath's taste. They had worked together on the attempt to negotiate entry to the European Economic Community in 1961–63, when Maitland had served as a Foreign Office spokesman. He shared Heath's commitment to Europe, although perhaps with more nostalgia for Empire.[38] Maitland had been head of the Foreign Office's News Department before serving as Principal Private Secretary to two Labour Foreign Secretaries (George Brown and Michael Stewart). He was a meticulous, civilised and essentially conservative mandarin of the old school. Maitland's appointment came as a surprise to him, and Heath's election victory in 1970 meant a hurried weekend evacuation from the turbulent and confusing world of Libyan diplomacy (he had been appointed Ambassador in 1969). He returned to an office in Number 10 on Monday, barely a hundred hours after the polls had closed. Maitland went on to serve as Chief Press Secretary for exactly three years, retiring in June 1973. He and Heath had always seen the office as a fixed-term three-year civil service posting: both men were scrupulously correct in such matters, thereby pre-empting the risk of a Chief Press Secretary becoming over-identified with a Prime Minister, as occurred under the tenure of Bernard Ingham (1979–90).

Maitland proved a crucial and most effective appointment. Heath had wanted to elevate the role of Press Secretary to cover European and foreign affairs. He was in favour of making the role of Press Secretary more open and public.[39] He had been impressed by the State Secretary that German Chancellor Willy Brandt had, and wanted Maitland to fill the same role.[40] Maitland became very highly respected in Whitehall, and by much of the media.[41] According to one insider,

38. James interview, Hosking interview.

39. James interview.

40. Maitland interview.

41. Colin Seymour-Ure, 'The Role of Press Secretaries on Chief Executive Staffs in Anglo-American Systems', in Colin Campbell *et al.*, *Executive Leadership in Anglo-American Systems* (Pittsburgh, 1991).

who worked in the Press Office under both Wilson and Heath, 'Maitland raised the intellectual level of Number 10's press operation. There was much less improvisation. With Wilson you were more at the mercy of external events so that policy was devised on the hoof, and policy sometimes became a reflection of expediency. You had to take chances on what government policy was sometimes. We reverted under Heath to more serious thought and study, to knowing the fuller facts before making a commitment.'[42] Henry James, himself later to be Chief Press Secretary in 1979, was brought in to balance Maitland's foreign expertise with some domestic background, and was given the formal title of 'Press Secretary'. Maitland learned fast on the domestic side, and gradually the office of Chief Press Secretary assumed its traditional, though powerful, role.[43]

The press team under Wilson had survived in rather cramped conditions in two ground-floor rooms overlooking Downing Street. Maitland was not satisfied with the accommodation whereby his own room, the larger of the two, doubled as Lobby briefing room ('ridiculous: I had to move all my papers each time they came in, and there was no room for everyone to sit'[44]). Eventually he negotiated a back office for himself on the first floor, while the Press Office regulars, under Henry James in 1970–71, occupied the front offices.[45] Lobby briefings continued in the room vacated by Maitland, with no solution to the problem of sitting room for Lobby journalists, especially problematic on busy occasions.

The office began work early in the day, preparing for the daily 11 a.m. briefing given by Maitland to the Lobby. Morning briefings were held at Number 10: the 4 p.m. briefings would again be conducted by Maitland and were held in the House of Commons. Issues arising from the twice-weekly Prime Minister's Questions would be brought up at this meeting. Heath never asked what had been said in Lobby briefings, and was less concerned than some premiers, such as Wilson and Major, about bad press. He kept a strict distance from influential media figures, was scrupulous about not having press favourites, and gave no journalists honours. Heath never complained himself if he felt errors had appeared in the media: Maitland would contact the journalist concerned, but never the editor. Ian Aitken, Ronald Butt, Peter Jenkins, David Watt and David Wood were among the political journalists most respected at Number 10.[46]

42. Maitland interview.
43. James interview.
44. Maitland interview.
45. Ibid.
46. Ibid.

The guiding principle of Heath's press relations operation was that 'comment was free but facts were key'. They would correct errors of fact from the government but not bother too much about adverse comment in the media.[47] Heath and Maitland were keen for the government's line to be communicated to the electorate directly, for them to make of it what they will, rather than for it to be sieved (and worse, distorted) by the media. This belief led to the most notable formal innovation in press policy during the Heath years – the Prime Ministerial press conference: two such press conferences were thus held by Heath during his years as premier.

The House of Commons has traditionally cavilled at government announcements being made first elsewhere, and some government information officers were sceptical about the press conference plan. The two were held at Lancaster House – one concerned Europe, and the other the second stage of the prices and incomes policy. As well as emphasising the authority of Heath as leader of the government, they were designed to show off to maximum advantage Heath's personal abilities. In Maitland's words, he had an impressive physical presence, was able to extemporise in concise and grammatical English, and he felt comfortable, almost arrogantly so, in dealing with questions from the floor.[48] Heath approved of press conferences, and thought that the House of Commons's *amour propre* would not be offended.[49] The press conferences risked dissent within the media as well, though only John Groser of *The Times* openly declared his hostility.

The early 1970s were a time of transition, in which the place of television – and the necessary repositioning of the press in British politics – was developing. As Donald Maitland puts it: 'This was a period when the written press was getting uneasy about the influence of television at their expense. We had to make use of the rise of TV without putting the press's nose out of joint.' Television arrangements at press conferences were a focus of this problem. Michael Wolff's note for the record on the 1973 conference shows that the BBC had asked for the right to televise edited highlights from the whole conference.[50] Donald Maitland sidestepped the issue by using live transmission of the statement and also not allowing television coverage of the question period, at the request of the written press who were extremely uncomfortable at the idea. The compromise was unhappy and, at the

47. Maitland interview; James interview.
48. Maitland interview.
49. *Evening Standard*, 25 May 1972.
50. Wolff papers, L3 'Press Conferences'.

request of the broadcasters, Maitland arranged for Heath to give private interviews in corners of the conference room.[51]

Further innovations for handling the media were also discussed, and met with no more success. The idea of an open, on-the-record briefing after Cabinet meetings was aired, consciously emulating the practice of Rudi von Wechmar, the German Staatssekretar, but to no avail.[52] Maitland and Henry James tried, without success, to interest the Lobby in the idea of induction tours of and talks on government departments. They hoped to prevent common elementary misconceptions, such as that the agenda for the Cabinet was always set by last night's news or that morning's 'Today' programme, from being propagated in print, but the offer was regarded with suspicion by the Lobby.[53]

The way in which government publicity was organised defeats neat management charts. The Prime Minister's press operation had at least three strands – speaking for the Prime Minister, speaking for the government as a whole (for which the Prime Minister was accountable), and making sure that departmental ministers and press officers were co-ordinated and were not contradicting each other and that key pronouncements would not be overshadowed by other stories. The third part caused particular difficulty.

Information officers from Whitehall departments met weekly on Mondays under the chairmanship of the Number 10 Press Secretariat. In addition there were three information co-ordination operations. One concerned Northern Ireland and was run out of the Ministry of Defence (MoD); one was about Europe and was run by Anthony Royle at the Foreign and Commonwealth Office (FCO), and the most complex, about prices and incomes, was run from Number 10 itself. Donald Maitland handled the tripartite prices and incomes conferences, but an officer, John Pestell, was recruited from the Ministry of Defence to handle the day-to-day business of making sure that Trade and Industry, Employment, the Treasury and Number 10 were working satisfactorily together.[54] These co-ordinating mechanisms proved not entirely successful – the style and methods of MoD information officers was not universally admired in Whitehall[55] and some thought Pestell's appointment unsuitable.[56] There was a multiplication of committees, including the 'Co-ordination of Government Information Committee'

51. Maitland interview.
52. Hosking interview. Letter to Anthony Seldon, 18 August 1995.
53. James interview.
54. Maitland interview.
55. Hosking interview.
56. Confidential interview.

which met roughly weekly from 1972, was composed, *inter alios* of Michael Wolff, John Pestell, Barbara Hosking, Geoffrey Johnson-Smith and occasionally Nicholas Scott, and seemed to deal mainly with the anticipation of events and announcements on a weekly cycle. As coal and oil crises broke in late 1973, it was proposed to set up yet another committee, to deal with energy presentation.[57]

The proliferation of co-ordination of publicity mechanisms was a source of concern for the political staff and ministers. In February 1972 a story circulated that William Rees-Mogg would be given a co-ordinating role, but the plan was not proceeded with.[58] Michael Wolff sent a memorandum to Heath in late 1973 entitled 'Government Publicity: Who's in Charge?' and Jim Prior on taking over as publicity co-ordination minister in late 1973 bemoaned 'the proliferation of co-ordinating machinery'.[59] Day-to-day responsibility for information control was vaguely divided between Number 10 and the Cabinet Office team under Geoffrey Johnson-Smith. Strategic co-ordination and relations with senior media executives were under the control of Robert Carr. Emergency response, the Lobby and party matters were co-ordinated by Prior as Leader of the House and a Party deputy chairman. Prior advocated concentration in one place, 'and this in effect means the [Downing Street] Press Office'.[60]

Some deterioration was felt to have occurred in the way in which the Press Secretariat operated. Maitland's departure in June 1973 saw Robin Haydon, another former Head of the News Department at the Foreign Office (1967–71), succeed him. Friends of Robin Haydon stress that he was 'unhappy' and that his appointment was 'a fundamental mistake'.[61] He was persuaded to leave a job he was enjoying, High Commissioner in Malawi, for one for which he had little natural aptitude. He was not cynical, or wily, enough to face the press corps successfully. It was his misfortune to run into the terminal crisis of the Heath government a few months into his tenure.

The deterioration of the Number 10 press machine and its relations with the media was a small contributing factor, as well as perhaps a symptom, of the collapse of the Heath government. James Margach, no friend of Heath, said that in his last few months at Number 10, Heath made desperate (and abortive) attempts to get on to good terms

57. Wolff papers, 'Co-ordination of information' minutes 1972–74, esp. 28 Nov. 1973, 5 Dec. 1973.

58. Campbell, *Edward Heath*, 504.

59. Wolff papers, Box L5 'Press and media'.

60. Ibid.

61. Confidential interview.

with Fleet Street.[62] The Conservative leadership suffered from fragmented organisation during the February 1974 election campaign. Douglas Hurd was fully occupied contesting his parliamentary seat of Mid Oxfordshire, although he managed to maintain a certain level of communication with the centre. Brendon Sewill was under civil service rules at the Treasury, the Cabinet were dispersed around the country and a plan to hold a mid-campaign cabinet meeting proved abortive.[63] A general inability of the Heath political team to respond quickly to events led to the election embarrassment of 'Figgures' figures' in February 1974.[64]

THE PRIVATE OFFICE

If, as the usual phrase goes, the Parliamentary Private Secretary was the Prime Minister's eyes and ears, the Private Office was his arms and legs. The Private Office was (and still is) situated through double doors off the opposite end of the Cabinet Room to the Political Secretary's small room. In the first part of the office worked the Principal Private Secretary and the Foreign Affairs Private Secretary: in a second room were situated the Diary Secretary and more junior Private Office staff. Robert Armstrong was the Principal Private Secretary with a comparatively small group of officers below him concentrating on particular aspects of policy and business. Peter Moon and, from 1972, Lord Bridges (son of Edward Bridges, a former Head of the Home Civil Service from 1945–56) worked on foreign affairs, foreign trade and defence. Christopher Roberts worked on Parliament and Peter Gregson (succeeded by Christopher Roberts and then Robin Butler, who had excelled in the Central Policy Review Staff, in 1972) on Home Affairs. The Private Office is traditionally regarded in the civil service as a staging post in the career of its brightest young officials, and in this Heath was served by two future Cabinet Secretaries and Heads of the Home Civil Service – Robert Armstrong (1979–87) and Robin Butler (1987–). Armstrong's own task as Principal Private Secretary consisted of general supervision of the Private Office and selection of Private Secretaries, oversight of the intelligence and security services, ministerial and other non-Church appointments, honours, relations with Buckingham Palace, constitutional issues and machinery of government. He was particularly involved with the European Economic Community

62. James Margach, *The Abuse of Power* (London, 1978), 166.
63. David Butler interview (confidential), 28 March 1974.
64. D. Butler and D. Kavanagh, *The British General Election of February 1974* (London, 1974), 100–103.

and, more generally, had to keep up to speed with whatever was concerning Heath at any particular point in time.[65]

Sandy Isserlis had been appointed Principal Private Secretary before the election in June 1970 after the premature death earlier that year of the incumbent Michael Halls, but was more suited to Wilson's personality than Heath's, with whom the chemistry did not work as well. Robert Armstrong replaced him after a few weeks. Armstrong's Treasury background, European orientation and economic fluency was of importance to Heath. As important in the eyes of William Armstrong, Robert Armstrong (no relation) loved music, so would have a head's start over some others in achieving a close rapport with Heath.[66] Robert had been Secretary to the Board at Covent Garden since 1968 and his father, the musician Sir Thomas Armstrong, had known Heath when he was the Organ Scholar at Balliol College. As John Campbell put it: 'Unquestionably, however, the bonds of music and family friendship created an exceptionally close – almost paternal/filial – relationship which further contributed to the warmth and camaraderie of the team in Downing Street.'[67] Heath became devoted to Armstrong, and found him one of the most intelligent, and companionable, officials he encountered in his career.[68]

Heath and the Private Office held each other in mutually high esteem; he took a personal interest in ensuring that the intake of extremely high quality civil servants was kept up.[69] Private Office staff were very highly rated by the other occupants of Number 10, Janet Whiting of the Press Office calling them 'a joy to work with'.[70] Christopher Roberts was the master of Question Time preparation and parliamentary business in general. One must, however, note a preponderance of graduates from Heath's own university, Oxford, among their ranks (though comparatively few, like Gregson, from Heath's college, Balliol). On returning to Downing Street in March 1974, Harold Wilson thought the Private Office was 'working far better than it ever did when I was here before', and invited Robert Armstrong to stay in his post, a position he held until 1975.[71]

The Private Office links the Prime Minister into the rest of Whitehall. It prepared briefs for Heath (when possible with twenty-four

65. Letter from Lord Armstrong to authors, 30 April 1995.
66. Ibid.
67. Campbell, *Edward Heath*, 490.
68. Authors' interview with Sir Edward Heath, 21 April 1995.
69. Armstrong interview.
70. Authors' interview with Janet Whiting, 21 April 1995.
71. Armstrong interview.

hours' notice before meetings), drafted official speeches, and generally ensured he was on top of the next day's business. Private Secretaries attended relevant items in Cabinet and cabinet committee meetings, and one travelled abroad with Heath on official business: Armstrong would travel on more important trips. Plane journeys were put to good use by the Private Office for the potential they offered to capture Heath for briefing sessions and obtaining decisions.[72] On a sidelight, the Heath period is of note for its establishment of 'red boxes' that were not red. To emphasise the separation of party and government business, material from Douglas Hurd was put into special black boxes. 'There was a friendly competition between my little black box and their multitude of red ones', which black usually won, according to Hurd.[73] The secret weapon of the Private Office was subsequently named 'Old Stripey' by Harold Wilson; Robert Armstrong invented a different coloured box – blue with a red stripe – for sensitive material to which only he, Lord Bridges, and Heath had keys. It was always the first thing the Prime Minister went to.[74]

The Private Office unsurprisingly played a particularly significant role in the centrepiece of Heath's premiership, negotiations with the European Community, above all over the Treaty of Accession. Heath took a very close personal interest in this and the Private Office worked directly with their counterparts in other European capitals. Heath's relations with his Foreign Secretary, Sir Alec Douglas-Home, were exceptionally trusting, although tensions existed at official level in the FCO, with fears in some quarters (recalling 1938–39) of Number 10 becoming too heavily involved in foreign policy. The centrality of Europe to the administration's agenda was reflected in the establishment of a European Secretariat in the Cabinet Office, sending a message to all of Whitehall to act and think in European terms.[75]

Not the least of the Private Office functions was to be on call during the night and at weekends. The Private Secretaries and press secretariat were on a rota: if a crisis blew up, the Duty Clerk at Number 10 would always ring them before obtaining the go-ahead to disturb the Prime Minister.[76] As weekends saw a focus on foreign affairs business, and entertaining of foreign leaders, Moon and Bridges had a large share of weekend duty.[77]

72. Authors' interview with Lord Bridges, 11 July 1995.
73. Hurd, *End to Promises*, 34.
74. Armstrong interview.
75. Letter from Lord Bridges to authors, 14 August 1995.
76. Whiting interview.
77. Bridges interview.

THE APPOINTMENTS OFFICE

Upstairs overlooking Downing Street, rather tucked away from the pressurised world of the work of the Prime Minister's Office, was the Appointments Secretary. The room, named after an otherwise long forgotten housekeeper called Mrs Perkins, housed one of the more quaint aspects of the work of the central executive – advice to the Prime Minister on recommendations to the Queen concerning crown appointments in the Church of England and in universities. These patronage powers included appointment of bishops and deans and Regius Professors at Oxford and Cambridge. The civil servant occupying this position is, invariably, a practising Anglican, and a gentlemanly (never a lady), old-world, courteous person. In Heath's time this was the province of Sir John Hewitt. In the words of Lord Bridges: 'John Hewitt was a tireless visitor to Anglican dioceses, and the common opinion was that he had a better personal knowledge of the higher clergy than anyone in the church.'[78] He was in the classic mould of Appointments Secretaries, and was left to do his work virtually undisturbed, before Prime Ministers took a close interest in the process and before the Church of England became restive about its place within the British establishment. He worked directly to the Prime Minister and was not part of the Private Office.[79] Hewitt was assisted by a small staff of three or four people, most notably Joan Porter who worked on appointments. She and the other Appointments Office staff had worked at Number 10 from before the time when posts there were more widely advertised around the civil service.[80]

THE CABINET SECRETARY

Heath was served by two Cabinet Secretaries, Burke Trend until the autumn of 1973 and then John Hunt. He and Trend were very different personalities; Trend the old-fashioned, quintessential mandarin, the embodiment of the traditions of the civil service, who had already in that capacity served three Prime Ministers before Heath: Harold Macmillan from 1962, Alec Douglas-Home (1963–64) and then Wilson, with whom he had relished working for six years. Heath was a man restless with tradition. Like Donald Maitland, Burke Trend had an emotional attachment to the Commonwealth, but unlike him he had

78. Letter from Lord Bridges to authors, 14 August 1995.
79. Letter from Lord Armstrong to Anthony Seldon, 30 May 1995.
80. Whiting interview.

little instinctive sympathy for the European ideal, nor the sensitivity or flexibility to adapt fully to a new Prime Minister. Heath certainly respected Trend, especially on intelligence matters with the US, where his knowledge of the players was *sans pareil*. But he found his approach to government business academic.[81] Burke Trend's enormous experience had imbued him with caution, thoughtfulness and a sense of history.

Trend was sceptical about some of Heath's innovations in Whitehall, notably the Central Policy Review Staff.[82] Heath and Trend clashed on a number of issues: one was over discussions with the Nixon administration. Heath wanted to ensure the British line was cleared with partners in Europe: to Trend, the approach was anathema. One anecdote serves to illustrate the difference in style between these two formidably able men. Heath was at Chequers and Trend submitted a brief for a cabinet discussion which ended with a paragraph proposing that the Cabinet ask itself the following questions. Heath rang Trend in a fury. 'How dare you put all these questions, wasting my time. If you don't know the answers you should bloody well find out.' Trend retorted 'No, this is the Socratic approach. These are perfectly logical questions that follow a logical sequence. If the Cabinet asks itself those questions in that order, it will ineluctably arrive at a conclusion.' Ted replied curtly 'That's not the sort of brief I want'.[83] Although relations were productive and always correct, there was no great personal warmth or rapport, and Trend's retirement was not unwelcome on either side.[84] John Hunt, who arrived in autumn 1973 from the key post of running the Cabinet Office's European Secretariat, found Heath good to work for, though demanding. Virtually his entire time was spent in crisis conditions; as he arrived, he recalled, 'It struck me that the smell of death was around'.[85]

The job of Cabinet Secretary during the Heath government was separate from that of the Head of the Home Civil Service, as it remained until 1981. During Heath's time the Head of the Home Civil Service was the more influential of the two offices, due mainly to the powerful personality of its incumbent, Sir William Armstrong.

81. Authors' interview with Sir Edward Heath, 21 February 1995.

82. Armstrong interview.

83. Hunt interview.

84. Ibid.

85. Symposium, 'Trade Unions and the Fall of the Heath Government', *Contemporary Record*, vol. 2 no. 1 (1988), 44.

HEAD OF THE HOME CIVIL SERVICE

Armstrong's formal responsibilities as Head of the Home Civil Service did not begin to encompass his role under Heath. The impression that he was embracing tasks outside the strict purview of a civil servant gathered weight after 1972 when he was seen to have played an instrumental role in the switch to incomes policy.[86] A phrase, which he came to bitterly regret, 'Deputy Prime Minister', had been coined by Bill Kendall of the civil service union, the Civil and Public Services Association (CPSA), at the press conference on 6 November 1972.[87] Armstrong and Edward Heath met at a kind of crossroads, as a committed, active civil servant and a highly pragmatic politician fascinated by structures of government. Heath has often been described as a Permanent Secretary *manqué*, a description some of those who worked with him assent to. But if he had been, he would have been in the mould of William Armstrong rather than of Burke Trend.

Heath and Armstrong were in some senses made for each other. Both were action men, doers rather than cogitators. By 1971 he had completed most of the managerial changes following the 1968 Fulton Report. As Frank Cooper, then Deputy Secretary at the Civil Service Department, put it, 'William got very bored with the whole thing . . . He was more and more diverted back into what he regarded as the mainstream of policy issues'.[88] Armstrong cast around for some fresh projects to occupy his formidable energies. Unlike Trend, he showed no signs of tiredness as his long official career approached its close. The first thought was that he would devote himself to the struggle against inflation, but that would have meant coming into the territory of Douglas Allen, Permanent Secretary at the Treasury, and a friend and colleague, so he backed off. Industrial relations and incomes policy then came up as the next suitable task, one he grabbed willingly. From mid-1972, it was taking the great majority of his time, relegating oversight of the Home Civil Service very much to his deputy.[89]

William Armstrong and Burke Trend came to be regarded with some unease by some of the more radical Heathmen such as David Howell, who commented, 'The low point of Burke's and William's influence was the return to incomes policy'.[90] Heath himself sees the relationship

86. Campbell, *Edward Heath*, 491.

87. P. Hennessy, *Whitehall* (London, 1989), 238–41.

88. Symposium, 'The Heath Government', *Contemporary Record*, vol. 9 no. 1 (1995), 212.

89. Authors' interview with Sir John Chilcot, 20 July 1995.

90. Howell interview.

differently. 'His part was in dealing with the prices and incomes policy, because he acted as secretary at the meetings with the trade unions and the employers. But all that has been greatly exaggerated . . . he wasn't dictating policy at all.'[91] As the story of the life and death of the Heath government after 1972 was increasingly that of industrial relations, his role was at once limited but absolutely central. In the final crisis the government proposed an institutionalisation of tripartite talks, which would have increased the role of Armstrong or his successor immeasurably, but the offer was declined by the TUC. John Campbell argues that Armstrong's apocalyptic line on the 1974 crisis contributed to Heath's failure to settle matters with the miners.[92] Armstrong's health collapsed in January 1974 contemporaneously with the government he served. It was an unfortunate ending to the career of one of the most brilliant and unusual civil servants of the postwar era. Dennis Kavanagh, however, believes that had Labour won the general election, Armstrong would not have been acceptable to the new Labour government.[93]

VICTOR ROTHSCHILD AND THE CPRS

Victor Rothschild was appointed Head of the Central Policy Review Staff. The CPRS belonged on the Cabinet Office side of the baize door separating Number 10 from the Cabinet Office. In its founding principles it was always made clear that it worked for the Cabinet collectively, although the Prime Minister had ministerial responsibility for its activities.[94] Its role overlapped a little with that later carried out by the Number 10 Policy Unit, but its collective role and licence to think the unthinkable in 1971–73 put it beyond the more loyal and tactical role of the Policy Unit after 1974. Another comparison would be with the work of the more partisan non-government 'think tanks' during the Thatcher and Major governments, such as the Centre for Policy Studies. Its two main functions during Heath's government were to prepare six-monthly reviews of government strategy, and to prepare studies of particular areas, such as consumer policy. It would occasionally take more direct suggestions from the Prime Minister, as from the Prime Minister on 24 December 1973:

91. Heath interview.
92. Campbell, *Edward Heath*, 490–92.
93. P. Hennessy and A. Seldon (eds), *Ruling Performance* (Oxford, 1987), 221
94. T. Blackstone and W. Plowden, *Inside the Think Tank: Advising the Cabinet 1971–1983* (London, 1988), 53–4.

> In the present situation the Government will necessarily have to take immediate decisions on a very wide range of questions. It will be important to ensure that these decisions are consistent with one another and relate as far as possible to a coherent strategy.[95]

The CPRS was to work closely with the departments to pursue these objectives. Part of the result was the report of 6 February 1974 on possible reform of the Industrial Relations Act, but nothing much happened to realise Heath's intentions.[96]

Victor Rothschild's informal, personal role hung between the Cabinet Office and Number 10. This was embodied by William Waldegrave, possibly the most political member of the CPRS in 1971–73. 'Victor Rothschild had a technique of using me as a sort of runner [to Number 10].'[97] Heath gave remarkable support to Rothschild in his official role, and listened to his private advice. He was an influential voice alongside Maudling in favour of the switch to incomes policy in 1972.[98] One insider observed, 'Though Victor's adversaries were the same as mine, at heart he was an old style Keynesian socialist on economics. On some micro matters he was helpful. That was all'.[99]

Heath used Rothschild in an *ad hominem* capacity for advice on intelligence and security matters. Relations with the Secret Services are always important to a Prime Minister as he alone in the government reads and hears about all major developments. Burke Trend jealously guarded the area, as had Sir Norman Brook before him. Another source of tension between Prime Minister and Cabinet Secretary, then, was Heath's use of Rothschild as a second source of advice to Trend's on these matters. Rothschild's MI5 background and his interest (even delight) in the intelligence world meant it was advice he was keen to proffer, including over Ireland and relations over oil with the Shah of Persia.[100]

Relations between Heath and Rothschild, however, declined after the occasion on 25 September 1973 when a sombre statistical discussion from Rothschild spoiled an upbeat speech on the economy from Heath. There were business-like apologies and the work of the CPRS continued as before, but the personal rapport was damaged.[101] A couple of months later Waldegrave was translated into the Political Office. Roths-

95. Wolff papers, minute M121/73, C1/18/CPRS.
96. Ibid.
97. Waldegrave interview.
98. David Butler interviews (confidential), 18 January 1974, 10 March 1973.
99. Howell interview.
100. Letter from William Waldegrave to Anthony Seldon, 19 August 1995.
101. Heath interview; Waldegrave interview; Blackstone and Plowden, 54.

child had some cynical, but economically justified advice on how to deal with the miners:

> Victor had various quite intelligent ways off the hook. His main contribution at that point was to suggest that the shift in oil prices meant that you should take all energy prices out of the statutory incomes and prices policy on the grounds that the whole thing was busted [because of the Middle East crisis]. But by that stage Ted wasn't in the mood to listen to advice like that.[102]

According to David Howell, the Parliamentary Secretary at the Civil Service Department, and a key thinker on machinery of government in the opposition years, the hopes of the CPRS providing a radical alternative source of advice to government from the civil service were stymied. 'The civil service hijacked it. William Armstrong and Burke Trend moved in round the Prime Minister early on.' He saw the spiking of the CPRS as part of a more general emasculation of his own radicalism. 'Armstrong and Trend moved in on me – lunch at the Athenaeum on the second day of the government. They said these were interesting ideas and they had also prepared a number of papers on how Whitehall could be run more effectively. And hey presto, it was all in their hands, not mine. And Ted ceased to have any time to keep the momentum moving.'[103] Ideas on civil service reform had been worked on in Whitehall before 1970. To those involved in this project Heath's decisions demonstrated the soundness of the principles they adopted rather than bureaucratic inertia.[104] To Howell, only in the 1980s did the ideas he expounded on reorganisation of government reach fruition. 'He had wanted to have people like me around him at Number 10. But the machine, and cabinet colleagues, moved around him. Momentum was lost as early as the first few weeks. I was a disappointed young man.'[105]

Overall, most insiders thought the CPRS was a valuable adjunct to government, and they were critical of Mrs Thatcher's eventual decision to abolish it in 1983. While it is indisputable that the CPRS was never more effective than it had been during 1971–73, its significance can be exaggerated. Its reports on individual areas had little effect on government policy, and its long-term strategic role failed to prevent the government being blown off course in 1973–74.

102. Waldegrave interview.
103. Howell interview.
104. Letter from Sir John Chilcot to authors, 3 August 1995.
105. Howell interview.

MICHAEL WOLFF AND SPEECH-WRITING

Another enigmatic presence was Michael Wolff. He had served Heath closely in opposition as speech writer and general fixer, and for a few days during the interregnum after the 1970 general election handled media relations at Number 10. He was met with a certain amount of suspicion by the civil servants in the Press Office, not necessarily because they were sympathetic to the outgoing Wilson government or because they feared that he would be a permanent appointment and the office would be lastingly politicised.[106] Both he and Heath were accustomed to the simpler arrangements of opposition but adjusted rapidly to the presence of the civil service machine and Wolff's involvement with press relations faded. He became instead 'Special Adviser to the Government'. His salary was paid by the Party and he flitted between Number 10 and Conservative Central Office with a wide, vague brief. Papers on virtually everything passed across one of his desks, although he took a particular interest in party and government propaganda. He worked closely with Douglas Hurd at Number 10 as a link between him and the Conservative Party more generally, and became something of a friend at court for younger MPs.[107] His was a diminishing influence over policy, though he continued to help Edward Heath with many of his speeches and pronouncements, including his message to the nation about entry to the European Economic Community.[108]

Heath did not like sitting down to write speeches. In theory, the Private Office looked at his programme every four months or so to see which major speeches were coming up, and decide what the focus of each should be. Then three weeks before, the Private Office presented him with a skeleton of the speech. Heath's response was often unenthusiastic, in part because he did not wish to focus on an event still so relatively far ahead and preparation for tomorrow had to take precedence over more distant events. Speech-writing thus often became a rather rushed, last minute affair, with regular input from Wolff and Hurd.[109]

106. Maitland interview; James interview.
107. Howell interview.
108. Wolff papers, L4 'Address on Europe'.
109. Bridges interview.

PERSONAL FRIENDS

Heath had several other personal friends who were regular visitors at Number 10 and on whom he could rely for support and advice about matters his officials could not really discuss. Sara Morrison was perhaps the closest and most valued source of advice on social matters and his personal dress and presentation. A trio of political wives, Rosemary Wolff, Araminta Aldington and Sally Kitson were also helpful.[110] Barbara Hosking, a holdover from the Wilson Press Office, developed a personal friendship with Heath based on a common interest in music.[111] A very close friend was his personal physician, Brian Warren (knighted 1974), who acquired an influence that can be compared to that of Lord Moran, doctor to Winston Churchill from 1940. Warren had contested the Brixton division of Lambeth in the 1959 general election. While Heath was at Number 10, Warren was a member of Westminster City Council, and was an influential figure in London local government and Conservative medical circles. Warren's importance was as a source of emotional support and comfort to Heath. Prone to mild hypochondria, he would call Warren in often, though as James Margach writes 'Edward Heath . . . was the fittest of all the Prime Ministers of the century and never had a day's illness worth mentioning'.[112] But, as with Moran and Churchill, Warren had no discernible political influence.

CONCLUSIONS

Heath's Number 10, as was intended, was a significant improvement on Wilson's in 1964–70. Several parts of it worked better, notably the Private Office and Press Office, at least until 1973. Relations at Number 10 were more harmonious, demarcation between government and party matters more meticulously followed, and professionalism more to the fore. The difference between Wilson and Heath as captains of Downing Street, as indeed between them as leaders of government, was rather less than was hoped back in June 1970. A representation of the influence on Heath of the key players at Number 10 is given in Figure 1 on the next page.

But the central question remains of how well an admittedly grand pair of back-to-backs knocked together could serve as the engine room for the leader of a modern industrial nation, the government of which

110. Maitland interview.

111. Hosking interview.

112. James Margach, *The Anatomy of Power* (London, 1979), 54.

FIGURE 3.1 *Relative influence of different figures at Number 10 on the Prime Minster*

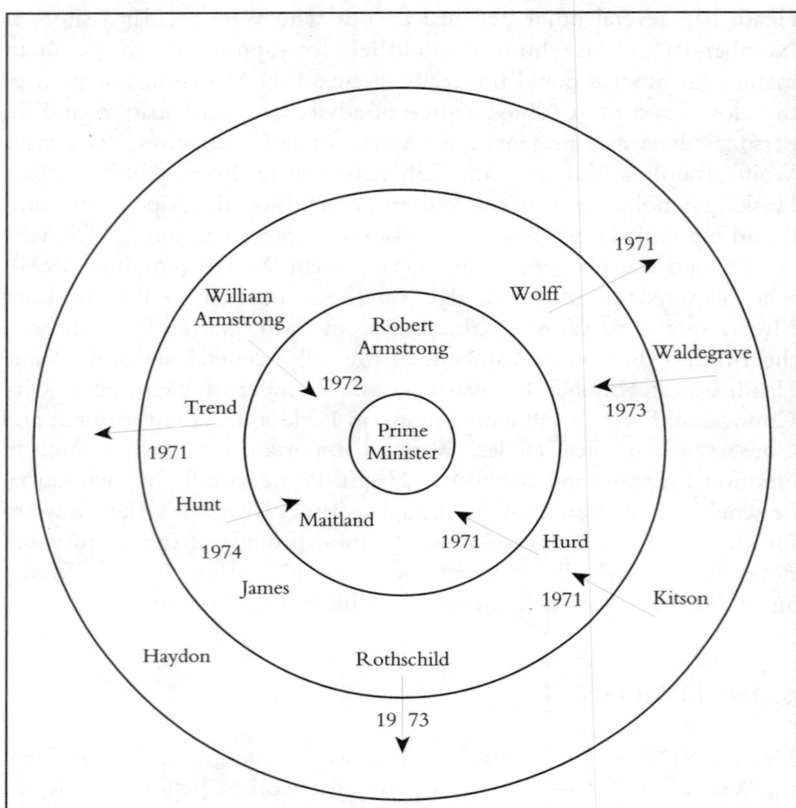

Note: The inner circle by the Prime Minister indicates greatest influence on the PM, the middle band less but still significant influence, the outer band little influence. Arrows indicate approximate dates when an individual's influence shifted. Excluded are figures like Hewitt, whose influence on Heath's thinking was minimal.

became even more complex with membership of the European Community half-way through Heath's premiership. Donald Maitland, on arrival, was struck by how amateurish the operation was.[113] Twenty-five years on, Number 10 is still a cause of concern about efficiency. Douglas Hurd still considers the centre 'ill-equipped', and would approve of an increase in the resources available to the Prime Minister.[114]

113. Maitland interview.
114. Hurd interview.

The overall number of staff employed at Number 10 did not change under Heath. In his May 1972 interview with the *Evening Standard*, Heath commented with equanimity that there were virtually the same number of people employed there as under Harold Wilson – sixty-three or sixty-four. Exactly the same number were employed at Number 10 by Mrs Thatcher in 1986.[115]

The prospects of the estabishment of a Prime Minister's Department were probably at their highest in 1970, but the option was not taken. Britain's central administration was being recast, with the establishment of the Civil Service Department in 1968 and the jumbo departments thereafter. Management reform was in the air. Edward Heath was perhaps the most personally inclined of all the Prime Ministers since Lloyd George to experiment with Britain's central institutions. He had no compunction about upgrading the office towards presidentialism in his relations with Parliament, in creating the Central Policy Review Staff, and in acquiring trappings of authority such as the press conferences. In William Armstrong he had an eager recruit for the office of first Permanent Secretary or Chief of Staff. David Howell had proposed a Prime Minister's Department on the lines of those in Germany, the USA, Canada, France and Italy.[116] The reasons why it did not happen are perhaps to be found less in civil service obstruction than in Heath's own unwillingness to create such a new body. Had he wanted to, he could have done so. He would have risked discontent in Parliament and allegations of rampant presidentialism.

But what might such a Prime Minister's Department have looked like? No agreed blueprint emerged under Heath's leadership. Any reformulation of Number 10 would have had to be based on what one needed it to *do*. Figure 3.2 examines the main functions of the Prime Minister, and the support provided by Number 10 for each. The clearest gap in support was in Heath's role as head of government policy: it was into this gap that William Armstrong fell.

Heath's Number 10 was clearly an important stage in the development of the institutions of the Prime Minister's Office. The Central Policy Review Staff, despite its institutional survival until 1983, was not the same after the fall of Heath, and is therefore in a sense the most transitory of the changes made to the central operations of the British government in 1970–74. The office of Political Secretary survived the change of government in 1970 and has become an accepted part of the institutional scene. Matching offices were developing in the

115. Hennessy, *Whitehall*, 382–7.
116. Howell interview.

FIGURE 3.2 *Prime Minister's Functions and Support*

Head of the Executive	Head of the Home Civil Service Cabinet Secretary Private Office
Head of Government Policy	CPRS (strategic planning) Press Office (communication)
Party Leader	Political Secretary (Central Office) Parliamentary Private Secretary (Parliamentary Party)
Head Appointing Officer	Appointments Secretary (Crown appointments) Head of the Home Civil Service (senior Whitehall jobs) Principal Private Secretary (ministerial appointments)
Leader of Party in Parliament	Parliamentary Private Secretary Private Secretary – Parliament
Senior British Representative Overseas	Cabinet Secretary (Commonwealth) Principal Private Secretary (Europe) Private Secretary – Foreign Affairs (all areas)

other ministries. The burden of that office, and the collective and long-term purpose of the Central Policy Review Staff, led to increasing realisation that there was a gap for a personal medium-term capacity at Number 10 working for the Prime Minister. The logical next step was to build on the embryonic office set up under Thomas Balogh in 1964.[117] According to Andrew Graham, this initiative provided the model for Harold Wilson when he asked Bernard Donoughue to establish the Policy Unit in 1974, situated significantly on the Number 10 side rather than the Cabinet Office side of the green baize door.

The lasting effects of Heath's tenure of Number 10 are perhaps subtle. By declining the option of a Prime Minister's Department, deciding instead to improve the existent system's effectiveness, he preserved the rather ramshackle Number 10 machine. Heath's path of cautious reform, which he inherited from Wilson, has been followed by all his successors to date.

117. Andrew Graham, 'No 10 Policy Unit', ICBH witness seminar, 13 July 1995.

CHAPTER FOUR

The Heath government, Whitehall and the civil service

Kevin Theakston

The civil service embodies and provides for continuity in government. When Edward Heath first entered Number 10 as Prime Minister on 19 June 1970, the civil service staff and private secretaries lined up in the entrance hall and, as is the tradition, applauded the new head of the government. Douglas Hurd, Heath's Political Secretary, was shown round his new office while Marcia Williams, aide to the outgoing Labour premier, was still upstairs in the building, frantically packing up Harold Wilson's files. As Heath and William Whitelaw, the Chief Whip, settled down to work into the small hours putting the finishing touches to the list of ministerial appointments, Sandy Isserlis, the Principal Private Secretary, made the arrangements for food and drink. The civil service had obviously got used to Wilson's style – to Whitelaw's dismay, beer and pork pies were served up.[1]

It did not take long for Heath to stamp his authority on the machine. New appointments were made in Number 10. A major reorganisation of government had been planned in opposition and steps were rapidly taken to introduce the Conservatives' reforms. Civil servants soon realised that Heath was a clear and decisive leader.

Stanley Baldwin, the interwar Conservative Prime Minister, once said the machinery of government was 'a subject distasteful or dull'. Heath was fascinated by it. He had actually been a civil servant for a year after the war, in the Ministry of Civil Aviation, and in many ways would have made an outstanding top permanent secretary. His approach to government was managerial, rational, and problem-solving. His critics accused him of being too much like a civil servant and felt that he was over-influenced by certain senior officials, particularly Sir William Armstrong, the Head of the Home Civil Service. Although he had a high regard for the civil service, he was convinced that reform of the

1. D. Hurd, *An End to Promises: Sketch of a Government 1970–1974* (London, 1979), 31.

Whitehall machine was urgently required to make government more efficient and to improve the quality of decision-making.

PREPARATIONS IN OPPOSITION

No party has entered office with such extensive and detailed plans for improving the structures and processes of the Whitehall machine as the Conservatives in 1970.

Reform of the machinery of government had appeared on the Conservative Party's agenda almost immediately after the 1964 election defeat. Hitherto, there had been little serious or sustained attention paid in Conservative circles to this issue. Though there were calls for a more commercially orientated civil service and for the use of 'modern scientific managment techniques' in the pamphlet *Change or Decay* published in 1962 by a group of Conservative MPs led by Airey Neave, and though Macmillan's government had undertaken important reforms of the Whitehall machine (reorganising the Treasury, introducing a new public expenditure planning system, and announcing plans to create a unified Ministry of Defence), with Douglas-Home privately considering a further shake-up if he were returned to office, the Labour Party and its Fabian allies had made most of the running on the fashionable subject of institutional modernisation in the early sixties.

At one level, the question after 1964 was how far the Conservatives could go along with the changes in the departmental structure and in the civil service introduced and occasioned by the Wilson government. Heath was scathing about Wilson's approach to the machinery of government, dismissing the Department of Economic Affairs and the Ministry of Technology as gimmicks that would be abolished and presenting his own plans and approach as 'rational' and efficiency-orientated. Some of Heath's advisers believed that serious-minded and extensive preparations for administrative reform might assist the Party in carrying conviction with the public and winning power (providing evidence that the Party knew how to do what it said it was going to do). And while not hostile to the Fulton committee on the civil service (1966–68), the Conservatives carefully made themselves independent of its report. Unlike the Labour and Liberal parties, the Conservative Party decided not to give evidence to the committee, though a number of Tory ex-ministers did so and Heath gave his views at an informal meeting with Fulton.[2]

2. Conservative Party, Public Sector Research Unit (PSRU), Progress Report: 12 January 1968, CPA CRD/3/14/8, CCO/20/26/6; G. Fry, *Reforming the Civil Service* (Edinburgh, 1993), 5.

At another level, it was for Heath not enough just to react to Labour initiatives in this field. Administrative reform was necessarily connected to the wider Conservative project. Heath insisted that he was not interested in playing with the machinery of government for its own sake but because he wanted to have the means of achieving his wider policy objectives. The 'war on inefficiency and waste' promised in the 1966 manifesto, and the argument that new management techniques would yield significant economies, was a way of squaring tax cuts with increased spending on favoured programmes. More fundamentally, the collectivist assumption (made by the Fulton committee, for instance) that the state would continue to be 'the great provider' was now questioned by the Conservatives, who linked their plans for Whitehall with a reduction in the scale and scope of central government. 'There is all the difference in the world between reform of government machinery and procedures under a party which believes in more government and under one which believes in less', argued David Howell MP. 'Under the latter it becomes . . . a key instrument in the drive for . . . economy and in the process of transferring functions and activities back to the private sector or running them down altogether.'[3]

The Conservative rethink on Whitehall after the 1964 general election was a rather disjointed exercise, with a number of different groups weighing in with advice and views at different times, though Heath's close interest in the issues involved was a constant. As early as November 1964, ideas about machinery of government reform were being aired at a Swinton College conference. While criticisms of 'amateur' mandarins were unsurprisingly rejected by a group chaired by Lord Normanbrook, the former Cabinet Secretary, the creation of some sort of 'central organisation' to focus on long-term problems and counter the tendency for governments to live from hand to mouth was mooted.[4]

Heath made his own views plain in a talk at that Swinton weekend, eight months before becoming Party leader. First, he wanted a smaller Cabinet committed to a clear set of priorities, and a system of larger, 'federal' departments. Second, he disliked the standard Whitehall committee practice of searching for the lowest common denominator of inter-departmental agreement and compromise, and wanted more use of trouble-shooting 'task forces' of the sort put together for the European Economic Community entry negotiations 1961–63. Third, the civil service was insufficiently dynamic and efficient:

3. D. Howell, *A New Style of Government* (London, 1970), 8.

4. 'Policy Group on the Machinery of Government: Cabinet Government and the Civil Service, weekend discussion on the machinery of government', Boyle papers, Brotherton Library, University of Leeds, MS.660/23776, folios 8–10.

> Far from the Civil Service running the Government, as the public sometimes believes, on too many occasions the Civil Service does not say plainly what it thinks policy ought to be . . . [It] is not equipped to take the initiative in so many of the technical fields today . . . specialists must be brought in on secondment . . . We may indeed have got to a stage where the whole system of minutes and letters has reached such a stage of perfection that it is in fact a block in the way of speedy and efficient work.

But, Heath warned,

> We must . . . be sensible about the size of the Civil Service. One of the things which worries me most about our period in Opposition is that we may become silly, as I believe we did between 1945 and 1951, about the size of the Civil Service. If we are going to be properly serviced in the modern world we have got to have the people to do it and pay them properly.

Finally, Heath suggested that a way had to be found to provide more support for the prime minister while avoiding the problems caused by a 'garden suburb' outfit.[5]

'Heath . . . hankered after a French-style Civil Service with highly trained officials not afraid to take a strong line', according to Peter Hennessy. What was wanted from civil servants was 'straight thinking', he told the Commons in 1968. They must 'identify problems and issues clearly, and . . . think out a policy which would lead to a solution as logically and clearly as possible.' His experience in Downing Street only strengthened his views. 'It's a Rolls-Royce machine and perhaps we could get along with something which wasn't quite so smooth', was his late-seventies verdict, and he complained of Whitehall's 'quality of inertia that leads to delay and a refusal to accept innovation.'[6]

The Party's policy group (chaired first by Heath and then by Sir Edward Boyle) had started to look at the Cabinet system and the machinery of government before the change of Party leadership and by the end of 1965 had formulated proposals, which were approved by the shadow cabinet, that largely prefigured the departmental pattern fashioned in 1970: there would be one economics department, a large industry ministry and amalgamations elsewhere to simplify the structure (in 1964 Heath had talked of merging Health, Pensions, and National

5. 'Talk by Mr Edward Heath at Swinton College weekend course on the Machinery of government', November 1964, Boyle papers, MS.660/23778.

6. P. Hennessy, *Whitehall* (London, 1989), 238; *House of Commons Debates*, 5th series, vol. 773, cols. 1572–3, 21 November 1968; E. Heath and A. Barker, 'Heath on Whitehall reform', *Parliamentary Affairs*, 31 (1978), 382; *The Times*, 8 May 1980.

Assistance into one Social Services federal department, as Wilson was to do in 1968).[7]

On a different front, Mark Schreiber of the Conservative Research Department and David Howell (nominally supervised by Ernest Marples) worked on new analytical and managerial techniques. They visited Japan and the United States in 1965 and came back enthusing about US Defense Secretary Robert McNamara's methods at the Pentagon and about Programme Budgeting (which was at that time all the rage in Washington DC). The idea of a central unit pushing for greater effectiveness and efficiency in government originated with Schreiber, who proposed a Public Sector Efficiency Unit in September 1965. In one form or another – a Crown Consultancy Unit, a Cost-Effectiveness Department (the 1966 manifesto version), and an Office of Government Reorganisation and Efficiency were other labels – the intention was to enable the prime minister to get a better managerial grip on the Whitehall machine.[8]

From March 1967 this work continued under the roof of the party's newly formed Public Sector Research Unit (PSRU). There were studies of the use of computers in the public sector, and of accountable management. Private-sector consultants were hired for particular projects: RTZ Consultants put together a report on government decision-making and Arthur D. Little looked at public procurement. At the same time, Howell strongly insisted that the Conservative goal had to be less government: his memos, articles and pamphlets were peppered with references to 'overloaded' government, 'rolling back the frontiers of the state', and winding-up activities or returning them to the private sector. He wanted to separate policy-making from administrative or management functions, 'hiving-off' the latter to autonomous agencies.[9] It was the PSRU which organised the important Sundridge Park conference on 'preparation for government' in September 1969, which brought together Conservative Party 'backroom' advisers, shadow cabinet members, former civil servants and outside business advisers for an extensive series of briefings and discussions on 'hiving-off', budgeting and management reforms.[10]

7. 'Policy Group on the Machinery of Government: Report on the Cabinet System', March 1966, CPA ACP(66)32; C. Pollitt, *Manipulating the Machine* (London, 1984), 83.

8. PSRU, Progress Report 12 January 1968, CRD/3/14/8; report on proposed Crown Consultancy Unit, Policy Group on Science and Technology, June 1969, ACP(69)62.

9. Howell, *New Style of Government*; *The Times*, 14 March 1967; 'Report on the work of the Conservative Party's Research Unit on Preparation for Government and Administrative Reform', by D. Howell, 22 January 1970, ACP(70)70.

10. 'Preparation for Government', PSRU seminar, Sundridge Park, 15–26 September 1969, CCO/20/26/8.

By late 1969 a 'Businessmen's Team' had taken shape, led by Richard Meyjes from Shell, to work in small groups on various projects including decision-making processes (what later became Programme Analysis and Review), procurement arrangements (Derek Rayner of Marks and Spencer taking the lead), and 'hiving-off'. The intention was that a number of these advisers would be 'loaned' by their companies to a Conservative government for perhaps two years after the election to translate their plans into practice.[11]

Heath commissioned additional personal advice from a number of former senior civil servants during 1968–69. A group chaired by the formidable former permanent secretary Dame Evelyn Sharp sent him three reports on the machinery of government including, at Heath's specific request, advice about the organisation of a possible 'Prime Minister's Department' – the group eventually recommending an 'Office of the Prime Minister and Cabinet' brigading the Cabinet Secretariat, the functions of the Civil Service Department and a new central planning staff to help establish and maintain a clear set of priorities.[12]

The impact that all this work and advice had on Heath and other leading Conservatives is not particularly clear. The PSRU team and the businessmen were not sure that shadow ministers fully understood their ideas and felt that some were actually very sceptical. The Sharp group came away from a meeting with Heath uncertain about his reaction to their recommendations. 'Ted has played this one rather close to his chest', noted one adviser in the files.[13] However, at Heath's instruction, the various proposals from the PSRU and the businessmen's team were brought together in an 'action plan' document (the so-called 'Black Book') just before the election in 1970. And the commitment to a 'new style of government' was prominent in the Party's manifesto in terms which Heath had foreshadowed in his October 1968 Party conference speech. Whatever his remarks in 1964, he had then pledged to 'prune drastically' the number of civil servants, and the manifesto was equally uncompromising: 'There has been too much government: there will be less.' There would be fewer civil servants, reduced spending and more efficient government.

11. Pollitt, *Manipulating the Machine*, 85–6.

12. Machinery of Government Group (chairman, Baroness Sharp, 1968–69), 'First Report to Mr Heath', February 1969, CRD/3/14/4–5; T. Blackstone and W. Plowden, *Inside the Think Tank* (London, 1988), 6–8.

13. J. Douglas to Lord Carrington, 16 October 1969, CRD/3/14/4.

THE HEATH GOVERNMENT AND THE MANDARINS

In contrast to the incoming Conservative governments of 1951 and 1979, the leading figures in the new government in 1970 do not seem to have been particularly wary or suspicious of the civil service after a period of Labour rule. There were doubts in some quarters. Keith Joseph, for instance, was privately concerned that ministers planning to cut back functions and staff would 'have to work against inertia – and worse'. And the PSRU warned Heath in a secret memorandum in June 1970 that 'many of the incoming political decision-makers are unlikely to know how to get things done in government. In some cases they will at once be absorbed into and run by the present bureaucratic system.' The lack of clear goals, the absence of information about the scope for cuts and the public expenditure resources available, the pressure of day-to-day business and crises, and the lack of analytical capability could together, the PSRU argued, 'minimise the impact of an incoming administration', adding that 'civil servants have plenty of well-tried and frequently successful techniques for diverting ministers from innovative behaviour which is too disruptive.'[14]

Heath had warned his shadow cabinet in December 1969 that they would need to 'challenge long-established official assumptions and viewpoints' and prepare thoroughly in opposition 'if they were not to be defeated by administrative difficulties at the outset.' But he seems to have felt that he could establish ministerial control. At the time of the Fulton committee, he had rejected arguments that ministers needed the support of *cabinets* and suggested that Labour ministers were too weak or too overwhelmed to get a firm grip on their departments. He always insisted that Whitehall was under firm political control during his administration. Three years after leaving Downing Street he told the Expenditure Committee that

> to say that the power of the Civil Service has been greatly increased or increased between 1970 and 1974 bears absolutely no resemblance to reality at all. It is the Ministers who have the power of decision, the Cabinet the collective power and I have not experienced situations in which Civil Servants, however high, have tried to persuade me against my will, or my colleagues against my will, to carry out policies which we did not accept or did not believe in or were not prepared to operate.[15]

14. K. Joseph to R. Carr, 3 March 1970, CRD/3/14/4; PSRU, *Action Plans: Proposals from Action Group 1*, 3 June 1970, 5–9.

15. G. Hutchinson, *Edward Heath* (London, 1970), 179–80; *The Times*, 20 January 1967; Expenditure Committee, *The Civil Service*, House of Commons Papers 535 (1976–77), qs. 1877, 1910.

The experience of the Conservative government 1970–74 provides evidence supporting this muscular image of ministerial dominance but in other ways also fuelled the controversy over civil servants' power. Heath's critics argue that the power of the civil service increased alarmingly during his time in office.

'Faced with a Conservative Government committed to a well-worked out and comprehensive reversal of national policy, the Civil Service shuddered – and then set to', was Richard Crossman's judgement on the transition of power in 1970. Jock Bruce-Gardyne, an unsympathetic Conservative chronicler, conceded that the Heath administration did indeed 'succeed in imposing itself on the departmental hierarchies' more than most governments up until then.[16]

The Conservatives had set out in opposition to make policy without civil service 'guidance', particularly in the fields of industrial relations and tax reform. Robert Carr arrived at the Department of Employment with a detailed programme already worked out that was virtually draft legislation. Some senior departmental officials were dubious about the Conservatives' proposals, but their objections were swept aside and the Industrial Relations Act quickly put onto the statute books. No-one could argue that the civil service thwarted the government's mandate, but – of course – the real lesson here, according to John Campbell, might be that 'policies determined inflexibly in opposition, in defiance of official advice, may lack realism when they come to be implemented in office.'[17]

At the Ministry of Housing, Peter Walker peremptorily brushed aside the arguments of his permanent secretary and made it clear that the Redcliffe–Maud local government reorganisation plan – commissioned by the Labour government and backed by the department – would not now be implemented. Local government reorganisation went off instead in a different direction, with Walker himself writing large parts of the Conservative's own White Paper. The new Education Secretary, Margaret Thatcher, turned up in her ministry with a page torn from an exercise book and a handwritten list of eighteen things she wanted done that day. (She was, however, talked out of killing off the Open University and, in the event, failed to halt the move to comprehensive schools.)

On the other hand, some Conservative right-wingers suspected that Foreign Office pressure or resistance contributed to the apparent failure

16. R. Crossman, *Inside View* (London, 1972), 48; J. Bruce-Gardyne, *Whatever Happened to the Quiet Revolution?* (London, 1974), 164.

17. B. Headey, *British Cabinet Ministers* (London, 1974), 202–4; J. Campbell, *Edward Heath: A Biography* (London, 1993), 221.

of the government's policy on Rhodesia and to the changes in policy on arms sales to South Africa and withdrawal from east of Suez. In opposition, Heath had berated the Foreign Office for its 'feebleness and bad faith' on withdrawal from the Gulf, but with the Treasury and the Ministry of Defence, as well as the Foreign and Commonwealth Office (FCO), unenthusiastic, and the resource-constraints remaining as powerful as ever, he had bowed to the inevitable by 1971. It is clear also that the Foreign Office disliked the idea of an Anglo-French nuclear partnership which had been floated by Heath in opposition, but this notion faded away more because the French were not interested and it was no longer relevant in the changed European situation the government faced in 1970–71 than simply because the diplomats were defending their entrenched positions.[18]

The failures of the Heath administration, and particularly the economic policy U-turn, encouraged a more fundamental criticism – that the civil service machine was in fact a significant obstacle in the way of the attainment of declared Conservative objectives. Nicholas Ridley (sacked as a Department of Trade and Industry minister in 1972) argued as much while the Conservatives were still in office. In a pamphlet published by the ardently free enterprise Aims of Industry in 1973, Ridley depicted Whitehall as an organised conspiracy against consensus-busting ministers. Many of his arguments about civil service obstruction and sabotage were similar to those of the Labour left, but Ridley's political point was that the mandarins 'made it hard for us to carry out some aspects of our Conservative policy', meaning the free-market policies of 1970. On this view, Heath had lacked the political determination to overthrow Whitehall's middle-ground conventional wisdom. Instead, his government succumbed to the mandarins' preference for public ownership and incomes policy.[19]

But it was not just Conservative right-wingers like Ridley who were critical of the civil service in the 1970s as the lessons of the Heath government were digested. The problem of 'an over-mighty civil service' with 'its own objectives' and with ministers often 'the creatures of their departments' also troubled a Tory intellectual like William Waldegrave (who had worked in the Central Policy Review Staff and in Number 10). And Douglas Hurd's experience as Heath's political adviser left him convinced that Whitehall's 'firm belief in the merits of action by the state' actually worked to the advantage of Labour governments and meant that the civil service was not a natural ally of the

18. Hurd, *An End To Promises*, 42; Bruce-Gardyne, *Whatever Happened?* 54–8.
19. N. Ridley, *Industry and the Civil Service* (London, 1973).

Conservative Party, especially if they were trying to cut back the public sector, as in 1970–71. 'The truth is that a party which believes in reducing the power of the state will always face serious problems with civil servants at all levels.'[20]

Heath's alleged pusillanimity in face of the mandarins – and its disastrous political consequences – was a key theme in Conservative thinking in the late 1970s, making the Thatcherites distrustful of and aggressive towards the civil service in and after 1979.

In the crucial economic policy field, however, Heath's political will was firmly asserted over the Treasury, traditionally the citadel of civil service power. Many prime ministers have been suspicious of (or have even feared) the Treasury. Heath certainly distrusted the Treasury and – in the view of former 'insiders' – interfered with it far more than he would have been able to do had Macleod not died. Heath was critical of the Treasury because of its gloomy economic growth and balance of payments forecasts, and because it was not fully behind him in its views about the economic consequences of EEC membership. (From the 1960s it had not shared his enthusiasm about joining Europe.) 'There was a certain amount of feeling that the Treasury was pulling against some of the main objectives that the Prime Minister [Heath] had', recalled Lord Croham, permanent secretary to the Treasury 1968–74. Cabinet Office 'keepers' were sent to accompany Treasury officials on some missions in case they handled things in discussions in Europe in ways that were not in line with Heath's approach.[21]

The Keynesian economic policy framework remained overwhelmingly dominant in the Treasury and Whitehall, though by 1973 parts of the Treasury were starting to look at the money supply and at domestic credit expansion. But the Treasury was dismayed that Heath would not axe the three 'jumbo projects' – Concorde, the third London airport and the Channel Tunnel – and, to its chagrin, large increases in public spending were pushed through from 1972 onwards. A critical sign of the Prime Minister's lack of favour was the way in which that expansion in public expenditure was organised not by the Treasury but by the Cabinet Office, and by William Armstrong working with William Nield (see below).

Significantly, in 1977 Heath backed the idea then being floated to split the Treasury, taking away its public spending responsibilities and

20. W. Waldegrave, *The Binding of Leviathan* (London, 1978), 74–5, 81; Hurd, *An End To Promises*, 29–30.

21. Institute of Contemporary British History (ICBH) witness seminar, February 1994, text published in 'The Heath Government', *Contemporary Record*, vol. 9, no. 1 (1995) 188–219.

leaving it as a Ministry of Finance, acknowledging that one aim would be to give the Prime Minister a bigger role as an economic policy arbiter.[22]

Heath's enemies attacked him as 'a civil servants' Prime Minister.' It is true that he had a high regard for the civil service as an institution and seemed to prefer to surround himself with the senior mandarins, and to rely upon them for advice, rather than looking to Cabinet colleagues, Party advisers or political cronies. The Thatcherite political analyst Martin Holmes argues that Heath's 'over-reliance on the civil service was a central feature of his Prime Ministerial style of government.'[23] But Douglas Hurd rejected the notion that this meant that civil servants shaped his ideas, a view shared by senior officials who worked closely with the Prime Minister. 'He used to get us all together to talk something through', recalled Sir Robert Armstrong. 'He would sit down and say nothing for half an hour. And suddenly he would say, "That's enough". He would listen to a talk and then he suddenly made up his mind. But I wouldn't say that any one person particularly influenced it.'[24]

If Heath was critical of the civil service it was for not being innovative or forceful enough. He disliked 'its reticence at moments of crisis' argues Peter Hennessy. 'In rough times, when existing policies have collapsed, a Prime Minister will find that the senior civil servants fall silent', Hurd discovered. At three critical moments he felt that the civil service 'fell below what was required': after Bloody Sunday in 1972, during the discussions on inflation in the summer of 1973, and in November 1973 as the coal crisis deepened. 'No one who was present at any of these three meetings could believe that the civil service runs this country' Hurd argues.[25]

Heath's immediate replacement of Sandy Isserlis, appointed Wilson's Principal Private Secretary in April 1970, had produced a Wilson-inspired but short-lived newspaper storm about 'fears of [a] civil service purge'. Although continuity in this post was the norm (as in 1964, 1974 and 1979), Whitehall accepted that on a change of government (or minister) private secretary posts may sometimes change because of the personal relationship involved. The indications are that Isserlis had been Wilson's rather than the civil service's choice and Sir William Armstrong had warned Isserlis that his might be only a caretaker

22. Expenditure Committee, *The Civil Service*, q. 1868.

23. M. Holmes, *Political Pressure and Economic Policy: British Government 1970–1974* (London, 1982), 131.

24. ICBH, witness seminar, February 1994, in 'The Heath Government.'

25. Hennessy, *Whitehall*, 238; Hurd, *An End To Promises*, 36, 117–18.

assignment until the election.[26] His replacement, Robert Armstrong, a brilliant Treasury 'high-flyer' (and later Secretary to the Cabinet and Head of the Home Civil Service), was famously skilful and efficient in this crucial post linking Number 10 and the official Whitehall machine, his close relationship with Heath cemented by a shared love of music.

Heath's other Downing Street appointments in 1970 signalled a change of style and tone from the Wilson 'kitchen cabinet' regime. In place of the highly political journalist Joe Haines, Heath chose as his Chief Press Secretary a career Foreign Office diplomat, Donald Maitland (with whom he had worked during the EEC talks in the 1960s and who was succeeded in 1973 by another Foreign Office man, Robin Haydon). Barbara Hosking, who had joined Wilson's Press Office from Transport House, was (surprisingly) kept on by Heath. In contrast to the situation with Mrs Thatcher and Bernard Ingham after 1979, the Downing Street press operation in the Heath years kept a scrupulously clear line between official government and party affairs. Maitland played a 'punctilious straight bat', in Heath biographer John Campbell's words, but – true to type – gave very little away: something which suited Heath, who was careless of his image and of personal projection. Douglas Hurd, Heath's Political Secretary (from 1967) also had a Foreign Office background and (unlike Wilson's aide Marcia Williams) did not upset any civil service applecarts, striking up a relatively smooth and cooperative relationship with the Number 10 private secretaries. Heath also took into Downing Street Michael Wolff as 'chief of staff', who functioned as a speech-writer.[27]

The absence of a 'kitchen cabinet' or a Downing Street Policy Unit of politically sympathetic advisers of the type instituted by Wilson in 1974 and copied by subsequent premiers, meant that Heath was, to a large extent, dependent on civil service advice. Although this suited him, it later turned out to be a weakness as the government ploughed on into turbulent political waters. Other Conservative ministers similarly depended predominantly on the official machine for advice and support. There had been some talk of ministerial *cabinets* but this came to little and, though some ministers took special advisers recruited from Central Office or the Conservative Research Department with them into their departments, these were not in the numbers found in later governments. At the Foreign Office, Sir Alec Douglas-Home was assisted by Miles Hudson, Brendon Sewill worked with Barber at the Treasury, John Cope advised John Davies and then Peter Walker at Trade and Industry,

26. *The Times*, 10 and 11 July 1970.
27. Campbell, *Edward Heath*, 290–1; Hurd, *An End To Promises*, 35.

and there were two or three others. But their impact was marginal and only towards the end of the government did Douglas Hurd manage to organise something of a political network with meetings of the advisers. One of the lessons of 1970–74, as John Campbell noted, was that governments needed more political advisers 'to prevent ministers becoming entirely smothered by the pressures of administration and to keep them in touch with their party.[28]

Heath's administrative approach to politics was seen in his experiments with 'mixed' committees of ministers and officials intermingled together (rather than the usual pattern of separate ministerial and civil service groups). Dennis Kavanagh's view was that this 'probably enhanced the political influence of civil servants',[29] though former 'insiders' seem more doubtful. 'It had a slightly forced atmosphere. Officials would not disagree with their Ministers', was the view of one participant. 'Mixed committees tend never to work', judged a former permanent secretary. 'Ministers and civil servants think differently; different things are important to them.'

The relationship between Heath and Sir Burke Trend, who was Secretary to the Cabinet for the first three years of his premiership, was at times strained. The problem was not that Trend (Cabinet Secretary since 1963) had been the despised Wilson's chief Whitehall adviser and aide, but that Heath was impatient of his classic and polished mandarin approach – self-effacing, carefully non-committal and detached, with 'Socratic' briefs indicating the key questions rather than making firm recommendations. Heath always wanted a definite view on what should be done, not an analysis of the options with their pros and cons. Trend's successor, Sir John Hunt, appointed in 1973, was more in the mould of dynamic managers and active fixer-doers favoured by Heath. Hunt was to make the Cabinet Office in the mid- and late-1970s a powerhouse, increasing its policy influence and (after the fall of William Armstrong) carving out a place for himself as the most powerful civil servant in Whitehall.

There is no question but that Sir William Armstrong was *the* dominant Whitehall figure during the Heath administration. Armstrong had been catapulted into the front rank when he was made Joint Permanent Secretary to the Treasury in 1962 at the age of 47. In 1968 he had become Head of the Civil Service, in charge of the new Civil Service Department, to push through the Fulton reforms, but by 1971–72 he

28. Campbell, *Edward Heath*, 326.

29. D. Kavanagh, 'The Heath Government, 1970–1974', in P. Hennessy and A. Seldon (eds), *Ruling Performance: British Governments from Attlee to Thatcher* (Oxford, 1987), 220.

was feeling that he had done about all he could on that front and was hankering after a central role in economic policy-making again. With the Treasury out of favour and the Heath–Trend relationship rather 'prickly',[30] he was able to establish a close rapport with the Prime Minister. 'William Armstrong was always at Number 10', recalled a former minister. 'He and Heath were closeted together the whole time.'[31]

As unemployment rose and Heath became convinced of the need for economic and industrial expansion prior to entering Europe, it was William Armstrong he turned to in November 1971 to organise the change of direction in policy. He was put in charge of a secret Cabinet Office committee, working with a handful of officials from the relevant departments and from the Central Policy Review Staff (CPRS) and reporting direct to the Prime Minister. Whitehall's 'need-to-know' principle was ruthlessly applied. Leo Pliatzky represented the Treasury – at the top of that department, Sir Douglas Allen and Sir Samuel Goldman knew about this operation but John Hunt and Peter Baldwin, the Deputy and Under-Secretaries on the public expenditure side, were not involved. As the committee put together a package of measures and prepared what was to become the 1972 Industry Act, it became 'difficult . . . to prevent excessively large numbers from being attached to every proposal through a sort of bidding-up process', Pliatzky recalled. 'The PAR approach, which was supposed to involve the costing of options and a comparison of inputs with outputs, had no place in this numbers game.'[32] Only a small number of ministers were kept in the picture and Heath decreed that the junior ministers at the Department of Trade and Industry – free-market men – must be told nothing.

Increasingly, Heath now leaned on Armstrong in the development of the government's economic policy and for general political advice. Theirs became one of the most extraordinary Prime Minister–civil servant relationships of recent times, but Armstrong's over-identification with Heath made him into a latter-day Horace Wilson. In the summer of 1972 there was press speculation that Armstrong would be put in charge of a new Prime Minister's Department, but though he dismissed this as 'silly season stuff' he did become something like the PM's chief of staff. The chief architect of the statutory incomes policy introduced at the end of 1972, Armstrong was labelled the 'Deputy Prime Minister'

30. Hennessy, *Whitehall*, 238.

31. Private information: interview with former minister.

32. L. Pliatzky, *Getting and Spending: Public Expenditure, Employment and Inflation* (Oxford, 1982), 109.

by union leaders after he had appeared sitting alongside the premier at Heath's Lancaster House presidential-style televised press conference in November 1972, at which was announced the ninety-day pay and prices freeze. (Armstrong later admitted this had been a bad mistake). He accompanied Heath at a meeting with the miners' union leadership in July 1973 which was kept secret from the Cabinet. And in the winter crisis of 1973–74, as the government and the NUM clashed, Armstrong was among the 'hawks', urging a tough line, and even giving advice on the highly party-political matter of election timing – something which he later acknowledged was crossing the boundary between civil service and political roles.[33]

William Armstrong, in the Heath years, clearly became a political official, 'not so much in the ideological sense as in his ambitious desire to embrace a policy without the civil servant's ultimate detachment', as Phillip Whitehead put it.[34] He cracked under the strain, a nervous breakdown removing him from the scene in February 1974 at the denouement of the crisis. His early retirement in March 1974 prevented any awkwardness with the incoming Labour government which had won the election he had advised Heath against calling, for Armstrong had become *persona non grata* with Labour.

A NEW STYLE OF GOVERNMENT

On 15 October 1970, less than four months after the election, the government unveiled its ambitious plans to overhaul the Whitehall machine in a White Paper, *The Reorganisation of Central Government*.[35] Five days earlier Heath had told the Conservative Party conference that his objective was to produce 'a rational structure of government' and a better way of taking decisions. The White Paper's managerialist language consciously expressed the new approach: the words 'strategy' or 'strategic' were used seventeen times in a slim document only sixteen pages long. The main reforms included two new 'giant' departments (Trade and Industry, and Environment), the establishment of the Central Policy Review Staff, the introduction of Programme Analysis and Review, and a commitment to 'hive off' and relinquish some departmental functions. Declaring that the government machine had been 'overloaded', the White Paper promised 'less government, and better government, carried out by fewer people.'

33. *The Times*, 15 January 1976.
34. P. Whitehead, *The Writing on the Wall: Britain in the Seventies* (London, 1985), 89.
35. *The Reorganisation of Central Government*, Cmnd. 4506 (1970).

The White Paper was a bold and optimistic document, and its explicit theorising about the machinery of government and its reform called to mind the Haldane Committee report of 1918. In many ways, Heath's was a very Fabian blueprint. (Revealingly, it was praised by William Robson, who took a swipe at Wilson's *ad hoc* approach.)[36]

The relatively quick and decisive action on the reform of the government machine owed something to the work done in the Party before 1970, but was also made possible because the civil service was receptive to the Conservatives' ideas and had itself been thinking in broadly similar terms. There were some crucial differences, but 'sufficient overlap and meeting of minds to ensure that things moved forward rapidly'.[37] The idea of large, 'functional' departments had wide support in political and bureaucratic circles. The Labour government's plans to create something like the Department of the Environment were well advanced (Anthony Crosland had been appointed as an 'overlord' minister in 1969), and a further expansion of the Ministry of Technology to take over the Board of Trade was on the cards. Inside the Treasury, there was a growing feeling that more effort had to be put into evaluating individual spending programmes and their results in the annual Public Expenditure Surrey Committee (PESC) public expenditure round. And, at the very top of Whitehall, Sir William Armstrong, Sir Burke Trend and Sir Douglas Allen (head of the Treasury) had for some time been talking over the need for a 'central capability' unit that could look to the long-term and take a strategic view. As Hennessy has put it, 'Heath's reformers were preaching to the converted.'[38]

The idea of splitting the Treasury had been intertwined with the plans for a 'central capability', with some Conservative advisers floating the separation of 'Ministry of Finance' from 'Bureau of the Budget' functions, but – crucially – this had never won the backing of the shadow cabinet or the Shadow Chancellor, Iain Macleod.[39]

The summer of 1970 saw a fair amount of pushing and pulling between the civil service 'insiders' and the Conservative reformers (based in the Civil Service Department: David Howell had become a junior minister, Mark Schreiber a special adviser, and the Businessmen's Team were also located there) as the White Paper was put together. Howell apparently prepared a first draft which was substantially rewrit-

36. W.A. Robson, 'The Reorganisation of Central Government', *Political Quarterly*, vol. 42 (1971), 87–90.

37. D. Howell, 'The Rocky Road to Government Reform', *Management Today* (September 1974) 60.

38. Hennessy, *Whitehall*, 221.

39. Howell, *New Style of Government*, 24–5; Pollitt, *Manipulating the Machine*, 92.

ten as it was processed through the CSD and Cabinet Office machine. Inevitably, the final product embodied some compromises (for instance, over the terms of the transfer of the Overseas Development Ministry to the Foreign Office) and some of the Conservative reformers' schemes were scaled down. Howell and others had intended the 'central capability' to be primarily a resource for the Prime Minister; Burke Trend was clear that it had to serve the Cabinet as a whole. Heath had actually wanted the new unit formally to be called the 'think tank' – the title Central Policy Review Staff came from Trend's ordered mandarin mind.

Heath's departmental amalgamations resulted in a Cabinet of eighteen compared with Wilson's twenty-one. The Ministries of Housing and Local Government, Public Buildings and Works, and Transport were brought together into the new Department of the Environment (DoE), while the Department of Trade and Industry (DTI) replaced the Ministry of Technology and the Board of Trade (with MinTech's aerospace functions going, as a temporary measure, to a Ministry of Aviation Supply which was itself wound up in May 1971 with the establishment of the Defence Procurement Executive). The advantages claimed were a capacity to develop a clear strategy for related functions, the elimination of duplication, and the resolution of policy conflicts within a unified line of management rather than by Heath's old bugbear, interdepartmental compromise.

The significance of the choice of Sir Antony Part from the 'free trade' Board of Trade rather than Sir Richard ('Otto') Clarke, a committed interventionist at MinTech, to be Permanent Secretary at the DTI was not lost on 'Whitehall watchers'. However, the DTI proved unwieldy from the start, not because of its size (only 18,000 civil servants) but because of the range and heterogeneity of its functions. Its having 75-or-so Under Secretaries indicated the wide spread of its policy responsibilities, and it had a team of nine ministers and – by 1973 – four Second Permanent Secretaries. These new superdepartments really needed a new type of executive minister to run them, delegating effectively to a team of political colleagues while pulling the threads of policy together. John Davies never got a strong grip on the DTI. Peter Walker – in charge of DoE and then, after November 1972, DTI – was more successful, using regular 'morning prayers' meetings of his ministerial team to keep everyone in touch and to co-ordinate policy. (When Rippon abandoned these sessions, the different 'wings' of the DoE began to drift further apart.)[40]

Although the White Paper had stated that the departmental pattern

40. J. Radcliffe, *The Reorganisation of Central Government* (Aldershot, 1991).

was expected to 'remain valid for a long time to come', it in fact started to unravel even before the government left office. The appointment of a second Cabinet minister at the DTI in late 1972 – Geoffrey Howe, responsible for trade, prices and consumer affairs – complicated the picture. Dissatisfied with the DTI's handling of the energy crisis, Heath decided to create a separate Department of Energy with its own Secretary of State in January 1974. Wilson and Callaghan completed the demolition of the original 1970 structure with the dismemberment of the DTI (1974) and the removal of Transport from the DoE (1976). And by the mid-1970s ministerial and Whitehall opinion had rather swung against the idea of 'giant' departments.

'I wanted to have something that would examine what was going on in a department, so that the minister could decide whether it was still necessary and whether it was still receiving the right priority', was how Heath explained the system of Programme Analysis and Review (PAR), introduced from 1971. PAR could be presented as a technique for more 'rational' management, involving the systematic and critical analysis of objectives, costs, outputs and new options. But its political purpose was clear. The government had pledged to cut out waste and eliminate unnecessary functions. David Howell saw PAR as helping to 'question the unquestionable . . . [and] kill off out-dated programmes'.[41]

In the event it was PAR itself that proved to be unwanted some time before it was finally killed off in 1979. One reason for its failure was that it fell victim to Whitehall's bureaucratic politics and power-play. The original plan to base PAR and its team of businessmen in the Civil Service Department (CSD) foundered on the opposition of the Treasury to encroachments on its territory. But, while the Treasury took it over, it was not enamoured of PAR. Treasury caution and the inter-departmental compromises brokered on the Whitehall steering committee (called PARC) meant that only a dozen or so programmes were reviewed each year. The Treasury inevitably saw the point as expenditure-reduction and did not take kindly to CPRS involvement sometimes complicating the picture with arguments that more resources would boost the effectiveness of a programme. Other departments, for the most part, reacted defensively – anxious to protect their empires, they would cannily offer up for review minor programmes or ones ministers would find it politically difficult to axe, or even deliberately put second-rate officials in charge of the reviews.

41. Heath and Barker, 'Heath on Whitehall Reform', 371; Howell, 'Rocky Road to Government Reform', 60.

Another problem was that, apart from Heath's backing, there was little heavyweight political support behind PAR. Most ministers seemed neutral or hostile. PAR did not fit ministerial timetables or help them in making their political judgements.

It was not surprising that the first rounds of PAR did not produce savings on the scale its proponents had anticipated. The government's U-turn and the turning-on of the public spending taps from 1973 then completely undermined the system. PAR became even less relevant when its political clients were no longer interested in 'rolling back the state'.

PAR lingered on under the Labour government after 1974, but there were no mourners when Thatcher formally abolished it in November 1979. The best that can be said for it is that the seeds were planted for Rayner's more effective 'efficiency strategy' after 1979. PAR's lessons were learnt and the later 'scrutiny programme' involved brisk 90-day inquiries and forceful 'action plans' put to ministers. What really made the difference in the 1980s, though, was that the public expenditure squeeze and the pressure for economy and efficiency in Whitehall was maintained.[42]

'The relinquishment of government functions seems to have been rather a mouse', according to Christopher Pollitt, and no major public-sector functions were privatised in the period 1970–74. In opposition a list of candidates for 'hiving-off' had been prepared, with businessmen to be brought in to run autonomous agencies on a more commercial basis and subject to 'input and output objectives'.[43] But here too there was only limited progress, with the Civil Aviation Authority 'hived-off' from the DTI in 1971. The government appears to have been persuaded that few activities were entirely suitable for this treatment (were largely self-financing, were not politically sensitive, etc.) and the strong opposition of the civil service unions was a further deterrent (staff not wanting to lose their status as civil servants). 'Hiving-off' was rejected for the Royal Ordnance Factories, which instead were put on a 'trading fund' basis (with profit and loss accounts).

Heath's businessmen had more success with the concept of 'departmental agencies' – separate units of accountable management operating within a departmental framework. The Defence Procurement Executive was established in the Ministry of Defence in 1971, with Derek Rayner as Chief Executive; the Property Services Agency was set up in the

42. A. Gray and B. Jenkins, 'Policy Analysis in British Central Government: the experience of PAR', *Public Administration* vol. 60 (1982), 429–50.

43. Pollitt, *Manipulating the Machine*, 101; 'Preparation for Government', CCO/20/26/8.

DoE in 1972; the Employment Services Agency and the Training Services Agency were created in the Department of Employment, with the Manpower Services Commission (initially opposed by officials) appearing in January 1974 (and later absorbing the other two agencies). These agencies turned out to be more durable than Heath's departmental creations. As with the seeds planted by PAR, Whitehall was not yet fully ready for this device, and the dramatic Next Steps initiative fifteen years later in part built on these early steps, but on a much larger scale and in a more thoroughgoing manner.

The Central Policy Review Staff (CPRS) – the think tank – was the most imaginative and successful product of Heath's 1970 reforms.[44] Starting work on 1 February 1971, it generated a certain amount of media hype because of the buccaneering style of its first head, Lord Rothschild, and because of its apparently glamorous role as a group of young and brilliant licensed free-thinkers at the heart of the government machine. The brief of the CPRS as set out in the White Paper, covered the clarification and monitoring of the government's overall policy strategy, the establishment of priorities and the analysis of alternatives and long-term problems. Members of its staff defined the role of the CPRS in more subversive terms as the grit in the machine, sabotaging the over-smooth functioning of Whitehall. 'Civil servants do not think the unthinkable', Heath's advisers had complained before the 1970 election in the secret 'Black Book' plan. This too became part of the CPRS's unofficial job-description, but with its small (fifteen to twenty) staff being a mix of outsiders and civil service 'high-fliers', the think tank showed that there was critical and creative talent available around Whitehall waiting to be tapped.

In opposition, Conservative advisers had been adamant that the 'central capability' should *not* be headed by a senior Treasury official – what was needed was 'an innovator from outside the Government Machine', a 'creative minded entrepreneurial type'.[45] The job of heading the CPRS was in fact offered to (and turned down by) two people before Burke Trend came up with Rothschild's name. The think tank's impact and success in the Heath years owed a great deal to this appointment. Rothschild was indeed a singular individual: politically a socialist, by training a scientist (head of research at Shell), a wartime bomb-disposal expert and intelligence operative (who still had links with the

44. Blackstone and Plowden, *Inside the Think Tank*; Campbell, *Edward Heath*, 317–24; P. Hennessy, S. Morrison and R. Townsend, *Routine Punctuated by Orgies: the Central Policy Review Staff 1970–83*, Strathclyde Papers on Government and Politics, no. 31 (Glasgow, 1985).

45. M. Schreiber to J. Douglas, 14 May 1968, CRD/3/14/4.

secret service), and no respecter of sacred cows. He established a close relationship with Heath (at least until the autumn of 1973) and also with William Armstrong, carving out a place as one of the most influential Whitehall advisers around the Prime Minister. At Rothschild's insistence, the head of the CPRS and his deputy were given the right – unique for civil servants – to attend and speak at ministerial meetings and Cabinet committees.

The CPRS operated in a number of ways. Heath had long been concerned that ministers were well-briefed on the business of their own departments but, as members of the Cabinet, had no independent advice about the proposals of other ministers and departments or about the wider problems facing the government. The CPRS circulated around fifty 'collective briefs' a year to the whole Cabinet – short notes analysing urgent issues (miners' pay or the collapse of Upper Clyde Shipbuilders, for instance) or pithy reviews of departments' papers (trying to relate the immediate issue or proposal to the government's general strategy, pointing out drawbacks, special pleading or weak spots in the argument). Departments generally resented what they saw as last-minute meddling by dilettante outsiders, so CPRS interventions probably produced 'more irritation than illumination', as Campbell says. Ministers mostly remained departmentally orientated but that is not to deny that this was an innovative attempt to address a genuine problem about collective decision-taking in government.

The CPRS was also deployed on more detailed and longer-term projects, including problems that cut across departmental boundaries.

> Before the end of the Conservative government (February 1974) it had conducted analyses of: the role of the City of London in the British economy; the British computer industry; Concorde [its report famously beginning, 'Concorde is a commercial disaster']; industries likely to suffer structural decline during the next ten years; roads and transport; energy policy, including energy conservation; prices and incomes policy; population; the future performance of the British economy relative to those of our EEC partners; and the presentation of information to ministers.[46]

There were many other of these CPRS inquiries. Burke Trend tried to bar the think tank from sensitive areas, particularly foreign policy and defence issues, but Heath authorised a report on Northern Ireland. The Treasury saw off CPRS attempts to get involved in fiscal policy and open up budget policy-making (the think tank once calculated that fifty per cent of the previous year's budget could have been leaked

46. Pollitt, *Manipulating the Machine*, 100.

without any economic damage), though it was centrally involved in the annual public expenditure round, its relationship with the Treasury being marked by strains and friction. It is not easy to assess the impact of these think tank studies. The main recommendations of the only one published in this period – Rothschild's 1972 report on the organisation of government research and development – were accepted by the government and implemented. But with others, it is possible at most to point to an indirect and longer-term influence on Whitehall thinking.

The CPRS's third role was as guardian of the government's overall strategy. Heath recalled that he wanted 'a piece of machinery . . . which would keep a continuous watch on the strategy of the Government and be able to tell the Government when they were departing from that strategy in any respect and analyse the reasons.'[47] Rothschild and his team organised presentations to the Cabinet at Chequers, using slides and charts, mapping out how the government had performed in relation to its declared aims and where it had fallen short of its objectives, and also looking at the problems looming over the horizon. The original idea was to hold these review sessions every six months but only three were actually held: in August 1971, May 1972 and June 1973. (A fourth, scheduled for November 1973, was cancelled.) The exercise would be repeated a few days later at meetings of junior ministers, chaired by Heath.

John Cambell has argued that these seminars were 'testimony . . . to Heath's surprising willingness to be told unwelcome things.' Wilson, in contrast, was willing to try this experiment only once when he returned to office in 1974, and Callaghan and Thatcher not at all. Douglas Hurd wrote admiringly of the think tank 'rubb[ing] Ministers' noses in the future', but some of Heath's Cabinet (including Peter Walker and Lord Jellicoe) seem to have regarded the strategy meetings as not very fruitful breaks away from their real work.[48]

One of the reasons why Labour was to be so suspicious of the think tank as a 'Tory Trojan Horse' was that it could seem to be playing a party-political role as guardian of the government's strategy. For their part, right-wing critics of the Heath government wondered about the constitutional propriety and the political wisdom of permitting a civil service unit (however unorthodox) to apparently take over what should be the Cabinet's central responsibility. Heath himself insisted that the CPRS gave ministers the information they needed to stick to their strategy, 'if we wished to do so' – an important qualification. Jock

47. Expenditure Committee, *The Civil Service*, q. 1875.

48. Campbell, *Edward Heath*, 319; Hurd, *An End To Promises*, 39; Pollitt, *Manipulating the Machine*, 101.

Bruce-Gardyne also made the point that the CPRS was 'not there to prevent governments being blown off course . . . It is there to make sure that Governments do not *steer* themselves off course – at least without realising that that is what they are doing.'[49]

The think tank's part in the government's U-turn on economic strategy remains difficult to pin down. Treasury critics of the CPRS talk of it 'whooping up public expenditure' and 'jump[ing] enthusiastically on the big-spending bandwagon'. But in 1972 it advised ministers against rescuing the 'lame duck' Upper Clyde Shipbuilders, and put together a report showing how government could disengage from detailed interference with the nationalised industries. This advice was in line with the strategy which the Cabinet had set out in 1970. Unfortunately, as John Campbell has noted, the government 'had changed its collective mind and was now rushing headlong in the opposite direction.'[50]

In other ways, however, the think tank weighed in with advice that may have helped to tilt the balance in favour of the adoption of a new course. This was the case in relation to the decision to float the pound in June 1972. More importantly for the political future of the government, former members of the think tank have claimed that 'CPRS advice was a major factor in encouraging the celebrated U-turn in relation to incomes policy in late 1972.' Inflation had been discussed at the May 1972 Chequers seminar. 'The facts were borne home to us, what we had promised and what was happening', one minister recalled. 'The statistics had been available to everyone before but no one had wanted to see them. Too unpleasant. We needed reminding how serious things were getting.'[51] While the CPRS strongly supported the introduction of a statutory incomes policy, external events and other powerful advisers inside Whitehall were also pushing in the same direction.

After Rothschild was carpeted in September 1973 for upstaging the Prime Minister with a public speech speculating about a future of national economic decline, the CPRS and its chief went out of favour with Heath. Think tank 'insiders' recall that it was 'largely excluded from centre stage' during the government's final crisis, 1973–74. Rothschild's ingenious proposal that the government could use the oil price

49. Heath and Barker, 'Heath on Whitehall Reform', 382; Bruce-Gardyne, *Whatever Happened?* 116.

50. Blackstone and Plowden, *Inside the Think Tank*, 64, 99; Campbell, *Edward Heath*, 322.

51. Blackstone and Plowden, *Inside the Think Tank*, 86; H. Heclo and A. Wildavsky, *The Private Government of Public Money*, 2nd edn (London, 1981), 316.

rise to justify giving the NUM a higher settlement was rejected, though it might have provided a way out of the conflict.

The CPRS was kept on after 1974, though neither it nor its subsequent heads (Rothschild left in September 1974) were to enjoy the same wide-ranging role and influence as in the 1971–73 period. With the appearance of the Downing Street Policy Unit after the February 1974 general election, prime ministers after Heath had an alternative – and more personally – and party-oriented – source of advice. The same applied to cabinet ministers with the appointment of a greater number of special advisers after 1974. The CPRS was absorbed into the Whitehall machine and pushed more into producing one-off reports (particularly on industrial issues). Politicians lost interest in the long-term and in overall strategy. And after 1979, 'conviction' politics drove out the sort of rational and analytical approach the CPRS stood for. Already badly damaged by the political furore over its controversial 1977 report on the diplomatic service, the think tank was further undermined by a spate of 'leaks' in the early 1980s. One of Mrs Thatcher's first acts after her 1983 election victory was to abolish it. It was clear that a unit like the think tank could achieve little without the full backing of the Prime Minister. Wilson and Callaghan were agnostic, Thatcher had no use for it; the creation and operation of the CPRS in the Heath years is perhaps testimony to a particular political style and circumstances, a remarkable but 'one-off' episode in British public administration.

THE CIVIL SERVICE UNDER HEATH

Heath seemed more interested in overhauling the machinery of government than in reforming the civil service as such. Some of the key recommendations of the 1968 Fulton Report on the civil service were implemented during his term of office but that process went ahead in ways relatively unaffected by the advent of the Conservative government in 1970. Over 1971–72 the civil service class and grading structure was reorganised according to a plan worked out by William Armstrong, the CSD and the civil service unions in Whitley Council negotiations: the Open Structure was created for the top three grades, the old Administrative, Executive and Clerical classes were amalgamated, and new groupings were put in place for scientists and for professional and technical staff. William Armstrong persuaded Heath and Lord Jellicoe, the Civil Service Minister, not to take unified grading any further than the top 800 officials, pointing to the complexities and costs involved. Heath's comments about the importance of retaining a 'high-flier' cadre and his view that the post-Fulton career opportunities for specialists appeared broadly adequate suggest that he was not greatly troubled by the grading issue (which was one that obsessed the champions of the Fulton Report).[52]

The Heath government was not antagonistic towards the civil service as an institution. The Review Body on Top Salaries was set up in May 1971, chaired by Lord Boyle, and made the first of its regular recommendations for substantial salary increases for higher civil servants in June 1972. The 1970–74 administration was the only one after 1964 that implemented in full the findings of the Priestley machinery for civil-service pay. Heath had used the opportunity of his first public engagement as Prime Minister – opening the Civil Service College at Sunningdale – to emphasise that his government intended to maintain 'fair dealings' with the civil service.[53] (In 1981 he was to oppose the abolition of the CSD on the grounds that the interests of the civil service needed 'properly looking after'). In 1971 legislation was introduced to give civil servants index-linked pensions. (A decade later the Thatcher government wanted to scrap these.) Only a minority on the policy group on public sector pensions set up in opposition had opposed this proposal, and Kenneth Baker, CSD junior minister, argued in 1972 that the government should take credit for this measure and for setting an example as a 'good employer'.[54]

Industrial relations in the civil service started to deteriorate in the early 1970s, however. Already in 1971 there were press reports of anger over pay, growing militancy among civil service unions, and the possibility of industrial action. The first civil-service strike occurred in 1973, a one-day stoppage involving 200,000 civil servants as a protest against the government's incomes policy.

The 1970 commitment to cut the number of civil servants was, for all practical purposes, quietly buried, though local Conservative parties and activists, as well as bodies like Aims of Industry, continued to demand swingeing cuts. Changes in statistics and classification complicate the picture somewhat. 'Hiving-off' reduced civil service numbers: the creation of the Civil Aviation Authority reduced the size of the DTI by around 5,000, and the creation of the Manpower Services Commission appeared to cut the size of the civil service by 18,000

52. Fry, *Reforming the Civil Service*, 272–3; *House of Commons Debates*, 5th series, vol. 773, cols 1572–3, 21 November 1968; Expenditure Committee, *The Civil Service*, qs. 1870–1872.

53. *The Times*, 27 June 1970.

54. Baker to J. Douglas, 25 July 1972, CRD/3/14/1, ACP (65) 18.

(but the MSC's staff regained their civil service status in 1975). On the other hand, policy changes, such as the introduction of Value Added Tax, increased numbers in some parts of Whitehall. Heath later claimed that his government brought about a reduction in civil service numbers of about 5,000 (in the context of a total of 700,000). He admitted that it had been 'a constant battle' to try to reduce the size of the civil service, disclosing that there had been nine separate Cabinet discussions about this in the first two years. By October 1972 the Central Office line was a defensive one: 'In general our plans for saving civil servants will be long term.'[55] In the short term, however, the government did not wield the axe with great ferocity.

OPENNESS AND SCRUTINY

The theme of 'open government' was strongly and persistently plugged by Heath and the Conservative opposition before 1970. Heath had made much of the need to open 'the opaque windows on to Whitehall' in 1966. 'Abandoning the secrecy obsession' and 'substantial reform, if not repeal, of the Official Secrets Act' were seen by David Howell as essential if government and the civil service were to be made more accountable and more managerially efficient.[56] The 1970 manifesto included a pledge to 'eliminate unnecessary secrecy' and to 'review the operation of the Official Secrets Act so that government is more open and accountable to the public.'

Once the Conservatives were in office, however, the issue seemed less urgent. William Whitelaw, the government's business manager, explained that 'open government' did not mean 'opening up to the public high-level policy discussions between ministers and their officials', but would involve 'providing more facts and if possible more information about the assumptions on which the Government is basing its policy.' But this commitment could mean little when, contrary to the assumptions and intentions of the business advisers team, a decision was taken that PAR reports would not be published.[57]

In February 1971 the defendants in the *Sunday Telegraph* secrets trial (initiated by the Labour government after embarrassing revelations about its stance during the Nigerian civil war) were acquitted, the judge declaring that Section 2 of the Official Secrets Act should be 'pensioned

55. Expenditure Committee, *The Civil Service*, q. 1895; Geoffrey Block to Lord Carrington, 6 October 1972, CRD/3/14/1.

56. *The Times*, 5 March 1971; Howell, *New Style of Government*, 36.

57. *The Times*, 7 February 1972; Pollitt, *Manipulating the Machine*, 86.

off'. The government's reaction was to appoint the Franks Committee to review the operation of the Act in April 1971. This move effectively kicked the issue into touch for the remainder of the government's term of office. In a hard-hitting report, published in September 1972, Franks called section 2 'a mess' and condemned its 'catch-all' character, proposing that criminal sanctions should instead apply to narrower and defined categories of information.[58] The Cabinet sat on the report until June 1973, when it announced that it accepted Franks's essential recommendations, but no further action had been taken before the government fell.

The 1911 Official Secrets Act actually remained on the statute book until 1989, when the Thatcher government eventually replaced it, by which time Heath had emerged as a prominent backbench critic of government secrecy, leading rebel MPs into the opposition lobby against a three-line whip on the measure and denouncing the absence of a 'public interest defence' in the new legislation.

The pattern of opposition promises and ministerial inaction and defensiveness was repeated on the related issue of improving parliamentary scrutiny of government. In 1968 Heath had argued that the modernisation of government involved three developments: 'more efficient and effective government; a more effective check by Parliament on the Executive; and more effective redress for the individual citizens of . . . grievances.' In the PSRU, David Howell had seen that 'hiving-off' managerial functions raised questions about public accountability and ministerial responsibility to Parliament. Establishing 'a clearly defined zone of managerial independence' would inevitably diminish ministerial accountability 'in the traditional sense', he argued. The answer was to make civil service managers answerable to parliamentary committees for their agencies' performance.[59]

The Labour government had been experimenting with investigative select committees in the 1960s and, following a report from the Commons Procedure Committee in 1969, had started a review of the next moves which was carried forward by the Conservatives and presented as a Green Paper in October 1970. From this came the replacement of the old Estimates Committee by a new Expenditure Committee, with wider terms of reference and with seven specialised sub-committees, in 1971. Heath had indicated his opposition to adding to ministers' burdens with powerful Congressional-type committees in 1964, and his

58. *Departmental Committee on Section 2 of the Official Secrets Act*, Home Office, Cmnd. 5104 (1972).

59. House of Commons Debates, 21 November 1968, col. 1579–80; Howell, *New Style of Government*, 33–6.

government's response to proposals to strengthen select committee scrutiny was grudging or dismissive. The Treasury opposed the creation of a select committee on taxation and economic affairs (though MPs were allowed to mount inquiries into corporation tax and the tax credit idea). The Expenditure Committee turned out, not surprisingly, to lack really sharp teeth and pressure built up throughout the 1970s for a reform of the select committee system which, in the event, was pushed through by Norman St John Stevas in the 1979 Conservative government.

The 1970 manifesto had talked of a 'better system of control and examination of decisions by civil servants' and of improved safeguards for citizen's rights, but interest in this issue also faded away once Conservatives got behind their ministerial desks. The idea of developing a more effective system of administrative law had long entertained Conservative lawyers – 'the Ombudsman is not enough', Lord Hailsham had once insisted – but ministers were not interested. Maudling put it bluntly in 1971: 'I have never seen the sense of administrative law in our country, because it merely means someone else taking the Government's decisions for them.'[60]

In contrast to its radicalism in relation to the machinery of government, the Heath government seems in practice to have been conservative and executive-minded on the issues of Whitehall secrecy and accountability (like other governments from both parties). David Howell's comments about the need for a new framework of accountability for executive agencies were prescient. The limited progress on 'hiving-off' meant that this was never a significant issue during 1970–74 but the problem returned to the agenda in the Thatcher years, and particularly with the 1988 Next Steps initiative.

Civil service ethics, another massively controversial subject in the 1980s and 1990s, also excited little interest at this time, though there were one or two disturbing incidents. Sir William Armstrong escaped remarkably unscathed after explaining – to a select committee investigating attempts to 'crowd out' Labour MPs' parliamentary questions – that the civil service did not act impartially between the government and the opposition and that civil servants routinely helped ministers to circumvent parliamentary scrutiny.[61] A tribunal investigating the collapse of the Vehicle and General Insurance Company let DTI ministers off the hook by pinning the blame on officials (accusing named civil servants of negligence and incompetence). But the serious questions

60. House of Commons, Standing Committee B (Immigration Bill), 25 May 1971, col.1508.

61. Select Committee on Parliamentary Questions, HC 393 (1972), qs. 133–225.

this raised about the meaning of the concept of ministerial responsibility in the age of 'giant' departments and 'accountable management', and about the constitutional roles of civil servants and ministers, were not properly addressed.[62] The First Division Association – the top civil servants' union – had set up a group in 1969 to look at the question of standards of conduct and the loyalties of officials, but its report in 1971 attracted little attention. Fifteen years later the Association was to be at the forefront of efforts to introduce a Whitehall Code of Ethics.

CONCLUSIONS

The reaction against the mandarins' prominence in policy-making under Heath and the critical edge to Conservative views about the civil service after 1974 were noted earlier. Mrs Thatcher was determined not to come unstuck in the same manner as Heath, and as Prime Minister underlined the subordination of the higher civil service to the elected government of the day (symbolically sending the Head of the Home Civil Service, Sir Ian Bancroft, into early retirement in 1981). She displayed much more antagonism towards 'establishment' institutions like the civil service than did Heath.

The Conservative government had entered office in 1970 with a clear policy strategy of its own, but once that had been abandoned it became heavily dependent on the civil service apparatus to work out the details of a new approach – the government's critics arguing that official influence extended to the direction of policy too. It is true that Heath tended to look for advice to senior civil servants rather than to his political colleagues, something which owed a great deal to factors of temperament and style. The absence of a Downing Street retinue of political and policy advisers (appointed by subsequent prime ministers) is also relevant here. Douglas Hurd felt that civil service advice was preponderant in Heath's premiership, and political advice crowded out. 'As problems mounted up and political nostrums failed [Heath] turned increasingly to the Civil Service to come up with new policies and new mechanisms to carry them out', observed John Campbell. The result was what Willie Whitelaw called the 'Armstrong syndrome' by late 1973, with Heath and his senior advisers deeply entangled in the administrative complexities of the prices and incomes policy. This

62. R.J.S. Barker, 'The V. and G. Affair and Ministerial Responsibility', *Political Quarterly*, vol. 43 (1972), 340–5; R.A. Chapman, 'The Vehicle and General Affair: Some Reflections for Public Administration in Britain', *Public Administration*, vol. 51 (1973), 273–90.

'over-administrative approach to government' and the neglect of the 'political dimension of national leadership' were major factors in Heath's downfall, Campbell suggests.[63]

The results of Heath's much-vaunted reforms of the machinery of government turned out in practice to be something much less than the 'new style of government' so optimistically talked about in 1970. 'Reforming and reorganizing British central government is a terrible business', David Howell concluded in 1974.[64] The new 'giant' departments (DTI and DoE) had been broken up or lost major functions within a few years of Heath's departure from Number 10. PAR was a damp squib. Little was 'hived-off'. Only the CPRS stands out as a really successful innovation and even its lustre had faded some time before it was disbanded in 1983.

Douglas Hurd believed that 'because of his justified respect for his senior advisers Mr Heath tended to exaggerate what could be achieved by new official machinery . . . a little more scepticism about machinery would have been wise.' John Campbell detected 'an element of wishful thinking' in Heath's belief that 'institutional tinkering was a solution to deep-seated economic problems.' Heath's approach and thinking and Wilson's were rather similar in this sense at least, whatever the differences in terms of character and personal style.[65]

'Heath initially had a vision of how he wanted Whitehall to work, but then he seems to have lost heart', a senior 'insider' recalled. Christopher Pollitt argued that the intensity of prime ministerial interest in the machinery of government began to recede soon after the appearance of the 1970 White Paper.[66] According to a former permanent secretary, 'Heath seemed to run out of interest eventually in about 1972/73, when so many other events came up . . . and [he] began to think that he was beating his head against a brick wall as far as reform was concerned.' At a dinner given for the business team in 1972, Heath reportedly commented: 'I am not at all sure about all this reform, and then of course there's Parliament, and that is impossible!'[67]

The business team had dispersed by the end of 1972. Richard Meyjes had reported to Heath that the initial series of projects had been completed. Heath's reluctance or inability to identify any new specific tasks he wanted to deploy them on, and his failure to give the sort of political 'steer' they were looking for, convinced them it was time to

63. Campbell, *Edward Heath*, 490, 492.
64. Howell, 'Rocky Road to Government Reform', 59.
65. Hurd, *An End To Promises*, 92–3; Campbell, *Edward Heath*, 222.
66. Pollitt, *Manipulating the Machine*, 96.
67. ICBH, witness seminar February 1994, in 'The Heath Government'.

go back to their companies. Progress on the Fulton reforms of the civil service petered out or was halted at around this time too – William Armstrong told his successor, Sir Douglas Allen, that he had decided to 'draw a line under Fulton'.

Inasmuch as the objective of the 'new style of government' was 'less but better government' (as promised in the 1970 manifesto and the White Paper), the U-turn on public spending fatally undermined it. The pressure to find more efficient, streamlined and economical methods was taken off. Political crisis management diverted attention away from reshaping the machine.

In some ways, Heath's attempted Whitehall reforms were ahead of their time and laid the groundwork for the changes of the Thatcher period. This was the case with the use of businessmen in government (Derek Rayner re-emerging as the Prime Minister's Efficiency Adviser in 1979), the interest in accountable management and the idea of separating policy and management functions and setting up agencies. In contrast to attitudes in 1970–74, however, Thatcher's interest in and commitment to overhauling the bureaucratic machine did not slacken, even though she had a significantly longer tenure of office. She also had a much more robust and confrontational attitude than did Heath to the civil service as an institutional interest, pushing through big reductions in staff numbers and moving to 'de-privilege' the service. Heath did not in practice fundamentally challenge or threaten the Whitehall status quo – Thatcher and Major have been very different in that respect.

CHAPTER FIVE

The Heath government and the British economy

Sir Alec Cairncross

The early 1970s ushered in a period of rapid inflation that came to take precedence as the central concern of policy over full employment, which had been the dominant aim since 1945. The 'Golden Age' in which unemployment had never – in any postwar year except possibly 1963 – averaged over 2.5 per cent was succeeded by one in which it never – from 1970 onwards – fell below that level (except briefly at the end of 1973) and eventually rose far above it. Inflation, which had averaged 4 per cent in the twenty years before 1970, accelerated thereafter and by the autumn of 1975 had reached a peak of 27 per cent – a rate without precedent in British experience. The exchange rate, previously fixed throughout the postwar years except for the two devaluations of 1949 and 1967, was allowed to float in June 1972 and continued to float until 1989.

The changes taking place in the United Kingdom in those years were common to nearly all industrial countries, although in the United Kingdom they were on a somewhat larger scale. In most countries, 1974 marked the end of full employment, the beginning of more rapid inflation, a slow-down in the growth of productivity and of output, and a rise in the importance attached to monetary growth. Few of these changes had progressed far when the Heath government fell, but the environment of policy was already being transformed in a world of floating exchange rates, rising commodity prices and increasing acceptance of monetarist ideas.

What was to prove the most important change was the onset of much more rapid inflation. The rise in hourly wage-rates in the seven leading industrial countries, which had averaged 7.3 per cent per annum in 1967–69, accelerated to 12.9 per cent in 1973 and 15 per cent in 1974. In the United Kingdom the acceleration was greater: from 6 per cent in 1967–69 to 12.9 per cent in 1973 and 17.1 per cent in 1974. The acceleration in consumer prices was also faster in the United Kingdom, rising from an average of 4.2 per cent in 1967–69 to 9.2

per cent in 1973 and 16 per cent in 1974 compared with an average for the seven leading industrial countries of 3.9 per cent in 1967–69, 7.5 per cent in 1973 and 13.3 per cent in 1974.

In other respects, too, the early 1970s were a watershed both in the United Kingdom and throughout the industrial world. The great surge in unemployment and slow-down in productivity growth did not occur in the United Kingdom or in other industrial countries until after 1973; but both were linked with the forces making for faster inflation that were already making themselves felt, and with the efforts to cope with those forces.

The Conservative government that took office in June 1970 had little thought of how the world was about to change. In most respects the economy was in a healthy and stable condition. Unemployment had changed little in the preceding three years. Consumer prices, after some acceleration in 1968 brought on by the devaluation of the previous year, had been increasing more slowly at about 5 per cent per annum in 1969. The finances of the public sector, for the first time since Stafford Cripps's budgets of 1948 and 1949, were in overall surplus, with a negative borrowing requirement. The money stock in 1969 had hardly changed if measured as M1; or, if measured as M3, had increased by less than 3 per cent. The current balance of payments, after a long succession of deficits, was in increasing surplus: in 1971 the surplus reached a peak of over £1,000 million. The anxieties that had attended economic policy-making throughout the 1960s appeared to be dissolving.

In three-and-a-half years of Conservative government, instead of dissolving, anxieties multiplied. Unemployment alone finished (in December 1973) below the level from which it started in June 1970; but it soon began to rise uncontrollably and never afterwards approached the low level to which it fell in 1973. Price inflation which began at a little over 5 per cent in 1970 had doubled by the first quarter of 1974 and it, too, went on to higher things. The borrowing requirement had risen to over 6 per cent of GDP and the money stock (M3) had grown during the previous year by 25 per cent. The balance of payments, hit by the first oil shock, was in deficit in the first quarter of 1974 at an annual rate of about £3 billion. Instead of having a single economic problem such as unemployment to tackle, the government was struggling with inflation, a large budget deficit and an enormous balance of payments deficit simultaneously.

The following account of developments in the economy under the Heath administration begins with a brief indication of its economic philosophy. It then outlines the development of macro-economic policy,

TABLE 5.1 *Economic Indicators 1969–74*

		GDP % increase p.a. over past half year	*Increase in unemployment (000s)*	*Increase in employment (000s)*	*% increase in consumer prices*	*Current balance of payments (£ million)*
1969	1	2.1	−10.4	−38	5.4	+155
	2	2.4	+23.0	−54	5.0	+327
1970	1	1.2	+17.6	−92	4.8	+495
	2	3.3	+19.7	−63	6.2	+326
1971	1	0.3	+132.8	−289	7.7	+496
	2	2.9	+123.3	−182	7.7	+618
1972	1	1.3	+7.4	+185	5.7	+311
	2	5.6	−89.6	+247	5.4	−128
1973	1	12.1	−154.7	+300	7.4	−286
	2	−0.8	−110.0	+77	8.9	−710
1974	1	−4.3	+38.5	+49	11.3	−1564

Source: Col. 1: Economic Trends Annual Supplement 1990, T1; Cols 2 and 3: Economic Trends Annual Supplement 1981, T105; Col. 4: National Institute Economic Review, various issues; Col. 5: Economic Trends Annual Supplement 1990, T30.

taking in turn fiscal policy, monetary policy, incomes policy and external economic policy. A brief concluding section draws together the more important conclusions.

THE PHILOSOPHY OF THE HEATH GOVERNMENT

The Conservative government, like its predecessor, began with high ambitions to transform the economy. As the Prime Minister told the Conservative Conference in Blackpool in October 1970: 'We were returned to office to change the course of history of this nation – nothing less.'[1] The ambitions of the Conservatives lay in a very different direction to those of the Labour Party. The economy was to be transformed by 'less but better' government. There was to be less intervention in industry; an improvement in the efficiency of the government machine by the use of new administrative techniques; tax reform; a reduction in trade union power through legislation; and

1. Quoted in F.T. Blackaby, 'Narrative 1960–74', in F.T. Blackaby *et al.* (eds), *British Economic Policy 1960–74* (Cambridge, 1978), 52. Apart from this work there is no really thorough study of economic policy and performance under the Heath Government. There are, however, many useful commentaries in the quarterly issues of the *National Institute Economic Review* and these have been drawn upon in this chapter.

a fresh effort to join the European Economic Community. An improvement in industrial relations and faster economic growth would follow.

The government's philosophy was one of disengagement on the one hand and self-reliance on the other. The role of government was to provide a framework within which free enterprise could flourish. The government should limit its activities, concentrating on what would otherwise not be done at all or done inadequately, while the individual should be encouraged to stand on his own feet and refrain from turning to the government for succour and support. The emphasis was less on the virtue of market forces than on the importance of individual responsibility. A corollary of this approach was a rejection of much of the intervention practised in the 1960s. There was to be no national economic planning, no pursuit of faster economic growth under government direction, no statutory incomes policy or intervention in wage settlements in the private sector. Agencies and instruments of policy associated with such activities were to be eliminated.

Examples of what the government had in mind were provided in the Chancellor's first budget in October 1970. The Industrial Expansion Act was to be repealed and the Industrial Reconstruction Corporation and the Land Commission were to be wound up. The Regional Employment Premium was to be phased out. Investment grants were to be replaced by tax allowances and the development areas were to be allowed the free depreciation originally introduced by Reginald Maudling in 1963. Partly in readiness for eventual entry into the EEC, import levies on foodstuffs were to be substituted for the deficiency payments previously made to farmers. Various subsidies were to be reviewed and reduced. To this list was added in November a decision to wind up the National Board for Prices and Incomes; the government looked instead to employers, prompted by their own self-interest, to resist excessive wage demands.

MACRO-ECONOMIC POLICY IN 1970–74

The last years of Labour government had been anxious ones and some indication of these anxieties is a necessary preface to an account of subsequent developments. What stands out is how thinking and action had been dominated by the balance of payments. In mid-1970 it was little more than a year since Roy Jenkins had been almost in despair in his struggle to overcome Britain's balance of payments difficulties and begin repaying the formidable aggregate of debt to the International

Monetary Fund (IMF), Bank of International Settlement and foreign central banks that had accumulated since 1964. In his Budget speech he confessed that he could not 'dismiss without thought the views of those who urge some entirely different strategy.' He went on to state it as his task that he should ensure that 'even a deviation in the wrong direction, would not leave us in an intolerable balance of payments situation'.[2]

By the end of the year he could look back dispassionately on perils that were past: 'the first D-mark crisis of May 1969 . . . the French devaluation of August 1969 . . . the second D-mark crisis of September 1969, crises or semi-crises [that] . . . were not caused by the problems of sterling.' But, he went on, 'so long as sterling remained weak this somewhat exacerbated each crisis for the rest of the world, while making them all immensely more dangerous for the United Kingdom.'[3]

All this was in the past. The long deflationary slog of 1968–69 had at last yielded a balance of payments surplus and one that was still increasing. Sterling had regained strength. A favourable swing of £500 million in the trade balance between 1968 and 1969 had been accompanied by a substantial improvement in invisible earnings. Exports had expanded strongly while imports, after a surprising leap in 1968, had been limited to a 2 per cent rise in 1969, in part by the scheme for a 50 per cent deposit on imported goods introduced in November 1968. The long-term capital account was in balance. Even the accounts of previous years had been given a slightly rosier tinge after the discovery that exports for some years had been systematically under-recorded. A beginning had been made with the repayment of external debt.

As 1970 opened, the domestic economy was expanding slowly. Output was growing steadily but at a rate of only 1.5 per cent per annum – about half the rate normally attainable. For some reason, however, this did not result in any very perceptible increase in unemployment, which remained a little under 2.5 per cent.[4] Consumer prices were rising at about 5 per cent. Wages in 1969 had risen, also at about 5 per cent, and earnings by about 8 per cent.

By the time the Conservatives took office in June, the main change

2. *House of Commons Debates*, 5th series, vol. 781, col. 1003, 14 April 1969.

3. Roy Jenkins, Speech to the British-American Chamber of Commerce, Chicago, 7 January 1970.

4. From the mid-1960s the unemployment statistics are an uncertain index of changes in the labour market. On US definitions, unemployment rose to 3.8 per cent in 1967 (not 2.4 per cent) with little change in the next three years. *National Institute Economic Review* (May 1971), 67.

in the situation was a decided speeding-up in the rise in wages. By the autumn of 1970, hourly wages were rising more than twice as fast as in the second half of 1969.[5] Many explanations were advanced for the acceleration. It clearly had nothing to do with unemployment and labour shortages, which had changed little. It could be due simply to the ending of incomes policy and the restraint which this had exercised on settlements. If there was any expectation of fresh restraints under a new government, workers would want to make larger demands while they had the chance of pressing them. Another possibility was that a new generation of trade union leaders, with no memories of the 1930s, and more accustomed to a world of inflation, were adopting a more militant attitude, free of the hesitations of their predecessors. If so, there was likely to be a continuing change in industrial relations and a more inflationary outcome to future wage-bargaining. On the other hand, labour might be reacting to the temporary pressure on real incomes that the transformation in the balance of payments had required. Higher taxation designed to facilitate such a transformation meant lower take-home pay. A further loss of real income resulted from the rise in import prices since devaluation – a rise outstripping export prices.[6] It was at least conceivable that wage-earners were seeking to restore their real incomes in compensation for these sacrifices. Which of these explanations carried most weight would decide how enduring would be the intensification of inflation.[7]

FISCAL POLICY

Roy Jenkins, in his final Budget in April 1970, had taken a cautious line for reasons largely unconnected with wage behaviour, and had given the economy only a mild dose of reflation, forecasting an increase in GDP over the following twelve months of about 3.5 per cent. Commentators, including the National Institute, took a less hopeful view and proved to be nearer the mark. The Treasury forecast implied

5. In the second half of 1969 hourly wages were 5.3 per cent higher than a year before; in each of the next four quarters the rise accelerated, reaching 14 per cent in the first quarter of 1971.

6. The average male worker's earnings, after deduction of tax and national insurance contributions and an addition for family allowances, was no higher in real terms in 1969 than it had been in 1966 but rose by over 13 per cent in the next three years. Income tax plus national insurance contributions rose from 13.7 per cent of average earnings in 1966 to 19.4 per cent in 1969 and were 19.6 per cent in 1972 *National Institute Economic Review* (May 1974), 20.

7. *National Institute Economic Review* (May 1970), 13.

a slow decline in unemployment, but in the second half of 1970 what happened was a gradual rise that persisted into 1971. In March 1971, before Anthony Barber introduced his Budget, unemployment had reached 2.9 per cent, and numbers of unemployed had increased since a year earlier by about 90,000. GDP was thought to have fallen between the second half of 1970 and the first half of 1971, although later estimates show a tiny rise.

At first it seemed that the slight easing in the labour market had moderated wage settlements, and the National Institute forecast an early de-escalation from a rise of 14.5 per cent in wages and salaries in the last quarter of 1970 to 9.6 per cent in the second quarter of 1971 and 8 per cent by the middle of 1972.[8] No such de-escalation occurred. In the middle of 1971 wages were still rising at nearly 13 per cent per annum and in 1972 rather faster (see Fig. 5.1).

The rise in wages disposed the new Chancellor to refrain from reflation. A mini-budget on 27 October 1970 made no attempt to influence aggregate demand. The Chancellor pointed to 'the rapid rise in costs and prices which we have experienced over the past year or so' in justification for taking no steps 'likely to increase further the pressure of demand.'[9] In his budget at the end of March he still thought it 'irresponsible' to take action to reduce unemployment by boosting consumer demand 'until we get a substantial reduction in the level of pay settlements' and contented himself with tax cuts that were calculated to allow output to grow at 3 per cent instead of 2 per cent. This, he assumed, would prevent a *fall* in the pressure of demand and maintain unemployment at a more or less unchanged level. The Selective Employment Tax (SET) was cut by 50 per cent as part of a move to go over to a value added tax; various reliefs and allowances were made in income tax; corporation tax was reduced by 2.5 per cent; and a number of concessions were made in capital gains taxation and estate duty. The various tax reliefs for the year ahead added up to about £550 million of which £290 million represented the cut in SET.

Again, the Treasury's expectations were too optimistic. Output at the end of 1971 was only 2 per cent higher than it had been eighteen months earlier and unemployment, instead of holding steady, had shot up throughout the year. By January 1972 it had reached a peak of 4 per cent – a level never before reached since the Second World War except in the depths of a particularly severe winter in February 1963.

8. *National Institute Economic Review* (February 1971), 27.

9. *House of Commons Debates*, 5th series, vol. 805, col. 1089, 4 November 1970, quoted in *National Institute Economic Review* (November 1970), 12.

FIGURE 5.1 *Hourly wage rates and consumer prices 1969–74 (Increase in past 12 months)*

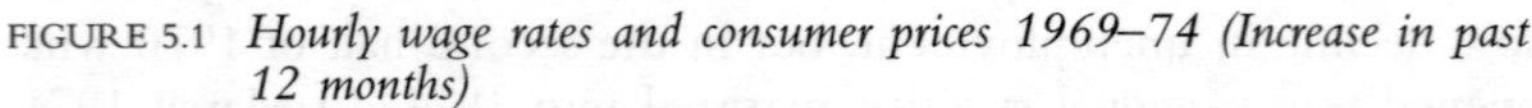

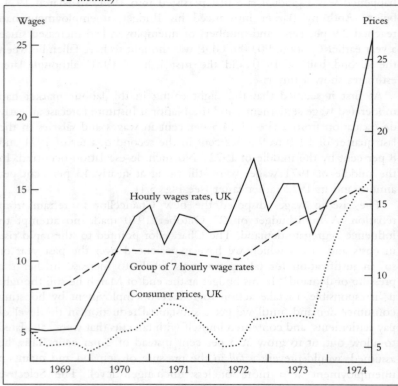

Why was it that the slight element of slack that had continued since 1967 grew so suddenly in 1971?

The initial fall in production in the first quarter of 1971 was largely due to labour difficulties. During the rest of the year production was never more than about 1 per cent higher than at the end of 1970. Inconsistencies in the figures make it difficult to attribute the slowing down to specific elements in demand but the evidence points to a sharp fall in stockbuilding as the main factor.[10]

Exports, on the other hand, were relatively buoyant in 1971 in comparison with the slowing down in most other industrial countries. Indeed, Britain's share of world exports of manufactures increased slightly in 1971 after falling almost continuously since soon after the

10. *National Institute Economic Review* (November 1973), 10, Table 2.

Data for Table 5.2 *Increase in hourly wages and consumer prices 1969–74*

		Percentage increase in hourly wage rates in UK	Increase in consumer prices in UK
1969	3	5.3	5.1
	4	5.3	4.9
1970	1	7.3	4.6
	2	9.4	5.3
	3	11.2	5.9
	4	13.3	6.4
1971	1	14.0	7.1
	2	13.3	8.2
	3	13.5	8.1
	4	13.0	7.3
1972	1	12.0	8.2
	2	12.1	6.2
	3	14.8	5.6
	4	17.1	8.0
1973	1	13.5	8.0
	2	15.6	8.8
	3	15.5	9.0
	4	11.9	8.8
1974	1	14.2	11.1
	2	16.9	14.1
	3	20.5	15.7

Source: National Institute Economic Review, various issues.

war. Well before the end of 1971, however, the buoyancy had gone and the volume of exports had begun to fall. Of the other elements in demand, consumption was an expanding element from 1970 to 1973 and government expenditure on goods and services also grew steadily over that period. It was investment that faltered most conspicuously in 1971. Fixed investment had been recovering in 1970 but the recovery was halted in 1971 and was not resumed until 1973. Investment in stocks, even on the official estimates, plunged downwards and in all probability fell even more heavily than is indicated by the figures. The essence of the matter is that exports were losing momentum, fixed investment was no longer booming and in 1971 stockbuilding appears to have taken a nosedive.

From the middle of 1971, economic policy began to change in two respects. On the one hand, the government began to look more favourably on reflationary measures and by the Budget of 1972 was anxious to bring down the level of unemployment, not just check an increase.

At the same time it abandoned its earlier approach to wage-inflation, actively seeking the help of the Confederation of British Industry (CBI) and the Trades Union Congress (TUC) to moderate first the rise in prices and then the rise in wages. When lengthy negotiations failed, it turned, like its predecessor, to statutory control. This change in attitude carried with it a new willingness to intervene to keep firms in business in areas of high unemployment: a willingness that expanded in other directions such as the encouragement of more investment in manufacturing industry.

The first indication of change came in the summer of 1971. Up to the middle of the year, the Treasury view seems to have been that output would keep pace with productive potential so that the rise in unemployment would peter out. In June £46 million had been made available over two years for house improvement grants, and in July a first instalment of £33 million had been announced as part of a programme of public works in the development areas which would amount in total to £100 million over the next few years. These developments were compatible with the government's stance; but a cut of £400 million in revenue from purchase tax on 19 July was not, and formed part of a bargain with the CBI. The removal of hire-purchase controls, which followed a recommendation by the Crowther Committee, was a further reflationary move.

A more radical change of policy was made in the 1972 Budget on 21 March. This made it an explicit aim to raise output by 10 per cent over a two-year period. The Chancellor hoped that by the announcement of a sustained rapid rate of growth, industrial investment would be stimulated and the rate of unemployment would be reduced to a more normal level. In his budget speech the Chancellor made it clear that he did not intend to be thwarted by the need to maintain an 'unrealistic' exchange rate, implying a willingness to devalue of which the financial markets took note.

In many ways the change of policy was badly timed. Although it was not very apparent in April, the leading industrial countries were all setting out together, as they had not done since the war, on a simultaneous expansion of production that put pressure on commodity prices more intense than at any time since the Korean War. It had already raised world commodity prices by 10 per cent in the first quarter of 1972 and two years later had doubled them. This meant that Britain was embarking on a major expansion at a time of world inflation and in the face of an adverse shift in the terms of trade of nearly 25 per cent over the next two years.

No doubt this could not have been foreseen (although something of the kind was forecast shortly afterwards by Wynne Godley).[11] What was foreseeable was the effect on inflation. The Conservative government had abandoned incomes policy; now it was abandoning the alternative to incomes policy – rising unemployment. Once it set about reducing unemployment as its first priority it had no option but to go back to incomes policy – and in unpropitious circumstances. Hourly wages had risen by 12 per cent over the past year although unemployment had grown by 140,000 to over 900,000 and was still increasing. Wage settlements for manual workers, it is true, had fallen over the year from a rate of increase of 14 per cent to one of 9 per cent but they were back to 14 per cent after the Budget.[12]

To encourage growth at 5 per cent per annum the Chancellor made large tax concessions, mainly in income tax. He did not reduce the standard rate of income tax but increased allowances by about £1,000 million and introduced a new unified system of personal direct taxation. He held out the possibility of a later amalgamation of personal tax allowances with social security benefits to yield what could be regarded as a negative income tax but nothing came of this. Cuts of £140 million were also made in purchase tax, which was to be replaced in April 1973 by a 10 per cent value added tax. The tax concession in a full year were estimated to be larger than the amounts quoted for 1972–73, reaching £1,200 million for direct and £175 million for indirect taxation. Adding in other concessions, the estimated reduction in tax revenue in a full year came to £1,800 million. Many other changes were made. The regional employment premium was to be phased out and a new system of regional development grants introduced. Depreciation allowance were to become more generous: all new and second hand plant and machinery would qualify for an allowance of 100 per cent in its first year. Concessions were made on estate duty and it was proposed to transform it into an inheritance tax. The Chancellor claimed that the change would create 'the most powerful combination of national and regional investment incentives . . . since the war'.

The tax concessions in the 1972 budget were larger than ever before but they were not as large as some commentators proposed. The National Institute, for example, argued in February that, in order to raise output by 5 per cent between the first half of 1972 and the first half of 1973 instead of the 1.9 per cent forecast, tax cuts operating solely on consumers' expenditure would have to amount to £2,500 million in loss of revenue. This was on the basis that there was a large

11. See p. 119–20.
12. *National Institute Economic Review* (February 1973), 40.

margin of slack in the economy amounting to 'between one and two years' normal growth'.[13] Later, the National Institute admitted that there had been rather less slack than it believed but it agreed that a 5 per cent rate of growth was the right aim.[14]

What the Chancellor proposed was that demand (nearly all consumer spending) should be given a boost sufficient to add 2 per cent to gross domestic product (GDP) in the first half of 1973 and maintain a rate of growth of 5 per cent per annum between the second half of 1971 and the first half of 1973. The selection of the second half of 1971 as a base was presumably designed to avoid including the first quarter of 1972 when output was depressed by the miners' strike and the three-day working week.

The implication of the target in terms of present-day official figures was that a rate of growth of 1.7 per cent in 1971 would accelerate in 1972, reach a rate somewhat in excess of 5 per cent for a time and then begin to slow down at some point in 1973. It does not appear to have been envisaged that the rate would go far beyond 5 per cent, as it did. Between the second half of 1971 and the second half of 1972 growth had reached only 3.5 per cent but was accelerating. There was then a headlong expansion by 6.1 per cent in the first six months of 1973 bringing the total increase in the eighteen months to 9.6 per cent. Unemployment, which had been rising in 1971, fell by 240,000; and employment, which had been falling, increased by 730,000.

There were many who felt that the pace was too hot and that the economy was being overheated. The pace was certainly very fast at the end of 1972 but it slowed down a great deal in the second half of 1973 and in the final quarter of the year production had begun to fall. Some, including *The Times*, maintained that 'the full employment level of unemployment' had risen since the mid-1960s and had been reached early in 1973. In July 1973 unemployment was down to 2.5 per cent and at the end of the year to 2.1 per cent. Perhaps these figures corresponded, as measures of the tightness of the labour market, to figures 0.5 per cent or even 1 per cent lower ten years previously?[15]

It was a question pursued carefully by the National Institute which examined eleven indicators of pressure on capacity from 1964 to 1973 and was satisfied in November 1973 that a margin of spare capacity

13. *National Institute Economic Review* (February 1972), 31.

14. *National Institute Economic Review* (November 1973), 24–33.

15. Professor A.J. Brown, in his *World Inflation since 1950: an International Comparative Study* (Cambridge, 1985), concludes that the full employment level of unemployment rose by about 2 per cent between the mid-1950s and 1979. My own impression in the late 1960s was that a change of this kind was then in progress.

FIGURE 5.2 *GDP 1969–74 (Rate of annual increase by half year)*

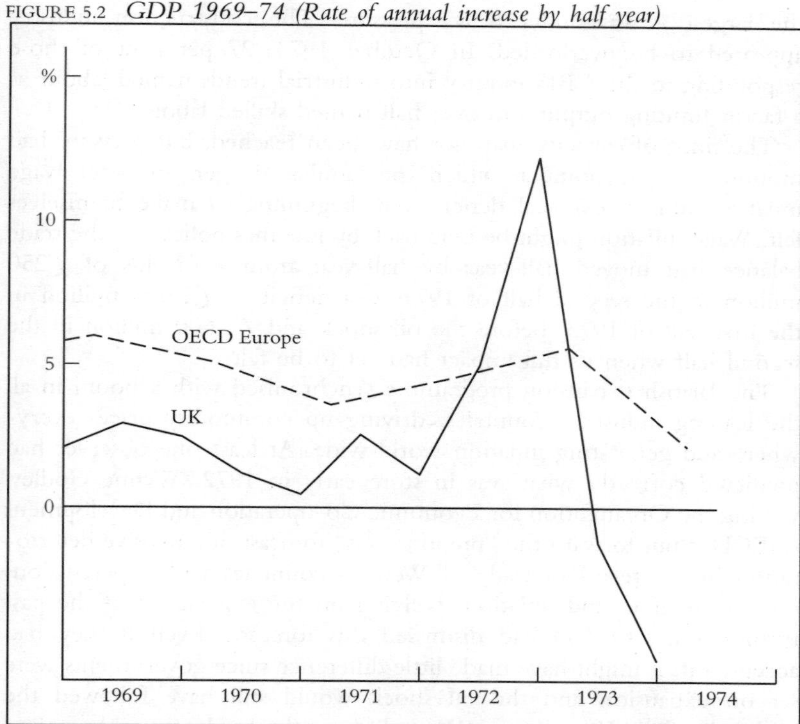

still existed.[16] In the light of later experience it may seem strange to be told that unemployment can be pushed below 2 per cent without overheating. But before 1970, 2 per cent was regarded as a relatively high rate. What makes one hesitate to accept the National Institute's conclusions is that vacancies at the end of 1973 were 1.6 per cent of the labour force and far above the highest level in the 1960s. The vacancy figures might be of doubtful reliability but there had been times (e.g. after devaluation in 1967) when they gave a truer picture than did unemployment figures. There were acute shortages of materials, components and plant capacity. Whatever the position in other parts of the country, the London and south-east region – by far

16. The National Institute was not alone in this, and throughout the Organisation for Economic Co-operation and Development (OECD) 'there was a conviction that there was much more slack in the economies than there turned out to be': comments of Andrea Boltho, at that time in charge of forecasting at the OECD, in F. Cairncross and A. Cairncross (eds), *The Legacy of the Golden Age: The 1960s and their Economic Consequences* (London, 1992), 129.

the largest – was under heavy pressure. The construction industry appeared to be overloaded. In October 1973, 27 per cent of those responding to the CBI's inquiry into industrial trends named labour as a factor limiting output and over half named skilled labour.

The limit of capacity may not have been reached; but pressure had mounted to the point at which the familiar dangers of faster wage inflation and an external deficit were beginning to make themselves felt. Wage inflation might be held back by incomes policy but the trade balance had moved half-year by half-year from a surplus of £250 million in the second half of 1971 to a deficit of £1,000 million in the first half of 1973, before the oil shock and £1,600 million in the second half when its full impact had yet to be felt.

The British expansion programme synchronised with a boom in all the leading industrial countries, driving up commodity prices everywhere and generating inflation world-wide. At least one observer had predicted correctly what was in store early in 1972. Wynne Godley, visiting the Organisation for Economic Co-operation and Development (OECD), 'put forward the "preposterous" forecast of a massive deterioration in the terms of trade of Western countries with repercussions on real incomes and inflation. Relying on the experience of the past twenty years, OECD had dismissed this forecast.' Even if they had accepted it, it might have made little difference since governments were set on expansion and the oil shock would still have followed the outbreak of the Yom Kippur War whatever the level of world pressure on primary produce.[17]

By the time the 1973 Budget was introduced a new and powerful influence on demand was at work. Import unit values had risen sharply – in the first two months 9 per cent above the average level in the second half of 1972; and this, as was soon apparent, was only the beginning. As had happened before – for example, in 1951 – a world commodity boom was pushing prices up, deflating the domestic economy and putting a brake on economic expansion.

The Budget took little account of the storm clouds already beginning to gather. It was designedly neutral and intended to prolong a fast rate of growth. Such changes as were made, apart from the introduction of Value Added Tax at 10 per cent, were largely in tidying up previous arrangements. The net effect was a small reduction in tax revenue from indirect taxation.

17. Bolitho, in Cairncross and Cairncross (eds), *The Legacy of the Golden Age*, 130. This was the period when the 'The Limits of Growth' was so popular: D.H. Meadows *et al.* (eds), *The Limits of Growth: A Report for the Club of Rome's Project on the Predicament of Mankind* (London, 1972)

The 5 per cent target was preserved for a year. But of course 5 per cent represented a slowing down compared to the figures for the last quarter of 1972, and it was difficult to judge how far the slow-down would go. Even in May the forecasts, official and unofficial, looked forward to the continuation of boomlike conditions at least up to the middle of 1974. Instead, by the third quarter of 1973 – ahead of the first oil shock – growth on all three measures of GDP was either flat or negative. Production in the second half of the year was unmistakably below the level in the first half. Unemployment continued to fall but this was quite a normal lag behind the turning point in output.

'At first sight', the National Institute remarked, 'it looks as though the familiar "stop–go" cycle has returned.' But very little of the slow-down was the work of government. Indeed, government expenditure was one of the two elements in demand that continued to grow, the other being exports. Consumer spending fell from the peak in the first quarter caused by a scramble to buy in advance of VAT and was checked by higher import prices. Stockbuilding reacted to the check and to general uncertainty in the second half of the year. Fixed investment was also checked but manufacturing investment, which the Chancellor had set out to encourage, remained a little higher than in 1972.

In May, when the Chancellor still imagined that output was growing at 5 per cent per annum, he had felt it necessary to make reductions in public expenditure, some in 1973–74, some in 1974–75 so as to clear the way for the continued expansion of other elements in the economy: additional industrial investment and exports in particular. Since there was still some spare capacity, the cuts in 1973–74 were to be modest – £100 million in road expenditure. In 1974–75 these were to be followed by a wide range of reductions totalling £500 million and extending from local government expenditure to industrial subsidies, defence projects, agriculture and the nationalised industries.

As 1973 progressed, ministers gradually abandoned the 5 per cent target. It was only too obvious that its achievement required a continuing intake of labour and other additional resources that were becoming increasingly scarce. There were complaints of shortages of materials and parts, the construction industry was overloaded, in the south-east there were more vacancies than unemployed, and the rise in wages and prices was beginning to accelerate. These symptoms of pressure were worrying enough. But the government's main anxiety had become once again the balance of payments which had swung from a small surplus in 1972 to a substantial deficit in 1973 as commodity prices rose faster than ever before and added to Britain's import bill. The shortages and the inflation in prices might be world-wide and not confined to Britain, but Britain was in a less favourable position to withstand inflationary pressure and maintain its standing in international financial markets than most other industrial countries.

From October onwards the government faced problems of economic management on the grand scale: restrictions on Middle Eastern supplies of oil and a trebling of its price on the one hand and a struggle with the miners on the other. The rapid progress of the previous eighteen months degenerated into an inflationary free-for-all.

The story goes far beyond demand management and must be told briefly. The Arab oil producers, reacting to the Arab–Israeli War which broke out on 6 October 1973, raised the posted price of oil by 66 per cent ten days later and decided to cut production by 5 per cent per month. Early in November they announced that supplies to the West would be reduced by a minimum of 25 per cent but modified this on 26 December to a cutback of 15 per cent on September production, having three days previously doubled the price of oil with effect from 1 January 1974.

On top of a threatened oil shortage was added the threat of a strike by miners and electricians. The miners had rejected an offer of a 7 per cent pay rise (as in 1971) on 11 October and the electrical power engineers had begun strike action at the end of the month in support of increases in standby payments. On 12 November the miners began an overtime ban and the following day the government declared a state of emergency. Various restrictions were imposed on space heating, floodlighting and supplies of petroleum and a speed limit of 50 mph was imposed. For the second time in two years, a three-day week came into operation.

At the same time financial conditions were tightened. On 13 November the minimum lending rate was raised from 11¼ to 13 per cent and Special Deposits from 4 to 6 per cent. On 17 December a mini-budget announced the introduction of 'the corset' – a new restriction on the growth of bank deposits (see p. 126) – and reintroduced hire-purchase controls which had been lifted in July 1971 after the report of the Crowther committee.[18] Additional taxation was imposed on property development and in the form of a surcharge on surtax. Public expenditure, which had been cut again in October by £115 million, was now reduced yet again (in the sense that the intended increase in 1974–75 was revised downwards). This time the cut was an all-time record of about £1,200 million.

18. J.H.B. Tew, 'Monetary Policy' in Blackaby, *British Economic Policy 1970–74*, 226–7.

The dispute with the power engineers was settled on 28 December but talks with the miners, including a meeting with the Prime Minister on 28 November, were unsuccessful. The subsequent history of the dispute is discussed elsewhere (see chapter 7). Here we need note only that after some apparent vacillation the miners called a strike to start on 10 February, the Prime Minister on 7 February called a general election, and the strike was brought to an end only after the Conservative government had lost power by a narrow majority and been succeeded by a Labour government under Harold Wilson.

It was fiscal policy that initiated the 1972–73 boom in the Budget of 1972. It was fiscal policy again in May, October, and December 1973 that was intended as the principal moderating influence. But in fact few of the measures taken had any effect in 1973–74; they were aimed almost entirely at a re-balancing of competing demands on the economy in 1974–75. So far as the boom was held in check by government policy it was through a tightening of monetary control. But the deflationary effect of rising import prices and a shift in the terms of trade was a good deal more important.

The Growth of Public Expenditure

The Conservatives had given much thought to fiscal policy while they were out of office and Iain Macleod in particular had prepared himself for a programme of extensive tax reform. His death after only a few weeks in office was a setback to such hopes but some elements of the programme, notably a move from purchase tax to a value added tax, survived. A Value Added Tax was introduced in the 1973 Budget, the initial rate being fixed at 10 per cent. Proposals were also made in 1972 for an amalgamation of tax allowances and social service benefits but nothing came of this. Various taxes introduced by Labour were faded out, some of them being replaced by grants. The Conservative manifesto had also promised cuts in taxation and in public expenditure but the pressures to increase both remained strong.

The Conservative government of 1959–64 had sought to keep total public expenditure within a fixed proportion of GDP so that it grew no faster than the growth of resources. In this they did not altogether succeed but the increase in the ratio (using Pliatzky's estimates) was under 1 per cent from 33.1 per cent in 1959 to 33.9 per cent in 1964. The Labour government had a similar aim, fixing on 4.1 per cent as the limit to the annual growth of public expenditure and setting 4 per cent as the target rate of growth for GDP. However, by 1967–68 the ratio of 33.9 per cent had grown to 39.9 per cent. Roy Jenkins' budgets brought this down to 37.5 per cent in 1969–70 but it then returned to 39.9 per cent in 1973–74 under the Conservatives. In the first two years of Conservative government the growth in public expenditure was comparatively modest and in line with the growth of output. But in the next two years public expenditure (at constant prices) rose by 6.6 per cent and 7.9 per cent – rates well above the growth in real resources.[19]

Public expenditure under the Conservatives consistently outgrew the revenue available to finance it. The financial deficit of the public sector grew year by year from £0.25 billion in 1970–71 to £3.5 billion in 1973–74 (and £6 billion in 1974–75). It was necessary to raise an increasing total in revenue from rates and taxes, national insurance and trading income, and borrow the rest. The rising deficit enabled revenue to lag behind expenditure, the proportion of revenue under all heads to GDP falling between 1969 and 1973 from 40.8 per cent to 37.1 per cent and the deficit growing from 0.34 per cent to 4.8 per cent. The growth of expenditure does not appear to have differed greatly between broad headings, expenditure on consumer goods and services, on capital formation and on grants and subsidies all rising by between 60 per cent and 70 per cent between 1969 and 1973 while debt interest rose by rather less.

MONETARY POLICY

Although it had been the practice in postwar years to rely primarily on fiscal policy to regulate demand and employment, with monetary policy in a subordinate role aimed more at preserving international balance, a new view was beginning to be heard under the Heath government. The more inflation accelerated and the more helpless demand management was to arrest it, the greater the urge to seek more effective weapons. If incomes policy had been tried and failed, perhaps it was time to try monetary policy. There had always been those who saw monetary policy as an independent instrument of policy endowed with unique powers for the control of inflation. Keynesians might argue that it was *demand* that governed prices and that the quantity of money was more a symptom than a cause of changes in demand. But an

19. These figures are all from L. Pliatzky, *Getting and Spending: Public Expenditure, Employment and Inflation* (Oxford, 1982) 218. Rather higher figures are given in the *Financial Statement and Budget Report 1994–95*, 115. (for example 1973–74 is shown as 43.5 per cent) but the changes over time are similar.

influential school of thought labelled 'monetarist' found a direct connection between the stock of money and the price level and insisted with Milton Friedman that 'inflation is always and everywhere a monetary phenomenon.' The idea that money would lose value the more of it there was in circulation had a strong popular appeal.

In 1970–74 monetarism's time had not yet come. It was not till the control of inflation became the overriding aim of policy, and financial markets reacted strongly to changes in the quantity of money, that governments adopted monetarist or quasi-monetarist ideas. In the 1960s the IMF had insisted on monetary targets as a condition of their credits. But the targets had been put aside even before the last debts to the IMF were repaid early in 1972 and were not revived until after the fall of the Heath government.

It was, however, the workings of the monetary system in the early 1970s that converted many to monetarism. It became a popular view that the acceleration of inflation in the 1970s was brought about by a rapid expansion in the stock of money beginning in 1971. This in turn was attributed to a change in policy by the Bank of England designed to enable the banks to engage more freely in competition with one another and with other financial institutions.[20] That the banks did lend more freely after the change of policy and that the quantity of money increased more rapidly is undoubtedly true. But there is equally no doubt that the great inflation of the mid-1970s, in which nearly all industrial countries participated, had more obvious causes than monetary growth. In 1973 and the first half of 1974 the dominant influence was undoubtedly rising import prices which were followed by rising labour costs. Both of these may owe something to an increase in the money stock but when world commodity prices (in dollars) nearly doubled in these eighteen months, monetary influences confined to Britain were obviously of secondary importance. It is much more reasonable to view the expansion in bank credit over that period as a natural *consequence* of rising prices rather than their cause.

It is the earlier period from 1971 to 1973 that is usually cited as evidence of the inflationary consequences of a faster increase in the money stock. It is true that the new Bank of England policy enabled the banks to increase their lending in 1973 by no less than 33 per cent and that between the first quarter of 1971 and the first quarter of 1973 £M3 grew by about 44 per cent. That certainly contributed to the pick-up in activity over those two years; but did it account for the more

20. The change of policy was explained in 'Competition and Credit Control', *Bank of England Quarterly Bulletin* (1971), 189–93.

rapid inflation? We should note first that M1 (i.e. notes and deposits) increased by only 20 per cent, or just a little faster than retail prices which rose by nearly 17 per cent. What we are discussing is greater success by the banks in competing to finance business at a time when business's need of credit was growing fast. Worldwide the export price of primary produce rose by 38 per cent and the export price of manufactures by 18 per cent (both in dollars). The running was being made in part by inflation abroad which added to the credit requirements of British industry at all stages. At the same time labour costs were mounting because of a 28 per cent increase in hourly wage-rates over the two years 1972–73, an increase that had been in progress at much the same rate since the autumn of 1970, well before any change in monetary policy. It is not possible to blame the acceleration in wages on an easing in monetary control; and the rise in commodity prices was worldwide, not confined to the United Kingdom, so that only the extra rise as the pound floated down could be attributed to monetary influences. Greater liquidity and lower interest rates may have helped to boost asset prices, with repercussions on spending and investment. But the faster rise in prices in 1971–73 can be explained without much emphasis on monetary factors; and in 1973–75 it was the rise in import prices and the consequent balance of payments deficit that dominated the picture.

Putting aside these broader issues, what role did monetary policy play in the early 1970s? Monetary policy consisted largely of a combination of debt management with operations in the money market involving changes in bank rate – or minimum lending rate, as it became in 1972. As the exchange rate strengthened in 1970–71 bank rate was gradually reduced from 8 per cent at the beginning of 1970 to 5 per cent in the autumn of 1971. From there it climbed to 9 per cent at the end of 1972, starting with a rise to 6 per cent in June when sterling was allowed to float. These changes were all responses to pressure on the exchanges, with the tightening of policy in 1972 running counter to the expansionary *volte-face* in fiscal policy.

In 1973, after some slight easing in interest rates in the first half of the year, the trend was reversed again in the second half as the balance of payments weakened and the pound began to sink. From $7\frac{1}{2}$ per cent in late June, bank rate moved up to $11\frac{1}{2}$ per cent a month later. There was then a rather extraordinary drop of $\frac{1}{4}$ per cent in October but in November the rate went up to 13 per cent as a state of emergency was declared. Many of the increases in bank rate – in November and December 1972, January, July and November 1973 – were accompanied by calls by the Bank of England for special deposits.

In December 1973 the Bank took stronger action to control the money stock, introducing what came to be called 'the corset'. This was designed to check the growth in broad money by a form of quantitative restriction penalising banks and finance houses that allowed interest-bearing deposits (in sterling) to grow too fast. The penalty would be compulsory deposits with the Bank of England, with no interest paid on them, and such deposits would become increasingly onerous the more the growth of interest-bearing deposits exceeded the prescribed rate, fixed initially at 8 per cent in the first half of 1974. Thus the removal of ceilings on bank lending in 1971 was succeeded by ceilings on the growth of bank deposits in 1974.[21]

The development of monetary policy was, however, more complicated than a succession of interest rate changes. A major change in monetary control was made in September 1971 when the Bank of England sought to promote freer competition among the clearing banks and between them and other financial institutions in accordance with the ideas it had set out in 'Competition and Credit Control'. First, all quantitative limits on bank credit – the ceilings so frequently applied – were to be removed and the banks freed to compete with other lenders not subject to those limits. Secondly, the cartel-like arrangements under which the clearing banks agreed on common deposit and lending rates linked to bank rate were to be abolished. These arrangements had suited the authorities in postwar years when it gave them some purchase over interest rates and was part of the understanding that the tender would always be covered by an agreed bid from the discount houses. But in the meantime other markets in funds had developed with no direct link to bank rate, such as inter-bank deposits, local authority temporary borrowing and certificates of deposit. The control afforded over short-term interest rates was, therefore, far less extensive and effective. Considerations of this kind led in 1972 to the replacement of an administered bank rate by a market-determined Minimum Lending Rate which was related to the Treasury bill rate and varied automatically with market rates.

A third change was the replacement of the reserve ratios observed by the banks by a new system. The London clearing banks were to hold 1½ per cent of their 'eligible liabilities' on deposit at the Bank of England without receiving interest, the change from an 8 per cent cash ratio corresponding to the exclusion in future of notes and coin

21. For an analysis of the forces governing bank lending (and hence the stock of money) after 1971 see J.C.R. Dow and I.D. Saville, *A Critique of Monetary Policy: Theory and British Experience* (Oxford, 1988), 180–90; and for the operation of the corset, *ibid.*, 153–7.

from the calculation of reserve assets. The larger finance houses were required to keep to a reserve ratio of 10 per cent.

Another important change, which the Bank of England had long resisted, was the withdrawal by the Bank from any obligation to support a weak market in government bonds. In the past the Bank had felt that in the interests of maintaining an active market in government debt it should intervene to prevent sharp falls in price and aim to sell as far as possible on a rising market. The Bank was now more willing to allow fluctuations in interest rates in order to retain a grip over credit creation.[22]

The immediate effect of the reforms was an unexpectedly large surge in bank lending. The banks clearly intended to use their new freedom with a vengeance and the authorities were soon made aware how limited were their powers of control. In the end the Bank was obliged to reintroduce quantitative restrictions in another form.

When the banks first began to feel pressure on their reserves in 1972, instead of restricting credit they bid for more reserve assets in the form of Treasury bills and for additional funds such as certificates of deposit and wholesale deposits which they could use in making loans. This so-called 'liability management' had not been envisaged in 'Competition and Credit Control' and raised the return on wholesale deposits and certificates of deposit relative to the yield on Treasury bills. One consequence was that the interest-bearing element in the money stock could rise as interest rates rose, because of the increasing differential in favour of time deposits. In this lay one of the reasons for the rapid growth in £M3, compared with M1 on which no interest was earned.[23]

During 1973 a more surprising development was what became known as 'round-tripping'. Liability management on the part of the banks raised the return on certificates of deposit to a point at which first-class borrowers could borrow from the banks at base rate plus 1 per cent and lend back in the form of certificates of deposit at a higher rate. This practice helped to inflate the growth of the money stock. It was partly in reaction to this situation that the Bank turned in 1973 from calls for Special Deposits to a more direct limitation of the growth in the stock of money.

22. N.H. Dimsdale, 'British Monetary Policy since 1945' in N.F.R. Craft and N.W.C. Woodward (eds), *The British Economy since 1945* (Oxford, 1991), 119.
23. Dimsdale, 'British Monetary Policy', 124.

EXTERNAL ECONOMIC POLICY

The 1960s had been punctuated with balance of payments crises that continued after devaluation in 1967. Year after year in the 1960s, recourse was made to foreign borrowing and, at the end of 1968, debts to the IMF and foreign central banks had reached over £8,000 million – more than three times the value of the exchange reserves. By the time the Conservative government took office in 1970, however, the balance of payments was in increasing surplus; confidence in sterling had returned and with it much of the capital withdrawn in the years of crisis; the repayment of debt had brought down the total outstanding to £3,626 million. A year later all debt to foreign central banks had been extinguished and in the following year outstanding debt to the IMF was also repaid.

Exchange Control

Exchange control had continued after the change of government much as before. Import deposits, introduced in November 1968 at 50 per cent of the value of the goods imported, were continued into 1970 and the rates were reduced in May and September before the scheme was withdrawn in December. For a few months at the end of 1971, when sterling was in demand, regulations were made to restrict various short-term capital inflows. In 1972 policy swung the other way and exchange control was extended for the first time to the sterling area. The same rules were applied as applied elsewhere: individual investors had to use investment currency bought at a premium, and direct investment had to carry the approval of the Bank of England. No doubt with the expected demise of reserve currencies, the rapid decline in the economic importance of the Commonwealth link and the approach of entry into the European Community, it was seen as anomalous to continue to discriminate in favour of non-European countries.

On the other hand, the restrictions on foreign investment had by then been relaxed to allow it to be financed out of foreign borrowing. This was true both of portfolio and direct investment abroad. Borrowing in foreign currency for private investment abroad had expanded rapidly in the late 1960s when it enabled investment outside the sterling area to continue without causing any drain on official reserves. By 1970 borrowing in foreign currency for investment abroad had risen to £265 million and in 1972 reached £980 million, with a slight reduction in 1973 to £869 million.[24] Private investors, however, were not allowed to make use of foreign borrowing for the purchase of securities until December 1970 and even then continued to use the investment currency market, paying a premium varying between 10 and 35 per cent over the official rate and surrendering 25 per cent of the premium to the reserves when they disposed of the investment. In 1972 this brought in £162 million to the reserves, indicating sales amounting to £650 million.

Up to September 1973 the United Kingdom also enjoyed a medium-term borrowing facility totalling $2 billion with a group of central banks operating in conjunction with the Bank for International Settlements in Basle. This was intended to meet the possible withdrawal of sterling balances by countries in the sterling area and was coupled with an exchange guarantee in dollars, underwritten by the group, covering 90 per cent of each sterling area country's official sterling reserves. When the agreement ran out in September 1973, it was replaced by a unilateral guarantee for the next six months. The exchange guarantees, in view of the fall in the value of the pound, proved expensive, costing £59 million under the Basle arrangement and £80 million under the unilateral guarantee.[25]

International Monetary Arrangements

In the early years of the Heath government it was the dollar that was under pressure. First there was something like a flight from the dollar with increasing quantities of dollar deposits leaving the United States. Then in August 1971 President Nixon suspended convertibility and imposed a 10 per cent import surcharge. A period of currency instability ensued in which most currencies were allowed to float. At the Bank/Fund meeting that followed, the Chancellor took the opportunity, as several of his predecessors at the Treasury had done over the previous decade, to put forward his own plan for international monetary reform.

At that stage he had nothing to say in favour of floating: a year earlier at Copenhagen he had dwelt at some length on the virtues of fixed exchange rates. He also wished to do away with reserve currencies. Instead, he proposed that the system should be reorganised around Special Drawing Rights on the International Monetary Fund, brought into existence through the agreement of its members. There were

24. Terence Higgins, comments in Cairncross and Cairncross (eds), *Legacy of the Golden Age*, 98.

25. Blackaby, *British Economic Policy*, 61.

intended to supplant – and perhaps even replace – gold as a form of international currency. Special Drawing Rights (SDR) would be the *numéraire* in which parities would be expressed and the main asset in which countries held their reserves. Gold would remain as an alternative reserve asset while currencies would lose their predominant position in reserves and shrink to working balances.

These ideas were elaborated in the Chancellor's address in Washington which dealt with some of the advantages and difficulties. He left open the question whether existing official holdings of reserves currencies should be converted into SDR and if so, how fast, but went on to urge just such a move 'on a considerable scale, probably by stages'. What he had primarily in mind were the holdings of dollars but he also saw his proposals 'as a way of running down over time the reserve role of sterling'. He had little to say, however, about the obligations that would be undertaken by the reserve currency countries in respect of the balances converted into Special Drawing Rights. He returned to the ideas from time to time but they soon faded and had little influence.

Floating Currencies

A few months later in 1971 came the Smithsonian Agreement on 19 December in which currencies were realigned and the surcharge withdrawn. Sterling was revalued at a fixed parity of $2.60 against the dollar. This was accompanied by the removal of restrictions, introduced at the end of August, on the payment of interest on additional deposits by non-residents. The new parity continued into 1972 until the rate was allowed to float at the end of June. At the end of April the six members of the EEC had taken what they regarded as a step towards European Monetary Union by limiting fluctuations on either side of their cross-parity with each member country to 2¼ per cent. On 1 May Britain joined 'the snake' as an intending member of the EEC and for a brief period of nearly two months was a member of a primitive Exchange-Rate Mechanism. The other members sought to continue towards their goal of monetary union and nearly succeeded. But one by one the currencies of the member countries were allowed to float and in the upheavals of the commodity boom and the oil shock of 1973, floating became the order of the day.

In 1971 sterling had become a strong currency. For the first time since 1958, there was a visible surplus, augmented by a surplus of nearly £900 million in invisibles, to yield a record current account surplus of £1,100 million. All danger from the balance of payments seemed to have passed. Yet half-way through 1972 funds were again draining away from sterling, imports were soaring, and in June the pound was allowed to float. Nominally this was a temporary float like that of the mark in September 1969 and October 1970. In the event, it lasted until 1990.

Why did this sudden transformation occur? One factor was a swing in the trade balance from an unprecedented surplus of £200 million in the second half of 1971 to a deficit of £250 million in the first half of 1972 – a swing in annual terms of £900 million in the space of a year. It was the beginning of a continuing deterioration in the current account, reversing the post-devaluation trend. The reversal indicated a decline in competitive power associated with wage settlements showing increases of 12–14 per cent from the spring of 1970 and an appreciation of sterling from 2.40 to 2.60 to the dollar under the Smithsonian Agreement. Export prices of British manufactures, for example, were estimated by the National Institute to have increased by at least 10 per cent in comparison to those of foreign competitors in the eighteen months to the first quarter of 1972. Import price competitiveness deteriorated simultaneously by 7.2 per cent. A second influence was the decline in manufacturing production brought about by the strikes and power cuts in the first quarter of 1972. Manufacturing production had in fact been in decline throughout 1971 and fell quite steeply in the first quarter of 1972 because of labour difficulties while imports, which were held back by various factors in 1971, accelerated in 1972.

Although rising costs and reduced competitiveness weakened the pound, the current account remained in surplus in the first half of 1972. It was speculative pressure – anticipating a further weakening, and in the expectation of a float – that created the exchange crisis in June. The Chancellor's remarks in his 1972 budget speech about not maintaining an 'unrealistic' exchange rate implied that he would stick to his expansion target of 5 per cent per annum whatever the effect on the balance of payments, and this was widely interpreted as a willingness to let the pound float downwards. It did not take long for the market to draw this conclusion and act accordingly. In May and June Britain was able to obtain $2,600 million in temporary support, mainly from other members of the 'snake', but the government was unwilling to go on borrowing in the manner of that done in the 1960s. By the last quarter of 1972 the pound had fallen against the dollar by about 9 per cent.

The pressure on the pound was no doubt intense but greater pressure in the 1960s had been withstood. The fact is that the Chancellor was already mentally prepared to protect his expansionary programme by a float, and speculators knew that this was so. Given his anxiety to reduce unemployment, he did not intend to be held back by the balance of payments and, as it was clearly heading for the red, a little devaluation might be just what was needed. Whether he seriously intended to go back to a fixed parity is not clear.

The fall in the exchange rate revived the volume of exports which had been flagging in 1971 and the first half of 1972. In 1973 there was an increase of 13.5 per cent by volume which almost exactly matched the increase in imports. The balance of payments, however, continued to deteriorate after the float because of the faster rise in import than in export prices. The swing in the terms of trade accounts almost entirely for the deficit in 1973 and again in 1974 when exports grew faster than imports. In the last quarter of 1973 the annual rate of deficit on current account was already in excess of £1400 million, with the full impact of higher oil prices still to come in 1974 when the current account deficit reached £3,359 million. To these results the falling pound may have contributed a little but what mattered far more was the world boom in commodity prices, including oil. Exports of primary products doubled in price between 1972 and 1974 and United Kingdom import prices did likewise.

In 1973 the Treasury found a convenient way of financing the deficit: they revived foreign currency borrowing. Nationalised industries and local authorities were encouraged to borrow in the Euro-currency market, using forward cover provided by the Treasury and paying the proceeds into the Exchange Equalisation Account. It could be an expensive form of borrowing if the exchange rate fell heavily. But in 1973 it brought in £1,000 million – enough to cover nearly the whole of the current deficit. Borrowing abroad by companies on two-year maturities, which had been banned in January 1971 (when borrowing was limited to five-year maturities), was also revived.

The crisis created by rising import prices and an enormous external deficit was not resolved until long after the government left office. The balance of payments dipped much further in 1974 and the current account took four years to return to balance. Inflation continued to accelerate until wage claims of nearly 40 per cent were being submitted in 1975.

INCOMES POLICY

Since incomes policy is dealt with at length in Chapter Seven, the account given below confines itself to an outline of developments.

What began as a dismantling of the apparatus of incomes policy gave way to a statutory policy on American lines aimed at holding in check the rapid increase in wages which from 1970 had become the main source of rising costs and prices.

In 1970–71 the government was unwilling to interfere in private sector settlements. It could not, however, escape responsibility for increases in the public sector. It based its policy in the first two years on 'the view that if the level of public sector settlements could be reduced, the level of private sector settlements would follow'.[26] Selwyn Lloyd had had a similar idea in 1961 but it had not worked. In the 1970s the government was able to claim some success initially but the policy foundered with the first miners' strike at the beginning of 1972.

Wages were already rising at 13 per cent per annum by the middle of 1970. In the second half of the year there were wage disputes with local authority manual workers, electricity supply workers and Post Office workers, all involving strike action and a Committee or Court of Inquiry. Each of these issued in an increase somewhat higher than the original offer but an offer of a 12 per cent increase was accepted by vote in November by the miners. The government's aim was to arrive at successively lower wage settlements (the 'n minus one' policy) and in 1971 wages and earnings did rise a little more slowly than in 1970. Wage awards in the public sector in the second half of 1971 were substantially lower than a year earlier, but there was no parallel moderation in the private sector.[27]

An informal agreement with the CBI in the summer of 1971 was designed to reinforce the policy from the prices side. Members of the CBI were invited to sign an undertaking to limit any unavoidable price increases over the next twelve months – to 31 July 1972 – to 5 per cent, while the government undertook to invite the nationalised industries to follow suit, regardless of financial targets. The CBI's initiative was predicated on the adoption by the government of a reflationary policy; and a succession of reflationary measures began in July.

From July 1971 to July 1972 retail prices rose by no more than 5.8 per cent compared with 10.1 per cent in the previous year, indicating a remarkable success so far as price inflation was concerned. But wages and costs continued along the same inflationary path, hourly wages rising by 12.5 per cent, only slightly less than the 13.8 per cent rise in the previous year. Not only so, but holding prices down laid up

26. Blackaby, *British Economic Policy*, 62.

27. J.H.B. Tew, 'Policies aimed at improving the balance of payments', in Blackaby (ed.), *British Economic Policy*, 334.

inflationary upsets later on when an adjustment had to be made to the movement of costs.

A wage dispute arose in the mining industry in the autumn of 1971 and, after an overtime ban in November, it led to the first national coal strike for nearly fifty years on 9 January 1972. The government declared a state of emergency, power cuts were made, and most of British industry adopted a three-day week, with $1\frac{1}{2}$ million workers laid off. When work was resumed after a seven-week strike and a report by a Court of Inquiry, average earnings were some 17–20 per cent higher. The government's policy had clearly failed.[28]

Inflation became the central preoccupation of economic policy in 1972–73. The CBI's pledge of voluntary price restraint was due to expire in mid-July 1972 and employers were in no mood to extend it without some reciprocal undertaking by the unions. The government hoped to devise an acceptable voluntary policy in negotiations with the CBI and the TUC which began on 9 March soon after the settlement of the miners' strike. The negotiations were highly protracted, not least because of the operation of the Industrial Relations Act which came into full effect at the end of February.

The trade unions demanded the repeal or suspension of the Act when this was clearly a matter for Parliament. Negotiations finally got under way in July 1972 but were curiously unreal. Each side wanted what the other side could not guarantee – limits on the rise in wages and prices. The government offered a limit of 5 per cent on increases in retail prices resulting from a rise in costs which, in the circumstances of 1972–73, it would have been hard put to secure. As the trade unions pointed out, this did not deal with increases in rents, changes in the exchange rate and the new food import levies. The trade unions, for their part, made no specific offers and tabled demands for everything imaginable. It was hardly surprising that negotiations broke down.

The most important outcome of the negotiations was the emergence of the idea of linking increases in wages and prices. Hitherto the government had carefully avoided this idea and the experience of the next two years was to demonstrate the wisdom of doing so. Apart from other difficulties, such a link meant that a rise in import prices that outpaced the rise in export prices – and so meant a reduction in real incomes – would be automatically translated in a *rise* in money wages instead of a fall. In 1974 a link of this kind, with predetermined additions to wages for every rise in retail prices above a threshold, was

28. Ibid., 352.

to play an important part in making inflation worse, contrary to the hopes of Edward Heath.

The first attempt to limit inflation had crashed with the miners' strike in 1972. A second attempt, this time to arrive at a voluntary policy, had failed. The government then introduced a statutory incomes policy such as it had earlier denounced, in three stages, beginning on 6 November 1972 with a 90-day standstill – subsequently extended to March–April 1973 – on pay prices, rents and dividends. The pay freeze caused few difficulties, average earnings rising over the winter by less than 1 per cent. Retail prices on the other hand rose at 5 per cent a year because of increases in the price of seasonal foods and imports.

In the second stage, beginning in April 1973, a Pay Board and a Prices Commission were set up, following an American model, to operate new wage and price guidelines. The result appears to have been a marked check to wage inflation and fewer strikes than in the previous years. For the year from November 1972 to November 1973 the rise in hourly wages works out at 11.6 per cent compared with 19 per cent in the previous year.

In the third stage, beginning in November, a limit was set on pay increases of £2.25 per head per week or 7 per cent with an individual limit of £350 a year. If the retail price index rose more than 7 per cent above the level in October 1973 a further addition of 40p could be made for every further rise in prices of 1 per cent. This provision would have been risky at any time, but proved disastrous in 1974 when increases in pay were triggered again and again between April and October.

That this was likely to happen should have been apparent by October when the limits were decided. The first mild tremors of the oil shock had already been felt. More important, import prices were rising fast. An international boom had raised them by 37 per cent since September 1972 and international commodity prices were still rising at a rate almost comparable with the rise in oil prices. It was a time when the prospect of accelerating inflation was plain to see.

Thus when the first oil shock hit the industrial countries, the United Kingdom was in a particularly vulnerable position. The government had given the economy a powerful boost just as its external balance was deteriorating. Now it was introducing an incomes policy that might accelerate, not moderate, inflation.

The latter stages of the government's incomes policy – and indeed of the Conservative government itself – were overshadowed by the dispute with the miners, who rejected an offer from the National Coal

Board equivalent to an average increase in pay of 13 per cent and began an overtime ban on 12 November. The simultaneous rise in oil prices by 66 per cent in October greatly strengthened the miners' position and was bound to affect the entire market for energy. There was, however, no adequate mechanism under the incomes policy for dealing with special cases; and indeed to allow special cases might take from the acceptability of the policy. The TUC did agree in January 1974 that this *was* a special case and would not be quoted in justification of other claims. But no action was taken and, when the Prime Minister announced a general election on 28 February, the dispute was still unsettled.

CONCLUSION

The 1970s were a difficult time for all European countries but the United Kingdom suffered a bigger setback than its neighbours. This was partly because when the oil shock occurred the economy was already out of balance: in substantial external deficit, suffering from rapid wage inflation, and experiencing increasing pressure on the economy to an unsustainable degree. Before balance could be restored there was a loss of control in 1974–75 which made the task still more difficult and opened the way to fundamental changes in economic management.

Yet if one looks simply at the rate of economic growth over the 3½ years of Conservative rule, leaving aside the chaos of the final months, the record bears comparison with earlier periods. Between the second quarter of 1970 and the final quarter of 1973 GDP increased by 11.1 per cent or by 3.05 per cent per annum, slightly faster than between 1960 and 1970. Too much of that increase, however, went in consumption and too little in investment; and too much of the increase was in the single year 1973.

From the point of view of policy, the interest lies in the twofold U-turn in the middle of the government's term of office. First it embarked on a boomlike expansion in the spring of 1972 in order to bring down unemployment; then it introduced a statutory incomes policy in November 1972 whereas it had earlier wanted rid of any formal incomes policy. In some ways the government's philosophy at the start had had much in common with Mrs Thatcher's in the 1980s. But there was one vital difference: Thatcher's had no employment policy. For her it was inflation that mattered and she was not deflected by the repercussions on employment of her efforts to limit inflation. The Heath Government on the other hand persevered with a 5 per cent growth target with faster inflation already looming up. In other directions there is a contrast in resoluteness. Where Heath talked of disengagement, Mrs Thatcher went for privatisation and was able to continue with policies requiring industry to be self-reliant and refrain from seeking government help.

At the same time Heath was conspicuously out of luck. The world boom of 1972–73 coincided at just the wrong time with his own little boom. He had no North Sea oil to free him from balance of payments difficulties. Instead the balance of payments was plunged into deficit by the higher price of oil, the terms of trade had already changed strongly against the United Kingdom, and his efforts to moderate wage-inflation were simultaneously knocked on the head by the miners. The one respect in which he did enjoy some luck was that General de Gaulle was no longer alive to thwart his application to join the European Community.

CHAPTER SIX

The Heath government, industrial policy and the 'new capitalism'

Robert Taylor

'The Conservative party is the party of free enterprise. Our approach is to say, how can we enable the free enterprise system to work better?'
Edward Heath, Conservative Party annual conference, 15 October 1966.

'All modern governments are involved in economic management and accordingly they cannot fail to take an interest in the workings of industry.'
Conservative Party *Campaign Guide 1974*, 107.

No issue has aroused more controversy over Edward Heath's government than its attitude towards industry. It is in that public policy area – so the critics claim – where the famous 1972 U-turn proved to be the most dramatic as well as the most disastrous. They argue Heath was elected with a clear mandate to disengage the state from industrial affairs, under the so-called philosophy of Selsdon man. After years of subsidy and over-regulation, private sector companies were to be made to fend for themselves in a thrusting market economy which rewarded risk-taking and business acumen. No longer could employers expect a benevolent government to rescue them if they fell into financial difficulties. If the new bracing no-nonsense approach forced some ailing firms to go to the wall, then this was a price well worth paying in order to convince others the state could no longer be relied upon as the source of their salvation.

Neo-economic liberals in the Conservative Party pointed to the robust rhetoric used by both Heath and John Davies, his first Secretary of State in the newly formed Department of Trade and Industry (DTI), as evidence that the new government initially promised a decisive break with past bipartisan practice in the making of industrial policy. 'Our strategy is clear', declared the Prime Minister at the 1970 party conference as he unveiled his 'quiet revolution'. 'It is to reorganise the functions of government, to leave more to individual and corporate effort, to make savings in government expenditure, to provide room for greater incentives to men and women and to firms and businesses.

Our strategy is to encourage them more to take their own decisions, and to stand on their own feet, to accept responsibility for themselves and their families'.[1] A month later Davies spoke derisively in the House of Commons about the 'soft, sodden morass of subsidised incompetence'. 'We believe that the essential need of the country is to gear its policies to the great majority of people, who are not lame ducks, who do not need a helping hand', he told MP's.[2] 'All seemed set to embark on the privatisation programme and the dismantling of the socialist state', recalled Nicholas Ridley later in his memoirs.[3]

But, Heath's opponents inside his own Party argued, the initial promise of radical change soon vanished as the Prime Minister crumpled under pressure in the early months of 1972 when faced with the alarming prospect of registered unemployment remaining above the politically unacceptable figure of one million. By then his government had already displayed alarming signs of industrial appeasement – his Conservative critics argued – both by its decision to take parts of the Rolls-Royce company into state ownership to prevent liquidation and more significantly by the rescue of Upper Clyde Shipbuilders after its workers staged a successful work-in to try to save the four yards on the Clyde from closure because of lack of orders and escalating costs. In the spring of 1972 – it is alleged – Heath, in close alliance with Sir William Armstrong, head of the civil service and by then increasingly the *de facto* deputy Prime Minister, bypassed the hapless Davies and his department to draw up the details of what became the infamous Industry Act. Tony Benn, Labour's shadow industry spokesman, described it as 'a massive measure of intrusion.' 'We shall make use of the powers of the Bill when we come into power again more radically than the right honourable gentleman will use them'.[4] By the final months of Heath's government Peter Walker, his comparatively youthful Trade and Industry Secretary, was talking enthusiastically about the emergence of a 'new capitalism' where a dynamic state was to be the catalyst for industrial change.

Heath himself never accepted that his government had performed a drastic U-turn in its approach to industry. It is true the Prime Minister was not transformed instantly from being a champion of industrial laissez-faire into an arch-corporatist who believed widespread state intervention was the way to cure Britain's industrial ills. There was certainly some continuity in his attitude to industry, particularly when

1. Conservative Party, *Annual Conference Report 1970*, 38.
2. *House of Commons Debates*, 5th series, vol. 805, col. 1211, 4 November 1970.
3. N. Ridley, *My Style of Government* (London, 1992), 4.
4. *HC Debs.*, 5th series, vol. 837, col. 1031, 22 May 1972.

related to government assistance to the regions. As a One Nation Tory Heath could be pragmatic, cautious and sensitive to the adverse social consequences of industrial change. There were sceptics, almost from the start, about just how ready the Prime Minister was to turn his free market rhetoric into practical action. 'The anti-lame duck approach did not guide government policy even in its earliest days, except in a very partial and one-sided way', observed Samuel Brittan, the *Financial Times's* economic commentator.[5] The events of early 1972 were a less sudden rupture in the government's industrial policy than the political hyperbole of the time might have suggested. Those who argue that Heath betrayed his own supposed convictions about the virtues of laissez-faire capitalism fail to recognise that his robust language about free enterprise hid a much more complex reality.

Moreover, as Davies displayed in his own tough-sounding speech to the 1970 party conference, he was well aware of the severe limitations that would be imposed on any industrial disengagement strategy pursued by the government. 'Simply to abandon great sectors of our productive capacity at their moment of maximum weakness would be folly', he told the Party faithful, although in the next breath he warned he would not 'bolster up or bail out companies where I can see no end to the process of propping them up' as this would mean 'reinforcing failure'. Even as he exempted the aircraft industry from his strictures (already aware of the gravity of Rolls-Royce's troubles), Davies went on to emphasise that he would 'not accept involvement as an open-ended liability'.[6]

Neither of the opposing views of Heath's industrial strategy – of disengagement betrayed by pragmatism or a continuity of belief in active state involvement – is completely accurate. In fact, both of them contain an element of truth. In practice, Heath turned out to be an often impatient and angry Prime Minister who used both activist measures and laissez-faire approaches to industrial policy in pursuit of one over-riding objective. This was to modernise British industry by creating, through different forms of state encouragement, a more competitive business climate designed to stimulate entrepreneurs to invest in new growth industries. In the words of Brendan Sewill, special adviser to the Chancellor of the Exchequer during the Heath government, 'the strategy was no less than an attempt to change the whole attitude of mind of the British people: to create a more dynamic, thrusting, go-getting economy on the American or German model'.[7]

5. S. Brittan, *The Economic Consequences of Democracy* (London, 1977), 134.

6. Conservative Party, *Annual Conference Report 1970*, 31.

7. B. Sewill and R. Harris, *British Economic Policy 1970–1974* (Institute of Economic Affairs, 1975), 30.

A determination to make UK companies both efficient and innovative was to be the driving force behind Heath's approach to industrial policy throughout the entire life of his government. What changed over time, however, were the instrumental means that were to be used in achieving that elusive goal, as Heath grew increasingly frustrated and disillusioned with the apparent failure of the private sector to respond in a positive manner to the bracing business environment he believed he had helped to create for entrepreneurs with cuts in corporate taxation and the removal of bureaucratic state controls. The shift to a more active statist industrial policy after 1972 was seen as necessary by Heath and others because of British capitalism's inability to respond effectively to the competitive challenge posed by the European Community after the UK became a member on 1 January 1973. Heath was a man in a hurry who felt let down by what he regarded as the timidity and sloth of too many British employers. Faced by the dangers of high unemployment and the lack of a private investment boom, he turned inevitably to a government-led growth strategy with a strong emphasis on public investment programmes, especially in infrastructure. If private industry lacked the self-confidence and dynamism to set the pace, then the state would have to step in and seize the initiative.

A SENTIMENT MORE THAN A POLICY?

Heath and his senior colleagues did not draw up a highly detailed industrial strategy for government during their years in opposition similar to that for industrial relations, 'The lame duck philosophy – that inefficient firms should be allowed to go bust – had a comparatively small place in our thinking in opposition, was never mentioned at the 1970 Selsdon Park meeting and achieved headlines only with John Davies's speech in October 1970', argued Sewill.[8] But this did not mean the Conservatives carried out no reappraisal between their electoral defeat in October 1964 and June 1970 on what the Party's approach towards industry ought to be.

A thorough examination of the future role of the nationalised industries was carried out by a policy group led by Nicholas Ridley who was to be appointed a junior minister under Davies at the Department of Trade and Industry. Its terms of reference were clear enough: 'to consider future policy regarding the existing nationalised industries, the scope for denationalisation and conditions required for the proper

8. Sewill and Harris, *British Economic Policy*, 37.

management of the industries remaining nationalised in a competitive economy'.[9]

The resulting report set out in precise and blunt language a future Conservative government policy towards state-owned industry. It is true that it did not suggest a wholesale roll-back by the state from the publicly owned sectors. On the contrary, as the report admitted 'whatever is done about denationalisation, it is clear a large public sector of industry will remain'. But Ridley's group was convinced that public corporations could not be managed as commercial undertakings, mainly because they operated with an 'implied government guarantee' of viability. The report proposed that there should be a clear division of responsibility between the state and the nationalised industries. Ridley and his colleagues argued that:

> Since the government must provide the capital, it has a very real and legitimate concern with the size and purpose of the nationalised industries. It must be able to make its will known and carried out in these respects. But having given the industries their instructions, as it were, it should not interfere nor bring hidden political pressures to bear upon the managers. They must be left alone to manage.

However, the report suggested that government needed to establish clear guidelines on how the state-owned industries should operate. These guidelines would provide details of the task that each industry should perform, 'including any deviations from the most profitable course of action' – for social, defence or political reasons – that the government wanted them to undertake. 'The government must decide where the responsibility of an industry begins and ends', said Ridley. The report also accepted that the state had 'always to control the size of the public sector by one arbitrary means or another'. It also meant the government should lay down – in either an annual binding directive or a five-year rolling programme – the policy for each public corporation on product diversification, its prices, purchasing and financial targets. The state needed a 'reserve power to increase the price of industries' products' although this should be 'a power of last resort, rarely used'. Ridley even favoured the creation of a number of small government-owned holding companies to act as a 'buffer' between the state and the nationalised industry sector. These would co-ordinate capital investment programmes as well as appoint managers. The report also backed the establishment of a ministry for the nationalised industries to co-ordinate the approach.

9. 'Report of the Policy Group on Nationalised Industries', chaired by N. Ridley, 11 July 1968, CPA ACP(68)51, CRD/3/17/12.

Such recommended levels of state intervention did not mean that the Conservatives took a benevolent view of the role of the nationalised industries in a mixed market economy. Quite the reverse. But as the Ridley report explained:

> The public sector of industry is a millstone round our necks. Real commercialism in the nationalised sector can never be achieved. Government interference is inevitable. Competition between private and public sector can never be fair. The problems of management and control can never be properly solved. We have a built-in system of misallocation of capital in our economy.

The document proposed selling off a number of state industries to the private sector. These included steel (which had been returned by the Labour government to public ownership in 1967), BEA and BOAC airlines, Thomas Cook the travel agents and the British Aviation Authority. Labour's plan to nationalise the docks was to be scrapped. State holdings in Short Brothers, the aircraft engine company in Northern Ireland and Upper Clyde Shipbuilders (described in the Ridley report as 'exactly the wrong sort of enterprise even for partial state holdings') were to be sold off on the market. Ridley and his colleagues also believed that state industries should no longer be allowed by government to diversify their business activities. It was suggested that the National Coal Board ought to be told to sell off its subsidiary businesses, including its activity in North Sea gas exploration, although the report admitted that 'political considerations would make denationalisation of coal an unrealistic proposition at least in the foreseeable future'. British Rail should be told to pull out of its shipping and hovercraft activities, it also advised. Postal services and telecommunications needed to be separated from each other and their monopoly power broken up, although both should remain in the public sector. The report doubted whether it was 'practicable' to denationalise gas and electricity but it looked favourably on the so-called BP 'solution' to nationalisation with its private–public business partnership approach.

Ridley and his colleagues visited a number of European countries – Italy, France and West Germany – to look at how their public industry sectors were organised. In November 1969 they produced a further report that recommended the introduction of government 'annual directives' for the nationalised industries and their profit maximisation. 'The politics of the matter appear to suggest we should denationalise some industries but avoid using that word', it concluded. The report insisted there were 'substantial economic reasons' to denationalise. 'There is a very strong case for embarking on a course of gradually dismantling the public sector as a whole', it added. Ridley believed this would not only ensure large savings in government expenditure and thereby help reduce taxes but also enable the spread of equity shares among the general public. 'We want shares widely held by as many of the public as possible', the report said. Ridley's group recognised it would be 'impracticable' to denationalise most of state industry but thought many public corporations 'might be – at some stage' after being put on a sounder basis and covered by 'suitable regulatory machinery'. The industries they had in mind were coal, buses, British Rail, electricity, gas, the telephone service and Cable and Wireless.[10]

Much of the radical thrust of the Ridley group was unwelcome to some senior Conservatives. The most sceptical response to their suggestions came from Sir Keith Joseph, the Party's shadow industry spokesman. He favoured a more prudent and pragmatic approach; as he wrote in February 1969,

> In my view we cannot disinterest ourselves altogether from the over-fragmentation of industry and from resisting overseas bids for companies in a very limited number of cases. And we certainly cannot avoid entanglement occasionally in a public industry, though our purpose should be to restore it to the market as fast as possible. The objective should be only to deal with situations which are very important where the need is clear but for some reason will not be achieved by normal market forces. All our method should be only to break a log-jam obstructing a market solution rather than to impose a solution of our own as the Industrial Rorganisation Corporation does.[11]

Heath himself seemed less than enthusiastic about any fundamental shake-up of the state industry sector. He warned in June 1969 that the Conservatives

> should be careful in future in proposing to introduce changes in the structure of everything in which the government was now involved. There would be a number of high priority matters and we would need all our time. We would get no thanks from the public for bogging ourselves down in massive structural changes in our early years in office.[12]

Joseph agreed with him. He believed the Party's approach to private industry must be concerned with helping firms to 'liberate energies by cuts in direct tax rates', abolishing the taxation of share options, and reforming corporate taxation. Joseph was not even sure whether the

10. 'Report of the Policy Group on Nationalised Industries'.
11. 'Government Intervention in Industry', memo by Sir K. Joseph, 28 February 1969, CPA LCC/69/221.
12. Leader's Consultative Committee, 16 June 1969, LCC/69/308.

Conservatives ought to commit themselves to the abolition of the Industrial Reorganisation Corporation, established by the Labour government to encourage corporate mergers. 'I am not convinced we should go as far as this', he wrote. 'We shall need a method by which Whitehall can keep in touch with industry.' 'There will occasionally be catalytic functions to perform in industries that respond very sluggishly to market needs', he added.[13]

However, other Conservative policy-makers were more enthusiastic about Ridley's robust approach to industrial policy. Iain Macleod, for one, told Heath he thought the group's proposals 'go a considerable way to meeting the demand for denationalisation without tying us to a fixed formula'.[14] The lack of detailed precision about future industry policy in the run-up to the 1970 general election troubled some leading Conservatives. Sewill wondered if they would not do better to spell out their strategy for the nationalised industries rather than maintain the party's 'present position of responsible silence'. 'While this subject (industry policy) is of no great interest to the general public, can we get through an election campaign without being more specific about our plans for the future of particular industries such as steel and the airlines?', he questioned.[15]

The 1970 Conservative election manifesto suggested that the language – if not the recommendations – of the Ridley report was of some political use to the leadership. The manifesto promised that:

> We will pursue a vigorous competition policy. We will check any abuse of dominant market power or monopoly, strengthening and reforming the machinery which exists. We reject the detailed intervention of Socialism which usurps the function of management and seeks to dictate prices and earnings in industry. We much prefer a system of general pressures, creating an economic climate which favours, and rewards, enterprise and efficiency. Our aim is to identify and remove obstacles that prevent effective competition and restrict initiative.[16]

The document may have fallen far short of any grand plan to disengage the state from industry but on the other hand it was much more than a collection of bland generalities. 'We will progressively reduce the

13. 'Industrial Re-organisation Corporation', memo by Sir K. Joseph, 4 December 1969, LCC/69/263.

14. I. Macleod to E. Heath, 12 March 1970, CRD/3/17/14.

15. 'Publication of Policy during 1970', memo by B. Sewill, 21 January 1970, for Shadow Cabinet weekend, 31 January – 1 February 1970, Selsdon Park Hotel, CPA Selsdon Park papers (filed with LCC papers), SP/70/12.

16. Conservative Party general election manifesto, *A Better Tomorrow* (Conservative Central Office, 1970), 11–12.

involvement of the state in the nationalised industries (e.g. steel) to improve their competitiveness. An increasing use of private capital will help to reduce the burden on the taxpayer, get better investment decisions and ensure more effective use of total resources', it suggested. Public–private partnerships were proposed in shipping, hotels, catering services and land development. 'Bureaucratic burdens imposed on industry by government departments, agencies and boards have steadily increased in recent years. We will see they are reduced', the manifesto promised. Ridley suggested that much of his group report, although 'suitably disguised', had been included in the Party's policy.[17] Sir Michael Fraser at Central Office agreed. As he wrote to James Douglas at the Conservative Research Department: 'In my view, the manifesto is sufficiently broad to give a mandate for as much of the Ridley–Eden policy as a Conservative government might wish to implement.'[18]

However, the thrust of the Party's industrial programme assumed an activist policy towards industry by government. Even Ridley's own recommendations required a high degree of state involvement. Nobody among Conservative policy-makers believed it was possible in 1970 for government to disengage itself completely from the country's industrial affairs. In practice, hardly anybody in the Conservative Party questioned the wisdom of managing the mixed economy. This does not mean to suggest that Heath and his colleagues were concerned with merely administering a Wilsonian industrial strategy of state control. The Conservative promise of 1970 was to adopt a technocratic approach to industrial policy concerned with the creation of a go-getting climate within which business could flourish. Heath believed the main way government could help private industry was to reduce public sector waste, cut out red tape and lift onerous tax burdens off the backs of companies to allow them to grow. This was regarded as a much more important way of stimulating industry than direct state intervention. But the inner Party debate among Conservatives suggested that Heath and his colleagues were readier to question a bipartisan approach to industry than seemed likely two years later. While the Conservatives may not have hammered out any highly detailed blueprint for industry, the leadership was convinced of the need to introduce a more robust, competitive spirit into the country's industrial affairs. Ridley's group may have gone further in their proposals than Heath and his colleagues believed to be politically sensible, but their approach was more in tune

17. Ridley, *My Style*, 4.
18. M. Fraser to J. Douglas, 18 May 1970, CPA CRD/3/17/14.

with the leader's thinking in 1970 than many on either side of the party were later prepared to admit.

THE LIBERATION OF INDUSTRY: THE QUIET REVOLUTION

The Heath government's initial decisions suggested a radical change of direction from that of the Wilson years in industrial policy. The Prime Minister decided not to appoint Joseph to the industry portfolio. Instead he made Geoffrey Rippon Minister of Technology with Ridley and Sir John Eden, a right-wing MP, as junior ministers. On Macleod's sudden death four weeks later, John Davies replaced Rippon who went off to head Britain's team negotiating the country's European Economic Community membership. Only recently elected to Parliament as MP for Knutsford, Davies was a former director-general of the Confederation of British Industry with no political experience. He was seen by many as very much a corporatist figure who had played an important role in the development of industrial tripartism during the 1960s. Davies was to head the newly conceived Department of Trade and Industry through the merger of the Board of Trade and the Ministry of Technology. The DTI was not a grandiose Heathite idea, but had been prepared in the final months of the Wilson government.

Within a short time Heath and his colleagues seemed intent on a drastic disengagement from industry. The National Prices and Incomes Board was abolished. After initial hesitation, so was the Industrial Reorganisation Corporation along with the Consumer Council. The Industrial Expansion Act with its state enabling powers was repealed. The Shipbuilding Industry Board closed down. Labour's proposal for a Design Council was dropped and a state grant for the British Productivity Council was scrapped. The National Economic Development Council was reappraised and, although it was reprieved, the Prime Minister decided to downgrade its importance by no longer chairing all its monthly meetings. Such moves to abolish most of the institutions that had administered the Labour government's industrial policy in the 1960s delighted those Conservatives who believed Heath and his colleagues were committed to a radical approach to industry.

But other early decisions taken by the Cabinet suggested that ministers lacked any coherent or consistent industrial strategy. Despite the escalating costs to the taxpayer, ministers agreed to persist with the expensive Concorde project. No doubt this was seen as a useful way of reassuring Georges Pompidou, the French president, at a time when his support was vital to smooth the way for UK membership of the European Economic Community. However, the government withdrew Britain from the European Airbus programme. At the end of November 1970, the Cabinet refused to provide a bridging loan for the Mersey Docks and Harbours Board. Instead a moratorium was declared on repayments and 30 per cent of its capital was written down. Ministers also agreed that Thomas Cook and Lunn-Poly travel agents and state-owned public houses in the Carlisle area and in Scotland should be returned to the private sector. However, Lord Robens refused to accept the offer of a further term as National Coal Board chairman when the government decided to pass legislation hiving off some of its non-mining activities such as brickmaking and its computer-ticket agency to the private sector. But plans to sell off the retail showrooms of the Gas and Electricity Boards came to nothing. The government also dismissed Lord Hall, the Post Office chairman, when he refused to pursue a more profit-oriented policy. Labour's plan to nationalise Britain's ports was quietly dropped, while the Cabinet agreed to hand over BOAC's west African routes to BUA/Caledonian private airways. Changes were also made to government regional policy with a move from investment grants to allowances and the introduction of free depreciation on plant and machinery as well as the abolition of the regional employment premium from 1974. The selective employment tax was also cut as a first stage towards eventual abolition.

Taken together, most of these decisions suggested that Heath and his colleagues were in the mood to adopt a much more hands-off approach to industry than that of the previous Labour government. But the Cabinet was not motivated by any strong ideological attitude. As in other policy areas, ministers revealed a familiar pragmatic, ad hoc approach. Moreover, they were not insensitive – even during their first months of office – to the wider social consequences of industrial policy. On balance, however, ministers were readier than they proved to be after the spring of 1972 to take a critical view of the state's role in industrial affairs.

From the start the Cabinet intervened in the running of the nationalised industries in ways that destroyed their commercial viability. While ministers sought to minimise the role of the public corporations, they felt obliged to determine their policies as part of the government's wider economic strategy. This was especially true of ministerial insistance on price restraint. It represented a clear change of policy. Before June 1970, successive governments had expected the nationalised industries to operate commercially, to borrow at market rates of interest and to achieve a return on capital in line with that of the private sector. But now, Heath and his colleagues manipulated the prices of the public corporations as part of their wider programme of renewal.

Whatever early hopes of industrial disengagement there might have been were quickly dashed by the appearance of two urgent and intractable industrial problems that pushed their way onto the Cabinet's agenda. The first concerned the future of Rolls-Royce, the highly respected, blue-chip company. Less than a week after coming to office, Fred Corfield, the aviation minister, was confronted by Sir Denning Pearson, the company's chairman, who told him that Rolls-Royce required an urgent government cash injection if it hoped to honour its £150m contract with the Lockheed Aircraft Corporation for the supply of Rolls-Royce RB-211 engines to the US company's 1011 airbus.

In November 1970 the Cabinet agreed to provide £60m towards a support package for the company, but the City of London's financial institutions failed to produce the £30m they were asked for to help. Unless the government agreed to provide further assistance, the company faced financial collapse. Early in February 1971 the government decided to allow Rolls-Royce to go bankrupt and then took most of its assets into public ownership in the national interest. After a prolonged and often acrimonious negotiation with the US government and Lockheed, which was facing severe financial difficulties itself, Heath and his colleagues agreed to accept a slightly revised contract for the RB-211 engines. 'Within a year the Cabinet had carried out the first new programme of nationalisation since the Attlee government', wrote Leo Pliatzky, then Deputy Secretary at the Treasury.[19]

But even Jock Bruce-Gardyne in his critical account of Heath's 'quiet revolution' accepted the Cabinet's decision to save Rolls-Royce was not 'the first of the government's tactical adjustments motivated by employment considerations'.[20] Margaret Thatcher in her memoirs said she did 'not think any of us doubted that on defence grounds it was important to keep an indigenous aircraft engine capability.'[21] All sides agreed it would have been unthinkable to allow Rolls-Royce to shut down with the possible loss of around 80,000 jobs. Certainly, such a step would have provoked a bitter row with President Nixon and soured 'the special relationship' between Britain and the United States. It would also have been a devastating blow to the international prestige of British industry.

A much more controversial Cabinet decision was the rescue of Upper

19. L. Pliatzky, *Getting and Spending: Public Expenditure, Employment and Inflation* (Oxford, 1982), 107.

20. J. Bruce-Gardyne, *Whatever Happened to the Quiet Revolution?* (London, 1974), 32.

21. M. Thatcher, *The Path to Power* (London, 1995), 207.

Clyde Shipbuilders following the disturbing course of events in west-central Scotland during the summer and autumn of 1971. This was regarded as the most blatant failure of the government's strategy of industrial disengagement. There is little doubt that ministers were overwhelmed by a growing fear of the consequences of mass unemployment that would follow the end of merchant shipbuilding on the Clyde. That anxiety was coupled with concern over the dangers of widespread civil disorder – a view expressed to them by David McNee, the local chief constable, who claimed he would need to recruit or mobilise an extra 15,000 police to uphold the rule of law if all the yards were closed.

In June 1971 Davies informed the Commons that the government had 'decided that nobody's interest' would be 'served by making an injection of funds into the firm as it now stands'.[22] Closure seemed inevitable as UCS needed an extra £6m of taxpayer's money to avoid insolvency, and the liquidator was called in. A report prepared for Davies by Lord Robens concluded that funding UCS 'in its present form would be wholly unjustified and in the end could cause serious and more widespread damage'.[23] It suggested that, while the Govan yard might be saved, both Scotstoun and Clydebank would have to close. The government initially accepted that bleak conclusion and appointed Hill Samuel the merchant bankers to work out how the rundown was to be achieved. In a report, they also concluded there could be 'no question of the establishment of Govan Shipbuilders (covering all the yards) being a proposition that could attract commercial support'.[24]

But UCS workers were unwilling to remain passive and accept their fate. They decided to occupy all the yards under the militant leadership of their senior Communist shop stewards – Jimmy Airlie and Jimmy Reid – and began a work-in. In her memoirs, Mrs Thatcher complained that the government 'allowed itself to be sucked into talks with the trade unions, who it was believed might be able to influence the militant shop stewards behind the occupation'.[25] She believed the Heath government's mistake was to agree to the provision of public money to keep the yards operating normally while the liquidator sought a long-term solution. Ministers accepted that their eventual willingness

22. *HC Debs.*, 5th series, vol. 820, col. 156, 21 June 1971.

23. *Report of the Advisory Group on Shipbuilding on the Upper Clyde*, chaired by Lord Robens, House of Commons papers, 554, (HMSO) 29 July 1971, 2–3; J. Foster and C. Woolfson, *The Politics of the UCS Work-In* (London, 1986), 192.

24. Report of Hill Samuel & Co. Ltd, Cmd. 4918, March 1972, 11, 15; Foster and Woolfson, *UCS Work-In*, 328.

25. Thatcher, *Path to Power*, 214.

to rescue UCS made no obvious business sense. But on 24 February 1972 the Cabinet was told that £35m would be provided by the government to save three of the four yards, the solution presented to it by its advisers. As Mrs Thatcher explained: 'Davies openly admitted to us that the new group had little chance of making its way commercially and that if the general level of unemployment had been lower and the economy reviving faster, he would not have recommended this course.' 'There was tangible unease', she recalled. 'It was a small but memorably inglorious episode'.[26] John Campbell, Heath's biographer, wrote that 'the government frankly gave in to the threat of violence . . . UCS was saved purely to preserve jobs'.[27]

THE RISE OF 'NEW CAPITALISM'

The rescue of UCS led inexorably to the 1972 Industry Act, the most substantial part of the Heath government's dirigiste approach to industrial policy and the symbol of his famous U-turn. As Edmund Dell, Labour MP for Birkenhead, argued in its Commons second reading debate: 'Our pragmatic Prime Minister, having marched his troops up the hill to laissez-faire and disengagement, is marching them down to selective intervention on a massive scale. With the enthusiasm of the convert, the government have moved at a stroke from the extreme of disengagement on the one hand to selective squandermania at the other extreme without precedent and without parliamentary control'.[28]

However, Davies had made clear the reasoning behind the Government's change of direction in its industrial policy: 'in a new and rapidly changing world industrial and commercial environment, the government cannot stand aside when situations arise which industry and the financial institutions cannot meet alone. We have decided to take powers to help industry to modernise, adapt and rationalise to meet these new and changing circumstances'.[29]

The main cause of the government's more interventionist industrial strategy lay in its determination to prepare British industry for the challenge of European Economic Community membership. But it was also partly influenced by growing fears over the soaring unemployment rate in the winter of 1971–72 and apparent dangers of widespread social disorder. Moreover, Heath was sensitive to the erroneous but wide-

26. Thatcher, *Path to Power*, 218.
27. J. Campbell, *Edward Heath* (London, 1993), 442.
28. *HC Debs.*, 5th series, vol. 837, col. 1096, 22 May 1972.
29. *HC Debs.*, 5th series, vol. 833, col. 1546, 22 March 1972.

spread charge that he was callous about the alleged human consequences of the government's economic policy. Nor could ministers be unaware of the political dangers of industrial disengagement. 'The electoral crunch will undoubtedly come on the problems of the declining industries', warned Central Office. 'If we fail to carry conviction on these, we shall have great difficulty in making our regional policy stand up'.[30] Yet even before the spring of 1972, ministers were moving away from an abrasive approach to industry. Davies told Heath as early as November 1971 that the government's 'disengagement policy' had been 'arrested'. He said his ministry would now be concentrating on modernising company law and developing more integrated measures to 'overcome problems of the declining areas'.[31]

In fact, most of the new Industry Bill was drawn up secretly in 10 Downing Street by Heath, Armstrong, and senior civil service colleagues Douglas Allen, William Nield and Leo Pliatzky. It emerged from the work initiated by the Prime Minister on how the UK should prepare itself for membership of the European Economic Community by modernising the country's industrial capacity and strengthening regional infrastructure. New regional development grants were to be introduced at a cost of up to £250m a year. But the Bill also provided sweeping powers for the Secretary of State to provide any form of financial assistance to industry whether inside or outside the assisted areas, where he was satisfied it would be of likely benefit to the economy, was in the national interest and the funds could not be obtainable from anywhere else. Under the measure, parliamentary approval would be needed for any project that exceeded £5m, while it was envisaged that up to £150m of assistance could be provided with four further possible tranches of £100m, with Treasury consent subject to Commons approval.

An Industrial Development Advisory Board was established to help the Secretary of State exercise his responsibilities under the Act. A number of senior captains of industry were appointed to that body which was chaired by Gordon Richardson, a future governor of the Bank of England. 'Virtually all the decisions taken by the board ended in success', claimed Peter Walker.[32] At the same time a new Industrial Development Executive was formed inside the Department of Trade and Industry. It established a strong regional organisation in close liaison with regional economic planning councils and boards. The measure

30. 'The Next Manifesto: Policy', memo by A. Newton and J. Douglas, 17 March 1972, CPA SC/72/11.

31. J. Davies to E. Heath, 8 November 1971, SC/70/21.

32. P. Walker, *Staying Power* (London, 1991), 95.

also provided tapering grants for the construction and equipment from 1972 to 1974 of new merchant ships of over 100 gross tonnes and mobile off-shore installations to a total cost of £50m of taxpayer's money. Cheap credit guarantees available to UK shipbuilders building for UK shipowners were raised from £700m to £1bn and up to £1.4bn with Treasury consent. By October 1973, over 18,800 applications for regional development grants had been received and £55m paid out. Nearly 1,800 applications had been made for selective assistance under section seven of the Industry Act, and £76.5m was offered to create 51,000 new jobs.

The significance of the change of direction in Heath's industrial policy was clear from the ministerial reshuffle in April 1972 when both Eden and Ridley were removed from the DTI. Chris Chataway was put in charge of the new Industrial Development Executive while Tom Boardman, a backbencher, was brought in to replace Eden. Michael Heseltine was given responsibility for aviation. Seven months later, the hapless Davies was replaced as Secretary of State by Peter Walker, articulate enthusiast for the 'new capitalism' and an ardent Heathite.

The government's fondness for more state intervention in industry was provided with some intellectual justification by Chataway in a lecture he delivered to the Conservative Political Centre in October 1972. Mainland European dirigiste experience appeared to have a considerable influence over the emerging strategy. Chataway pointed out how close European cooperation was required between governments and private companies in the high technology sector such as computer manufacture and aircraft production. He also argued that it was in the national interest for the state to give 'temporary support to an industry' which had to 'adapt to drastically changed circumstances' but was being hit by 'severe market dislocation, a surge of imports or heavily subsidised overseas competitors'. Chataway added that state backing for industry could be justified on 'social considerations'. 'To allow a major firm to collapse in an area of high unemployment where the cost of putting the firm on its feet will definitely be less than the cost of paying unemployment benefit, is clearly bad economics as well as bad social policy', he insisted. However, Chataway was anxious to dispel any suggestion the government was ready to assist any ailing firm. 'It is not in anybody's interest to prop up on a temporary basis bad managements and firms with no prospect of viability. There can be no future in taxing the efficient in order to subsidise the effete', he warned.[33] By

33. C. Chataway, *New Deal For Industry* (Conservative Political Centre, pamphlet 515, October 1972).

early 1973 the government had developed a coherent and robust view of what the state's role should be in the development of an industrial policy. As a memorandum to the leader's Steering Committee explained: 'Government has a clear responsibility to see that industrial affairs are conducted in line with the broader interests of the community'. This would involve a highly dynamic approach to the nationalised industries. 'We may wish to develop the idea of the public sector using its purchasing power throughout the economy to shape the development of exportable products based on a strong home market', it reasoned, citing transport and civil engineering as examples. If the Conservatives won the next general election, the document argued, 'the state would continue to provide the greatest possible encouragement for British industry, trade and commerce to expand both at home and overseas.' 'We shall pay particular attention to the need for a rising level of investment to sustain the progress now being made'.[34]

At the 1973 party conference, Walker spoke enthusiastically about the creation of a 'new capitalism' as he laid out the next steps in the government's strategy with the creation of a Minister of Consumer Affairs and an Office of Fair Trading. The Secretary of State also promised to make insider dealing a criminal offence and introduce legislation to increase disclosure in companies to ensure employers took their responsibilities to their own workers as seriously as they did to their consumers and shareholders. Walker worried over 'the failure of capitalism to appeal to the idealism of man'. He called for the 'ruthless' pursuit of equality of opportunity and urged the holders of corporate power to grow more 'socially responsible'.[35] 'The object of the "new capitalism" is the harnessing of economic growth to the creation of a civilised society', declared Walker.

Further specific and expensive industrial measures followed from the government's new approach. The Cabinet agreed (although not without doubts from Heath and in the face of Treasury resistance) to support the British Steel Corporation's ambitious ten-year strategy for the modernisation and expansion of steel production capacity. It backed the move to concentrate investment in five giant steel plants at a cost of £570m over a four-year period. But this was less of a U-turn than many people realised. As early as June 1971 Davies had accepted that bulk steel-making should remain within the state-owned company. Moreover, this involved the closure of obsolete plants such as Shotton,

34. 'Future Policy', discussion paper, 15 February 1973, SC/73/18.
35. Conservative Party, *Annual Conference Report 1973*, 29.

Ebbw Vale and East Moors in Wales with resulting job losses although these were not to occur while Heath was in office.

The state-owned coal industry also secured Cabinet approval with a highly generous £1.1bn of state financial assistance. 'We may fairly claim to have given the coal industry the tools to enable it to establish itself on a secure long-term basis and to make an appropriate contribution to the country's energy needs', declared Boardman.[36] Under the 1972 Gas Act, the government placed the gas industry under one national body – the British Gas Corporation – while it took powers over the Central Electricity Generating Board to ensure that no new power stations should be constructed without ministerial approval. In 1972 the government established British Nuclear Fuels Ltd which was enabled to seek finance from the private capital market while the state kept 51 per cent of its share-holding. A Nuclear Power Board was also set up to advise ministers on civil nuclear energy strategy. The British machine tool industry received £16m in support from the state in 1972 through a bringing forward of public sector orders. In July 1973 Chataway announced that £25.8m of 'launching aid' support was to be pumped into ICL, Britain's only large computer manufacturer. The textile industry also benefited substantially from assistance under the Industry Act. In a White Paper published in July 1973, the government set out its ideas for a new Companies Bill which would have given further powers to the state to take a highly interventionist role.

Walker and his colleagues at the DTI also displayed a Heathite zeal to shake up the private sector. Under Heseltine's influence, business breakfasts were introduced to enable ministers to invigorate employers with pep-talks before the start of their working day. 'Heseltine said if we organised those they would all feel they had to come. If ministers were ready to get up, the industrialists would think they should be ready to do so', wrote Walker. 'Once the briefing was over, the only place they could go on to was their office. If you excited them, they would go straight back and do something about it'.[37]

The more dynamic approach took Walker and his DTI team into boardrooms across the country, but what they often saw did nothing to encourage optimism about industrial revival. In his memoirs Walker complained about the poor quality of professional management in industry and the lack of toughness among employers in competing effectively in export markets. These were familiar enough observations that can be found scattered across much of British twentieth-century

36. T. Boardman, Standing Committee on Statutory Instruments, 18 July 1973, quoted in *The Campaign Guide 1974* (Conservative Central Office, 1974), 117.

37. Walker, *Staying Power*, 99.

business history. It is not surprising that by 1973 Heath seemed to prefer the company of trade union leaders more than he did that of industrialists and financiers. His exasperated public rebuke to Lonrho as the 'unpleasant and unacceptable face of capitalism' reflected his increasing disillusionment, even personal sense of betrayal, caused by what he saw as the lack of success displayed by British industry in taking advantage of his government's high-risk dash for economic growth in 1972–73. He grew more convinced that large public investment infrastructure projects, such as the planned third London airport at Maplin and the Channel Tunnel, were necessary despite the already huge growth in public expenditure. If the private sector could not lead the way in industrial expansion despite government encouragement, then instead the state would have to seize the initiative.

It is doubtful whether Heath's approach to industry would have succeeded if he had won the February 1974 general election. The deeper the state commitment to an activist industrial strategy, the worse grew the condition of the public sector's finances. The price restraints imposed by the government from June 1971, in alliance with the voluntary price freeze initiative of the Confederation of British Industry, heralded a persistent government interference, motivated more by political considerations than any concern with the commercial well-being of the nationalised sector. The resulting accumulated debts were to hamper the Labour government's efforts in the late 1970s to introduce financial prudence to the public corporations. 'The year 1973 was a turning point for the nationalised industries', wrote Richard Pryke. 'By the mid-1970s their finances were chaotic as they became instruments of economic and social policy, not commercial undertakings'.[38]

CONCLUSION

Heath's industrial strategy had certainly changed by the time he lost office in March 1974, but the question is just how sharp a U-turn had taken place. The Conservatives came to power in June 1970 without any detailed promise to roll back the frontiers of the state. The more radical ideas of Ridley's study group were unacceptable. But even Margaret Thatcher did not win office in May 1979 on a programme to privatise the nationalised industries. If Heath and his colleagues stopped well short of wanting to end the mixed market economy, they were still keen to make private industry more productive and competi-

38. R. Pryke, *The Nationalised Industries* (London, 1981), 262.

tive through government action. With cuts in corporation tax and the removal of regulatory burdens on business, they hoped to encourage corporate modernisation. But this involved only limited disengagement. Moreover, the government intervened constantly in the pricing of products and services in the nationalised sector with damaging consequences for the financial viability of many public corporations. Ministers did not doubt they had a key strategic role to play in the making of industrial policy. Moreover, under the pressure of events they accepted that the state must bail out large private companies in financial trouble. The saving of Rolls-Royce was justified on grounds of national interest. The rescue of Upper Clyde Shipbuilders was more controversial, and a political response to the feared prospect of an outbreak of civil disorder and mass unemployment in west-central Scotland which might result from the closure of the yards. The Industry Act underlined what had already become obvious by the spring of 1972: the Heath government was not prepared to press ahead with a laissez-faire industrial strategy where lame ducks were to be sacrificed as a lesson to others. Across a wide range of industries – steel, coal, shipbuilding, textiles, computers, machine tools – the state was to play a substantial direct or catalytic role in promoting corporate change by accepting high levels of public investment. In the publicly owned utilities the government took the initiative in pressing modernisation programmes.

Heath and Walker believed British business suffered because the country lacked a clear strategy that involved industry and the state working together in partnership. Their approach – if it had been allowed to continue – might have succeeded in transforming traditional political attitudes in Britain towards industry. They looked enviously at the corporatist system operating at that time with success in Gaullist France, Social Democratic West Germany and Liberal Democratic Japan. In doing so, Heath and Walker were challenging the limited strategic role the British state played in industrial affairs. As Andrew Shonfield explained in 1965: 'Anything which smacked of a restless or over-energetic state, with ideas of guiding the nation on the basis of a long view of its economic interest, was instinctively the object of suspicion'.[39] The 'new capitalism' championed by the Prime Minister had almost revolutionary implications for the creation of a social market continental-style political economy in Britain. After 1975 the Conservatives under Margaret Thatcher tried with ill-disguised relief to abandon any commitment to the industrial dirigisme practised by the Heath government. The Prime Minister's policy may have proved over-blown

39. A. Shonfield, *Modern Capitalism* (London, 1965), 88.

as the postwar consensus began to collapse in the world economic blizzard caused primarily by the quadrupling of oil prices. It did much to discredit the use of taxpayer's money in assisting industry to modernise. The 'new capitalism' was, however, a brave if ultimately doomed attempt by government to transform Britain's industrial base to meet mainland Europe's competitive challenge. The satirical magazine *Private Eye* used to mock what it called Heathco as a gigantic folie de grandeur. Heath's successor had no intention of following his example. In reality, however, it remained unclear how far the state could withdraw from the demands of industry without provoking high unemployment and widespread bankruptcies of concern to the national interest. State-owned enterprises like British Leyland, British Steel and the British Shipbuilders all benefited from substantial state financial support in the early 1980s under Margaret Thatcher. Taxpayers' money was used to restore the well-being of state industry finances before their eventual sell-off to the private sector. In the mid-1990s, Michael Heseltine at the Department of Trade and Industry demonstrated that state engagement with British industry remained an important Conservative approach. The Heath experience after March 1972 may have upset the neo-liberals in the party, but it did not discredit interventionism by the state in the making of industrial policy.

CHAPTER SEVEN

*The Heath government and industrial relations: myth and reality**

Robert Taylor

Edward Heath's premiership was dominated – almost without respite – from its 'glad, confident morning' to bleak, ignominious end by the seemingly intractable problem of trade union 'power'. No other government after 1945 was forced to deal with such a sustained level of labour militancy, especially in the unionised public sector. Less than a fortnight after his arrival in 10 Downing Street, the new Prime Minister had to face a national dock strike, not of his making, which forced the Cabinet to declare a State of Emergency under the 1920 Emergency Powers Act. Over the next three-and-a-half years, Heath and his colleagues were to use that controversial legislation on no fewer than four further separate occasions which helped to focus national attention on the gravity of the country's industrial relations troubles. Strikes often appeared to be synonymous with Heath's relatively short period in office. The official statistics reveal the aggregate number of working days lost because of labour stoppages never fell below 10m from 1970 until 1973, a persistent level of industrial conflict not experienced in Britain since the immediate aftermath of the First World War. It is true that worker unrest at that time was not confined to Britain. It was a phenomenon to be seen across much of the western world at the end of the 1960s. But the particular virulence of its outbreak in Britain cannot be denied. Only Italy, Canada and Australia among industrialised countries experienced a worse strike record. Indeed, by the winter of 1973–74, some commentators had started to question whether the country's democratic institutions could survive in the face of what they saw as the brutal use of industrial power by monopolistic producer

* I should like to thank John Monks, the TUC's general secretary, for access to the Trades Union Congress archives for the period. Other primary material used came mainly from the Conservative Party Archives.

interests with proven strength to paralyse the market economy and defy the national interest. Much of the blame for the bitter strife of the time was placed firmly on the shoulders of Edward Heath himself. He was portrayed as a stubborn, insensitive, uncaring Prime Minister intent on the destruction of the supposed postwar social settlement between capital and labour based on a government commitment to the maintenance of 'full' employment and the 'voluntarist' system of free collective bargaining. Between June 1970 and March 1972, Heath – it was claimed – 'came to be loathed by many workers in a powerful and specific way. The feeling about him was that he was 'unfair', 'uncharitable', 'faceless and heartless'.[1] Such contemporary comment, however, provides a misleading and over-simplistic impression of Heath's approach to industrial relations. In fact, contrary to the myth-makers' claims, the Prime Minister was rarely seen by national trade union leaders as the enemy of organised labour waging class war against the workers. A former Minister of Labour himself for a short time under Harold Macmillan, Heath had no personal wish to either marginalise or neuter the trade unions. Jack Jones, the left-wing general secretary of the Transport and General Workers Union, recognised his genuine commitment to working with and not against the interests of organised labour. As he wrote in his memoirs:

> No Prime Minister, either before or since, could compare with Ted Heath in the efforts he made to establish a spirit of camaraderie with trade unions and to offer an attractive package which might satisfy large numbers of work people. At the outset I thought he represented the hard face of the Tory party but over the years he revealed the human face of Toryism, at least to the trade union leaders who met him frequently. It is doubtful whether the public gained that view of him, partly because, as he himself admitted at one of the Downing Street meetings, he was a bad communicator. Amazingly, he gained more personal respect from union leaders than they seemed to have for Harold Wilson, or even Jim Callaghan.[2]

Similar benign feelings towards Heath were also expressed by Vic Feather, the TUC's canny and manipulative General Secretary until September 1973, who believed the Prime Minister was a man that Congress House could do business with. Even Heath's most dangerous foe – Hugh Scanlon, president of the engineering workers' union – testified later to the positive and fair way the Prime Minister conducted his relations with trade union leaders. Employers' leaders in the Confed-

1. A. Barnett, 'Class struggle and the Heath government', *New Left Review* (January–February 1973), 5.

2. J. Jones, *Union Man* (London, 1986), 259.

eration of British Industry often gained the impression Heath much preferred the social company of the TUC establishment to their own. Heath's own advisers confirmed his stoical bonhomie with union leaders. They stressed, in particular, his rationality and endless patience in dealing with them. As Douglas Hurd, then the Prime Minister's political secretary, noted in 1976:

> We had a Prime Minister who believed passionately realism should prevail if facts were reasonably presented. We had a Cabinet which, representing the modern Conservative party, realised that in no way could that party prosper by setting class against class, however many warlike telegrams its supporters might send. Of all the charges now made against the government, the charge that it sought or welcomed confrontation with the trade unions is the most absurd.[3]

Other confidants such as Jim Prior and Michael Wolff confirmed Heath's inexhaustible capacity to try to secure trade union cooperation with his government. They believed that no other Conservative Prime Minister – not even Harold Macmillan – strove as much as he did to persuade the TUC to play a direct role in helping to run the British economy through what later came to be known as a social partnership. Heath's innumerable enemies inside the Conservative party (though most with hindsight) condemned what they saw as his reckless strategy of appeasement towards organised labour. They argued that Heath proved too accommodating in his benevolent response to the insatiable demands of sectional interests. Rather than confronting the trade unions with robust action – they complained – he was over-keen to make agreements with them. But instead of accepting his behaviour as far-sighted and magnanimous, union leaders interpreted it as a sign of his weakness. Once they had forged a 'social contract' with the opposition Labour Party in 1972, there was no obvious reason why the TUC should want to sign a comprehensive agreement with Heath, especially if such an achievement helped to secure him a second consecutive term in office. The painful lesson most Conservatives drew from Heath's defeats at the hands of organised labour was the need to find a credible way of weakening trade union power without provoking a return to the kind of industrial conflict that scarred the early 1970s. At first sight, Heath's relationship with the trade unions looks riddled with contradiction. How could such a supposedly well-meaning and sympathetic conciliator preside over a government that became a byword for industrial confrontation? In fact, the Prime Minister was both the

3. D. Hurd, *An End to Promises: Sketch of a Government 1970–1974* (London, 1976), 104–5.

luckless victim of adverse circumstances and an over-ambitious moderniser who believed he could 'solve' the country's industrial relations problems through the use of comprehensive legislation to regulate trade union behaviour. Above all, Heath was an impatient technocrat with a single-minded determination to use the power of government to make the British economy dynamic and competitive enough to seize the tactical advantage of its new position after 1 January 1973 as a member of the European Economic Community. Trade union reform through the stimulus of the law has to be seen as only part of a much wider national strategy designed to modernise the country. Like so many of his contemporaries, Heath came to believe trade unions had grown obstructive to the achievement of higher economic growth and incapable of change through their own efforts. He wanted the trade unions to become more disciplined and responsible organisations, capable of cooperating with employers in the negotiation of belated workplace change that would boost productivity, dampen down inflationary wage-push pressures and above all provide a clear command structure inside their organisations to curb workplace militants. Heath's ambitious industrial relations strategy assumed a substantial intrusion by the state into the conduct of workplace life, still dominated by the instinctive belief that 'most workers want nothing more of the law than that it should leave them alone'.[4]

PLANNING FOR TRADE UNION REFORM

Heath was elected to office in June 1970 with a detailed industrial relations policy already drawn up over the previous five years mainly by Conservative lawyers, most notably Geoffrey Howe, who as Solicitor-General played the key role in piloting the Party's legislation onto the statute book within twelve months. What was proposed aroused little opposition among Conservatives. The only doubts expressed came from Joseph Godber and Viscount Blakenham (formerly John Hare) who had been Ministers of Labour. They questioned whether a complex and comprehensive piece of legislation was the most sensible way of improving trade union behaviour. Few employers took part in the internal debates over Conservative industrial relations policy, even if it was they who would be asked to use the new laws in their dealings with trade unions. Howe himself led a fact-finding visit to the United States in 1969 to look at the American labour experience at first-hand.

4. W. Wedderburn, *The Worker and the Law* (London, 1986), 1.

But surprisingly little attempt was made to seek out and listen to the opinions of either side of British industry, and even Conservative trade union activists were treated with scarcely disguised condescension by the Party leadership.

However, the party leadership was sensitive to any suggestion that the Conservatives were planning draconian laws to shackle the trade unions. 'If we are to publish proposals in the autumn for trade union reforms we do not want it said this is entirely an anti-trade union move cooked up by the middle classes', Edward du Cann, the Party Chairman, warned Brendan Sewill, head of the Conservative Research Department in April 1965.[5]

The July 1965 document drawn up by Viscount Amory's working group on trade unions may have asserted that 'the sanctity of agreements must be the basis for industrial peace in a modern economy' and may have called for 'a new, comprehensive trade union Act to clarify the present confused, uncertain and out-dated legal enactments', but it also warned that it was 'undesirable that the major piece of legislation we envisage should be capable of being presented as a Bill directed against the trade unions'.[6] The group believed there was 'a considerable political and psychological advantage in getting away from legislation dealing exclusively with trade unions'. This could be done – it suggested – by also extending policy to cover the training and retraining of workers, improving workers' pension rights and strengthening independent conciliation and arbitration.

The virtually exclusive focus by the group on the problem of trade union power troubled Keith Joseph, when shadow employment secretary. In a paper he wrote in January 1966, he emphasised the 'pro-union' proposals in the new policy. These included a legal provision on employers to recognise trade unions, state backing for the check-off system of paying union dues through the pay packet, a voluntary code laying out 'good' employment practice, the right of an individual worker to take legal action against an alleged 'unfair' dismissal and the introduction of workers onto the supervisory boards of private companies. As Joseph explained to Shadow Cabinet colleagues, the Party's plans to regulate the internal behaviour of trade unions through a new strong and independent Registrar and the introduction of codified legal provisions enforceable through the courts were 'all deep intrusions into the trade union movement's position above the law'. 'What we intend is in the public interest', he agreed. 'But we must not allow the unions

5. E. Du Cann to B. Sewill, 27 July 1965, CRD/3/17/19.

6. 'Policy Group 20: Trade Union Law and Practices', chaired by Viscount Amory, draft report, 2 July 1965, CPA CRD/3/17/20, PG/20/65/45.

to pose as political victims or martyrs in a class war'. This was why he suggested that the Conservatives ought to make 'at least a gesture' by introducing employee co-determination on the West German model into companies over a certain, unspecified size.[7]

Nothing came of that proposal. But other senior Conservatives also raised occasional doubts about the credibility of the new approach to industrial relations reform. They were painfully aware of their lack of experience in that complex policy area. Only four Conservative parliamentary candidates in the 1966 general election were trade union activists, while few of the party's trade union advisory committees still functioned by the end of the 1960s. There were only fourteen full-time industrial organisers and a 'one man operation' in Central Office's almost defunct industrial department. Nonetheless, Heath and his colleagues insisted in public that their proposals would strengthen not weaken the trade unions. It is true that the closed shop was to be declared unlawful and that workers were to enjoy the legal right not to join as well as join a union. In tune with Conservative tradition, the individual was to be protected from any possible coercion from the collective organisation. But that libertarian approach was to co-exist with a more corporatist attitude designed to help not undermine 'sensible' trade unionism. 'Our policy is to support and encourage constructive trade unionism which we believe to be an aid to industrial progress', declared a Conservative Research Department paper in October 1966. Its aim was to 'help transform the character of trade union leadership at all levels, turning it into an ally of a progressive, free enterprise society rather than a bastion of out-dated Socialism'. Policies had to be developed that would encourage a 'responsible, and constructive, authoritative, trade union leadership' and create 'a steady change in the character of trade unionism.'[8]

Heath and his colleagues believed their legislation – once understood – would help union leaders to restore their lost authority over the workplace by enabling them to discipline dissident shop stewards. The new law's purpose was to promote 'positive co-operation between management, employees and trade unions to secure both industrial peace and progress', said the Party's Industrial Relations Policy Group in November 1967. It was also intended to remove 'barriers to efficiency and higher productivity', by protecting 'the individual and the enterprise

7. 'Industrial Relations Policy: Matters for Further Consideration', memo by Sir K. Joseph, for Policy Group on Trade Union Law and Practices, 1 January 1966, CRD/3/17/20, PG/20/65/60.

8. 'Conservatives and Trade Unionists', memo by S. Abbott, 26 October 1966, CRD/3/12/21.

from excessive, unfair or harmful authority exercised by organisations and pressure groups whether of employers or work-people'.[9] The Party leadership accepted that most trade union activists disliked the new industrial relations strategy, but also believed they would accept it when the new Bill became law. 'Once they begin to trust the underlying motives behind our policy the more moderate (at present apathetic) will become active in their unions', they reasoned. 'Once it is a "done thing" to be a good trade unionist without being a Labour party supporter, the move towards us could snowball rapidly.' But as the general election drew nearer, Carr began to express his concern about what a Conservative government would do if trade unions simply refused to accept the introduction of legally binding contracts with employers, as they would be able to do under the proposed legislation. As he explained: 'Trade unions may issue firm instructions to their negotiators not to sign any agreement without a clause "opting out" of enforceability. This would present grave problems for employers – most of whom would choose the peaceful way out.' But Carr was reluctant to insist that contracts should have legal force if both parties to them disagreed. 'We have consistently said we believe in "free" collective bargaining. It could hardly be this if agreements had to be legally binding regardless of the parties' wishes. With this provision we would be turning the law on its head', he reasoned.[10]

Leading Conservatives continued to believe that the trade unions would swallow the new legislation and not seek to defy the rule of law. 'Most citizens, including trade unionists and union officials prefer most of the time to be on the right side of the law', said Geoffrey Howe. 'Prisons are not wildly congenial and martyrdom is not enormously fashionable. As the modern Liverpool workers say in "Maggie May" when told of the defiance of a pioneer trade unionist: "They don't do that today, then do they? They don't"'.[11] Such insouciance was not shared, however, by Quintin Hogg, the Party's shadow Home Secretary. In June 1969 he warned his shadow cabinet colleagues that they 'should be prepared for possible confrontation with the unions'. 'We should not get involved in legislation until our emergency plans were ready', he advised. But Carr retorted: 'It would be dangerous to delay legislation

9. 'Report of the Policy Group on Industrial Relations (Part 1, Chapters 1–6)', chaired by R. Carr, 17 November 1967, CPA ACP(67)42.

10. 'Enforceability of Collective Agreements', memo by R. Carr, for Policy Group on Industrial Relations, 19 February 1970, CRD/3/17/2, PG/20/66/103.

11. 'Injunctions and Industrial Disputes', memo by G. Howe, CRD/3/17/20, PG/20/65/64.

to a point where it might mean not getting the Bill to the House during the first session'.[12]

From time to time Heath and his colleagues admitted – at least privately among themselves – that their industrial relations strategy was motivated in part by an attempt to weaken union power. This is certainly clear from the verbatim notes taken of the famous weekend conference the shadow cabinet held at the Selsdon Park Hotel in Surrey at the end of January 1970. Industrial relations policy was not on the agenda at that controversial meeting, nor was how a future Conservative government should handle pay demands in the unionised public sector, but Heath made his own views clear enough on both issues in some robust remarks that do not really square with his reputation as the great conciliator. According to the minutes he said:

> If we had trained men in the right place we would not have trade union monopoly. Employers will be prepared to spend if they know chaps won't strike. Never talked about this in public, perhaps we ought to. Point of industrial relations change is to redress the balance between employees and employer. Up to 1939 the balance was on the side of the employer. After 1945 the balance was on the side of the unions and it is still on the side of the unions.[13]

He went on to discuss wage bargaining prospects:

> I have come more and more to the conclusion we should say we are going to look after the government sector, our responsibility. But responsibility of private sector to deal with their own wage negotiations and no point in them coming to us saying why didn't we do something. Throw it back at them. If they don't like wages going up, don't put them up.

Margaret Thatcher, shadow education secretary, chipped in: 'They will', while Reginald Maudling, deputy leader, said it would be hard to say 'our trade union policy was to reduce buying power'. 'Employers have to be free to introduce new plant and get rid of men', insisted Heath. 'And all the pressure of increased wages is to make them more efficient. The trouble at the moment is they cannot get rid of men.' At Selsdon Park the shadow cabinet began to recognise that they could face a showdown with organised labour if the Party won the next general election. Carr admitted they might have to confront a strike 'because of our industrial relations reform'. 'We need someone in a major sector to take a strike and not wilt', he said, suggesting the need for contingency planning. But Heath intervened: 'Better not to talk about it.

12. Leader's Consultative Committee, 23 June 1969, CPA LCC/69/310.

13. Minutes of 6th session, 1 February 1970, Shadow Cabinet weekend, Selsdon Park Hotel, CPA Selsdon Park papers (filed with LCC papers).

Even Cabinets don't.' Hogg added 'until management is able to sack without facing a ruinous strike we will go round and round the mulberry bush.' Carr and Joseph both agreed with Heath's wish to provide the Monopolies Commission with powers to investigate restrictive trade union practices. By the spring of 1970, concern over wage push inflation with the disintegration of Labour's statutory incomes policy began to dominate Conservative thinking. The answer appeared to be: stand firm against excessive union pay demands. As a January policy paper explained:

> There can be little doubt that the main influence on the wage cycle could come as a result of the action the new Government takes on the first few major strike threats. It can be expected that the balance of payments will be sufficiently good to make a firm stand possible. Clearly the time when such a stand is most likely to be credible, and therefore successful, is within the first few months of the new government . . . After the election . . . the emphasis should be less on exhortation and more on quiet, decisive, no-nonsense government.[14]

CONFRONTING THE UNIONS AND THE MAKING OF THE INDUSTRIAL RELATIONS ACT

Once in Downing Street, Heath lost no time in rushing forward with industrial relations reform. Only two months were allowed for consultation in the autumn of 1970 on the proposed legislation, and Carr as employment secretary told a TUC delegation in September that the main pillars of the new legislation were non-negotiable. The Prime Minister believed he enjoyed a clear electoral mandate for what was needed. But the speed with which the massive new Bill was drawn up did little to encourage any rational debate on its complicated contents. Moreover, the TUC felt increasingly antagonised by the government's so-called 'N minus one' public sector pay policy which, in a crude and threatening way, suggested that public sector pay deals should each be one per cent less than the one before. Heath told a meeting he held with the TUC General Council on 2 September that the government would refuse to allow the nationalised industries to pass on any inflationary pay deals with price increases. But the Prime Minister's resolve proved to be short-lived, with the first set-piece public sector strike that autumn producing a wage settlement that incensed the Prime Minister. The local government manual workers – in pursuit

14. 'Controlling Prices', CRD memo, 21 January 1970, LCC Selsdon Park papers.

of a £30-a-week minimum wage – secured a 14.5 per cent pay rise – thanks to a committee of inquiry under that well-known arch-conciliator Sir Jack Scamp. The electricity power workers followed in the public sector pay offensive by imposing a work-to-rule and overtime ban that aroused widespread public anger. The government declared a State of Emergency but also agreed to set up a committee of inquiry under Lord Wilberforce, a High Court judge, to examine the power worker's case. Not only did the resulting report give the power workers pay rises of 15 to 18 per cent, but Wilberforce and his colleagues concluded that the power men could hardly be expected to accept lower increases if all others in the labour market did not moderate their pay expectations as well. It is true that Heath won a victory when the postal workers were forced back to work after a six-week strike in early 1971 with a 9 per cent wage settlement. But this failed to set an example of pay moderation for other groups, and the private sector employers paid little attention to government exhortations about wage restraint.

The pitched battles over pay in the public sector undoubtedly worsened the atmosphere surrounding the passage of the Industrial Relations Act onto the statute book. It was a huge piece of legislation with 163 clauses and nine schedules in its 160 pages. In his memoirs, Lord Howe blamed Sir John Fiennes, the parliamentary draftsman, for turning his 'plain English' drafts into complex legal jargon. 'If we wanted our Bill quickly – and we did – then we had to have it his way or not at all', wrote Howe. 'Carr and I were furious but in truth unreasonable. We had a case, of course, but not one that could be achieved in such a timescale – least of all by an office that was grossly understaffed and overworked.'[15] Howe claimed he wanted the bill to be a 'law with a human face'. But it is hard to see how this was possible, given the measure's ambitious and sweeping character. Carr himself was later to admit he did not really understand the bill and had to rely on briefs from his advisers to explain it. 'If it was complex to me, one of its main authors, what it seemed like to other people I dread to think', he admitted.[16] 'I don't believe the substance of the measure was wrong. But we tried to do too much in one Act of Parliament. We would have liked to have defined trade union powers and privileges in a positive way'. The real trouble, however, lay not so much in its detailed clauses as in the broader and yet confused general assumptions that lay

15. G. Howe, *Conflict of Loyalty* (London, 1994), 60.

16. P. Whitehead, *The Writing on the Wall* (London, 1985), 71; 'Symposium: The Trade Unions and Fall of the Heath Government', Institute of Contemporary British History witness seminar, *Contemporary Record*, vol. 2, no. 1, (1988), 40.

behind the legislation. 'The philosophy of the Bill was muddled', Margaret Thatcher admitted in retrospect. She believed it was 'in part corporatist and in part libertarian'. The measure sought to strengthen the individual worker against the union but also to strengthen the union as a regulated institution in the workplace.[17] Her first employment secretary, Jim Prior, thought that, apart from Carr, 'scarcely anyone in the Party understood industrial relations or knew industrialists, let alone any trade unionists'. He blamed Howe in particular for taking an 'extreme' legalistic approach 'with no appreciation of what made the unions tick or the real world of the shopfloor'.[18]

Its authors argued repeatedly that the Act was not meant to replace the existing industrial relations system – based on voluntary agreement – with a highly regulated one. As Carr told the Commons

> The best and probably only way of determining pay and conditions of work in a free society is by a voluntary system of negotiation, free from state control, between employers and employees and that is normally achieved by collective bargaining with strong trade union representation of the employees concerned.

Carr seemed to be suggesting that the 'serious defects' in the existing system requiring 'urgent need of renewal and reform' could be dealt with by laying down 'national standards for good industrial relations' set out in a Code of Practice. But he also admitted that change would only come slowly through 'steady and persistent treatment', perhaps over a ten year period.[19] So, it might be asked, why was there a need for urgency to force the measure onto the statute book in less than twelve months? Carr's long-term view contrasted uneasily with the stated ambitions of the measure. A Party memorandum in March 1971 tried to explain why the Act did not 'bash the unions.' 'Quite the reverse', it insisted. The purpose was to recreate 'strong and responsible unions' with clearly established rights. Asked if the bill would create offences that could lead to workers going to prison, the paper retorted 'Absolutely not,' although it acknowledged that workers might be jailed if found in contempt of court. 'The aim throughout is to strengthen and encourage good voluntary practices in industry. Legal proceedings and enforcement are provided only as a fall-back when the voluntary system has failed', it argued.[20] There was little expectation that the

17. M. Thatcher, *The Path to Power* (London, 1995), 204.
18. J. Prior, *A Balance of Power* (London, 1986), 72.
19. *House of Commons Debates*, 5th series, vol. 807, col. 632, 26 November 1970.
20. 'Industrial Relations Bill: Misrepresentations', memo, 9 March 1971, CPA CCO/20/1/19.

unions would resist as strongly as they did. Certainly the government did not want a prolonged battle with the TUC. 'Once the Act is on the statute book the main need will be for a period of reconciliation and bridge-building so as to enable all the moderate elements in the trade union movement to put on one hat instead of two and get on with their real job again', explained Sir Michael Fraser from Central Office.[21]

In fact, the Act contained serious flaws. It provided the means for hostile trade unions to avoid its provisions quite lawfully. First, the measure recognised that collective agreements would have no legal enforceability if either employers or unions said so. The Confederation of British Industry and other employer organisations had wanted the state to impose legally binding disputes procedures against any party that broke them, but the Party leadership rejected this suggestion, arguing that it would 'involve bureaucratic intervention inconsistent with Conservative philosophy' as well as 'weaken the resolve' of employers themselves to 'stand firm' by enabling them to pass responsibility onto government to decide what to do in a dispute.[22] Heath and his colleagues acknowledged that the trade unions might 'issue firm instructions to their negotiators not to sign any agreement without a clause "opting out" of enforceability'. It was recognised that 'this would present grave problems for employers – most of whom would choose the peaceful way out'. But the leadership pointed out that they had 'constantly said we believe in "free" collective bargaining. It could hardly be this if agreements had to be legally binding regardless of the parties' wishes. With this provision we would also be turning the law of contract on its head'. In practice, no legally binding collective agreements were signed during the period of the Industrial Relations Act. Surprisingly, the government made no effort even to require the nationalised industries to insist on this. Heath pulled back from any suggestion of compulsion from the beginning. The CBI actively encouraged its member companies not to use the Act. It argued: 'Resort by employers to the legal processes in the Act may well be less effective than good voluntary practices.'[23]

Second and more important was the vexed question of registration. Trade unions were required to remain on the new proposed Register that would emerge from the old one if they wanted to enjoy legal

21. 'Current Political Situation and Outlook', memo by Sir M. Fraser, 7 May 1971, SC/71/3.

22. 'Enforceability of Collective Agreements'.

23. Confederation of British Industry, *Guidance to Employers on the Industrial Relations Act* (London, 1971), 41.

protections, to avoid crippling financial damages from the National Industrial Relations Court and to secure themselves tax advantages under the Act. But they were perfectly entitled to leave the register if they so wished. Heath and Carr were convinced that unions would in time see the advantages to themselves of registration, but they were mistaken. 'I certainly had a blind spot about this', Carr admitted later. 'I never expected the unions would oppose the Bill on the question of registration. From their narrow short-term point of view it was a damnably effective tactic'.[24] Howe, at a late stage of the Bill's passage through Parliament, amended the measure by ensuring that trade unions who remained on the newly formed 'provisional' register would be automatically transferred to the new permanent one unless they took the positive step of requesting their removal from the register. 'By placing the onus on unions to de-register the government created enormous problems for the TUC. This single amendment came close to destroying the campaign of opposition to the Act', Michael Moran argued.[25] In retrospect, it is easy to argue that the Act was doomed from the start – thanks to most employers who sought to avoid its use and trade unions who campaigned effectively to render the legislation harmless. But this outcome was by no means so apparent at the time. It was the combination of a number of unforeseen circumstances that wrecked the measure's credibility in the summer of 1972, less than six months after most of its provisions came into force.

The Trades Union Congress may have been united in its opposition to the Act, but it was unsure of how to confront the legislation effectively. From the start, Jones and Scanlon led the main resistance among those on the TUC General Council who wanted to have nothing to do with the measure. They wanted the TUC to 'instruct' affiliate trade unions to deregister and to boycott the National Industrial Relations Court as well as the other bodies designed to administer the Act. But such an absolutist position was hard to sustain in practice. At a special Congress at Croydon in March 1971, the TUC agreed that unions should seek to try to nullify the Act. Affiliates were 'strongly advised' not to remain on the register and not to serve on the new statutory bodies. The unions were also promised financial indemnification by the TUC in 'exceptional circumstances' before the court when defending themselves under the Act. However, the TUC rejected by 5,055,000 votes to 4,284,000 an attempt by its left-wing affiliates to 'instruct' unions to deregister or face the ultimate sanction of expul-

24. Whitehead, *Writing on the Wall*, 93.
25. M. Moran, *The Politics of Industrial Relations* (London, 1976), 123.

sion from the TUC. Even the more moderate position adopted at Croydon was hard to sustain. On the eve of the 1972 Congress the general council noted that

> many unions were interpreting the Croydon registration decision as passive and had not endeavoured to implement it. Six months after Croydon unions were still sitting on the fence and as a result there was disarray. Very soon, if the policy was not tightened up, a large number of unions which intended to carry out the Croydon registration request would reconsider their position.[26]

Less than a week later, the left defeated the TUC establishment when Congress voted for a motion that instructed affiliates to deregister, with 5,625,000 votes for and 4,500,000 against.

This was, though, by no means the end of the matter. The passage of a toughly-worded resolution at Congress did not mean its automatic acceptance by all the unions. Many union leaders were reluctant to take any action that meant either breaking the law or placing their own financial assets in danger. The TUC itself was quite clear on that point. Its finance and general purposes committee agreed in April 1972 that 'It would be wrong for the TUC deliberately to court actions by putting itself in a position where it was clearly contravening the law just as it would be wrong for the TUC deliberately to encourage unions to break the law.'[27] Jones and the TGWU executive council forced the TUC to face that dilemma when their union was fined £5,000 for contempt and a further £50,000 for a refusal to attend the NIRC or to obey the court's order to stop the unofficial picketing and blacking, by its docker members, of goods being transported to the new container terminals by Heatons, a road haulage company on Merseyside. Under the clear threat of a sequestration of their entire funds, the TGWU sought the TUC's advice on what to decide. The TUC finance and general purposes committee told Jones his union would have to pay the fines. 'The whole movement could not be expected to meet fines arising from an unofficial action which was also in defiance of specific advice from the union', it reasoned.[28]

Two months later, the same committee went further and warned that 'trade unions existed to protect the interests of their members and this implied they should defend themselves against attacks in the bodies established by the Industrial Relations Act.'[29] Feather told the TUC

26. TUC General Council, 2 September 1971, TUC archives.
27. Finance and General Purposes Committee, 26 April 1972, TUC archives.
28. Finance and General Purposes Committee, 1 May 1972, TUC archives.
29. Finance and General Purposes Committee, 24 July 1972, TUC archives.

General Council in April 1972 that 'there was a danger unions would not be lame ducks but sitting ducks. He expected the great majority of trade unionists would expect trade unions in certain circumstances to defend themselves before the new courts.'[30] Such views alarmed Scanlon, who warned that the TUC general council was 'on a slippery slope which would lead to co-operation with the NIRC, injunctions and involvement of the Act into the trade union movement'.[31] But Fred Hayday, a senior official in the General and Municipal Workers Union, suggested that the unions 'must move away from a situation of defying institutions of the Act and facing endless fines which unions could not meet. It would be better to reconsider and reassess the situation at this juncture rather than have a reconsideration forced on them later by force of circumstance.'[32] By 15 votes to 11 against, the General Council rejected a call by the left for a recall Congress.

At the end of June 1972, as many as thirty-eight trade unions were still listed on the 'provisional' register. These included large affiliates such as the shopworkers, the electricians, Clive Jenkins's ASTMS and the ISTC steel workers. The left led by Scanlon began to press the TUC to start disciplinary action against the errant unions. The TUC facade of outward unity against the Act seemed close to the point of collapse. Events, however, came to the rescue of Congress House. The TUC was saved by the explosive consequences of the confrontation that erupted between the dockers picketing Midland Cold Storage terminal in east London and the new law that brought about (to the dismay of the government) the imprisonment of their unofficial leaders in Pentonville jail for contempt of court. The crisis was precipitated by the bizarre judgment of Lord Denning and his colleagues in the Court of Appeal, who overturned a lower court judgment which had ruled the TGWU itself was liable to meet damages for not repudiating the action of its shop stewards in the blacking of container lorries. The Court of Appeal argued that the opposite was the case and that the union was not liable for the behaviour of its stewards. The decision, in the words of Carr, came like 'a torpedo below the waterline'.[33] It led to the very outcome the Cabinet had believed was impossible under the Industrial Relations Act – that an employer could seek redress in compensation for unlawful action from his own workers and not from their trade union.

The spectacle of trade unionists being sent to prison in such circum-

30. TUC General Council, 26 April 1972, TUC archives.
31. TUC General Council, 4 May 1972, TUC archives.
32. TUC General Council, 4 May 1972, TUC archives.
33. Whitehead, *Writing on the Wall*, 78.

stances threatened to provoke widespread sympathy strikes. A triumphant Scanlon told a shocked TUC General Council that, while he did not want to see 'confrontation, revolution or general strike', the unions could 'not permit the imprisonment of five dockers however misguided they may be'.[34] The volatile situation was calmed, however, first by the sudden appearance on the scene of the Official Solicitor who had the five dockers leaders released from jail although none of them would purge their contempt, and secondly by the intervention of the House of Lords who overturned the Court of Appeal judgment in rapid time. But the turbulent events of July 1972 had dealt a fatal blow to the Act's credibility. Moderate unions like the electricians and shopworkers decided to deregister as a mark of their disapproval at the imprisonment of the dockers. Their action ensured that the vast majority of the TUC would remain united in resistance to the Act as non-registered bodies, but the outcome had been a much more close-run thing than it might have seemed at the time. A total of thirty unions were subsequently expelled from the TUC for staying on the register, but none of them were large ones.

Other parts of the Act also ran into rapid trouble. Its 'cooling-off' provisions were soon discredited. In April 1972 Maurice Macmillan, who had succeeded Carr as employment secretary, went to the National Industrial Relations Court – very much on Howe's advice – to secure a fourteen day 'cooling off' period to prevent the start of a national rail strike. The rail unions obeyed the court's ruling, but no progess was made in the two weeks to secure agreement. At the end of the designated period the government applied to the court and obtained an order enforcing a secret ballot of railway workers to find out whether they backed their union or accepted British Rail's pay offer. By a three-to-one majority they gave impressive but predictable support to their union. The government's original decision to go to court was seen as short-sighted. In a remarkably short length of time the Act – heralded as a cure for Britain's industrial relations troubles – had become a liability that threatened to plunge the country into yet further labour conflict.

THE SEARCH FOR CONSENSUS

By the spring of 1972, Heath and his Cabinet were already reassessing the consequences of their economic policy. Two events were especially

34. TUC General Council, 26 July 1972, TUC archives.

crucial in bringing about the government's famous U-turn. First, the government feared that registered unemployment would not only rise above one million but stay there, with the resulting danger of social upheaval and electoral unpopularity. The second and even more traumatic event was the humiliating outcome of the six-week-long national miners' strike which dealt a devastating blow to Heath's government, from which many believe it never really recovered. The sudden eruption of the National Union of Mineworkers onto the national scene came as a surprise to many observers. 'We just didn't know the miners', Carr later recalled. 'They hadn't been to St James's Square, the old home of the Ministry of Labour, for nearly fifty years.'[35] The revolt on the coalfields reflected a deep frustration and anger among the miners caused by the enormous wave of pit closures and redundancies that hit the industry from the early 1960s. The coal industry seemed to be in irreversible decline, and those miners remaining saw their real earnings falling sharply. The NUM demanded a 47 per cent pay rise for its members with a £35-a-week minimum rate for face workers. With a narrow pithead ballot vote in favour, the union declared a national stoppage and launched an aggressive offensive through the use of flying pickets who laid siege to power stations and coal depots. The new mood of the once stoical miners was symbolised by the battle of Saltley coke depot in Birmingham where an estimated 15,000 workers forced the police to close its gates. 'Here was living proof that the working class had only to flex its muscles and it could bring governments, employers and society to a complete standstill', asserted the young Yorkshire leader Arthur Scargill, who led the pickets at Saltley.[36]

The Cabinet looked on helplessly at the menacing course of events. Officials wondered hysterically how the government would be able to deal with rioting in the streets, epidemics and a complete breakdown of public order. 'At the time many of those in positions of influence looked into the abyss and saw only a few days away the possibility of the country being plunged into a state of chaos not so very far removed from that which might prevail after a minor nuclear attack', recalled Brendan Sewill.[37] 'The government is now vainly wandering over the battlefield looking for someone to surrender to and being massacred all the time', moaned Douglas Hurd.[38] The Cabinet raised the white flag by setting up a public inquiry under the ubiquitous Lord Wilberforce

35. Whitehead, *Writing on the Wall*, 74.

36. A. Scargill, 'New Unionism', *New Left Review* (July–August 1975), 19–20.

37. B. Sewill and R. Harris, *British Economic Policy 1970–1974* (Institute of Economic Affairs, 1975), 50.

38. Hurd, *End to Promises*, 103.

to provide the terms of capitulation while at the same time introducing a three-day working week. The resulting report, produced in less than a week, went a long way to meet the NUM's demands but, to add to their humiliation, Heath and his colleagues were then forced to make further concessions across the table in 10 Downing Street when confronted by the union's executive. The alternatives facing the Prime Minister had been horrendous – the use of troops, a possible general election, with the resurgence of bitter class feelings across society. Many of Heath's colleagues believed the outcome of the miners' strike was a disaster for the government. But the Prime Minister chose to take a more optimistic view of future prospects as he resolved in a broadcast to the nation that there had to be a 'more sensible way to settle our differences'.[39]

Between March and November 1972, Heath made valiant efforts to establish a new form of economic management that would bring the TUC and the CBI into a close partnership with government. Virtually out in the cold for nearly two years, the TUC was encouraged by the Prime Minister to drop its public hostility and seek an understanding with the government. The new spirit of reconciliation can be seen in the minutes of the meeting Heath held with senior TUC leaders in 10 Downing Street on 9 March. As he explained to them, the 'discussions' he had in mind would be 'wide-ranging without any limitations on the subjects concerned'. While he pointed out that the government had been elected 'to do certain things, at the same time, government policies did develop'. Heath 'hoped problems could be considered not only in relation to the immediate situation but in terms of common objectives in the longer term and the changing needs of an industrial society'. From the start, the Prime Minister was keen to spell out the economic situation to them. As he argued: 'There is a need to get away from "stop–go" and place the emphasis on a sustained and steady expansion of the economy, a decrease in unemployment (the government had never expected or wanted unemployment to reach its present level) and a steady rise in living standards. The prime need is to maintain competitiveness and bring prices under control.' Heath added that the government was 'not attracted to the idea of a formal, statutory incomes policy or guidance and a declaration of intent which had not been too successful in the past. Beyond this he said he had no preconceived notion and proposed to consider suggestions with an open mind, including those contained in the TUC's own economic review'. He even suggested that the government and TUC positions had 'coincided

39. J. Campbell, *Edward Heath* (London, 1993), 420.

on a number of issues, such as progress on an annual review of pensions'.[40]

At a further meeting, on 26 April, Heath told the TUC economic committee that it 'was a pity it had not been possible to have a detailed joint discussion on industrial relations when the Conservative Party had been in opposition or shortly after it had taken power'. But he refused to accept the TUC's call for the Industrial Relations Act to be either repealed or put on ice. 'The government wanted cooperation with the trade union movement but it also had a responsibility to the country as a whole', he reminded them.[41] However, at his meeting with the TUC General Council on 24 July, Heath tried to meet some of their objections to the Act. 'The main cause of the serious strikes which had occurred was not the Act but the desire of workers for high money wages', he told them. 'Much of the tension in British industry could be attributed to the present inflation rate.' He added that the government hoped the Act 'would only be used as a matter of last resort' and that if the TUC would be willing to work with the legislation, then 'in the light of experience' changes could then be made to it. Heath believed that both the government and the TUC wanted to maintain 'free collective bargaining', but he warned that there was also 'a common need to avoid confrontation and inflation'. The Prime Minister said they faced three choices: reaching a 'voluntary agreement, statutory procedures or confrontations'. 'We strongly favour voluntary methods of resolving the problem and have never sought confrontation', he assured them.[42]

Serious discussions between the government, the TUC and the CBI did not really begin until after the Trades Union Congress in September. The union leaders were pleasantly surprised at Heath's conciliatory approach. On 27 September he laid out his proposals. These involved a government commitment to a 5 per cent annual growth rate for the next two years, voluntary price restraints and acceptance that pay would not go up by more than £2 a week, the introduction of threshold payments to protect workers from price inflation, a better deal for the pensioners, and the creation of an independent public body 'to help the traditionally low paid industries to achieve greater efficiency as a basis for higher wages'. He added that he hoped they could see their

40. Note of meeting with Heath, 9 March 1972, report to TUC General Council, TUC archives.

41. Note of meeting with Heath, 26 April 1972, report to TUC General Council, TUC archives.

42. Note of meeting with Heath, 24 July 1972, report to TUC General Council, TUC archives.

way forward into what he said would be a 'new era of cooperation'.[43] But it must remain doubtful how genuine was the willingness of all the TUC team to reach any national economic accord with Heath. In response to his proposals, Congress House drew up their own long shopping-list of demands, including statutory price controls, suspension of council house rent rises, renegotiation of the EC's common agricultural policy, a wealth tax and a capital gains surcharge as well as dividend controls, a large flat-rate pension increase and rise in family allowances as well as the suspension of the Industrial Relations Act.

At his meetings with the TUC and CBI from 26 to 30 October, Heath emphasised that Parliament 'would not agree to unilateral price control and he would not be able to carry his own party on this. The government and the CBI would accept a voluntary policy with enabling or fall-back powers to be operated if necessary but this would have to apply to wages as well as to prices'. Heath said that the government was 'not saying statutory control on prices was impossible' but he pointed out to the TUC that covering commodity prices and in particular food posed a problem of 'credibility'. In essence, he moved very little beyond his September proposals despite TUC pressures.[44] The government was fearful that the power workers might take industrial action in pursuit of an inflationary pay claim, so there was some relief when a deal with them was reached on the eve of the collapse of the tripartite talks. On 6 November, Heath was forced reluctantly to announce an immediate 90-day freeze on wages, prices, dividends and rents. This was to be followed by the imposition of a statutory prices and incomes policy. Two public bodies were created to administer the new economic strategy – the Price Commission and the Pay Board. The TUC denounced what was proposed but there was to be no confrontation. 'In the end, whatever their previous claims to a share in government, union leaders found it easier to have terms imposed by the government than to persuade their own members to accept what a majority of them regarded as necessary', noted Keith Middlemas.[45]

Heath's admission of defeat on establishing a voluntary agreement and his imposition of wage and price controls aroused misgivings among some Conservatives but nobody resigned from the government. 'It is an extraordinary comment on the state of mind that we had reached

43. Note of meeting with Heath, 27 September 1972, report to TUC General Council, TUC archives.

44. Note of meeting with Heath, 30 October 1972, report to TUC General Council, TUC archives.

45. K. Middlemas, *Power, Competition and the State: Volume 2, Threats to the Postwar Settlement: Britain, 1961–1974* (London, 1990), 357.

that, as far as I can recall, neither now nor later did anyone at Cabinet raise the objection that this was precisely the policy we had ruled out in our 1970 general election manifesto', noted Mrs Thatcher in her memoirs.[46] For the next twelve months unions protested but did little to breach the statutory policy which enjoyed widespread public support. The Prime Minister did not give up hope of securing TUC backing for his economic strategy despite their opposition to statutory wage restraint. He pursued a highly conciliatory and activist employment policy which assumed close future union involvement. The TUC was asked to play an important role in the tripartite Manpower Services Commission created in 1973 to promote a more efficient employment service. Other bipartisan measures were prepared in the Department of Employment with the proposed creation of hived-off public agencies in areas like health and safety, conciliation and arbitration, sex and race discrimination. These organisations were to emerge under the Labour government, but much of the preparatory work on their creation took place under Heath.

Other steps were also taken in the government to demonstrate how much ministers wanted to avoid any conflict with organised labour. In a party memorandum to the leader's Steering Committee on 17 March 1972, it had been suggested that it would be 'particularly valuable if we can develop the "positive" side (of the Industrial Relations Act) in terms of employee information and consultation'.[47] 'We need something to put forward which recognises management's responsibility to its employees as well as shareholders', Carr told the Steering Committee in February 1973. Heath agreed that 'it was right to be wary of too much public talk solely directed at the militants which could risk a hardening of attitudes'. Lord Carrington, the Defence Secretary, wondered whether it might be possible for the government 'to pass European legislation on industrial relations and company law on the German pattern' but Carr doubted whether that would be 'right for Britain'.[48] However, ministers were moving towards acceptance in principle of legislation on employee participation that would protect trade unions as well as workers. A consultative document was promised on the subject for the autumn of 1973, but it became a casualty of the crisis that led on to the government's electoral defeat.

The benign sensitivity of Heath and his colleagues to the demands of organised labour was also apparent in their determination to maintain

46. Thatcher, *Path to Power*, 224.

47. 'The Next Manifesto: Policy', memo by A. Newton and J. Douglas, 17 March 1972, SC/72/11.

48. Steering Committee, 28 February 1973, SC/73/19.

the dash for economic growth as well as pay and price controls. But they recognised that this would involve a more dynamic approach to the labour market. 'Employment services are being brought up to the standards we need to attract both employers and workers to use them and to eliminate forever the dreary image of the dole queue at the labour exchange', the government argued. 'We shall make sure no one need be out of work through a failure to match unavailable jobs with available skills.'[49] However, the commitment to price and pay controls aroused profound misgivings inside the government. Ministers were aware that efforts to restrain wage expectations in a free society by means of a permanent statutory incomes policy could provoke a serious industrial confrontation between the state and a powerful section of the workforce such as the miners or the power workers. A strategy paper to the leader's Steering Committee explained in February 1973 that:

> A policy which ultimately depends largely on social pressures for its efficiency requires in the long-term the support of a good deal more than a half to two thirds of the people. As a temporary expedient to deal with a critical situation most people are probably prepared, if reluctantly, to submit their demands to the procrustean judgement of a statutory authority but few people are in the long-term going to be prepared to leave it to the government to decide the remuneration appropriate to their work. The prodigious extension of the powers of the state which this would represent would be distasteful to a large section of the middle class while that third of the working class on which we depend for success at the polls might well think if the government is going to settle their wages they would do better with a government of their own kind.[50]

But, as the paper acknowledged, it was 'unlikely' that the country could return to free collective bargaining for some years until there had been 'some fundamental change in the techniques of economic management' which provided 'a completely new solution to the problem of cost-push inflation'. This raised a severe problem, as the state had to take exclusive responsibility for price and incomes control. As the document explained,

> Traditional collective bargaining provides institutions through which the representatives of employers and employed in one sector of the economy can bargain with each other. However what most people and most members of trade unions are concerned about are relativities of pay and income. The present situation is that bargains struck in one industry affect all industries through their effect on prices but there are no institutions

49. 'Future Policy', discussion paper, 15 February 1973, SC/73/18.
50. 'The Strategic/Tactical Situation in 1973', memo by Sir M. Fraser *et al.*, 14 February 1973, SC/73/17.

> through which bargaining can take place and agreements reached about relativities as between industries. As a temporary expedient the power of the state can be invoked to bridge this gap. But in a free society that provides considerable safeguards against people being forced to work under conditions they do not accept as fair, the responsibility for deterring what is a fair basis of remuneration as between one occupation and another needs to rest on a broader base than a government ruling or even an Act of Parliament.

The paper envisaged a new body charged with dealing with pay relativity problems, but nothing was done about that until later in the year when the government was locked in a further conflict with the miners. Prophetically, the strategy document also warned that the government would face serious trouble if it called a snap general election on the question of trade union power. 'With a modern mass electorate ever since World War One no general election has been confined to a single issue', it observed. 'There is no guarantee the electorate or significant parts of it will not decide to vote about something else with possibly disturbing results'. It cannot be said that Heath had not been warned.

THE FINAL DAYS

Heath announced stage three of his government's statutory prices and incomes policy on 8 October 1973 in the ornate surroundings of Lancaster House with Armstrong at his side. He announced that wage increases for the next twelve months from 1 November were to be limited to £2.25 a head or seven per cent for a group of workers, with a £350 annual limit per person. A further one per cent flexibility margin was to be made available to negotiators to remedy any anomalies caused by the policy's first two stages. Extra payments were permissible when genuine savings could be proved and price stabilisation achieved. Progress to equal pay was allowed, while higher London weighting allowances were accepted as well. In a gesture to the TUC Heath also announced the introduction of threshold payments to safeguard living standards. Wages were to be allowed to go up by an extra 40p a week during the twelve-month period once the retail price index reached seven per cent and by a further 40p a week increase for every one per cent price rise over that level.

Premium payments were also possible for the working of 'unsocial hours'. Pensioners secured a £10 Christmas bonus, and the 5 per cent limit on dividends was to remain in force, as were price controls. 'The policy was as much an elaborate and comprehensive conciliation exercise to avoid confrontation in the 1973–74 wage round as it was a counter-inflation operation', explained Sir Denis Barnes, permanent secretary at the Department of Employment.[51] The TUC General Council expressed its opposition to the wage controls, arguing that they were unacceptable and probably unworkable, but most union leaders were convinced there would be little rank-and-file resistance to what Heath proposed. At his Party conference a week later the Prime Minister spoke warmly about his regular meetings with national union leaders. He told Conservatives he now met them in 'a calm atmosphere to discuss future policy' and no longer 'in the heat of a crisis'. 'Too often in the past a strike was the only way for a union to make its views known', he told the party faithful. 'Those days are past. Our talks in Downing Street are held regularly before there is a dispute. They have had more influence on policy than any number of demonstrations or strikes'.[52]

It was to be Heath's last speech as leader to the Conservative conference. Within three days the whole premise of the government's ambitious economic growth strategy was undermined with the announcement by the Organisation of Petroleum Exporting Countries (OPEC) to restrict oil production and quadruple oil prices in response to the Yom Kippur War. All the economic assumptions that lay behind the statutory prices and incomes policy were thrown into serious doubt. More critically, the squeeze on oil strengthened the bargaining position of the National Union of Mineworkers. Heath and Armstrong were convinced that the elaborate commitment in stage three to 'unsocial hours' payments provided the flexibility needed to ensure that the miners would settle within its terms. They thought they had secured the backing of NUM president Joe Gormley for this when the Prime Minister met him on 16 July in the garden of Downing Street, unknown to either the Cabinet or the NUM executive. This turned out to be a profound mistake. Gormley had wanted a special deal for the miners, particularly the faceworkers, that could not apply to anybody else. What Heath proposed failed to meet that demand.

Once again the Heath government and the NUM were set on a collision course. This time – unlike in 1972 – the Cabinet decided to declare a State of Emergency on 13 November, the day after the NUM imposed a national overtime ban on the coalfields. Ministers were concerned about industrial conflict among power engineers as well as train drivers. There is little doubt that Heath wanted to avoid another

51. D. Barnes and E. Reid, *Governments and Trade Unions: The British Experience* (London, 1980), 177.

52. Conservative Party, *Annual Conference Report 1973*, 136.

damaging miners' strike, and over the weeks running up to Christmas he made efforts to find a way out of the looming crisis. But his promise of a wide-ranging review of the coal industry with the hope of better pay and benefits to come, and a clear indication that the Pay Board's forthcoming pay relativities report would provide more money to the miners, failed to win any support on the NUM executive where moderates and militants appeared united. Gormley was defeated by 18 to 5 on the executive when he urged that the Coal Board's stage-three pay offer to the miners should be tested in a pithead ballot. The NUM president's attempt to secure a deal based on extra cash for the miners for waiting and bathing time collapsed when Labour leader Harold Wilson raised the idea as his own in the Commons and made it politically impossible for Heath to accept it. Many ministers were convinced that the conflict with the NUM was political and not industrial, an ideological attempt by Communists and other extremists to destroy an elected government. On 13 December, Heath announced that the country would go on to a three-day working week after the Christmas holiday break. It was a pre-emptive move to try to conserve dwindling coal stocks at the power stations as the overtime ban cut into production levels.

The TUC was growing increasingly concerned at the course of events and, on 9 January 1974, launched an initiative to try to resolve the crisis at the regular monthly meeting of the National Economic Development Council (NEDC). As TUC chairman Sid Greene, general secretary of the National Union of Railwaymen, told ministers: if the government was 'prepared to give an assurance that they will make possible a settlement between the miners and the National Coal Board, other unions will not use this as an argument in negotiations on their own settlements'.[53] Murray admitted later that the TUC offer had been neither formalised nor agreed by the General Council. They had not known exactly what they were putting forward, but they had been suggesting a negotiating position which might result in a joint suggestion for a future course of action. Barber reacted negatively to what was proposed. He asked whether it implied the TUC would accept stage three and, when told it did not, he suggested the offer was 'not of great substance'. Denis Barnes admitted later: 'The rejection may not have been tactically sensible but it was not totally unreasonable'.[54]

Next day Heath met Murray and senior union leaders to discuss the TUC's offer. Scanlon recalled that the Prime Minister was 'more amen-

53. National Economic Development Council, minutes, 7 January 1974, TUC archives.

54. Barnes and Reid, *Governments and Trade Unions*, 180.

able to some of the things we were trying to say than unfortunately some of his ministers were. He listened like no other minister'.[55] But Heath remained sceptical. A special TUC conference of executives backed the initiative on 16 January. Congress House explained its position to that gathering in a document which said

> When unions negotiate, employers are insistent the settlement shall have regard to the circumstances in those industries and shall be based on the merits of each case. That is what employers demand and that is all the TUC is asking for. In the circumstances facing British industry in 1974, it is straining the bounds of credibility to assume trade unions are going to base claims on a settlement in the mining industry.

However, the TUC paper did concede that the pay problems in coal were not unique, and pointed to potential troubles in electricity supply, motor manufacturing and the ambulance service. The TUC showed no desire to recommend to affiliates pay restraint on the lines of stage three. It argued against 'a rigid framework where essentially what is needed is a minimum degree of flexibility'.[56]

Heath still refused to grasp the limited opening offered to him by the TUC. 'Is there anything we can do to convince you this is a genuine offer? Is there anything you'd expect us to do beyond what we've offered to do already?' asked Scanlon when they met him five days later.[57] The Prime Minister did not reply to the question. He continued to worry that there was no guarantee the TUC could honour its promise in ensuring that other unions did not press for wage rises beyond the stage-three norm once the miners had secured special treatment. Ministers later argued that they had been concerned that the Electricians' Union would not have accepted the TUC position and would have broken stage three as well. They remembered how close they had come to a disastrous power strike in late October 1972 before the imposition of stage one of the incomes policy. Frank Chapple, the union's general secretary, denied this view angrily in his memoirs. 'The TUC opened the door and the government slammed it shut', he wrote. 'The Prime Minister was wrong in every way, politically, industrially, tactically, even morally. Ted Heath's pigheadedness and his refusal to pick up the TUC olive branch in those Downing Street talks was his biggest error.'[58] However, Jack Jones believed Heath may have had half a point. Describing Chapple as 'the maverick in the

55. Barnes and Reid, *Governments and Trade Unions*, 180.

56. *TUC Congress Report*, 1974, 156.

57. TUC note of meeting with Heath, 21 January 1974, report to TUC General Council TUC archives.

58. F. Chapple, *Sparks Fly!* (London, 1984), 136–7.

park', he added that the government had, however, 'misunderstood his influence and power'.[59] In truth, the electrician's union was not the dominant force at the power stations.

In those final days Heath was seen by union leaders as a troubled, agonised man looking for certainty. He was to be the last of the inner group in the cabinet who believed that an appeal to the country with a general election was the only option left open to the government to resolve the crisis. But even Mrs Thatcher was to admit Heath should have taken up the TUC's peace offer. 'We might have done better to accept it and put the TUC on the spot', she reasoned.[60] Murray thought it was foolish of the government not to accept the offer because if they had done so they would have been in a position of either being able to boast of their success in getting the unions into line or to have found extra justification for a tough line against the unions. The trouble was that nobody in the Cabinet was ready to contemplate – let alone risk – another humiliation like February 1972 at the hands of the NUM executive. Too often since that decisive moment, ministers reasoned, they had tried to make deals with the TUC. They feared that Heath had too great a faith in rationality when it came to trying to reach agreements with the trade unions.

Confusion and doubt in the government continued to the finish. The Pay Board published its wage relativities report on 30 January and Heath accepted its recommendations. He called on the miners to resume normal working and agree to a stage-three pay deal with immediate talks to be held on their longer-term pay arrangements in line with the relativities procedures. At a meeting with a TUC delegation on 4 February, he suggested that the relativities report 'offered a way of building on the TUC initiative.' Heath told them it was 'not true to say the government had rejected' the initiative 'although he did not consider it offered an effective safeguard for dealing with the present situation'.[61] In the event, the NUM rejected his suggestion. On 7 February, Heath called on the Queen to dissolve Parliament. However, on that very same day William Whitelaw, Secretary of State for Employment, agreed to refer the miners' wage claim to the Pay Board to see if they should have a larger wage increase from 1 March under stage three. Here was the way out of the crisis; calling a general election over the issue at the same time made little obvious sense. Moreover, Heath was reluctant to make trade union power the dominant theme

59. J. Jones, in 'Trade Unions and Fall of the Heath Government', 40.

60. Thatcher, *Path to Power*, 232.

61. TUC note of meeting with Heath, 4 February 1974, report to TUC General Council, TUC archives.

of his election campaign, unlike some of his colleagues who believed he should have a showdown with organised labour.

The Conservative election manifesto spelt out a stark choice for the voters over 'the danger from within'. It warned that acceptance of the NUM's pay demands would 'mean accepting the abuse of industrial power to gain a privileged position'. The Party also sought, however, to reassure the voters that it wanted Britain to be a country 'united in moderation, not divided by extremism; a society in which there was change without revolution'. After consultations with both sides of industry, Heath promised amendments to the Industrial Relations Act, 'in the light of experience'.[62] The Central Policy Review Staff in Downing Street proposed a number of key changes in the measure in a paper presented to the Prime Minister. It provided a bleak assessment of a measure many had believed would transform industrial relations. The report advised the abolition of registration, believing that that would not involve 'abandonment of any basic principle' and would form 'a useful concession to the unions'. It also suggested legalising the post-entry closed shop with safeguards for the individual worker, and the abolition of emergency powers provided for the state. The report favoured the National Industrial Relations Court (NIRC) being given investigative powers in disputes, the creation of a system of local courts with right of appeal, and ways of enabling the unions to say what rights should be protected in an industrial court, and conceded that

> It is unlikely any amendments to the Act could command open acceptance or support from the union leaders, who have, at least in public, consistently opposed both the Act and the NIRC. But if many of the unions' more reasonable and substantial objections could be met, resistance to the Court would decline as its value to employees in protecting their rights was increasingly realised and given greater publicity.

However, the CPRS also believed the establishment of 'a legal framework to regulate industrial relations' was a 'considerable achievement', and should be retained. 'The achievement is the baby in the bath', it added; 'though a certain amount of water can be thrown away, the baby must at all costs be kept safely in the bath'.[63]

Such conciliatory attitudes were not to the liking of all senior Conservatives, but they reflected Heath's hopes of avoiding any further

62. Conservative Party, general election manifesto, February 1974, in F.W.S. Craig (ed.), *British General Election Manifestos* (London, 1976), 161–5.

63. Central Policy Review Staff, 'Industrial Relations Act: Feasible Options', 28 January 1974, Michael Wolff papers, to be deposited at Churchill College Archives Centre, University of Cambridge.

conflict with organised labour after his expected election victory. However, he was wrong-footed by the intervention of CBI director-general Campbell Adamson who claimed unhelpfully that the Industrial Relations Act had 'sullied every relationship at national level between unions and employers'.[64] Nor was he helped by the Pay Board's sudden revelation that the figures on which the stage-three offer to the miners had been made were based on wrong calculations. Heath's cause also suffered from the shrewd way in which the NUM conducted itself during the miners' strike. There were to be none of the tumultuous scenes witnessed two years earlier outside many of the country's power stations.

CONCLUSION

The downfall of Heath was a personal tragedy, although he never aroused much public sympathy for his plight. Neither hard-hearted authoritarian nor the soulless technocrat of legend, he was to be a transitional figure in Conservative politics. A One-Nation Tory who wanted to modernise the trade unions and the economy, he failed to find a national language of persuasion that could shake people out of their apathy and complacency at a time of deepening crisis. Heath's slogan 'Action not words' reflected his administrative rather than political approach to policy-making. He lacked an intuitive and imaginative grasp that would convince the wider electorate about the wisdom of his strategy. Some union leaders looked back with nostalgia to the Heath days when they were wined and dined by government ministers. But for all his dogged desire to make rational deals with the TUC, Heath failed to recognise that Britain's trade unions were neither structurally nor ideologically capable at that time of delivering the kind of agreement he wanted, one which would help in transforming the UK into a European social market economy. One overriding conviction was to emerge from the wreckage of his industrial relations strategy to influence Margaret Thatcher's own approach to the problem of organised labour five years later. It was Hurd who suggested that Heath had been broken by 'the brutal exercise of trade union power'.[65] That view haunted senior Conservatives until the defeat of the National Union of Mineworkers under the messianic leadership of Arthur Scargill in

64. D. Butler and D. Kavanagh, *The British General Election of February 1974* (London, 1974), 85.
65. Hurd, *End to Promises*, 150.

March 1985 after an epic eleven-month strike. As a result of this perception, Heath's successor moved more cautiously in a so-called 'step by step' strategy to tilt the balance of power in labour law away from the unions and towards employers. No further attempt was made to try to impose a comprehensive measure like the Industrial Relations Act on a hostile trade union movement. Instead, Mrs Thatcher worked with the grain of the voluntarist system in weakening trade union power and she did so with considerable success. But the experience of the Heath government with the trade unions was to have profounder consequences for the future of British politics. It was his Herculean attempt to maintain statutory wage and price controls that convinced many Conservatives it was no longer possible for government to reconcile pay bargaining with low inflation and full employment. An increasingly influential body of neo-liberal economic opinion cast doubt on such devices as incomes policies and demand management. Instead, they called for a tight control of the money supply, laws to curb union power and the introduction of supply-side measures to create an efficient, deregulated labour market. Above all, they were willing to abandon the commitment to full employment as a political priority of economic policy. The ideological change did not flow inevitably from Heath's failures either to solve the trade union 'problem' or to defeat roaring wage-push inflation, but change became more likely as the old tripartite approach to industrial relations no longer seemed credible in a society where social consensus was fast disappearing in a desperate wages war of 'all against all'.

CHAPTER EIGHT

The social policy of the Heath government

Rodney Lowe

In social policy, as in so many other areas, the record of the Heath government appears to be a catalogue of broken promises. The commitment to reduce government expenditure was followed by the highest rise in social expenditure of any postwar government. The commitment to reduce the size of government was followed by a 10 per cent increase in public employment and the extravagant reorganisation of both the National Health Service and local government, which later Conservative administrations had to amend.[1] The commitment to restore honesty to government was followed by an electoral pledge to increase family allowances, which was immediately broken. The commitment to restore incentives was followed by the knowing creation of a 'poverty trap', which discouraged social security claimants from raising themselves out of 'dependency'. Finally, a government committed to provide special care for the most needy acquired a reputation for hard-heartedness and for furthering the interests of the rich.

How can such apparent contradictions be explained? *Was* the government hard-hearted and uncaring, as claimed by those on the left of British politics? If so, why did social expenditure rise so steeply and why were there so many small acts of generosity, such as the granting of pensions to the over-80s and attendance allowances to the disabled? Did the government, at the first sign of trouble in 1972, cravenly betray its principles as claimed by those on the right? If so, what was the precise role of high-spending ministers who were later to be the government's leading detractors – most notably Sir Keith Joseph at the Department

1. Social expenditure rose in real terms by an annual average of 6.8 per cent, whereas it increased by 4.2 per cent between 1951 and 1964, 5.9 per cent under the Wilson governments of 1964–70, and a mere 2 per cent under Labour between 1974 and 1979. It also rose fastest in relation to gross domestic product (GDP) under Heath. Public employment rose by 432,000, equally divided between central and local government. See A. Walker (ed.), *Public Expenditure and Social Policy* (London, 1982), 30, and *Economic Trends*, 446 (London, 1990), 95.

of Health and Social Security and Margaret Thatcher at the Ministry of Education? Alternatively, at a critical point in the development of collective welfare in all western countries, when declining rates of economic growth coincided with an escalating demand for welfare (generated by ageing populations, rising public expectations and enhanced professional standards), did the Heath government boldly seek a new set of priorities to ensure the continuation of both economic growth and generous welfare provision? Did it actually succeed, particularly in social security and housing policy, in designing and implementing a 'coherent, selective strategy' which was to prove 'of enormous importance for the future'?[2] Have such objectives and achievements merely been obscured by more momentous historical events, such as the oil crisis, by the intransigence of a conservative electorate and by later commentators concerned more with their own ideological presuppositions than with the historical record?

It would be foolish to pretend that either in the planning for government or during government itself social policy enjoyed the importance accorded, for example, to the reform of industrial relations or entry into the EEC. Nevertheless, it was always central to the government's fortunes. Its vast cost, amounting to over half of public expenditure, restricted the government's freedom of action elsewhere – particularly in relation to tax reform. Its direct relevance to all voters also made any change in policy highly sensitive. However, policy had to change. Were no economies to be effected, public expenditure and thus both taxation and the predominance of government in society would rise. This would have been anathema to Party activists. On the other hand, were cuts to be made, public expectations would be disappointed with damaging electoral consequences. The purpose of this chapter is to examine how, in the shadow of more glamorous events, a logical solution was sought to this dilemma in each core area of social policy.

THE OBJECTIVE

The remodelling of social policy was an integral part of the extensive planning process carried out by the Party while in opposition between 1964 and 1970. The basic principles of reform had been agreed by the time of the 1966 election. They were then applied to specific areas of

2. H. Glennerster, 'Social policy since the Second World War', in J. Hills (ed.), *The State of Welfare* (Oxford, 1990), 20; M. Hill, *The Welfare State in Britain* (Aldershot, 1993), 91.

welfare by various policy groups, the most important of which for social policy were the groups on education and housing (chaired by Sir Keith Joseph), both of which reported in 1968. By that time, officials within the Conservative Research Department were growing alarmed that the mass of detailed recommendations might not only conflict with each other but also obscure the broad objectives of Party policy. The drafting of *Make Life Better* for the 1969 conference was an attempt to establish priorities. Until the build-up to the 1970 election, however, the Shadow Cabinet showed no such urgency and it was only at the Selsdon Park meeting in January 1970 that a determined attempt was made to finalise policy. From such an extenuated planning process, did a coherent social services philosophy emerge and were the specific recommendations for social reform compatible with each other and with the government's overall objectives?

To maximise welfare in its broadest sense, the Heath government planned to 'trust the people' with the greatest possible amount of political and economic power. To reinvigorate society, the role of government was to be reduced and everyone given greater control over – and responsibility for – their own lives. To reinvigorate the economy, and thereby halt relative decline, individual initiative and enterprise were to be encouraged and more fully rewarded. The key was to be a restructured tax system. A switch in personal taxation from earnings to spending would stimulate individual initiative. Taxpayers would retain a higher percentage of their income and decide for themselves how, if at all, it was to be spent. Savings, it was hoped, would be increased, turning Britain into not only a property-owning but also a capital-owning democracy. Similarly, a switch in corporate taxation from profits to costs would encourage industrial efficiency and international competitiveness. Tax reform, in other words, was intended to attain simultaneously three broad goals. Politically, an extension of private property would strengthen the individual against the state. Economically, more extensive savings would counter inflation and facilitate industrial investment. Finally, individual welfare would also be enhanced by a greater sense of personal freedom and achievement. Attitudes would be permanently changed and the vicious circle of dependency and economic decline transformed into a virtuous cycle of political independence and economic advance.

This adaptation of 'One-Nation' Toryism to changing economic and social circumstances provided a distinct alternative to both contemporary socialism and later Thatcherism. In sharp contrast to Labour Party assumptions, high taxation was portrayed as the 'arch-enemy of the social services' because it penalised 'the very enterprise and initiative which create the wealth needed to pay for social advance'.[3] In contrast to Thatcherism, tax reductions were not equated with minimum government. The core commitment of the postwar settlement – to full employment – remained as strong as ever. Unemployment was recognised to be both a personal tragedy and a waste of economic resources. It also deterred rather than stimulated economic efficiency because, as in the 1930s, both sides of industry would react defensively and adopt restrictive practices. A measure of government planning was also acceptable both to provide a framework for industrial expansion and as a substitute for the market in areas – such as town and country planning – where it had patently failed. Finally, state intervention was required for those in genuine need because, as Iain Macleod had warned the 1966 Party Conference, in a more dynamic and competitive society 'we are not all pace-setters, we are not all competitors and . . . change when it comes as it must is often a very cruel thing to an individual or to a township or to a community. So competition needs compassion'.[4] The resulting 'One Nation' ideal was succinctly summarised in *Make Life Better.* It was 'a free society in which men and women are free to make the most of their individual talents . . . free to achieve and to excel, free to sustain variety and choice in their lives. *But it is a society – not a collection of individuals*: a society in which the young are cared for as well as the old, the backward as well as the pace-setters, the deprived as well as the high flyers'.[5]

This ideal, it was admitted, could not be achieved painlessly – especially in the medium term before economic growth had restored to government the income forfeited in tax cuts. Consequently, the corollary of tax reform was greater selectivity in the provision of social services. Selectivity, however, was one of those broad principles embraced in 1966 which later proved increasingly difficult to define. It acquired three conflicting meanings. As promoted by the Institute of Economic Affairs (IEA), it entailed greater reliance by the majority on private services with state provision (and perhaps finance) reserved for the poor.[6] Alternatively, it meant a continuing monopoly of state

3. Official Group, 'Policy document – second draft', 30 May 1968, CPA SC/68/9, f.35.

4. R. Shepherd, *Iain Macleod* (London, 1994), 438; such reasoning was remarkably close to that of Richard Titmuss.

5. 'Policy document – second draft', f.55.

6. The Institute of Economic Affairs did, of course, recommend vouchers. These were rejected on grounds of practicality – how would they cater for differences in the regional costs of services and in the cost of, for example, technical and secondary modern education? If selective, they would disadvantage the middle class; if universal, they could hardly be called selective.

services with the increased use of means-testing to ensure that only the most needy received them. Finally, at its most limited, it meant the maintenance of access to existing services but the targeting of any additional resources on the most needy.

Selectivity in all of these guises was advocated on a variety of grounds. First, services could not be maintained at existing standards if there were to be no increase in taxation. This was because of the rising dependency ratio: the escalating number of children in full-time education and of old people. Secondly, even existing standards of service were inadequate because of rising public expectations, scientific advance, higher professional standards and the relative neglect of many needy groups such as the disabled. Some form of rationing was therefore inevitable. Thirdly, the existing system was inefficient and inflexible. Not only did high taxation depress economic growth and thus government revenue but, in the absence of any charges, consumers were unaware of costs and continued to demand improved services whilst resisting tax increases. Finally, given the scarcity of resources, social justice demanded that those who could pay for services should assist those who could not. Increased prescription charges, for example, were justified if more kidney machines could thereby be financed for dying children. Greater reliance on private provision, as advocated by the IEA, could bring additional benefits. It could increase personal responsibility and choice. It could alert consumers to the true cost of services and thereby initiate an informed debate between consumers and producers of welfare on the efficiency of services. Parents, for example, might take an increased interest in the quality of education. Private provision was also more likely than state monopolies to pioneer new practices. Above all, it would pull in extra resources as individuals chose to forgo other consumer goods in favour of welfare services which would be to their direct advantage.[7]

Persuasive though many of these arguments were in theory, in practice the application of 'selectivity' to specific services – particularly in the guise of increased private provision or means-testing – aroused mounting opposition. The major objection was the perceived electoral consequences. Universal services in the Beveridge mould continued to be regarded by the majority of voters with affection and pride. Consequently any attack upon them involved considerable electoral risks, of which at least one Party official doubted the wisdom. In a direct challenge to the IEA he questioned: 'Are we trying to slavishly follow

7. Many of these arguments were summarised in 'Social Priorities: Report of the Working Group on Selectivity and Private Provision in the Social Services', 14 July 1967, CPA ACP(67)38.

the American industrial ethos? It could be that the British are naturally a more collaborative and less competitive nation than the Americans and that, given the right attitudes and terms of reference, we might progress as quickly and with less waste of scarce resources as others do by competition'.[8] The erosion of universal services would also break contractual obligations arising from past insurance payments, disappoint expectations and above all threaten the sense of security enjoyed not only by the needy but also by the middle class. Indeed, when detailed estimates were made of the redistribution of resources likely to arise from the tax cuts (which largely favoured the rich) and the targeting of benefits (which benefited the poor), the main losers were identified as the family man on an annual income between £560 and £1750.[9] This was precisely the target voter in elections and the type of person the Party sought most to attract to Conservatism through the promise of an 'opportunity' state.

Universalism, as opposed to selectivity, was justified on other practical grounds. Government had a direct interest in the quality of service provided. Economic efficiency, for example, was dependent on a mobile, educated and healthy workforce and so on the quality of housing, education and medical provision. Universal insurance contributions ensured that everyone contributed towards the cost of his or her old age, thus avoiding the problem of 'free riders' inherent in all private insurance schemes. Any greater division between public and private welfare would also, as in the 1930s, be highly divisive – although there was a total rejection of Labour's contention that universal services symbolised common citizenship. 'We do not accept the "badge of citizenship" argument', insisted a Party report on selectivity in 1967, 'we do not want to see a one class society being brought about at the expense of freedom, choice and diversity'.[10] Common citizenship was best expressed freely through voluntary service or hard work to generate the wealth which would fund more generous state relief. Finally, there were doubts (to be substantiated in the 1980s) concerning the willingness of the market to accept bad risks without substantial subsidies, the granting of which would have undermined the very financial and moral purpose of reform.

As a result of all these reservations, selectivity was finally adopted only in its most limited form: the targeting of additional resources on the most needy. The structure of state provision was to remain

8. 'Notes for the Official Group', memo by D. Clarke, 6 December 1967, CPA OG/67/12.

9. J. Douglas to E. Heath, 20 May 1968, CPA CRD/3/7/26/41.

10. 'Social Priorities', report of Working Group on Selectivity, f.8.

broadly the same. Charges might be marginally increased while additional private provision was to be encouraged by tax relief on contractual savings, such as mortgages, occupational pensions, life assurance and subscriptions to BUPA. The resulting package was somewhat confused. Private provision was to be encouraged for the majority in housing and occupational pensions, but only for a minority in private education and health. Charges were to be levied on drugs and nursery education, but not on hospital care or higher education. Additional services were to be provided in some cases by categories of need (such as disablement) but in others after a test of means (as in supplementary benefit). Pragmatism of necessity took precedence over principle and, in consequence, social policy was left vulnerable to further calls for economy.

Such calls intensified in 1969, when the incipient conflict between tax cuts and the spending commitments sought by various social policy groups was belatedly acknowledged by the Shadow Cabinet. The conflict had been exacerbated by the enforced withdrawal, in the face of strong Party opposition, of proposals to maintain the progressiveness of the tax system by the introduction of either a wealth tax or a payroll tax. The former, it was argued, would break up estates and prevent both farms and small businesses from being inherited by children. This directly contradicted the Party's drive to reward personal initiative and promote savings. It would provide a hostage to fortune which Labour might exploit (just as Labour's introduction of charges into the NHS in 1950 had been exploited by the Conservatives). Moreover, it would be difficult to administer and raise little revenue unless applied to those on middle incomes. On the other hand a payroll tax – which, as on the continent, would have directly recouped from employers the cost of the social services for their workforce – was also rejected because it appeared too similar to Labour's Selective Employment Tax, which the Party was committed to repeal. Moreover, by adding to industrial costs, it angered small businessmen and ran counter to the Party's commitment to improve international competitiveness and promote exports.

Without the buoyant revenue to be raised from these two taxes, the Shadow Cabinet had no option other than to consider the introduction of value added tax (VAT) – which was refundable on exports – and 'draconian' cuts in public expenditure.[11] Certain economies might be anticipated from the traditional promise of all opposition parties to eliminate waste, a promise made the more credible by Heath's personal

11. M. Fraser to E. Heath, 'Key issues in economic policy', 21 April 1969, SC/68/12. Opposition to the wealth and payroll taxes is best summarised in the series of briefs for Anthony Barber, 30 July 1970, CRD/3/7/26/37.

commitment to introduce modern management techniques. However, the Shadow Cabinet was under no illusion that major changes in policy were also required. Macleod's eventual package of tax and expenditure cuts, which was agreed after Selsdon, proposed savings of some £1,500m – ten times the amount that, in 1965, it had been estimated tax reform would require.[12] 63 per cent were to be found in social policy – most notably from the withdrawal of universal family allowances, the taxation of short-term benefits, the removal of subsidies for school meals and transport, and the obligation on employers to finance the first four weeks of sickness benefit. The drive for long-term competitiveness was to take an immediate toll on compassion.

In opposition, therefore, the foundations were laid for a coherent social services philosophy based on competition and compassion. It acknowledged the scarcity of resources, exacerbated by a declining rate of economic growth and a rising demand for welfare. It was also distinctive from Labour Party policy. A positive role was preserved for government, particularly in the maintenance of full employment, but the market was increasingly to be the principal provider of welfare – either directly through enhanced rewards or indirectly through generating the government revenue to finance more generous social provision. In consequence equity was to replace equality as the primary goal of policy. Individual welfare would rise in line with individual effort. It would not, as under Labour, be levelled down to the same standard for everyone regardless of effort.

The basis for a coherent philosophy existed, therefore, but how fully was it – and its practical consequences – accepted within the Party or even within the shadow cabinet? The varying definitions of selectivity, the abandonment of the more radical tax reforms, and the conflict between tax cuts and social expenditure in Macleod's final taxation package suggest that many issues remained unsolved. The simultaneous achievement of competition and compassion clearly required hard political choices. Had the winners and losers from such choices been identified? Had the likely electoral consequences been accepted? Was it realised that more modern managerial techniques in government could increase as well as reduce alienation? Was it possible consensually to achieve the desired revolution in public attitudes, which required both the abandonment of security and the embracing of enterprise? While the Party was in opposition, it would appear that questions such as these were never fully answered. A thorough-going revolution, it was tacitly assumed, could be achieved without casualties or political

12. Brief to Barber, CRD/3/7/26/37.

disruption. With the Party in government between 1970 and 1974, these unresolved questions dogged each area of social policy.

THE RECORD

Social Security

Social security was by far the most costly welfare service, consuming over one-third of social expenditure and, throughout the Heath government, was the responsibility of one of its leading later detractors, Sir Keith Joseph. It might have been expected to be, therefore, a prime target for economy and, in the incipient battle between 'One-Nation' Toryism and more radical policies, a focus for bold experiments in selectivity. It was not. Expenditure upon it rose by an annual average of 3.1 per cent and, in Campbell's words, there was only a 'tentative groping for greater selectivity within the norm of ever-improving universal provision'.[13] The major characteristics of policy were rather a series of small acts of generosity, dishonesty and incompetence in the handling of child poverty, and an ambitious but unconsummated attempt to reform pensions. What did this signify?

The acts of generosity included the granting of pensions to the over-80s (some 110,000 people who, having retired before 1948 without paying insurance contributions, had never had the right to a state pension); a Christmas bonus and annual upratings for all pensioners; pensions for widows under 50; and attendance allowances for the disabled. Each might be dismissed as a cynical and inexpensive act of electoral bribery or, in Heath's own words, 'coups de théâtre'.[14] More expensive commitments were dropped, such as the uprating of pensions in line with average earnings (rather than prices) and enhanced pensions for those over 75. Both had been promised in the 1964 manifesto. Plans for a disability pension, immediately revived by Geoffrey Howe as shadow social security minister in 1974, were also shelved. However, such cynicism is unjustified. Concern for those in need had been a consistent feature of Conservative planning throughout the 1960s and the personal commitment of senior ministers was unquestionable.

13. J. Campbell, *Edward Heath* (London, 1993), 383.

14. Steering Committee, 28 February 1973, SC/73/19. Heath's own abandonment of increased pensions for the over-75s, on the grounds that it would be a universal payment not targeted on need, is recorded in Steering Committee, 12 March 1970, SC/70/10.

Macleod, for example, was a founder of Crisis at Christmas and Joseph himself an early benefactor of the Child Poverty Action Group (CPAG). The legislation was a genuine expression of the government's compassion.

The broken election pledge to increase family allowances was altogether less creditable, particularly in the light of the manifesto's emphasis on honesty and Joseph's long-standing association with CPAG. The Party had been concerned about family poverty since its 'discovery' in 1965 by CPAG, but characteristically no remedy had been agreed. *Make Life Better* was incisive in its support of selectivity. 'Adequate family allowances will go to those families that need them', it pronounced, 'other families would benefit through reduced taxation'.[15] At Selsdon, Macleod endorsed the abandonment of universal payments in his search for economies. A net gain of £150m could be achieved even after the allocation of an additional £100m to means-tested supplementary benefit to compensate the poorest families. Other ministers were less sanguine. Although opinion polls confirmed that family allowances were widely regarded as an 'expensive and most unpopular social service', it was feared that their actual withdrawal from the middle class and particularly from mothers would be electorally damaging. It was also indefensible, argued Joseph, to withdraw automatic entitlements from poorer families while making tax concessions to the rich. Moreover, there were practical problems. As even Mrs Thatcher acknowledged, the stigma of means-tested benefit would reduce take-up.[16] families in which there were wage-earners were also ineligible for supplementary benefit, although CPAG had demonstrated that many contained children in poverty. The requirements of compassion, in other words, clashed directly with the drive to create conditions favourable to competitive efficiency. The discussion ended inconclusively with Heath significantly observing that 'we do not seem prepared to do what is required'.

The 1970 election reopened the issue. CPAG published a pamphlet asserting that 'the poor get poorer under Labour' which Macleod could not resist exploiting. It had the potential to hit Labour where it was most vulnerable and to disillusion Party workers. He met a delegation from CPAG and agreed to increase family allowances substantially. Any

15. 'Family Allowances', memo by B. Hayhoe, 28 January 1970, CRD/3/9/92, SP/70/8; Shadow Cabinet weekend, Selsdon Park Hotel, 'transcript of 9.15 meeting', 31 January 1970, CRD/3/9/92, SP/70/8.

16. Mrs Thatcher did assert, however, that family allowances encouraged large families, to which Quintin Hogg retorted that he 'did not see people procreating just to get these small allowances': Shadow Cabinet weekend, 'transcript of 9.15 meeting'.

additional benefit this gave the better-off would be reclaimed, as CPAG recommended, through the tax system. 'We accept', he confirmed in June, 'that . . . the only way of tackling family poverty in the short term is to increase allowances and operate the clawback principle'.[17] This appeared directly to contradict the manifesto (which had repeated the wording of *Make Life Better*) as well as Macleod's own stand at Selsdon. However, since January he had acknowledged that supplementary benefit could not aid working families and had commenced the re-examination of negative income tax as a permanent solution to the problem. His pledge to CPAG was explicitly short-term. After Macleod's death, however, Joseph immediately broke it and introduced a new means-tested benefit (Family Income Supplement – FIS) as the temporary solution for those in work. His justification for this *volte face* was that family allowances did nothing to help the first child and would spread the available money too thinly. Moreover, because inflation under Labour had eroded tax thresholds, many living below the poverty line were now liable for income tax. CPAG's expedient of clawback from all tax payers could thus hit the very people increased payments were intended to help.[18]

However, the fatal flaw of FIS, which had been devised not within the Party but by the Treasury under Labour, had already been identified by Peter Walker at Selsdon. This was the poverty trap. FIS paid claimants half the difference between their take-home pay and the level of supplementary benefit to which they would have been entitled had they been unemployed. As take-home pay increased, so payments declined along with other means-tested benefits (such as free school meals). Once claimants also became liable for tax, their additional earnings became subject to an effective rate of 'taxation' higher than that experienced by surtax payers. In extreme cases, income could actually decrease. This was no way to encourage the low-paid to work harder.

The theoretical solution to the problem was a merger of the tax and benefit systems. This had long been the holy grail of selectivists within the Conservative Research Department and had taken a number of guises from the original minimum income guarantee of the early 1960s, to a negative income tax in the late 1960s, and finally to the system of tax credits as proposed by the 1972 green paper. The ultimate objective was simple. All social entitlements – be they tax allowances, cash benefits or benefits in kind such as education – should be provided

17. F. Field, *Poverty and Politics* (London, 1982), 39; see also M. McCarthy, *Campaigning for the Poor* (London, 1986), chapters 6–7. The proposed addition was of 50p, to a basic allowance of 90p.

18. T. Raison, *Tories and the Welfare State* (Basingstoke, 1990), 73.

through the tax system. Were an individual's entitlements to exceed their tax liabilities, the difference would be paid directly to them in their pay packet. The complex system of child support (including child tax allowances, family allowances, family income support and a variety of other means-tested benefits such as free meals) was the obvious initial focus for reform.

The attractions of a merger were clear. Much administrative duplication and thus cost would be eliminated. Payments would be targeted on the most needy and paid automatically. In the absence of stigma, take-up would be high. Moreover, an individual's smooth transition from credit to debit would preserve incentives. However, as its various mutations suggested, there were an equal number of practical and political problems. In practice, the system depended upon a test of income rather than need and so how could regional variations in the cost of living and, in particular, differing housing costs be met? If someone fell ill, how could their income be speedily supplemented? Above all, how could unwaged mothers retain their right to family allowances?[19] It soon became clear that the system would have to be restricted to cash benefits and that a residual Supplementary Benefits Commission would be needed to meet emergencies. The prospect of simplicity and administrative savings duly faded. Politically, there were serious potential problems, particularly with alienation. The new system would break the relationship between insurance contributions and benefits and thus claimants' much-valued contractual right to benefit. Moreover it would create one all-powerful government department and, more ominously, an all-powerful government. As Mrs Thatcher unburdened her soul to the *Building Societies Gazette* in October 1967:

> Those who are so ready to equate tax reliefs with cash benefits should realise that according to their contentions there is no difference between (a) the State agreeing that a person should keep more of his own money and (b) the State taking away more from the citizen and then bountifully handing some of it back, usually in equal amounts regardless of income. It implies that all income is ultimately vested in the State with the individual entitled to nothing. The concept of personal ownership and even more important personal responsibility would cease.

This might have been in keeping with Labour's ideals. Was it really the kind of society selectivists wanted?

In the end, there were three main reasons why a negative income

19. The reformers were wholly insensitive on this point. As Hayhoe remarked at Selsdon, 'it really is neither necessary nor desirable for the State to concern itself with a compulsory transfer of income from fathers to mothers': Shadow Cabinet weekend, 'transcript of 9.15 meeting'.

tax proved to be fool's gold. It was too managerialist. This had been identified immediately by a computer expert brought in to vet the initial proposals of 1965. 'The idea of the computer revolutionising the machinery of government', he warned, 'is mistaken. Only major policy decisions revolutionise the machinery of government'. Among the vital decisions to be resolved was the question of who should lose or gain from reform. The Heath government decreed that there should be no losers and so the proposals grew unacceptably unwieldy. Finally, no variation of negative income tax could resolve the fundamental issue of incentives. As a 1972 Conservative Research Department succinctly summarised the problem:

> Given the present income distribution and the current supplementary benefits level (i.e. the minimum poverty level considered socially tolerable), any government faces the dilemma of either reducing the supplementary benefit level or alternatively imposing higher taxation further up the scale, not so much to pay for the supplementary benefits themselves, but in order to avoid a heavy disincentive as an earner approaches the tax threshold.[20]

In other words, the Party's principal objectives were in conflict. Compassion demanded that no-one live below a 'socially tolerable' poverty line. Competition demanded the maintenance of incentives and thus only the gradual withdrawal of benefits from low earners as they improved themselves. This, however, required the heavier taxation of the higher-paid 'dynamos' in society, upon whom economic growth depended. This was the basic dilemma which stalled reform not just in Britain but in all western countries which flirted with the concept of a negative income tax.

Pensions offered the other principal opportunity for radical reform. The catalyst was, as ever, rising costs. Ever since Attlee, against Beveridge's advice, had granted full pensions to those whose insurance contributions did not actuarially justify them there had been potential financial problems. In 1959 they had been temporarily relieved by a limited experiment in graduated pensions. Graduated contributions were used to meet the escalating cost of the basic state pension. By the late 1960s, however, concern had started to grow over how to pay the graduated pensions themselves. Conservative and Labour proposals were superficially similar. Both, agreed that everyone should have two pensions: one to guarantee subsistence and the other to provide an earnings-related supplement. Both also agreed that there should be a

20. J. Hough to B. Sewill, 21 December 1965, CRD/3/7/26/13; 'Dealing with Poverty', memo by J. Douglas, 11 May 1972, ACP(72)76.

right to contract out of the second state pension into a private occupational scheme. It was over the terms of contracting out that the Parties fundamentally diverged. In order to contain government and maximise individual freedom, the Heath government wanted the second pension to be as far as possible both private and a form of genuine savings. In contrast to Labour's proposals, therefore, generous terms for contracting out were to be offered so that the role of state scheme would become merely residual. Moreover the contributions to both the private and state schemes were not to be used to pay existing pensions, as under Labour, but to fund future commitments. This would both restore financial propriety and provide a buoyant source for industrial investment.

There were inevitable drawbacks to these proposals, which were approved by Parliament in the 1973 Social Security Act. The principal one was cost. The proper financing of both current and future pensions would have placed an immense additional burden on wage-earners and taxpayers, already hit by higher insurance contributions and rising prices (in part the consequence of VAT). The terms were unfavourable to part-time workers and especially to women. Moreover, private enterprise itself was not enthusiastic. Employers particularly resented the insistence that pensions should be transferable, because the historic objective of granting occupational pensions had been to retain key workers. Insurance companies were equally suspicious of government regulation. The practicality of the proposals, however, were never put to the test as the legislation was repealed by the incoming Wilson government before it became operative.

Social security may be likened to an oil tanker which it is difficult to divert, let alone halt, within a short period of time. During the three-and-a-half years of the Heath government, humane additions were made at the margin of policy. Pensions legislation and the introduction of earnings-related contributions for all benefits also promised greater financial integrity. However, more radical proposals such as the 'hiving-off' to employers of both the financing and administration of the first month of sick leave were shelved. Consequently, policy remained an 'unholy muddle' of universal and selective benefits – a muddle compounded by the creation of a poverty trap which was privately acknowledged to be 'an affront to common sense'.[21] The outcome of policy therefore reflected the evasion by government, and by Keith Joseph in particular, of the hard political choices to be made

21. 'Dealing with Poverty'; 'Preliminary draft of a "normal" manifesto', memo by A. Newton, 17 December 1973, SC/73/24.

if the twin objectives of competitiveness and compassion were to be attained. Problems, it was unavailingly hoped, could be resolved not by politicians but by computers.

Health and Welfare

The NHS, as Heath admitted at Selsdon, represented a major gap in the Party's planning. Its importance was acknowledged. It consumed one-fifth of public expenditure and employed one-thirtieth of the workforce. Moreover it was the prime example of a service where policy could not stand still. Were no additional resources to be found, the standard of care would inevitably decline because of deteriorating facilities and rising demand. The trouble was that selectivist reforms long favoured by Party activists would have been ineffectual, while radical initiatives were impractical.

Two of the most favoured traditional reforms were hospital boarding charges and tax exemption for private health insurance. The former would recoup costs from those most able to pay while the latter, it was hoped, would both reduce demand on the NHS and attract additional resources into health care. However, boarding charges would have raised little extra revenue at considerable administrative cost and public inconvenience. Demands would have been made on people when they were emotionally and financially at their most vulnerable. Similarly tax exemption on private insurance, even in the most unlikely event of its increasing subscribers tenfold, would have brought into health care additional resources equivalent to only five per cent of the overall income of the NHS.[22] Greater inequality of provision would, therefore, have been very hard to justify as a public good. Foremost among the more radical proposals was the revival by Maurice Macmillan of an idea favoured by his father in the late 1950s. The NHS should be put more fully on an insurance basis with everyone required to cover themselves against a given minimum of health needs, including visits to GPs and hospital out-patient departments.[23] This would reduce the direct burden on taxpayers and, by bringing home the true cost of health care, help to limit further both demand and abuse. However, as Macleod – despite his desperate search for economies – pointed out at Selsdon, the trouble

22. 'Health', memo by B. Sewill and C.E. Bellairs, 22 January 1970, CRD/3/9/92, SP/70/7.

23. Heath fully endorsed charges for visits to GPs: Steering Committee, 12 March 1970, SC/70/10. The irony was that the contribution of insurance contributions to the National Health Service budget fell from 10.2 to 7.9 per cent between 1970 and 1973.

with such a proposal was that it would double the cost of compulsory insurance for those on average wages. This was a demand they could not afford and would not tolerate.

Despite the acknowledged urgency of financial reform, therefore, neither in opposition nor in government could the Party agree on any practical changes. There were, typically, even additional burdens placed on the service after 1970 by marginal improvements such as the availability of contraception on prescription. Nevertheless, there was one area where radical action was taken, albeit at considerable cost: administrative reorganisation. The principle of reorganisation was itself uncontroversial. There was a recognised need for the greater unification of the tripartite system inherited from Bevan, clearer lines of management, closer relations with social workers, and greater openness in decision-making. The original intention had accordingly been to establish about forty managerial Area Health Authorities staffed equally from among the nominees of central government, local authorities and the professions. Largely as a result of lobbying by vested interests, however, three tiers of administration – regional, area and district – were eventually established with a large number of representative appointees. Each of the original objectives was duly lost. GPs, who were the vital link between hospitals and social work, were not formally incorporated into the authorities. Managerial lines of communication were confused by the divided loyalties of appointees. Even the Ombudsman and the Community Health Councils shadowing the district authorities appeared little more than token gestures to consumer power. 'An attempt to please everyone', as Klein has concluded, 'eventually satisfied no one'. The fundamental weakness of reform was its excessive bureaucracy which, to its authors' shame, had been identified from the very start. As John Silkin had memorably remarked on the Reorganisation Act's progress through Parliament: 'if you have tiers, prepare to shed them now'.[24] This was advice immediately endorsed by the 1976–79 Royal Commission on the NHS and implemented with the abolition of Area Health Authorities in 1982. Joseph's reorganisation, in other words, despite the opportunity to digest the lessons of twenty-five years of national administration, lasted for less than half the time of Bevan's necessarily hasty improvisations.

Administrative extravagance was repeated in the reorganisation of the personal social services where between 1972 and 1974 alone the number of senior supervisory staff and social workers employed by local authori-

24. R. Klein, *The Politics of the NHS* (2nd edn, London, 1989), 99; Raison, *Tories and the Welfare State,* 81.

ties increased by over forty per cent.[25] This reorganisation was admittedly initiated not by the Heath government but by Labour in the aftermath of the 1968 Seebohm Report. Nevertheless expansion was not halted in 1970 and was even redoubled during the reorganisation of local government in 1973. As with the NHS, the need for reorganisation was not controversial. Indeed it had been demanded by Sir Keith Joseph and Margaret Thatcher in a joint memorandum to the Shadow Cabinet in 1965.[26] By enabling those in need to be cared for at home, social work had the advantage over institutional care of being both more humane and more cost-effective. Moreover, it could provide a positive expression of common citizenship by acting as a focus for formal voluntary, neighbourhood and family care. In opposition, therefore, Joseph and Thatcher had sought the creation of a humane local service entrusted with the positive duty to seek out need and to co-ordinate benefits in cash and kind. The trouble was that, in the realisation of this service in office, Joseph sought once again to evade hard political decisions. Given the insufficiency of resources to meet all needs, clear spending priorities had to be established. They were not. Moreover, no service could simultaneously serve the conflicting interests of government, of the community and of the clients it served. Where did power ultimately lie? Issues such as these remained unresolved, with the result that much public money and human effort were expended to little good effect. As in the NHS, staff morale plummeted, public disillusion grew and standards of care failed to noticeably improve.

Housing

Housing was the area of the government's most radical experiment and yet, on its own admission, was also the area of its 'greatest failure'.[27] This was reflected by the massive increase in land and house prices following the relaxation of credit which had been intended to stimulate industrial investment: easier and larger profits, it was soon found, could be made from property speculation. As a result the price of a new house more than doubled and, with the mortgage rate rising to 11 per

25. E. Younghusband, *Social Work in Britain 1950–1975*, vol. 1 (London, 1978), 298; see also P. Hall, *Reforming the Welfare* (London, 1976), 122–30.

26. 'Pensions and care for the elderly', memo by K. Joseph and M. Thatcher, 16 February 1965, CPA LCC/65/12.

27. Robert Carr, in Steering Committee, 28 February 1973, SC/73/19. The statistics in this section are taken from the appendix of M. Boddy, *The Building Societies* (London, 1980), and J.R. Short, *Housing in Britain* (London, 1982), 118.

cent, average initial mortgage payments increased from 26 to 42 per cent of average wages. In 1970 Peter Walker, who was soon to assume responsibility for housing policy as Secretary of State for the Environment, had attacked Labour on the grounds that it had become 'impossible for the average wage-earner to buy an average priced house'.[28] This prospect retreated still further in the next three-and-a-half years, and owner-occupation rose only marginally from 50 to 52.7 per cent of housing stock.

Owner-occupancy nevertheless remained, as it had been since 1945, the primary objective of policy. In the broadest political sense, it was regarded as the prerequisite for a strong property-owning democracy capable of resisting over-powerful government. In narrower party terms, it provided the key to the breaking-up of heavily subsidised council estates where tenants tended automatically to vote Labour. Financially, in an area where (because of high construction costs) some state subsidy was inevitable, limited support for the purchase of houses was seen as a cheaper alternative to the payment of the full capital and current costs of rented accommodation. Consequently a range of additional incentives, from low-start mortgages to loans to building societies to offset interest rate rises, were introduced, but they had little effect because of the disincentive of escalating prices.

This did not mean, though, that the government deserted the owner-occupier. On the contrary, the real value of existing incentives escalated with the explosion of house prices. Principal among the incentives was tax relief on mortgage interest repayments. Its cost to the Treasury doubled to £556m by 1973–4 and for the first time the annual subsidy to mortgage holders, at £76, exceeded that for council tenants at £56. In addition, there was the exceptional exemption of the main home from capital gains tax (at an estimated cost by 1975 of £550m); the withdrawal of tax on imputed rent which had been levied before 1963 (£200m); and use through improvement grants of public money to increase the value of private property (£300m). Such subsidies might be justified on the grounds of encouraging personal incentive. They were, nevertheless, a controversially high price to pay for a government committed to economy and to targeting the poor.

Their legitimacy was brought even more into question by the stricter application of selectivist principles to the rented sector through the 1972 Housing Finance Act. It was here that the government broke new ground because the aim of policy was nothing less than the abolition of all existing housing subsidies and rent controls. Every local

28. Leader's Consultative Committee, 23 March 1970, LCC/70/357.

authority was instead required both to charge 'fair rents' to all their tenants, in line with practice in the private rented sector, and to participate in a national rent rebate scheme to help those in both the public and the private sector who could not pay. Through a complex series of regulations, central government would make good any deficiency in a council's housing account (arising from rebate expenditure exceeding rent income) while recouping half of any surplus (to ensure some redistribution of income from rich to poor areas). The clear objective was to oblige council tenants to pay more economic rents for their housing while giving subsidies, for the first time, to tenants in the private rented sector – who were often far poorer. This established two principles which had until recently been opposed within the Party: the tying of subsidies to individuals rather than to property and the subsidisation, however indirectly, of private landlords.

The resulting increase in council rents provoked outrage and, in a rare example of postwar non-compliance, a housing commissioner had to be appointed in the Derbyshire district of Clay Cross to implement the legislation. In fact this outrage was hardly justified, because rents rose on average only from 8 to 8.6 per cent of average wages. There were, however, two more justifiable reasons for criticisms of the Act. First, as with all the government's grandiose schemes of reorganisation, it led to administrative chaos and increased expenditure. This was because of exacerbation of the poverty trap by means-tested rebates, and because of the confusion of responsibility between local authorities and the supplementary benefits system over responsibility for the unemployed. More importantly, the Act eroded local democracy. Local authorities lost the right to determine the level of their rents, for which a centrally appointed Rent Scrutiny Board became ultimately responsible. They also lost the freedom to subsidise tenants if they so chose or to use surpluses in their housing account to subsidise other services. Such centralist tendencies had been incipient in Party policy since the 1968 report of the Housing Policy Group, chaired by Sir Keith Joseph and attended by Margaret Thatcher. Its impatience with local government (as both housing and planning authority) had been evident in a series of recommended restrictions (especially on building) and compulsory obligations (including the payment by councils of removal expenses to tenants who had bought their own council house).[29] Although the ultimate objective was to liberate the housing market, such tendencies were as contradictory for a Party committed to decentralisation as was the increased assistance of owner-occupiers

29. Report of the Policy group on Housing, 16 July 1968, ACP(68)50.

for one committed to selectivity. The full logic of housing policy had been either not thought through or not explicitly acknowledged.

Education

The final area of policy, education, is of particular interest because it remained throughout the government the responsibility of Margaret Thatcher. Within the Party while in opposition, hostility to existing educational practice had grown as a result of Labour's accelerated programme of comprehensivisation and rising student unrest. It peaked with the publication of two Black Papers in 1968 and the enforced resignation of the Party's spokesman, Edward Boyle, first as co-ordinator of policy-planning in 1968, then from active politics in 1970 and finally from the Party itself in 1972. The time appeared ripe for radical change. Instead, however, education expenditure continued to rise faster than GDP and in 1972 a White Paper significantly entitled *Education: A Framework for Expansion* promised even faster growth over the following decade (Cmnd 5174). Each area of education was to benefit. Free nursery education was to be provided to all who required it. The number of teachers was to be increased by 150,000 – allowing teacher–pupil ratios to drop from 1:22.6 to 1:18.5. Participation in higher education was also to increase from 15 to 22 per cent of the relevant age group.

Such planned expansion seems, on the surface, remarkable not only for a Party sceptical of current educational practice but also for a government whose initial act of withdrawing milk from primary school children had branded it – albeit unfairly – as 'pre-Disraelian'.[30] There were nevertheless good reasons, at least within revised 'One-Nation' Toryism, for educational expansion. Education, as Macleod had argued even as shadow chancellor, was a 'programme which can and must rise more than the average' because it held the key to the twin objectives of equality of opportunity and economic efficiency.[31]

The former was Mrs Thatcher's principal objective as minister. Nursery and primary schools were scheduled for expansion, particularly in Education Priority Areas, to help break the 'cycle of deprivation' with which Keith Joseph was becoming increasingly concerned. To honour a pledge originally made in the 1944 Education Act, the school leaving

30. Former Labour ministers who made these charges had themselves withdrawn free milk from secondary schools. The Conservatives' objective was, moreover, not to cut educational expenditure but to re-prioritise it.

31. Shepherd, *Macleod*, 478.

age was finally raised in 1972 to 16. Most surprisingly of all, the Open University was saved from extinction. Both Macleod and Boyle, despite being leading advocates of equal opportunity, had sought its abolition mainly because experience in the USA suggested that there would be high drop-out rates. Not yet having admitted any students, it also represented a soft target. Moreover, Heath himself was convinced there were already too many universities. Nevertheless, Mrs Thatcher secured its survival. Her permanent secretary has since claimed that she regarded it, somewhat ironically, as an economy measure: it could produce graduates at half the cost of Oxbridge. However, Hugo Young's contention is the more plausible that the essential reason for survival was its provision of 'educational opportunity for those prepared to work for it'. After all, it was for this reason that at Selsdon Mrs Thatcher had called it, rather than the projected private University of Buckingham, 'Thatcher University Ltd'.[32]

It was on the second criterion of economic efficiency that the record of education expansion appears more blemished. With the Party in opposition, for example, a report of its Education Policy Group in 1968 had recommended, in line with selectivist principles, the expansion of nursery education only in Education Priority Areas and on a fee-paying basis. Mrs Thatcher's eventual decision to introduce a free nationwide service raises fundamental questions not only about her commitment to public expenditure restraint and thus tax reform but also about priorities within the education budget. Was the competitive efficiency of the economy best served by a concentration of resources on social need amongst the youngest age group? This question was given added power by her regret, expressed immediately on leaving office, that more thought and resources had not been given to the needs of those kept on in school by the raising of the leaving age.[33]

It was, however, the reorganisation of secondary schools which provided the government with its greatest challenge. Labour's requirement that all local authorities should adopt comprehensive schooling was set aside. Nevertheless, the momentum of reform continued so that, between 1970 and 1974, the proportion of secondary school children in comprehensives rose from 32 to 62 per cent. Mrs Thatcher rejected only 326 of the 3612 reorganisation proposals submitted to her and sanctioned the closure of more grammar schools than had any other education minister. Her actions did not necessarily conflict with the

32. B. Simon, *Education and the Social Order 1940–1990* (London, 1991), 464; H. Young, *One of Us* (London, 1989), 69; Shadow Cabinet weekend, Selsdon Park Hotel, transcript of meeting on education, 1 February 1970, LCC/42 (uncatalogued).

33. 'Housing', memo by M. Thatcher, 1 May 1974, LCC/74/13.

policy of local diversity, which had been developed by Boyle in the 1960s. Boyle had rejected, on clear educational grounds, selection by ability at 11 and had welcomed orderly change consistent with expressed local wishes and available resources. Above all, dogmatism was not to be met by dogmatism. Each plan was to be scrutinised to ensure that, in the manner best suited to each locality, high academic standards were maintained while educational opportunity was widened. Reorganisation between 1970 and 1974 observed no such exacting criteria. Plans were accepted without conviction and covert support was lent, wherever possible, to their opponents. In addition, little positive thought was given to the content of education.[34] It was indeed Heath who, when presented with the 1972 White Paper, asked searching questions about educational output.[35] Under Mrs Thatcher, only tentative steps – such as the commissioning of the Bullock Committee on reading standards – were taken in this direction. To what extent, therefore, did education policy in these years become more cost-effective or advance economic competitiveness?

The problems facing education policy epitomised those facing all other social policies. Given the scarcity of resources, hard political decisions had to be taken to realise the twin objectives of revised 'One-Nation' Toryism, competition and compassion. In the background, there existed a more radical critique of state provision which supported the economies canvassed by 'One-Nation' without embracing their positive purpose. These economies, well-aired in the 1960s and to be revived in the 1980s, included the greater use of teaching assistants and – in higher education – the introduction of student loans, two-year degrees and the reorganisation of the university year. Between 1970 and 1974, however, no hard decision on economies, other than the withdrawal of school milk, was taken to help finance rapid expansion. Heath recognized the danger. 'It is encouraging', he wrote somewhat pointedly to Mrs Thatcher in 1972, 'that you expect to be able to hold out the prospect of further development on all fronts, despite the very difficult problems of priorities which confront us in this field'.[36] However, Mrs Thatcher continued in her role as a conventionally strong departmental minister, maximising resources for traditional ends. She failed to break new ground by resolving the long-standing weakness of

34. Simon, *Education*, 405–19; Boyle's principles are best expressed in 'Secondary school reorganisation', 9 February 1967, LCC/67/127.

35. Sir William Pile, at Institute of Contemporary British History witness seminar, February 1994, text published in 'The Heath Government', *Contemporary Record*, vol. 9, no. 1 (1995), 188–219.

36. E. Heath to M. Thatcher, 15 June 1972, SC/72/11.

education provision (technical and vocational education) or by anticipating the predominant theme of future Party policy (parent power). On neither One-Nation nor on more radical criteria, therefore, could she be called a conviction politician. In the field of education, that politician was Edward Boyle.[37]

CONCLUSION

In the relatively unglamorous and unquestionably complex field of social policy, two burning issues arise from the record of the Heath government. Were the twin goals of competition and compassion compatible? What was the precise role in government of those high-spending ministers, Sir Keith Joseph and Margaret Thatcher, who were later so to disparage it? In opposition under Heath's leadership the Party was courageous in rising to the challenge of adapting welfare services – designed to resolve the problems of interwar depression – to radically change economic and social conditions. Its new objectives were not hard-hearted, as superficially claimed by Labour. Rather, they were liberating. Individual welfare was recognised to exceed material well-being and to include, among other things, political freedom and the opportunity for self-enhancement. The market as much as the State was the guarantor of this broader concept of welfare, and so competitive efficiency and economic growth had to be assured. They were needed, moreover, to generate the resources to fund more generous state welfare for those whose welfare the market, as in the past, was ill-equipped to provide directly. In the twin objectives of competition and compassion the Party had identified realistic and distinctive policy goals. In tax reform it had also identified an effective means for their achievement.

Success depended, however, on a revolution in public attitudes and institutional practice. Postwar policy had reinforced a popular preference for security over the rigours of competition and, in addition, created a complex network of vested interests. In the reordering of priorities, therefore, the Party faced major internal and electoral problems – all the more so because its natural supporters within the supposedly independent middle class were among the major beneficiaries of universal welfare services and tax allowances. These problems were likely to be particularly acute in the medium term, before accelerating economic growth restored to government the revenue lost in tax cuts. Neither

37. Just as he resigned on principle from the government after Suez, so he resigned from the Party in 1972.

when the Party was in opposition nor when it was in government were these problems faced with sufficient clarity of purpose or administrative skill. The abandonment of the wealth tax and the massive increase in subsidies for owner-occupiers, for example, raised major questions about the real willingness and ability of the Party to encourage initiative, to target benefits and, above all, to create a genuine 'One-Nation' society. In welfare administration there was the disaster of the grandiose reorganisation of the NHS and sheer incompetence in both the payment of housing benefits and the creation of a poverty trap. The chimera of a negative income tax typified the government's unavailing search for a painless revolution. The ultimate failure of social policy, therefore, cannot be explained by external 'shocks' such as Macleod's early death or the oil crisis. The fundamental reason was insufficient ruthlessness in the determination of priorities.

Two of the highest spending social service ministers might, of course, have been expected to play a full part in the determination of these priorities. This they noticeably failed to do. Joseph, while displaying genuine compassion and integrity (particularly in pensions legislation), showed little steel in the identification and implementation of selective economies. He was also responsible for the worst administrative disasters. Mrs Thatcher pursued an expansionist programme with little apparent determination or ability to remedy past failings (such as technical education) or to target resources in areas which would advance competitive efficiency. The ultimate failure of social policy between 1970 and 1974 may finally have persuaded them that collective welfare was no answer to Britain's economic and social ills. They themselves, however, bore considerable responsibility for that failure. Neither was prepared to make the hard choices, advocated by Macleod, to achieve a new constructive balance between economic and social policy. The tragedy was that when the necessary changes were made after 1979 they had little of the positive purpose, the compassion or (from both the country's and the Party's point of view) the long-term political realism which had been the goals of 'One-Nation'. Toryism.

CHAPTER NINE

Immigration and the Heath government

Zig Layton-Henry

INTRODUCTION

The legacy that Heath inherited in the areas of immigration and race relations was to prove particularly difficult and troublesome for him to manage, both as Leader of the Opposition from 1965 to 1970 and as Prime Minister. The exploitation of racism and anti-immigrant feeling for party advantage was abhorrent to Heath[1] but it was to prove a great temptation to some Conservative politicians in the 1960s and 1970s. Immigration was to play a major role in the battle between the major parties during the whole period of Heath's leadership. Most explosive of all was the fact that immigration was to provide the detonator in the titanic struggle between Heath and his arch opponent Enoch Powell.

During the 1950s a number of right-wingers, notably Cyril Osborne and Norman Pannel, had waged a long and ultimately successful campaign to mobilise support in the Conservative party for immigration control legislation.[2] This was eventually conceded by the Party leadership in 1961 by the introduction of a Commonwealth Immigrants Bill which made Commonwealth immigration subject to control for the first time through a system of employment vouchers. These vouchers had to be obtained before immigration was permitted. These were the first controls on Commonwealth immigration. The Bill had considerable support among Conservative Party activists but also among the electorate as a whole, two-thirds of whom supported the legislation.[3] Initially the Bill provoked vehement opposition from the Labour Party and considerable unease among Conservative leaders, but by the time of the 1964 general election the support of the electorate for immigration controls was so strong that even the Labour leadership had accepted the need for such

1. See for example D. Hurd, *An End to Promises: Sketch of a Government 1970–74* (London, 1979), 50.
2. Z. Layton-Henry, *The Politics of Race in Britain* (London, 1984), 30–43.
3. Lord Butler, *The Art of the Possible* (Harmondsworth, 1973), 207.

controls. During the election campaign, Sir Alec Douglas-Home had attempted to tap this support for the Conservatives by claiming credit for the government for passing the Commonwealth Immigrants Act and as a result substantially reducing immigration.

The deep prejudices that could be aroused by immigration surfaced locally in the 1964 general election in a number of Midland constituencies. This was an embarrassment to the Tory leadership, but Sir Alec was not embarrassed enough to repudiate the electoral successes of Peter Griffiths in Smethwick and Wyndham Davies in Birmingham, Perry Barr.

Support for tougher immigration controls strengthened on both sides of Parliament during 1965, encouraged by Labour's defeat in the Leyton by-election in January and continuing pressure from the Conservatives. On 3 February, Sir Alec in a speech at Hampstead advocated assisted repatriation of immigrants and the vigorous pursuit of illegal entrants. Two days later the Home Secretary, Sir Frank Soskice, took powers to tighten the immigration regulations covering the entry of dependant relatives and to deport illegal entrants. On 2 March, Sir Cyril Osborne proposed to the House a private member's Bill on immigration. It requested that

> leave be given to bringing in a Bill to make provision for the fixing of periodic and precise limits on immigration into the United Kingdom (until local authorities have dealt with the urgent problems arising from previous immigration); to stop the widespread avoidance of existing regulations; to provide for the repatriation of immigrants who enter the United Kingdom illegally; to make further provision regarding deportation of immigrants who have been convicted of offences punishable by imprisonment; to provide for assisted passages for immigrants who wish to return to their own country; and for purposes connected with the matters aforesaid.[4]

This motion was supported by 162 Conservative MPs including Sir Alec Douglas-Home, Peter Thorneycroft, Enoch Powell and Edward Heath.

The Conservative front bench continued to press the issue during 1965. On 5 March, Peter Thorneycroft, the Shadow Home Secretary, made a speech to the Home Affairs Committee of the Conservative Parliamentary Party advocating the end of mass immigration. In a debate in the House on 23 March, he urged a drastic cut in the number of immigrants.[5] On 21 May, Powell made a speech to the women's

4. *House of Commons Debates*, 5th ser., vol. 707, col. 1132, 2 March 1965.
5. *HC Debs.*, 5th ser., vol. 709, col. 334–6, 23 March 1965.

section of his constituency association in Wolverhampton emphasising the dangers of the expansion of the immigrant population through natural increase.

The election of Heath as leader of the Conservative Party in July resulted in the replacement of Thorneycroft as Home Affairs spokesman by Quintin Hogg. This resulted in a softening of the Conservative position on immigration. The major concern of Heath and Hogg was to prevent immigration becoming a matter of political dispute, partly because it was an issue that divided the Party but also because they felt it would damage race relations.[6] They were naturally well aware that anti-immigrant feeling was directed against West Indian and Asian immigration and that the terms 'immigrant' and 'immigration' had become coded ways of referring to black immigrants and non-white immigration. The Labour government, which felt exceedingly vulnerable because of its tiny majority, was equally concerned to exclude immigration from the agenda of party politics for fear of losing votes. In August the government introduced a new White Paper 'Immigration from the Commonwealth' which drastically cut Commonwealth immigration, increased the government's powers to deport illegal entrants and imposed additional health checks on immigrants.[7] The White Paper was very popular with the electorate, and the Gallup Poll in September 1965 found that 88 per cent of the electorate supported its proposals.[8]

The Unilateral Declaration of Independence by Iain Smith in Rhodesia on 11 November 1965 threw the Conservative Party into disarray and enabled Wilson to exploit Tory divisions. In the vote on oil sanctions on 21 December, for example, the Opposition split three ways. The shadow cabinet decided to abstain but could not hold the party together. Fifty Conservative MPs voted against the order and thirty voted with the government. On the right of the Party there was considerable sympathy for Iain Smith and the white minority in Rhodesia, described by Lord Salisbury as our 'kith and kin'. On the liberal left of the Party there was equally strong opposition to support for a white minority regime which had seized independence unconstitutionally. The Rhodesian problem was to remain a thorn in Heath's side for the whole period of his leadership. The Party remained deeply divided about what action to take, and any move to compromise with the illegal Smith regime brought Labour accusations of pandering to racism and of giving succour to an illegal and unconstitutional regime.[9]

6. J. Campbell, *Edward Heath* (London, 1993), 237–8.
7. Immigration from the Commonwealth, Cmnd. 2739, 1965.
8. Social Surveys (Gallup Poll) Ltd, September 1965.
9. Campbell, *Edward Heath*, 205.

The growing support in the Conservative party for tougher controls was reflected in the Conservative Party's 1966 manifesto *Action Not Words*. The immigration proposals began on a positive note affirming the Party's commitment to equality of citizenship but went on to include proposals aimed at reassuring those demanding more stringent controls. The manifesto commitments were to:

- Ensure that all immigrants living in Britain are treated in all respects as equal citizens and without discrimination.
- Introduce a conditional entry system which will control the initial time during which a new immigrant may stay, until permission is granted whether permanently or for a limited period.
- Strengthen the arrangements for health checks for immigrants.
- Require all immigrants to register the names of any dependants who might at any time wish to join them, so that their numbers will be known. In the case of new immigrants the number of dependants will be an important factor in deciding whether entry will be permitted.
- Help immigrants already here to rejoin their families in their countries of origin, or to return with their families to these countries, if they so wish.
- Combine stricter control of entry with special help where necessary to those areas where immigrants are concentrated.[10]

Immigration played almost no part in the general election of 1966. To the Labour Party's great relief all the parliamentary seats where racism had appeared to influence the result in the 1964 election were recaptured from the Conservatives. The absence of the issue from the election campaign was partly due to Heath's insistence that the issue should not be exploited by Conservative parliamentary candidates. It was also a result of Labour's strategy of supporting and introducing tough immigration controls to deny the Conservatives the opportunity of exploiting the issue electorally. This strategy was so successful that at the time of the general election, 61 per cent of voters were unable to detect any appreciable differences between the parties on the issue.[11]

This bipartisan consensus was to be relatively short-lived. Two new issues arose in 1967 which were to re-establish immigration and race

10. *Action Not Words: The New Conservative Programme* (Conservative and Unionist Central Office, 1965), 13.

11. D.T. Studlar, 'Policy Voting in Britain: The Coloured Immigration Issue in the 1964, 1966 and 1970 General Elections', *American Political Science Review,* vol. 72 (1978), 46–72.

relations as major sources of conflict on the national political agenda. The first was new Race Relations legislation. The large Labour majority provided a political opportunity for the Home Secretary, Roy Jenkins, to strengthen the Race Relations Act. He was already convinced this was necessary and had encouraged the Race Relations Board and the National Council for Commonwealth Immigrants to sponsor research into racial discrimination and American race relations legislation.[12] In April the report on racial discrimination was published, and this was followed in October by the Street report on anti-discrimination legislation. The first report, commissioned from Political and Economic Planning, revealed much higher levels of discrimination than had previously been thought to exist and there were widespread demands, particularly in the press, for urgent action. The Street report argued that voluntary conciliation was not effective and that legal sanctions were necessary for anti-discrimination legislation to be effective.[13] The report by Political and Economic Planning was decisive and Jenkins was able to persuade the Cabinet of the need for a stronger race relations Bill; in May he announced the government's intention to introduce new legislation.

The second issue was Asian migration from Kenya. In 1963 Kenya became independent, and residents of the new country had two years to decide whether to take Kenyan nationality or remain citizens of the UK and colonies. Many Kenyan Asians uncertain of their future in an independent Kenya chose to retain their British citizenship. As Kenya did not allow dual citizenship this meant that they were vulnerable to Kenyan government policies to give preference to Kenyan citizens in employment and business. As Asians lost their jobs and licenses to run businesses they began to migrate to Britain. In January 1968 the Kenyan government introduced new laws concerning the employment of non-citizens: work permits could be issued for a maximum of two years after which non-citizens would be expected to leave Kenya.

In the autumn of 1967 Enoch Powell and Duncan Sandys initiated a campaign to control this new source of immigration. At Deal on 18 October, Powell argued that 'it is quite monstrous that an unforeseen loophole in legislation should be able to add another quarter of a million or so . . . without any control or limit whatever.'[14] As had occurred in the early 1960s, the campaign itself stimulated immigration

12. Layton-Henry, *Politics of Race*, 66.

13. Political and Economic Planning, *Racial Discrimination*, April 1967, H. Street, G. Howe, and G. Bindman, *Report on Anti-Discrimination Legislation*, Political and Economic Planning and Research Services LTD, October 1967.

14. P. Cosgrave, *The Lives of Enoch Powell* (London, 1990), 240–1.

as Kenyan Asians with British citizenship rushed to come to Britain before restrictions were imposed.

The campaign came to a head with major speeches by Sandys on 8 February and Powell on 9 February demanding controls. On 12 February Sandys tabled a motion calling on the government to take immediate action and on 18 February Malcolm MacDonald was dispatched to Kenya to negotiate a modification in Kenyan government policy. MacDonald's mission was unsuccessful and immigration from Kenya rose rapidly, some 10,000 people arriving in the last two weeks of February. On 20 February, Sandys tabled another motion requesting legislation and 90 Conservative MPs signed it. More surprisingly, 15 Labour MPs signed an amendment agreeing that some kind of control legislation was necessary.[15]

On 22 February the Cabinet met and decided to impose a quota on the number of British Asians from Kenya allowed to enter Britain each year. This bill was a betrayal of people who had kept British citizenship for their own protection in an uncertain situation. If they had been 'kith and kin' like the white settlers in Kenya, they would have been welcomed with open arms.

The decision by the government to control Asian immigration from Kenya caused a dilemma for Heath as it was a Conservative administration that had granted independence to Kenya and had allowed the white and Asian minorities to retain their British passports. Iain Macleod, the Colonial Secretary at the time, was positive that the Asians had been promised free entry to Britain: 'We did it', he wrote in the *Spectator*, 'we meant to do it and in any case we had no other alternative.'[16] Powell and Sandys disagreed with Macleod arguing that the Asians were Kenya's responsibility.

The shadow cabinet had to balance the widespread support among Conservative MPs for controlling the immigration of the Kenyan Asians with the moral obligations most believed Britain had to them. The shadow cabinet decided to support the Bill. This was justified by Heath on the grounds that there would be serious social consequences if they were to come at a rate which could not be satisfactorily absorbed.[17] The Bill was rushed through Parliament, receiving overwhelming support in the Commons with only small rebellions on both sides. Fifteen Tory MPs, including MacLeod, voted against the Bill as did thirty-five Labour MPs. The Bill was fiercely criticised outside the House by the voluntary agencies concerned with race relations, the quality press and

15. D. Steel, *No Entry* (London, 1969).
16. I. Macleod, 'A Shameful and Unnecessary Act', *The Spectator*, 1 March 1968.
17. *The Times*, 22 February 1967.

the churches. Auberan Waugh, writing in the same issue of *The Spectator* as MacLeod, described the bill as 'one of the most immoral pieces of legislation to have emerged from any British Parliament'.[18]

The campaign by Powell and Sandys had been stunningly successful. They had caused the British government to restrict the rights of entry of British nationals with British passports, and this action had been supported by the shadow cabinet. Powell now turned his attention to the Race Relations Bill which he strongly opposed. However, the betrayal of the Kenyan Asians had made both government and opposition front benches more sympathetic to the Race Relations Bill as a measure complementary to tough immigration controls, and one that would aid the integration of the settled black population. The shadow cabinet was divided in its response to the bill and decided on a reasoned amendment declining to support the bill and expressing support for equal treatment. As Powell had helped to draft the amendment, he was expected to support the shadow cabinet's position.[19]

This was the background to Powell's dramatic Birmingham speech where in apocalyptical terms he described observing the annual inflow of immigrant dependants as being like watching a nation busily engaged in heaping up its own funeral pyre, and warned that the Race Relations Bill would allow immigrants to overawe and dominate their fellow citizens. He predicted large-scale racial violence unless the tide of immigration were not merely halted but reversed. This was the meaning of his concluding sentences. 'As I look ahead, I am filled with foreboding, like the Roman, I seem to see the River Tiber foaming with much blood. That tragic and intractable phenomenon that we watch with horror on the other side of the Atlantic but which there is interwoven with the history and existence of the states itself, is coming upon us here by our own volition and our own neglect.'[20]

Powell's speech was a major challenge to Heath, but also to other members of the shadow cabinet. In particular it trespassed on Quintin Hogg's area of responsibility without his agreement, and it was also a slight to Willie Whitelaw who, as Chief Whip, was responsible for party unity. It outraged many members of the shadow cabinet who supported the policy of not making immigration an issue of dispute between the parties. Boyle, Carr and Macleod were all outraged at the content and tone of Powell's speech. Heath could only maintain his

18. A. Waugh, 'The Victory of Autochthonous Racism', *The Spectator*, 1 March 1968.

19. W. Whitelaw, *The Whitelaw Memoirs* (London, 1989), 64.

20. E. Powell, 'Text of Speech Delivered to the Annual Meeting of the West Midlands Area Conservative Political Centre, Birmingham, 20 April 1968', in B. Smithies and P. Fiddick (eds), *Enoch Powell on Immigration* (London, 1969), 35–43.

authority as leader by dismissing Powell from the shadow cabinet. He did this, criticising Powell's speech as 'racialist in tone and liable to exacerbate racial tension'.[21]

The dismissal of Powell strengthened Heath's position in the shadow cabinet and to some extent in the parliamentary Party, but Powell's speech and the publicity it received made him a national political force. He had tapped the deep-seated popular frustration with the bipartisan approach to immigration and race relations issues. The leading opinion polls indicated huge levels of popular support for Powell ranging from 67 per cent in NOP to 82 per cent in ORC. They also showed that two-thirds of the public felt Heath had been wrong to sack him.[22] Powell received an avalanche of over 45,000 letters, almost all supporting his views, while Heath received thousands of letters of criticism, some of which were extremely abusive.[23] The Chairman of the Conservative Party also received hundreds of letters from constituency associations, party members, factories and individual voters overwhelmingly supporting Powell.[24]

The popularity of Powell's views, especially within Conservative Constituency Associations, forced Heath to toughen Conservative immigration policy to reassure the electorate that their concerns were being acted upon by responsible politicians, but he was also at pains to emphasise the importance of racial harmony. In September in a speech at York just before the Party conference he said 'our main purpose must be to maintain racial harmony. More and more will this become necessary as children of immigrants born British citizens receive their education in British schools and seek to take their rightful place in every walk of British life.'[25] He went on to condemn Powell's April speech, saying 'yet for a few days last April it was touch and go whether Britain would not be torn apart by the same sort of racial hatred that has brought such damage to the United States.'[26] The cause of the outcry, he argued, was a deep-rooted feeling among large sections of the country that there was a problem affecting them personally in their daily lives and over which the government had little or no control. He promised that the Conservatives would introduce permanent legislation

21. Whitelaw, *Memoirs*, 64.

22. Cosgrave, *Lives*, 253.

23. M. Laing, *Edward Heath, Prime Minister* (London, 1972), 198; D. Spearman, 'Enoch Powell's Postbag', *New Society*, 27 June 1968.

24. Chairman's Office, Correspondence on E. Powell's Race Relations Speech, CPA CCO/20/66/1–11.

25. Rt. Hon Edward Heath, 'Immigration and Racial Harmony', Public Meeting, St George's Hall, York, 20 September 1968, CCO/20/66.

26. Ibid.

involving strict and effective controls, that Commonwealth immigrants would only be able to enter Britain under the same conditions as aliens and that dependants would also be subject to controls.[27]

Powell continued his campaign at the party conference and afterward in another dramatic speech at Eastbourne in November. In December the Conservative Political Centre carried out a survey of its 412 constituency groups and found that 327 wanted all immigration stopped indefinitely and a further 55 favoured strictly limited immigration of dependants combined with a five-year ban on new immigration.[28] This confirmed that Powell's views had very strong support among Conservative Party activists.

In January 1969 Heath made a major speech on immigration which set out in detail the new tough immigration policy of the Party. Commonwealth immigrants, like aliens, would have no automatic right to permanent residence. They would be allowed into Britain only for a specific job, in a specific place and for a specific time. Their permit to stay would have to be renewed annually and work permits would have to be renewed every time they changed jobs. There would be no absolute right to bring in relatives, however close. The decision on entitlement to enter would be made in the country of origin and not on arrival in Britain.[29] While these proposals represented a considerable hardening of Conservative Party policy, they no longer would satisfy Powell who now advocated repatriation as a means of reducing the immigrant population in Britain. At the annual Party conference in October, Heath said 'we shall make funds available to assist immigrants who wish to return to their own country of origin. But we are not going to press them; we are not going to harry them; we are going to do everything to prevent a climate being created which will make them wish to leave against their own free will'.[30]

THE GENERAL ELECTION OF 1970

The general election campaign was notable for the lack of attention immigration and race relations issues received from the party leaders. The Conservative manifesto reflected Heath's recent policy statements. It emphasised the importance of good race relations and equality of treatment for all citizens and urged that additional funds should be

27. Heath, 'Immigration and Racial Harmony'.
28. M. Walker, *The National Front* (London, 1977), 111.
29. *The Observer*, 26 January 1969.
30. *The Campaign Guide 1970* (Conservative and Unionist Central Office, 1970), 469.

made available to local authorities to assist integration. It promised that the Conservatives would establish a new system of control over all immigration from overseas and in future work permits would not carry the rights of permanent settlement. No further large-scale permanent immigration would be permitted. Assistance would be provided to Commonwealth immigrants who wished to return to their country of origin.[31] Few Conservative candidates, with one notable exception, raised the issue. The exception, of course, was Powell. He fought his own election campaign independently of the Party machine and, on key issues such as entry to the EEC and immigration, was substantially at odds with Heath. On immigration, he demanded a complete halt to new immigration, a new citizenship law to distinguish UK citizens from everyone else and voluntary repatriation. Otherwise, he argued, the immigration problem could bring a 'threat of division, violence and bloodshed of American dimensions.'[32]

Powell's strategy appears to have been to make a major impact during the campaign, support the Conservative cause despite being at odds with the party leadership and position himself to challenge Heath for the leadership after the widely predicted defeat. This strategy collapsed when the Conservatives won the election and Heath became Prime Minister. Many commentators believe that Powell contributed significantly to the Conservative victory and therefore to the success of his major political rival.[33]

THE IMMIGRATION ACT 1971

The new government, realising the intensity of feeling in the party over immigration, acted quickly to fulfil its manifesto commitments. On 2 July in the Queen's speech, it was announced that legislation would be introduced on Commonwealth immigration and that more assistance would be provided for areas of special need, especially those in which large numbers of immigrants were settled.

In the debate on the Queen's speech, the Prime Minister argued that the aim of the government's immigration policy was 'justice to all those who are already in this country, whatever their race, creed or colour may be, to set the public mind at rest on this issue so that there cannot be any further justification for existing passions and so that

31. *A Better Tomorrow: The Conservative Programme for the Next 5 Years* (Conservative Central Office, 1970), 23–4.

32. D. Schoen, *Enoch Powell and the Powellites* (London, 1977), 51–2.

33. Cosgrave, *Lives*, 286–90.

there can be absolutely no reason for apprehension on the part of immigrants who are already settled here'. Heath paid tribute to the part which Roy Jenkins as previous Home Secretary had played in trying to reach this objective.[34]

The Immigration Bill which the government published in February 1971 was a major departure from previous legislation on Commonwealth immigration. It was to repeal the temporary 1962 Commonwealth Immigrants Act and replace it with permanent legislation. In future, citizens of Commonwealth countries who wished to immigrate would have to apply, like aliens, for work permits instead of employment vouchers. Work permits would not carry the right of permanent residence or the right of entry for dependants. Secondly, the Bill introduced a new term 'patrial' into immigration legislation. A patrial was a person who had the right of abode in the UK and was completely free of all immigration controls. A patrial was defined as a citizen of the UK and colonies whose parents or grandparents were born in the UK; as a citizen of the UK and colonies settled in the UK for five years; and finally, as any Commonwealth citizen who had a parent or grandparent born in the UK.

Introducing the Bill on its second reading the Home Secretary, Maudling, argued that the Bill gave the government greater control and flexibility over immigration and would allow them to carry out their undertaking of the election that there would be no further large-scale immigration.[35] Callaghan, for the opposition, argued that Commonwealth citizens were now to be treated as aliens for immigration purposes. They would lose their statutory right to bring in wives and children under the age of 16 years. This would become an administrative right and thus easier to change, though the Home Secretary argued that there was no intention to do so. Dependants would now be admitted only if the husband and father could provide accommodation as well as financial support. Commonwealth citizens who had been settled for five years could in future be deported on the same basis as aliens. Finally, Commonwealth citizens settled for five years would no longer be able to register as citizens automatically; registration would be at the discretion of the Home Secretary.[36]

In the debate Enoch Powell argued that what was really needed was not an immigration bill but legislation which defined UK citizenship. He did not believe that the Immigration Bill would settle the issue. He had a number of specific criticisms of the Bill, notably the definition

34. *House of Commons Debates*, 5th ser., vol. 803, col. 94, 2 July 1970.
35. *HC Debs.*, 5th ser., vol. 813, col. 56, 8 March 1971.
36. *HC Debs.*, 5th ser., vol. 813, cols 57–60, 8 March 1971.

of patriality which he felt was too broad and divisive. It would include many thousands of Anglo-Indians with one British-born grandparent and divide Australians, for example, into those who were patrials and those who were not. Powell was also disappointed that the Bill did not include stronger provisions for repatriation.[37]

There were a large number of amendments introduced into the Bill at committee stage, the most important of which was a change in the definition of patrials so that only Commonwealth citizens with a British-born parent, rather than grandparent as originally proposed, would qualify as patrials. The government also accepted a large number of Lords amendments, including one which confirmed that Commonwealth immigrants would have the statutory right to bring in their wives and children. This was strongly opposed by Powell. At a late stage the government dropped the provision that non-patrial Commonwealth citizens would have to register with the police. The Bill received the Royal Assent on 21 October 1971.

Powell regarded the Immigration Act as a step – but only a small step – in the right direction. He felt it did not fulfil the commitment to end large-scale immigration, and the powers to operate a voluntary repatriation scheme were woefully inadequate in his view. Two events occurred shortly after the Act was passed to intensify the conflict between him and the leaders of the Conservative Party. The first was the conflict in East Pakistan which resulted in the creation of Bangladesh and the secession of Pakistan from the Commonwealth on 30 January 1972. The second was the expulsion of British passport holders from Uganda in the latter part of the same year.

PAKISTAN'S DEPARTURE FROM THE COMMONWEALTH

The secession of Pakistan from the Commonwealth and the creation of the new independent state of Bangladesh provided the British government, according to Powell, with an unique opportunity to remedy the consequences of the 1948 Nationality Act. This Act had allowed citizens of independent Commonwealth countries, even those that had decided to become republics, to remain British subjects. However, the withdrawal of Pakistan from the Commonwealth meant that Pakistani citizens in the UK ceased to be British subjects and thus they became aliens. Pakistanis therefore, Powell argued, lost the right to vote

37. *HC Debs.*, 5th ser., vol. 813, cols 76–85, 8 March 1971.

and to bring their dependants into Britain. He also argued that the new state of Bangladesh should not be admitted to the Commonwealth and that its citizens should be regarded as aliens too. This would enable the British government to proceed with a repatriation policy returning Pakistani and Bangladeshi nationals to their home countries and remedying in part the 'monstrous occurrence – the implanting in Britain without the assent or even knowledge of her people of a large and growing Asian, West Indian and African population.'[38]

Heath and the Cabinet, however, were strongly opposed to Powell's views. In a press conference in Dehli on 9 February 1972, Sir Alec Douglas-Home said that Pakistanis living in Britain would not suffer as a result of Pakistan leaving the Commonwealth. 'It would not be just', he said, 'if Pakistanis in Britain were made to suffer.'[39] Pakistani voting rights in Britain were allowed to continue, even though it would have been advantageous for the Conservatives to treat them as aliens and remove the right. In 1973 the Pakistan and Bangladesh Acts were passed. The Bangladesh Act recognised Bangladesh as a member of the Commonwealth, thus confirming the voting and other rights of Bangladeshi citizens resident in Britain. The Pakistan Act allowed Pakistani citizens in the UK the rights they had had before Pakistan's withdrawal from the Commonwealth, for a generous transitional period, and also allowed them to continue to register as citizens of the UK and colonies. The Heath government therefore rejected Powell's advice to seize the opportunity to confer alien status on hundreds of thousands of Asians resident in Britain, and to begin the process of their repatriation.

Powell's advice, if taken, would have had immensely damaging effects on community relations in Britain and would have greatly increased the insecurity of Pakistani and Bangladeshi settlers in Britain. It would have legitimated pressure on them to return to their countries of origin and reduced future immigration. These no doubt were Powell's objectives, but the government rightly decided to safeguard community relations by protecting the rights of Pakistani and Bangladeshi permanent residents within the UK and to maintain good relations with Bangladesh and other Commonwealth countries.

The hopes of Heath and other Conservative leaders that the Immigration Act 1971 would finally reassure public opinion and defuse the immigration debate once and for all were brutally shattered on 4 August

38. R. Ritchie (ed.), *Enoch Powell: A Nation or No Nation? Six Years in British Politics* (Kingswood, Surrey, 1979), 70.

39. 'Effects on Pakistan citizens resident in the UK of the withdrawal of Pakistan from the Commonwealth', Conservative Research Department brief for Home Affairs Committee, 14 February 1972, CPA CRD/4/9/18, HAC(72)2.

1972 when President Amin of Uganda announced, to some of his troops, that he would ask the British government to take over responsibility for all Asians in Uganda who were holding British passports, because they were sabotaging the economy.[40] The Foreign Secretary estimated that there were some 57,000 British passport holders in Uganda and he accepted that the British government had an obligation to them.[41]

THE UGANDAN ASIANS

The announcement that Britain might receive some 57,000 Asian immigrants from Uganda, all at once, was greeted with horror in the media and by some politicians, particularly Powell, who claimed that Britain was not responsible for the Asians in East Africa and that they should be returned to India or Pakistan. There was considerable public disquiet about the prospective influx and considerable lobbying of MPs and even the Home Office, which received very substantial mail on the issue. Some local authorities, like Leicester, were reluctant to receive any more Asian immigrants.[42] However, the government decided that if diplomatic efforts to get President Amin to change his mind were unsuccessful, then Britain would keep its word and observe International Law by accepting the British passport holders. On 31st August the Foreign Secretary confirmed this in a ministerial broadcast on television and announced the setting up of a Ugandan Resettlement Board, under Sir Charles Cunningham, to assist their reception, dispersal and integration.

The details of the government's diplomatic response were announced by Robert Carr, the Home Secretary, on 8 September. He said that the government had protested officially to President Amin, it had asked him to treat the Asians with dignity and allow them to leave with their possessions, that they had pressed the Commonwealth and other governments to bring pressure on Amin to change his mind, that they had suspended a £10 million loan to Uganda and suspended new aid. The Government had been in touch with fifty other governments and twelve had offered to accept some Ugandan Asians. It was also in touch with the United Nations and refugee agencies. In Britain the Ugandan Resettlement Board and local authorities would take the lead in settling the refugees. Extra funding would be available to local authorities

40. HC Debs., 5th ser., vol. 842, col. 1260, 7 August 1972.
41. HC Debs., 5th ser., vol. 842, cols 1263–4, 7 August 1972.
42. D. Humphrey and D. Ward, *Passports and Politics* (Harmondsworth, 1974).

through the rate support grant, section 11 funding and the Ugandan Resettlement Board.[43]

The expulsion of the Ugandan Asians and the government's acceptance of its obligation to settle them in Britain received considerable publicity in the media It was a major boost to anti-immigrant organisations both within the Conservative Party, such as the Monday Club, and those further to the right and outside the Party, such as the National Front. The Monday Club, a right-wing group formed to oppose decolonisation in Africa, started a 'Halt Immigration Now' campaign. The Rhodesian crisis and Ugandan Asian immigration provided the Club with popular issues among right-wing Conservatives which enabled it to expand its membership and influence. It claimed 2,000 members of its national organisation including 34 members of parliament and 55 university groups, and an exaggerated 6,000 members of its regional organisation.[44] The Monday Club was very hostile to many of Heath's policies and was particularly obsessed with immigration, where it was very sympathetic to Enoch Powell's views. The National Front, an ultra-right-wing party founded in 1967, exploited the issue for all it was worth, and particularly for the fact that it was a Conservative government, committed to ending New Commonwealth immigration, that had accepted its obligations to the Ugandan Asians. The Front claimed that this was a betrayal of the Conservative Party's electoral promises. The National Front hoped to exploit popular anxieties over immigration and the deep prejudices that Enoch Powell's campaign had revealed by presenting itself as the only anti-immigration party worth supporting. The expulsion of the Ugandan Asians by President Amin enabled the National Front to begin a period of membership growth and electoral advance which gave it a degree of publicity and notoriety which lasted throughout the 1970s until its decisive failure in the general election of 1979.

The divisions within the Conservative Party over the decision to admit the Ugandan Asians reached their climax at the annual Party conference in October when the leadership was presented with a major challenge. A motion on immigration was voted on to the agenda by conference delegates and moved by Powell in his capacity as President of the Hackney South and Shoreditch constituency association whose motion had been successful in the ballot. (It is usual practice at Conservative Party conferences for space on the agenda to be left open for one motion to be selected for debate by representatives in a secret

43. *The Times*, 9 September 1972.
44. Walker, *National Front*, 118.

ballot.) The motion was similar to the one passed in 1969 and declared 'that this conference is convinced that the Conservative Party's declared policy on immigration is the only solution likely to be successful and should be implemented by this Government at the earliest opportunity'.[45] Unfortunately for the Conservative leadership, Powell made it clear that his interpretation of Conservative policy was that new Commonwealth immigration should be halted, even reversed by voluntary repatriation, and that as there was in his view no legal obligation to accept the Ugandan Asians, they should be included under this policy. He warned that the electorate would not forgive a party which left its promises unfulfilled.[46]

However, the Young Conservatives and the Federation of Conservative Students, both under progressive leadership at this time, came to the rescue of the Party leadership. They mobilised their generous conference representation behind an anti-Powellite resolution. David Hunt, the National Chairman of the Young Conservatives, moved an amendment to Powell's motion, deleting all the words after 'successful' and inserting 'and congratulates the Government on its swift action to accept responsibility for the Asian refugees from Uganda'. The Young Conservatives' amendment was carried and the amended resolution won by 1,721 votes to 736, a majority of 985. It was a rare but substantial victory for liberal conservatism which must have delighted the Party leader. But the defeat infuriated many Conservative right-wingers who felt it was the result of a Young Conservative and Conservative Students' coup. This view was expressed in an interview to the author by Anthony Reed-Herbert, who resigned from the Conservative Party after this conference and joined the National Front. He was subsequently to become a leading member of the National Front in Leicester.

The anger felt by many right-wing Conservatives with government policy on immigration led to increasing cooperation between members of the Monday Club and the National Front, and it appeared that this was not only due to common sympathies but also to National Front infiltration of some branches. At the Monday Club rally on 16 September in Central Hall, Westminster, there was ample evidence of National Front participation. Also, during the Uxbridge by-election in December, the West Middlesex branch of the Monday Club was dissolved for endorsing the National Front candidate. There also appeared to be support by members of the North Kent branch of the Monday Club for the anti-Common Market candidate at the Sutton and Cheam

45. Conservative Party, *Annual Conference Report 1972*, 72.
46. Ibid.

by-election which the Tories lost to the Liberals.[47] These activities helped to discredit the Monday Club as an influential group within the Conservative Party and most of its prominent members quickly resigned. The Club then became increasingly involved in an internal struggle over its leadership which was to leave it a spent force by 1974.

THE CRISIS OVER THE IMMIGRATION RULES

Shortly after the annual Party conference the government was dramatically defeated in the House of Commons over the introduction of new immigration Rules. This was a dramatic reverse for the government and has been described by a leading parliamentary expert as 'the most important government defeat on the floor of the House in post-war parliamentary history'.[48] It was the first defeat by a postwar government on a three-line whip. The defeat was brought about by a rebellion of at least 56 Conservative backbenchers, seven of whom, including Enoch Powell, voted against the Rules.[49]

The new immigration Rules were introduced to implement the Immigration Act 1971 and also to bring in changes required by Britain's accession to the Treaty of Rome and membership of the European Economic Community. The government had agreed during the passage of the Immigration Bill that the new Rules, which would be required as a result of the Act, would be subject to the negative resolution procedure and the debate on this was held on 22 November.

The main change introduced by the Rules was to give effect to the sections of the Treaty of Rome laying down Rules for the free movement of workers between European Community countries. These Rules therefore incurred the hostility of many backbenchers, such as Powell, who were opposed to Britain's accession to the Treaty of Rome and membership of the European Economic Community. A consequence of the new Rules was to give European Community nationals easier access to Britain than non-patrial Commonwealth citizens, who were subject to immigration controls. This also antagonised those Conservative MPs who wished to retain the close ties between Britain and the old 'white' Commonwealth countries – particularly Canada, Australia and New Zealand. Outside Parliament, Sir Max Aitken, an enthusiastic supporter of imperial ties, waged an effective

47. Humphrey and Ward, *Passports*, 129–31.

48. P. Norton, 'Intra-party dissent in the House of Commons: a case study of the immigration Rules 1972', *Parliamentary Affairs*, vol. 29 no. 4 (1976), 404.

49. Ibid.

campaign in the *Daily Express* against the new immigration Rules on these grounds. Many Conservatives felt that the Commonwealth had been badly let down by Britain's decision to join the European Community and they mounted a campaign for discrimination in the immigration Rules in favour of the old Commonwealth countries. This campaign had the support of many of their constituents with relatives in these countries. Sir Bernard Braine tabled an Early Day Motion in the Commons arguing that ties with Australia, Canada and New Zealand should not be weakened by vexatious immigration controls and this was signed by 42 Conservative backbenchers.

A third factor in the Government's defeat was back-bench resentment at what was regarded as Heath's high-handed and authoritarian leadership. Conservative backbenchers felt railroaded into support for the EEC. Some were sympathetic to the illegal Rhodesian regime and were resentful at the lack of progress in negotiating a settlement. Many MPs were angry at the government's impotence in the face of President Amin's expulsion of the Ugandan Asians. The government failed to recognise the strength of back-bench feeling and refused to make any concessions. The government whips believed that the Rules would command a small majority, but to ensure maximum support the Home and Foreign Secretaries opened and closed the debate for the government. In spite of this, the immigration Rules were rejected by a majority of 35. Harold Wilson then asked the Prime Minister if he was going to resign but Heath replied, 'The House has rejected two statements made in accordance with Acts passed by the House. Statements to replace them will be laid in due course.'[50]

After extensive consultations with backbenchers, new Rules were laid before the House on 25 January 1973. The major changes introduced were that anybody with a grandparent born in the UK would not need a work permit before immigrating to the UK. This, in effect, widened the definition of patriality to that originally proposed in the Immigration Bill. Also, it was agreed that the working holidaymaker scheme for Commonwealth citizens would normally be for a minimum period of 12 months. These changes were sufficient to satisfy back-bench feelings and the new Rules were easily passed on 21 February 1973 when the government had a majority of 43. However, many backbenchers felt that Heath and his government had been taught a much needed lesson in party management and that the original defeat over the immigration Rules would make the Prime Minister more sensitive to the need to consult and carry his backbenchers with him.

50. *HC Debs.*, 5th ser., vol. 846, cols 1458–9, 22 November 1972.

In December there was a wide-ranging debate in the Commons on Immigration and Race Relations, ostensibly to discuss three important reports from the Select Committee on Race Relations and Immigration. These were concerned with housing, police–immigrant relations and education.[51] However, Robert Carr, the Home Secretary, used the occasion to outline government policy and in particular to reassure his Party that the 1971 Immigration Act was working and that immigration controls were effective. He argued that the four principles of government policy were first, that Britain should have no second-class citizens; second, that further permanent immigration must be cut to a small and inescapable minimum; third, that new immigration must be reserved for close dependant relatives of those lawfully settled and also for the UK passport holders to whom obligations are owed; and finally, that illegal immigration must be halted. Carr argued that immigration was declining, including that of dependants.[52] The opposition accused the government of using administrative delays to influence the immigration figures and of failing to take action to promote harmonious community relations.[53] Some Conservative backbenchers felt the government was underestimating the potential of further New Commonwealth immigration and Enoch Powell continued his fierce criticism of government policy.[54]

CONCLUSION

The Heath government inherited an extremely difficult legacy in the area of immigration and race relations. On the one hand, Heath abhorred racism and was determined to promote good community relations and integration. He was resolutely opposed to Powell's inflammatory language and extreme policy proposals such as large-scale repatriation. On the other hand, Heath and his advisers recognised that there was considerable support in the Conservative Party and among the electorate for Powell's policies on immigration. Powell's speeches and the publicity they received had intensified public anxieties about immigration, increased support for tougher controls and generated support for anti-immigrant and racist groups such as the Monday Club

51. House of Commons, Select Committee on Race Relations and Immigration, Session 1970–71, Housing, 22 July 1971; Session 1970–71, Police/Immigrant Relations, 3 August 1972; Session 1972–3, Education, 24 July 1973.

52. *HC Debs.*, 5th ser., vol. 865, cols 1469–70, 6 December 1973.

53. *HC Debs.*, 5th ser., vol. 865, cols 1485–98, 6 December 1973.

54. *HC Debs.*, 5th ser., vol. 865, cols 1531–7, 6 December 1973.

and the National Front. Heath was forced to recognise the widespread support for Powell, especially among Conservatives, and so agreed to tough new policies before the 1970 general election. Ironically, Powell's campaign for an end to Commonwealth immigration helped to win the general election for his implacable rival.[55]

Heath's strategy was to reassure public opinion and reduce Powell's momentum by acting quickly to introduce the 1971 Immigration Act. However, Heath was not able to control international events, and the announcement by President Amin that British Asian passport holders would be expelled from Uganda provoked an unexpected immigration crisis. The crisis was greatly exaggerated by the media as the number of Ugandan Asians was not large and they were a skilled and well educated community. Also their reception and settlement was well managed by the government. Nevertheless the impression was created that immigration was not under the government's control. The election promise that large-scale permanent immigration would be ended appeared to have been broken and this was exploited by anti-immigrant groups.

The acceptance of the Ugandan Asians by the Heath government was not a change in immigration policy but an acceptance of Britain's obligations to British passport holders who had become the victims of an arbitrary and brutal regime. Heath had the cabinet behind him and much of the Party, as could be seen at the annual party conference, but Powell had the support of an uncomfortably large minority.

Heath took a considerable personal interest in immigration and race relations issues. He was appalled at the willingness of some of his colleagues to exploit these sensitive and emotional issues for party advantage. He consistently did everything he could to prevent this, even when it was to the electoral disadvantage of his Party. While he supported tough immigration controls and introduced the 1971 Immigration Act, he strongly opposed both Powell's rhetoric and his inhumane policy proposals, on one occasion denouncing Powell as 'unchristian' and as 'an intolerable example of man's inhumanity to man'.[56] The verdict of history is likely to be that Heath's policies in this area were courageous and consistent. He acted as a national statesman and not merely as the leader of a political party.

55. Schoen, *Enoch Powell*, 45–68.
56. Cosgrave, *Lives*, 270.

CHAPTER TEN

The Heath government and Northern Ireland

Paul Arthur

HEATH, POWELL AND THE NORTHERN IRELAND PROBLEM

Hindsight is a useful commodity for a politician; it serves as a safeguard against the slings and arrows of outrageous commentary. Edward Heath may have had more recourse to it than most recent Prime Ministers because posterity has not been kind to his governance. Admittedly he had to confront several unexpected problems during his years of office as well as the constant crises which face any government. Included among the latter were a harrowing confrontation with the trade union movement; the debilitating battle within Parliament (and within the Conservative Party) to ensure UK entry into the EEC; and a spate of social protests induced to some extent by a Prime Minister intent on modernisation and redefining Britain's place in the world. All of these might be described as discretionary items on the political agenda. It was the required items which may have tipped the balance against the return of a Heath government in February 1974. They included the sudden death of Iain Macleod – a politician of real weight and a counterpoint to Heath – less than five weeks into office; the disastrous effects of the aftermath of the Yom Kippur War on energy policy and on the continuing battle against inflation; and the growing and exhausting impact of the Northern Ireland conflict. Indeed John Campbell has concluded that the first two months of 1972 'must rate as the most dreadful short period of concentrated stress ever endured by a British government in peacetime – at any rate before the autumn of 1992'.[1] In early 1972 the Conservative ministry faced a six-week miners' strike; unemployment figures of over one million – the highest since 1947; a fiercely contested parliamentary battle on enabling legislation to take Britain into the EEC; and a huge surge in violence in Northern Ireland.

1. J. Campbell, *Edward Heath: A Biography* (London, 1993), 406.

If we are to examine Heath's policy in Northern Ireland, we need to be conscious of this pressure-cooker environment. We need to employ hindsight because, arguably, the Prime Minister can take the credit for having mapped out the parameters which have shaped policy towards the Anglo-Irish question in the intervening years. Much of the attention has focused on his first Secretary of State, William Whitelaw, but he was Heath's man and there is no question that the Prime Minister invested a huge amount of political and moral capital on the whole issue after, it has to be said, he had delivered the country on the question of Europe. Posterity may conclude that Europe and paradoxically, Ireland were the most successful of Heath's policies. They have to be taken in conjunction with industrial relations as the dominating themes of these years. Interestingly, Europe and Ireland were to be the obsessions of Heath's chief Conservative rival, Enoch Powell. Policy and personality loomed large in the Heath years.

When Stormont was prorogued in March 1972 and direct rule imposed from Westminster it was the first time since 1921 that Parliament had accepted full and exclusive responsibility for legislation for Northern Ireland; and when the British and Irish governments signed the Anglo-Irish Agreement on 15 November 1985 it was the first time that Parliament had recognised in a treaty registered at the United Nations that the government of the Republic of Ireland had a constructive role to play in the governance of Northern Ireland. The buckle which joined both of these events together was the Sunningdale conference of December 1973 – it was what Enoch Powell would have called 'a pre-play'.[2] Sunningdale was the pre-play to the Anglo-Irish Agreement, and the 'key figure in Heath's private office',[3] Robert Armstrong, his Principal Private Secretary, was (as Cabinet Secretary) the individual who played a major role in persuading Mrs Thatcher to sign the 1985 Agreement. The irony would not have been lost on Heath who acknowledged as much when he spoke in the Commons debate on the Anglo-Irish Agreement: 'The Leader of the Official Unionists said yesterday that there is nothing in the agreement that was not in the Sunningdale agreement, and that is right.'

Heath went on to expound on his own interests in Irish affairs. Interestingly, he traced them to his time as Chief Whip and the beginning of the European Community entry negotiations when he went to Belfast in 1961 (and antagonised some Unionists then by refusing to

2. Cited in J. Ranelagh, *Thatcher's People: An Insider's Account of the Politics, the Power and the Personalities* (London, 1992), viii.

3. Campbell, *Edward Heath*, 488.

countenance a permanent Northern Ireland observer in his delegation) through to the culmination of negotiations in 1972:

> It is because I believe that the present Government of the Republic has been the most helpful of all the Governments with whom I have had acquaintance that I thought it was right – I said so at the time – that the government should accept the settlement of the common agricultural policy, which gave a considerable advantage to the Republic. We were helping our friends. Some of the encouragement has borne fruit and will continue to do so. The great threat is violence in Northern Ireland and this agreement can lead to much closer cooperation between the two Governments in dealing with violence. Why should we want to maintain barriers when we are working more closely with such a large part of the world? I fail to understand the outlook of people who want to keep the barriers and indeed to profit from the barriers that exist today.[4]

This statement encapsulates not only his policy towards Ireland but his general outlook during the time he was Prime Minister. It was a position he had alluded to already in October 1963 when he appeared on 'Panorama' to pay homage to Harold Macmillan, the retiring Prime Minister. He singled out 'in particular his "extraordinary constructive imagination", his "power of concilation", his "recognition of interdependence as being the most important feature of this part of the century" and his sense of history.'[5]

History may well judge that Heath possessed three of those qualities but failed in the area of conciliation and of communication. In relation to Ireland his sense of history, awareness of interdependence and a constructive imagination all played their role in fashioning the most radical attempt since 1920 to get to grips with the conditions which promoted political violence in Ireland. It was not, he admitted, an easy task: 'I have tried to understand these different points of view over a long period . . . I confess that I have always found the Irish, all of them, extremely difficult to understand.'[6] Be that as it may, his contribution may prove to be profound in the longer term. At the very least he set the standards and established the parameters which were to shape British policy towards the wider Irish question over the following two decades.

It is conceivable that Enoch Powell would share that judgement but would not read it in so positive a light. He, too, had a constructive imagination and a sense of history and of continuity. But he parted company on the question of interdependence. In the last election in which he stood as a Conservative candidate he described the 'great

4. *House of Commons Debates*, 6th series, vol. 87, col. 898, 27 November 1985.
5. Campbell, *Edward Heath*, 147.
6. *HC Debs*, 6th series, vol. 87, col. 898, 27 November 1985.

dangers facing Britain' as 'Commonwealth immigration, the Common Market, and Socialism, in that order'.[7] Within a few years he was to invite the electorate to vote Labour, and 'Northern Ireland' had joined his list. Needless to say his understanding of Heath's policy towards Northern Ireland shared little with that of the conventional wisdom. In a debate on the Northern Ireland Act 1974 (Interim Period Extension), he argued that in imposing direct rule 'it was not the intention in doing so to bring Northern Ireland into congruence with the rest of the United Kingdom. The object was to establish in Northern Ireland a more susceptible or more manageable form of local administration which would still serve the purpose of arriving at some sort of accommodation with the Irish Republic and its desire for the amalgamation of the North of Ireland':

> That is what direct rule is about. It is not the consequence of Northern Ireland being recognised as part of the United Kingdom, for it is the consequence of a continuing determination to apply what used to be de Valera's formula for reuniting Ireland, the combination of Ulster autonomy with the English interest. Hon. Members may take that phrase and apply it as the key to the political history of the relations between the Government in the United Kingdom and that Province of the United Kingdom from 1920 onwards. If they do so, they will find that the key fits the lock.[8]

Here, then, are two interpretations of how the Northern Ireland problem was being handled. Both were enunciated with a sense of history but with competing perspectives. One asserts that the decisions of the 1970s and 1980s can be found in the flawed Government of Ireland Act 1920 with its devolutionist bias; the other is set in the geopolitical circumstances of the contemporary world. Interdependence was to be the way forward in the Heathite version; it was to be a weasel word in Powellism: '. . . the opposition to its policies in every sphere – immigration, Ulster, Rhodesia and the economy (as well as Europe) – was spearheaded by Enoch Powell . . .'[9]

Northern Ireland may not have been part of Powell's election concerns in 1970 but it would be foolish to imagine that he was not conscious of its significance to the 'identity' of the United Kingdom. He raised it in a speech in North Wales in September 1968 – that is, before the 'Troubles' had broken out – in the context of the debate about devolution inside the United Kingdom. He did not return to it

7. A. Alexander and A. Watkins, *The Making of the Prime Minister 1970* (London, 1970), 175.

8. *HC Debs.*, 6th series, vol. 63, col. 110, 2 July 1984.

9. Campbell, *Edward Heath*, 512.

publicly until the early 1970s but there is evidence that he had a deep interest in what was happening inside the province before then.[10] In that respect he was ahead of the mainstream of the Conservative Party for whom Northern Ireland was unknown territory. Insofar as it was known it was assumed to be safe Conservative *and* Unionist territory which was best left to its own devices. Hence when the Tories did come into office they adopted a strategy which was dissimilar to that of their Labour predecessors, with a greater emphasis on security than on reform. Northern Ireland was the concern of the Home Secretary, Reginald Maudling, but Maudling was no Jim Callaghan. The 'Troubles' had thrown a lifeline to Callaghan and offered him an escape from other policy failures: he realised its potential in terms of his own career. Maudling had no such incentive; nor did he share the advantages of being an interventionist, because by 1970 the complexities and the historic animosities of the problem had come to the surface. Labour's reform programme had created a revolution in rising expectations among Catholics and a sense of betrayal in the Protestant community. Maudling had enough on his plate with rising social protest and growing concerns over immigration. Northern Ireland was a place apart. Besides, the government was going to need whatever help it could get from Unionist MPs.

THE GENESIS OF DIRECT RULE.

Traditionally, relations between Stormont and Westminster had been cosy rather than intimate. The memoirs of politicians and officials clearly capture this complicity. This interpretation is confirmed by William Fitzsimmons who had held various portfolios in different Unionist administrations. He maintained that communication between both governments was extremely limited until the outbreak of the Troubles:

> Until Heath imposed direct rule, I hardly knew Westminster existed. Whenever I was appointed to a job, I would go over and meet the relevant minister in London. He would give me a glass of sherry and we would have a little chat for twenty minutes. Then I would go home and forget all about Westminster until the next time. And the money kept flowing in.[11]

10. I base this on conversations I had with Unionists who were in touch with Mr Powell at the time. For some of his public utterances see E. Powell, *Still To Decide* (Surrey, 1972), 170–89.

11. Quoted in J. Downey, *Them and Us: Britain, Ireland and the Northern Question 1969–1982* (Dublin, 1983), 14–15.

Unionist MPs at Westminster were careful not to make waves. Indeed, such was their profile that very few of them reached even the lower ranks of government. With the exception of Robin Chichester-Clark, the totality of Unionism's contribution to government amounted to one Parliamentary Secretary and three Parliamentary Private Secretaries between 1921 and 1970. Chichester-Clark, elected in 1955, had been Lord Commissioner of the Treasury in 1960, Comptroller of the Royal Household 1961–64 and chief Conservative spokesman on Northern Ireland 1964–70. He was close to Heath and acted as his polling agent for the leadership contest, but he was not rewarded until 1972 when he became Minister of State at Employment, a post he held until the February 1974 election for which he had not sought renomination. During the period of the Heath premiership, his was a pivotal position because he was Chairman of the Unionist MPs at Westminster 1971–74 and was the brother of James Chichester-Clark who was Northern Ireland's Prime Minister between May 1969 and March 1971. During this period both brothers kept in close touch; and in the matter which led to the Prime Minister's resignation – 'ineffective' security policy – he voted against the government in January 1971.

On the other hand, the Social Democratic and Labour Party (SDLP), the constitutional nationalist opposition, believed that too much emphasis was being placed on security, thereby alienating the Catholic community and (inadvertently) acting as recruiting agents for the Provisional Irish Republican Army (IRA). In the competition between Sinn Fein and the SDLP for the hearts and minds of the Catholic community, repressive security policies damaged constitutionalism. A tougher security policy was evident within two weeks of the Conservatives taking office. On the weekend of 3–4 July 1970, 1500 troops imposed a curfew on the Catholic Lower Falls area of Belfast. The result was the alienation of the nationalist population – an alienation which could be seen in the figures for loss of life from violence in Northern Ireland between 1969 and 72. There were 15 in 1969, 25 in 1970, 173 in 1971 and 474 in 1972 – the highest number to die in any single year of the Troubles. These figures cannot be studied in isolation from the wider political process but are mentioned in this context simply to illustrate the deepening security crisis . . . and the temptation to seek a response based purely on security considerations.

Indeed a case can be made for suggesting that security policy was the issue which led to the imposition of direct rule. The introduction of internment in August 1971, followed by allegations of brutality in army bases and, as the last straw, the impact of Bloody Sunday on 30 January 1972, had the cumulative impact of persuading the government that it needed to take full responsibility for Northern Ireland policy. Yet it was something which both Labour and Conservatives had been anxious to avoid. It had been mooted as early as August 1969, but, as James Callaghan recalled in his memoirs, the government was too well aware of its ignorance of Northern Ireland and was uncertain as to how the police and indigenous civil service would react to its introduction. When the Conservatives took office, the Prime Minister's attention was directed towards other matters. Internment was probably the first occasion on which he had had to give sustained thought to the question.

While he was sluggish in confronting the question, he began to take a closer interest once Brian Faulkner had succeeded James Chichester-Clark as Prime Minister in March 1971. He 'responded immediately to his energy, decisiveness and professionalism', a view which was reciprocated. Yet the decision on internment created his first real doubts about Faulkner: 'Heath was anxious about the decision. He was right to be. He should have put his foot down and disallowed it. But he was impressed by Faulkner. He wanted to support him, and he wanted to smash the IRA if it could be done.'[12] The Prime Minister may have been influenced by a threat from Robin Chichester-Clark in July to withdraw Unionist support altogether unless there were a tougher anti-terrorist policy. In the short term he continued to give full support to Faulkner and told him at Chequers on 19 August that he had no intention of imposing direct rule. Nonetheless, internment had been a disaster and a marvellous bonus for the IRA. The time was fast approaching when what Harold Wilson had called 'a council of despair', the imposition of direct rule, had to be contemplated.

It might also be said that the security response was a council of despair. The facts were that the Royal Ulster Constabulary (RUC) and their auxiliaries had long since lost all sympathy and support in the Catholic community. They were perceived as being an armed militia of the Unionist establishment, a perception given some weight in government reports and also in the opinion of Sir Arthur Young (who had been brought in from the Metropolitan Police to take control of the RUC) when he complained of 'a conspiracy of silence' inside his own force after a particular incident. Government came to rely more and more on the Army, but it lacked local intelligence and training in civilian control and used inappropriate riot-control agents such as CS gas. A circularity of violence was being induced whereby confrontation led to security force over-reaction which led to growing support for

12. Campbell, *Edward Heath*, 426, 427.

the IRA which led to government's desire to bring the violence under control. It was in these circumstances that internment was introduced.

Internment had been moderately successful as a security measure in 1921–24, 1938–45, and 1956–62 (when Faulkner had been the Minister in charge). It began on 9 August 1971 when over 300 men were detained, and lasted until 5 December 1975, by which time 2,158 'graduates' had passed through the internment camps. It led to huge resentment and failed to control the violence: of the 172 who died violently in 1971 only 28 were killed before internment was introduced. The bulk of IRA activists escaped the security swoop largely because RUC security files were out of date. Many of those detained in the first swoop had not been involved in the current troubles and so the operation was seen by Catholics as yet another attack on their community.

Direct rule was imposed simply because governments (in Belfast and London) were

> unable to perform that classic function of government, the provision of public order, which was essential if the United Kingdom state was to become an object of allegiance on the part of ghetto Catholics . . . Whereas in 1969 Stormont had lost this monopoly in Catholic territory largely because it lacked agencies of physical force capable of treating Catholics as citizens rather than as enemies, the events of 1969–72 demonstrated that even when ethnically neutral forces were placed at its disposal the regime was incapable of devising policies which would transform mere force into effective authority.[13]

In short, the policy of direct rule by proxy had failed. Westminster could neither rule nor properly control events at a distance. The fiasco of internment had proved that; and allegations of Army brutality in its aftermath compounded the need to take drastic action. As a consequence of the allegations, the Home Secretary set up a three-man enquiry to review interrogation procedures under Sir Edmund Compton. Its report in March 1972 carried a minority rider from the former Lord Chancellor, Lord Gardiner, who 'strongly condemned them as "secret, illegal, not morally justifiable and alien to the traditions" of British democracy. Heath, to his credit, accepted Gardiner's minority report and promised that the use of "intensive techniques" would cease.'[14] That cannot have been an easy decision – a Conservative Prime Minister with a good war record was accepting criticisms of army

13. D.W. Miller, *Queen's Rebels: Ulster Loyalism in Historical Perspective* (Dublin, 1978), 148–9.

14. Campbell, *Edward Heath*, 428.

behaviour and siding with what would have been interpreted as a nationalist interpretation. Here was a rare example of moral courage from a leading politician.

Most commentators assert that it was Bloody Sunday – 30 January 1972, when paratroopers shot dead thirteen (a fourteenth died some time later) unarmed civilians in Londonderry – which made direct rule inevitable. There may be another consideration. In the welter of activity surrounding Bloody Sunday, few recognised the significance of a legal decision which had arisen following the arrest under the Special Powers Act of two Stormont opposition MPs for refusing to obey the order of an Army officer. They won their appeal to the Northern Ireland High Court on the grounds that s.4(1) of the Government of Ireland Act 1920 did not permit the Special Powers Act to cover the actions of British troops. The matter raised doubts about other major security operations and demonstrated that the legal basis of army operations had never been clarified. Precisely one month before the prorogation of Stormont, the government introduced the Northern Ireland Bill which

> specifically authorised the Northern Ireland Parliament to legislate in respect of the armed forces of the Crown in so far as that was necessary to the maintenance of peace and order in Northern Ireland, and conferred *retrospective* validity on any actions taken before the passing of the act which would otherwise have been invalid.[15]

The bill became law within a matter of hours without a division on the Second or Third Readings. The government's alacrity owed much to concerns about international opinion and, with the fall-out from Bloody Sunday, made direct rule inevitable. When one considers that troop levels rose from 7,000 in 1970 to 21,000 in 1972, then the government's desire to have absolute control was understandable. Add to that the wide array of powers the security forces possessed to deal with the emergency; and the series of reports chaired by members of the judiciary examining areas of security force activity – Cameron, Scarman, Hunt, Gardiner, Compton. Direct rule was a council of despair.

Reaction to it was predictable. The Taoiseach, Jack Lynch, welcomed it as being sufficient to create the climate within which solutions to the Irish question could be found: the initiative, he said, 'imposed the obligation of a response touching constitutional, legal, economic and social matters'. That was a shrewd analysis which was to be confirmed within the year in the Green and White Papers which followed. The

15. K. Boyle, T. Hadden and P. Hillyard, *Law and State: the Case of Northern Ireland* (London, 1975), 132, my italics.

SDLP moved once again towards the mainstream of politics and, before the end of May, called on those Catholics who had withdrawn from participation in public affairs as a protest against internment to return and, in effect, cooperate with the direct rule administration. The republican movement failed to read the signs and assumed that 'one last heave' would see the departure of the British. In fact the opposite was the case. The unionist population was outraged by the decision. Many years later the UUP leader, James Molyneaux MP, was reflecting republican thinking when he told the Commons on 26 November 1985 the 'IRA naturally regarded the decision [to prorogue Stormont] as the first payment of the Danegeld.'[16] One unionist association (Foyle and Londonderry) described it as 'the most complete betrayal since Lundy' (i.e. the siege of Derry of 1689). The Government Committee of the Presbyterian Church 'deplored' the decision. But it was the former Prime Minister, Faulkner, who was most shaken. He firmly believed that he had the confidence of Heath. When they met at Downing Street on the fateful day of 22 March, Faulkner was taken aback to find that the Cabinet had unanimously endorsed the decision to prorogue Stormont: 'It took Faulkner some time to grasp that Heath was not "making an opening bid to soften us up, but . . . was presenting what amounted to an ultimatum".'[17] He reacted by supporting a two-day loyalist strike on 28–9 March which paralysed most of industry; and he told a mass rally at Stormont that he and his ministers not only understood their feelings but shared them.

DIRECT RULE AND THE NORTHERN IRELAND OFFICE

The imposition of direct rule created a democratic deficit – although republicans would maintain that the very creation of Northern Ireland was itself an act in democratic deficiency. Government had to move quickly to impose the conditions for stability. One well informed commentator wrote that when 'the Heath Government took over direct rule of Northern Ireland on 28 March, private estimates in Whitehall of the amount of time that had been "bought" for a peaceful settlement ranged from three to six months.'[18] In an attempt to overcome the problem of lack of accountability, the Secretary of State (who governed through three junior ministers and a newly created Northern Ireland Office [NIO]) told the Commons on 25 May that he had appointed

16. *H.C. Debs*, 6th series, vol. 87, col. 764, 26 November 1985.
17. Campbell, *Edward Heath*, 432.
18. D. Watt, *Financial Times*, 27 April 1973.

an advisory commission of eleven Ulster 'notables' composed of seven Protestants and four Catholics. But it made little impact in the community at large who considered it a sideshow.

The authorities were blessed in the appointment of William Whitelaw as Secretary of State for Northern Ireland. He faced huge administrative and political difficulties. Administration was partially a question of structure: two locations, Belfast and London; two sets of Departments and two civil services co-existing within the one ministry. The office had to be built up incrementally and it needed to be sensitive to inherited animosities. The memoirs of former Northern Ireland civil servants uncover tensions within the indigenous service in the period following direct rule. One Permanent Secretary (who was the second Catholic in the history of Northern Ireland ever to have reached that level) praised both the quality of the NIO team and the performance of the Northern Ireland Civil Service in the difficult days surrounding the imposition of direct rule. But he noted that senior civil servants found themselves 'more closely involved with political matters than is normal':

> Occasionally I felt that in these deliberations bearing on political happenings and initiatives some of my colleagues (particularly when their judgement of events was not in harmony with mine) revealed a less than adequate understanding of past political developments from which some of our contemporary difficulties had, in my view, sprung. They knew almost no Irish history and it must be said that some who had come to us from across the Irish Sea showed that they had aquired more knowledge of Ireland's past than had many of the native-born officials.[19]

Another senior civil servant recorded that relations with the Home Office in the period prior to the establishment of direct rule were a matter of great difficulty. When Whitelaw arrived on 25 March he won the confidence of the civil servants at once. Another problem concerned the intimacy of the local political culture. Successive direct-rule ministers commented on the easy access of interest groups to centres of power which 'encouraged a style of instant politics that concentrates attention on the immediate without adequate concerns for the future.'[20] It was precisely to avoid this that Heath had appointed the Central Policy Review Staff (CPRS). Its input into the Irish conundrum at this time was nonexistent – 'Victor Rothschild was anxious

19. P. Shea, *Voices and the Sound of Drums: An Irish Autobiography* (Belfast, 1981), 191.
20. Lord Windlesham, 'Ministers in Ulster: The Machinery of Direct Rule', *Public Administration*, 51 (1973), 270.

to avoid the big issues of Northern Ireland and defence', in the opinion of one very senior insider.

Politically, the new administration faced massive problems. The IRA felt that history was on its side and extreme loyalists reacted by joining the Ulster Defence Association (UDA) – founded in September 1971 as a paramilitary organisation with the ostensible aim of defending its territory from the IRA. It has been estimated that its numbers grew to 26,000 dues-paying members by the end of 1972, making it the largest paramilitary grouping in the western world.[21] Its reaction to direct rule was hyperactive, ranging from illegal marches by masked and becudgelled men to the creation of loyalist 'no-go' areas. There was an increase, too, in what the authorities called 'motiveless murders' – 80 Catholics and 38 Protestants were murdered before the end of the year. By early 1973 loyalists were being interned alongside republicans and in February they called a one-day strike which led to the deaths of five people. Similarly, the IRA had rejected the prorogation of Stormont as too little too late.

In all of these circumstances the establishment of the NIO was a triumph over adversity. It was conceived as a temporary phenomenon; it was an exercise in crisis management; and it operated under the impact of political violence and the ensuing political uncertainty. Administrative evolution had to follow the more pressing security and political problems, although there was the bonus in efficiency – security policy was now the sole responsibility of the UK government. Direct rule came into force on 30 March 1972 following the enactment of the Northern Ireland (Temporary Provisions) Act 1972. The NIO was staffed by officers mainly on loan from the Home Office, the Ministry of Defence, and the Foreign and Commonwealth Office and was paid for out of the Home Office budget. This caused some problems for officials in Belfast:

> The secretary of state's Northern Ireland office in Belfast was understandably staffed for the greater part with officials from London and was quite separate from our Northern Ireland departments . . . Bill Neild recognised the danger at once . . . We therefore advised ministers and the secretary of state direct; and the Northern Ireland Office concentrated rather on security, parliamentary matters, and preparations for the constitutional settlement that was to come.[22]

Despite these tensions, the transition to direct rule was reasonably

21. S. Bruce, *The Red Hand: Protestant Paramilitaries in Northern Ireland* (Oxford, 1992), 59.

22. J. Oliver, *Working At Stormont* (Dublin, 1978), 104.

smooth. The business of government went on as normal; it was political control that had changed. The 15,100 members of the Northern Ireland civil service carried out their normal work and the Cabinet Office at Stormont remained. The real change was the replacement of the Northern Ireland Cabinet structure with meetings chaired by the Secretary of State and attended by his ministers, by the principal civil advisers and usually by the heads of the security forces. Over time, the two civil services were to become more integrated. Most commentaries on the period have concentrated on security and political change but it is important to record what was in effect an administrative revolution conducted under very difficult circumstances when trust was at a low premium. One indication of the levels of suspicion can be found in Cecil King's diary. On 6 April 1971, for example, he records Peter Carrington as being 'appalled by the bigotry, drunkenness and stupidity of the Unionist Party'. The diary records the same sentiments being expressed by William Whitelaw on 26 May 1972: 'He is appalled by the bigotry and fear so much in evidence among the Protestants . . . Willy says his civil servants are excellent, but are quite irrational at the prospect of being absorbed into a united Ireland . . .'[23]

It is important to be aware of this atmosphere because the major difficulty was not so much with the machinery of government as with the nature of the problem. The Heath government may have had all the necessary contingency plans for imposing direct rule but he and his team were neither psychologically adjusted nor intellectually prepared for what was to come. Again Cecil King can act as our guide: 'Ted evidently knew no Irish history [but he] had laid down the policy to be pursued and that was that' (16 October 1970). Over tea with the diarist on 6 March 1971 Heath confessed that 'he disliked Enoch Powell more than somewhat, and that he had never considered a comprehensive solution of the Irish problem'. By August he was beginning to turn his attention to Ireland, consulting both King and Cardinal Heenan, although on 3 December 'Ted is reiterating his determination to find a military solution, in spite of all the evidence from the past . . .' With the introduction of direct rule they were to find that it was emotionally draining for those who came to the issue for the first time and that it was incredibly time-consuming. Douglas Hurd, who worked in Heath's private office between 1970 and 1974, describes the effect it had on the prime minister: '. . . the subject had a very high emotional content. To those who dealt with it, including the Prime Minister, it

23. C. King, *The Cecil King Diary 1970–1974* (London, 1975), passim.

was clearly the most important matter of the moment.'[24] The same impression is conveyed in Campbell's biography when he writes that over their four years in office they probably spent more time on Northern Ireland than on any other single subject; and he quotes Heath at the 1972 Conservative Party conference as saying that in 'terms of human misery' Ulster was 'the most terrible problem that we as a Government . . . have had to face. It haunts us every day.'[25]

The Irish problem interfered with European business and in the very serious coal miners' strike. It led him to postpone a vital cabinet reshuffle until November 1973 and to question whether he should call a general election in February 1974. It put the hastily assembled NIO into fourth place in the Commons league table of hours consumed in parliamentary business in the first fourteen months of its existence, ahead of such giants as the Home Office and the Foreign Office. With the prorogation of Stormont the remainder of the legislative programme for the 1971–72 session was transferred to Westminster. But, above all, the problem was 'different in kind from any other, because it touched the very integrity of the United Kingdom'.[26] A new constitutional architecture was needed; and, since direct rule was considered to be temporary, it was decided to proceed by way of Order in Council. This allowed for pre-legislative discussion but curtailed parliamentary debate and ensured that draft Orders could not be amended, only approved or rejected. That was a source of discontent to Unionist MPs who had been used to the easygoing ways of Stormont and to a convivial relationship with their Tory counterparts.

THE 'PRE-PLAY' OF NEGOTIATIONS

It was left to Whitelaw to feel his way through this political minefield. He did so assiduously and kept lines open to the two communities. He pursued a policy of steady release of IRA internees – but not at such a rate as would offend Protestant opinion absolutely. As a *quid pro quo* he stressed the economic advantages of the Union – in May 1972, for example, he announced a £35 million expansion plan for the ailing Belfast shipyard which would provide extra work for its overwhelmingly Protestant force. All these efforts won him the (not entirely hostile loyalist) epithet of 'Willy Whitewash'.

24. D. Hurd, *An End to Promises: Sketch of a Government 1970–1974* (London, 1979), 102.
25. Campbell, *Edward Heath*, 423.
26. Ibid., 423.

Whitelaw made one serious attempt to woo republicanism. In June 1972 he introduced 'special category status' into the prisons at a time when an IRA leader was close to death on hunger strike. Special category status enabled them to distinguish themselves from ordinary criminals and allowed them to organise their own prison regime. The IRA took this as sign that the government was prepared to parley with it *even* against the advice of the Irish government. On 26 June a ceasefire was called, and early in July secret talks were held in London between Whitelaw and republicans including IRA Chief of Staff, Sean MacStiofain, Gerry Adams and Martin McGuinness. They demanded *inter alia* that the government should declare its intention 'to withdraw all forces from Irish soil' by January 1975. Two days after the talks, the IRA broke the truce by staging a confrontation with the army, and then it broke the news of the secret talks.

The results of these initiatives were paradoxical. Whitelaw concluded that the immediate impact of the granting of special category status 'was limited and it was later found to have been a misguided decision'. Certainly it laid the foundations for the hunger strikes of 1980–81, events which poisoned Anglo-Irish relations and probably caused more bitterness between the two communities within Northern Ireland in the short term than any other single decision. On the other hand, as a result of the meeting with the IRA, he 'gained from what might easily have proved a dangerously mistaken decision.'[27] His reasoning was based on the fact that it was the IRA which appeared to be intransigent whereas the government was perceived as conciliatory. Indeed, one of his most senior officials confessed that 'the negotiations were not serious or substantive: "It was a case of letting the dog see the rabbit".'[28] All of this enabled Whitelaw to establish a much warmer relationship with the SDLP, which augured well for a constitutional settlement. However, that has to be set against a context in which there was growing concern in government about the outgrowth of 'no-go' areas where the rule of law no longer prevailed, in both loyalist and republican ghettoes. Matters came to a head after 'Bloody Friday' (21 July 1972) when the IRA set off a series of bombs in Belfast, killing ten civilians and three soldiers. 'Operation Motorman' followed ten days later when, in a huge military exercise, the army moved into no-go areas removing barricades and restoring the semblance of normality.

Government was involved in a twin-track approach, and some would argue that it moved into its most creative phase since partition

27. W. Whitelaw, *The Whitelaw Memoirs* (London, 1990), 121, 131.
28. Downey, *Them and Us*, 113.

between mid-1972 and March 1973. Northern Ireland became an adventure playground for constitutional experts and policy-makers. During this period the balance of power shifted away from the Unionist Party towards the SDLP and the Irish government. This shift needs some explanation. We know that the Prime Minister started with a minimalist approach towards the problem. Insofar as he had any prejudices they were in favour of the status quo and support for the dyanamic leadership of Brian Faulkner from March 1971. But that support was dissipated on security-related matters. Internment and all that ensued had been a public relations disaster. 'Bloody Sunday' brought down international opprobrium on the Heath government. In the meantime, with European legislation safely behind him, Ted Heath began to give sustained attention to Northern Ireland. He had already revealed that a Prime Minister 'has to decide himself in which spheres he is going to concentrate . . . It's then up to him to limit those and so organise himself that he can deal with it'. The three issues on which he chose to concentrate were Europe, Northern Ireland, and prices and income policy. These, he believed were matters on which only the Prime Minister had the authority to deal with the parties concerned.[29]

His train of thought was brutally unveiled in Downing Street on 22 March 1972 when he had his fateful meeting with Faulkner and his colleagues. The result was the prorogation of Stormont and what appeared to be a petulant reaction by the unionist leadership. Heath was now in the business of seeking new allies. He was not to find it among republicans and he found most loyalists to be uncongenial. When he made his first extended visit to Northern Ireland in November 1972, he made no attempt to hide his exasperation; in March 1973, he told an Ulster Television interviewer

> how much offence it gives to the rest of the United Kingdom to hear people who are prepared to say they will not work the institutions, they will not abide by the law which was passed at Westminster, that they will wreck this or wreck that. To describe them as 'loyalists' is completely untrue . . . they are in fact disloyalists.[30]

By this stage Heath had abandoned all hopes of finding a purely internal settlement to the problem. After a shaky start he began to build a rapport with the Irish Taoiseach, Jack Lynch. Each was genuinely suspicious of the other. Some members of the Fianna Fail Cabinet had been arraigned before the courts (and acquitted) on charges of gun-

29. Campbell, *Edward Heath*, 486–7.
30. *Irish Times*, 30 March 1973.

running for beleaguered Catholics in the north after August 1969, and Fianna Fail had proudly proclaimed itself a republican party. Equally, the Irish government believed that Heath was in thrall to unionism when he took office in 1970. Megaphone diplomacy did not help. Although Lynch had told the United Nations on 22 October 1970 that he placed his trust in 'quiet diplomacy and personal conversation', that was not always possible with his need to balance hawks and doves within Fianna Fail. Hence, when Faulkner visited Chequers in August 1971, Lynch sent Heath an open telegram demanding reforms in Northern Ireland and an alternative to the security solution. Heath replied in kind, telling him that he had no right to interfere in the affairs of the United Kingdom. Within a matter of weeks, however, the Taoiseach was at Chequers.

The two-day prime ministerial summit at Chequers on 6–7 September between Heath and Lynch was highly charged:

> This meeting turned out to have a significance that we never suspected at the time. Indeed I do not think that Jack Lynch has ever had proper acknowledgement for successfully persuading Heath to adopt a major change of policy. Until then Heath had listened almost exclusively to Faulkner, who sold him the line that internment would solve the IRA problem, halt the violence, and make everything else fall neatly into place. After the Chequers summit things changed . . .[31]

Garret FitzGerald also acknowledges that it was 'a meeting that marked a significant advance on the British side since it recognised the Irish Government's legitimate interest in a situation threatening the security of both parts of the island'.[32] In its turn, that led three weeks later to the first tripartite prime ministerial meeting at Chequers which Campbell describes as 'the first acknowledgement by a British Government of an "Irish dimension" to the Ulster problem'.[33] All of this might suggest that Heath's Irish policy was already in place before the imposition of direct rule. But that would be to leap too far ahead in the narrative. We know that he worried about the impact of security policy on his European partners and feared even that it could interfere with EEC negotiations. We know, too, that he maintained a bipartisan policy with the Labour opposition. We are informed, too, that 'Heath always had a sympathy with the SDLP – dating back to a private meeting with Hume in his Albany flat, when Heath was Opposition

31. P. Devlin, *Straight Left: An Autobiography* (Belfast, 1993), 162–3.
32. G. FitzGerald, *All in a Life: An Autobiography* (Dublin, 1991), 99.
33. Campbell, *Edward Heath*, 428.

leader . . .'[34] But it would be too deterministic to assume that Irish policy was written already in tablets of stone. The more likely explanation for the shift in emphasis lay in failed security policies and a greater concentration on the politics of interdependence.

In that respect he was in tune with constitutional nationalism even after a change in government in Dublin in March 1973. In his first major policy speech as Minister for Foreign Affairs, Garret FitzGerald told the Dail on 9 May 1973 that it was time to formulate new general guidelines for future foreign policy because of the movement towards greater interdependence in the world economy, the 'evolving situation in Northern Ireland', and 'the accession to membership of the European Communities'. Heath would have concurred with all of that. Indeed, there is evidence that there had been a degree of collusion between the British and Irish governments over the contents of the White Paper, 'Northern Ireland: constitutional proposals' (Cmd.5259) of March 1973. An Irish coalition government had come into office on 14 March 1973 to be told that the Heath government was putting the final touches to its White Paper and would be making a final decision within 48 hours. FitzGerald set to work immediately on a draft document which, he told the Dail on 9 May, 'I understand, from my subsequent contacts, to be taken fully into consideration and to influence the shaping of the White Paper'. It was this Paper which gave formal recognition to the concept of an 'Irish dimension'.

Earlier in the same debate the Taoiseach, Liam Cosgrave, had expounded on the parameters of that dimension:

> The full measure of the problem of Northern Ireland is that reconciliation between its two communities cannot be brought about successfully in isolation from the larger issue of reconciliation within the island as a whole. The two issues are inseparable . . . This is the real meaning of the 'Irish dimension' . . . It is a 'dimension' – an essential, and not a secondary, aspect of the problem. This means that it must be faced if the problem is to be solved. It is primarily as an institution which could respond to this need, and not simply as a means of smoothing out minor overlapping problems deriving from a common border, that a Council of Ireland seems to be called for.

What Faulkner had considered to be a 'nonsense',[35] included simply to bring the SDLP into negotiation, the Taoiseach saw as an 'essential . . . aspect of the problem'. Whoever was correct, there could be no doubt that Dublin's influence had moved considerably from the Downing

34. B. White, *John Hume: Statesman of the Troubles* (Belfast, 1984), 146.
35. B. Faulkner, *Memoirs of a Statesman* (London, 1978), 229.

Street declaration of August 1969 which affirmed that 'responsibility for affairs in Northern Ireland is entirely a matter of domestic jurisdiction'. Heath moved on another sacred cow in the Westminster–Stormont relationship when both the Green (of November 1972) and White Papers acknowledged (tacitly) that the Westminster model wasnot appropriate for a deeply divided society like Northern Ireland.

To assuage unionist fears, a Border Poll had been held earlier that month – the SDLP boycotted it but 58 per cent of the population voted to remain within the United Kingdom. That seemed to be enough to enable Brian Faulkner to get majority support from the Ulster Unionist Council to contest Assembly elections. The results made interesting reading. Parties in favour of power-sharing won two-thirds of the seats (with the SDLP running a close second behind the Ulster Unionist Party, but a majority of unionists had actually voted against Faulkner. That was to haunt him after the Assembly came into existence in January 1974.

POWER-SHARING AND THE ASSEMBLY

Nemesis appeared in other shapes as well. Relations between Heath and Faulkner were under an obvious strain after March 1972. That strain was extended to the wider unionist family following the publication of a White Paper which underlined the unionist sense of impotence. In 1972 they had lost control of security, of 'their' Parliament and government and then of their Governor; and in 1973 they were being offered the sop of an 'Assembly' and an 'Executive' to be headed by a mere 'Chief Executive' who, in any case, had to share what passed for power with a disloyal minority, all of which was being overseen by a 'colonial' Secretary of State. In a polity where symbolism mattered and under which one party had been used to untrammelled power for more than half a century, all of this was too much. And there were those in the wings who were willing and able to articulate the fears of a people who felt a fundamental loss of identity. Add to that an ambiguity about the distance between politics and violence which has been a feature of life in the North of Ireland from the beginning of the nineteenth century.[36]

One of the key officials concerned with moving the process forward described the White Paper as 'too clever by three-quarters' (private

36. J. Darby, *Intimidation and the Control of Conflict in Northern Ireland* (Dublin, 1986), passim.

interview). One can see his point if we examine the fate of the power-sharing Executive established in January 1974. It survived the fall of the Heath government in February – a demise assisted by his failure to win enough support from Ulster Unionist MPs at Westminster to keep his government in office – but had fallen itself by May. Unionists believed that Heath was intent in driving them down the Dublin road – hence their cleverly alarmist election slogan in that general election, 'Dublin is only a Sunningdale away'. The result was that eleven unionists not in favour of power-sharing were returned on just under 51 per cent of the poll with the SDLP leader, Gerry Fitt, being the only member of the power-sharing Executive to be returned. When Heath tried to split this ultra bloc (and more importantly keep himself in office) by sending a telegram to the seven Ulster Unionists led by Harry West on Sunday 3 March, he received a non-committal response. Within 24 hours he had resigned as Prime Minister.

It would be a nonsense to suggest that it was solely the Northern Ireland conflict which led to the collapse of the Heath government, but there was no question that had he had the trust of that small group of unionist MPs he could have remained in office. His fateful relationship with that community was established with the imposition of direct rule and was sealed in the Sunningdale talks in December 1973. Hindsight enables us to trace the deterioration in that relationship. The October 1972 Green Paper had moved outside the Westminster model in search of a constitutional solution by stressing the concept of power sharing in divided societies (para. 58) and emphasising the significance of an 'Irish dimension' (para. 76–8). It implied a reluctance to covet the Union actively – 'no United Kingdom government for many years has had any wish to impede the realisation of Irish unity, if it were to come about by genuine and freely given mutual agreement and on conditions acceptable to the two communities.' All of this was reinforced in the March 1973 White Paper with the announcement that government favoured 'and is prepared to facilitate the formation of [a Council of Ireland]' (para 110). Following the mixed messages conveyed in the Assembly elections of 28 June, negotiations to establish power-sharing culminated in the creation of an Executive-designate on 22 November. The final stage was a meeting between the putative Executive and the two Governments at Sunningdale in Berkshire on 6–9 December 1973. In the interim the Northern Ireland Constitution Act was enacted. The key issues in all of these documents were 'the status of Northern Ireland, the nature of its internal institutions of government, the degree of participation by different sections of the community in those institutions, and the relationships between Northern Ireland and the Irish Republic'.[37]

All of these elements were contained within the Sunningdale package. From a Unionist perspective the most worrying feature was the putative 'Council of Ireland' because it suggested Dublin 'interference' in the internal affairs of Northern Ireland. The price to be paid by the Irish Government was an acceptance of majority consent in Northern Ireland as essential to any constitutional change. In any case the form of the Council was to depend on further discussions between north and south which never materialised. One formulation spoke of a two-tier structure in which the top 14-member executive Council of Ministers (seven from each jurisdiction) would operate on a unanimity principle. Another piece of unfinished business was that entailing discussions on policing and judicial change to encompass both parts of Ireland. Unionists resented the fact that the SDLP continued to withhold wholehearted support for the RUC and yet they were pushing an agenda with an all-Ireland policing component. There was little doubt, too, that the Irish and the SDLP played a better negotiating game than the Unionists. Above all, the symbolism attached to Sunningdale, and the level of unfinished business, conspired to work against its success.

Twenty years later these were precisely the same issues being addressed – albeit under burgeoning developments within the European Union. What that reveals is again the crucial importance of time scales: those who fashioned the 1974 policy had cause for some (very) short term satisfaction but were to learn that the accretions of prejudice could not be removed in a matter of a few months. That view is encapsulated by Harold McCusker MP who is quoted as having said

> . . . it was more likely to put their children into a united Ireland in 25 or 30 years time. I said that the agreement was designed not to kick us out of the United Kingdom but to change our attitudes, to swing our gaze slowly from . . . London towards Dublin and by slow process to change the attitude of the loyalist people so that one day they might believe the myth of Irish unity which so bedevils many people in Northern Ireland.[38]

The Provisionals had rejected already any such political movement when they reacted to the White Paper which was not 'a basis for a lasting and just solution for the conflict in occupied Ireland'. That

37. K. Bloomfield, *Constitution-Making in Northern Ireland: A Look Around the Monuments*, Bass Ireland Lecture, University of Ulster at Jordanstown, 28 February 1991, 24.

38. Cited in Keith Kyle, 'Sunningdale and After: Britain, Ireland and Ulster', *World Today*, vol. 31, no. 11 (1975), 443.

would not come about until 'Britain recognises that the Irish people, and the Irish people alone, have the right to rule Ireland . . .'[39]

Despite such protestations, an Executive representative of nationalists and unionists was installed in Belfast on 1 January 1974 for the first time since Northern Ireland was established. Its collapse in May, ostensibly because unionists rejected the Irish dimension,[40] was perhaps inevitable once the Heath government lost office in February. William Whitelaw and Francis Pym (Whitelaw's successor since November 1973) had argued against a February general election, as had the SDLP who had been consulted confidentially by Heath.[41] But there may be more specific reasons. One body of opinion holds that nationalists had been too successful in the Sunningdale negotiations, leaving Brian Faulkner with too little to sell to his own supporters. Oliver Napier, leader of the Alliance Party and one of the Sunningdale participants, asserted 'the two people I blame – and both were superb at Sunningdale – are Garret FitzGerald and John Hume. They were going out to negotiate the best possible deal they could get from Faulkner for the nationalist tradition and to hell with everything else, and they did it very well'. He maintained that he would have traded the Council of Ireland for recognition by the Irish government of Northern Ireland's status and for a treaty on extradition.[42] There was the view, too, that the British negotiators at Sunningdale were exhausted by more pressing domestic and foreign affairs and came to negotiations not fully prepared. Certainly Whitelaw's absence was noticed; his more nuanced and sensitive approach might have had a restraining influence on the Prime Minister's impatience to get a deal done.[43]

39. *Irish Times*, 24 March 1973.

40. The reaction was based more on emotion and on symbolism because, as the former Head of the Northern Ireland Civil Service wrote, if 'you read today that part of the Paper [which refers to the Irish Dimension] you will see, I think, that these passages of the document represent in large measure a recognition of reality rather than a declaration of policy': Bloomfield, *Constitution-Making*, 30. It raises the degree to which Northern Ireland was a relatively mild and insulated form of 'paranocracy' – 'in which the basis of power was the successful appeal to paranoid fears in the Protestant electorate about the political, social, philosophical and military potential of their Catholic neighbours'. Cf. K. Heskin, *Northern Ireland: A Psychological Analysis* (Dublin, 1981), 100–2.

41. Devlin, *Straight Left*, 226.

42. *Sunday Tribune*, 7 October 1984. This analysis is confirmed in White, *Hume*, 146; and in Devlin, *Straight Left*, 204–10. See, too, Campbell, *Edward Heath*, 549–53; and FitzGerald, *All in a Life*, 196–221.

43. See S. Fay and H. Young, *Sunday Times*, 29 February 1976.

AFTERMATH AND CONCLUSIONS

That which was agreed at Sunningdale began to unravel from January 1974. The Ulster Unionist Council rejected the Faulkner approach by 454 votes to 374 on 4 January and he resigned three days later as Party leader but continued as Chief Executive. The general election led to a Labour administration which did not have the same commitment: indeed, the new Secretary of State had recorded in his diary of 27 September 1973, 'We would have to face up to the fact that the new constitution could not work'.[44] On 7 January an action was brought by a former Fianna Fail minister before the High Court in Dublin seeking an injunction to set aside the Sunningdale Agreement as unconstitutional. The action was rejected eventually but only after doing great damage to Faulkner's credibility among unionist voters. Although the record of the Executive suggests that relations among its members were largely amicable and constructive, the fact remained that they had entered office with too many major issues – security, constitutional status, conflicting economic ideologies – unresolved. In the fullness of time these could have been tackled, but the Executive did not have that luxury. Like the Heath government itself, it sank without fulfilling its promise.

The qualities which Heath had brought to his premiership – tenacity, vision and a conceptual outlook – were utilised to the full in his handling of Ireland. Once he grasped the problem conceptually, he went to huge lengths to try to implement it. As with the miners, he could not understand why others would not follow his reasoning. He possessed neither the patience nor the diplomatic skills to get underneath the accretions of prejudice. He was a leader who looked forward, negotiating with some who had a predeliction to look to the past. He was one who had a passion for 'Europe' and an appreciation of interdependence, whereas there were those in Ireland who were more used to contemplating their own navels. He had an understanding of the bigger issues but little tolerance for those who were concerned with questions of identity and of security.

Ultimately Heath's failings were political and personal. He had the misfortune to be a visionary when the United Kingdom was going through a very difficult period of transition. It might have been wiser simply to keep the ship of state afloat rather than attempt a major overhaul. But that was not part of his temperament. In keeping his eye on the horizon he missed the significance of the quotidian, and he was

44. M. Rees, *Northern Ireland: A Personal Perspective* (London, 1985), 31.

overwhelmed by one damned problem after another – industrial relations, inflation, immigration and Ireland. But the visionary may have the ability to see into the future; and in the matter of Ireland he outlined the parameters to the problem long before virtually everyone else. The thinking which went into the Anglo-Irish Agreement (November 1985), the Joint Declaration of the British and Irish Prime Ministers (December 1993) and the Framework Documents (February 1995) can trace its genesis back to the Heath era. Before there can be solutions, there has to be an acceptance of the nature of the problem. That was Heath's contribution to what was in effect an Anglo-Irish problem.

CHAPTER ELEVEN

The Heath government and British entry into the European Community

John W. Young

HEATH AND THE AMBITION TO 'ENTER EUROPE'

Francis Pym once said that, for Edward Heath, European Community (EC) membership was 'the jewel of the crown' of the 1970 government; Kenneth Baker considered it the 'most important decision that Ted Heath's Government made . . .'; and John Campbell has judged it to be 'the one unquestionable success of his premiership'.[1] The significance of the issue for the government, for the Prime Minister personally and for the future of Britain is thus universally recognised. Once elected as premier, there was little doubt that Heath would pursue entry into the 'common market' – as the EC was then generally known – with vigour; Conservative critics have complained that this was the only issue on which he kept up the businesslike determination which characterised his early months in power.[2]

By 1970 Heath was already closely identified with the ambition of entry. He himself saw this as being shaped by his experiences in early life, especially his visit to Europe as a student before the Second World War and his military service in France and Germany at its end: European unity was the way to prevent another such conflict.[3] His maiden speech in 1950 supported British involvement in talks on the Schuman Plan, the French proposal for a European Coal–Steel Community. This was the foundation-stone for the European Economic Community, created by the Treaty of Rome in 1957.[4] These early signs of a deep-

1. F. Pym, 1970s Archive, British Library of Political and Economic Science; K. Baker, *The Turbulent Years: My Life in Politics* (London 1993), 35; J. Campbell, *Edward Heath* (London 1993), 352.

2. For example N. Tebbit, *Upwardly Mobile* (London 1988), 106, 117.

3. E. Heath, *Travels* (London 1977), 115; evidence of Sir Donald Maitland, Sir Timothy Kitson and Lord Armstrong, Institute of Contemporary British History, (ICBH) witness seminar, February 1994 text published in 'The Heath Government', *Contemporary Record*, vol. 9, no. 1 (1995), 188–219.

4. *House of Commons Debates*, 5th ser., vol. 476, cols 1959–64, 26 June 1950.

seated Europeanism should not be exaggerated. Although he was born near Dover, Heath did not visit France until his teens, he never learnt a foreign language and, after supporting the Party line in the Schuman Plan debate, no more was heard from him on European issues until Macmillan appointed him Lord Privy Seal in July 1960. Nonetheless, Macmillan is unlikely to have chosen Heath for this post unless the latter were well-disposed to the Community, and it may have been Heath's work in the Whips' Office which prevented him from speaking out as a pro-European. Instead, the Lord Privy Seal kept his views largely to himself and, when asked by journalists, claimed to have no particular European commitment.[5] Macmillan gave Heath responsibility for the first British negotiations on EC entry in 1961, and Heath grasped this opportunity to make a name for himself. He acquitted himself well in the talks, mastering complex issues, travelling widely in Europe and winning great respect there, not least for the dignified way in which he faced the eventual veto of the application, in January 1963, by France's General de Gaulle. Even de Gaulle predicted, privately, that Britain would eventually enter the Community under Heath's leadership, for it was now obvious that entry was the latter's life ambition.[6]

Heath was determined to reverse the 1963 veto which had been a great personal setback,[7] and he recognised numerous powerful reasons why EC membership was vital to British interests. Within weeks of becoming Conservative Party leader in 1965 he received a report by a study group, under Lord Carrington, on foreign policy which began by urging membership as the way to secure a role in an economic and political grouping of enormous potential, which might match the power of the US and USSR. Such a step need not involve the surrender of historic British interests, but would rather allow them to be defended more successfully in a new context. For, once inside the Community, Britain could press policies which were in its own interest, secure greater trade and aid for the Commonwealth and make the EC a 'magnet' to draw in other countries, including those of the Eastern bloc.[8] These were aims which the new leader very much shared. In particular, on the economic side, he believed that Britain could only become more competitive and secure higher growth by entering the

5. According to N. Beloff, *The General Says No* (London, 1963), 97; but I am grateful to John Barnes of the London School of Economics for comments on Heath's pro-European views in 1960–61.

6. Campbell, *Edward Heath*, 132, and see 116–34 in general.

7. Evidence of Sir Donald Maitland, 'The Heath Government' witness seminar, 188–219.

8. 'Report of the Policy Group on Foreign Affairs', chaired by Lord Carrington, 6 August 1965, CPA ACP(65)20.

common market, a belief shared by most large companies in the Confederation of British Industry (CBI). EC membership offered the chance of technological cooperation and gains from economies of scale; it had an essential role in Heath's vision of a more efficient British economy. On the political side, he hoped for 'a Europe which could act politically as one' in the world, with a common foreign and defence policy, and he 'saw Britain in Europe as being the way back to being a Great Power.'[9] The economic and political gains of entry were mutually reinforcing, for a stronger economy would help Britain to retain its world role and strengthen the Atlantic alliance.[10]

It is pointless to ask whether Heath's enthusiasm for the common market amounted to support for European 'federalism'. Among postwar British premiers he may have held ideals closest to the Community's founders, but like most of his countrymen he was also a pragmatist and hoped that the EC would evolve gradually, rather like Britain's own unwritten constitution. In 1967, when speaking in America, he said that it was in Britain's interest, as a potential member, that the Community should be an 'effective' organisation with certain central powers, but he recalled a meeting in which Jean Monnet himself had said that no major power in the EC should be outvoted by others on 'a vital matter of national interest'. Heath considered arguments over federalism to be 'at best a sterile debate and at worst a positive hindrance to European progress' since the EC should develop gradually, creating new institutions and laws as they were required; it would take 'a long time' to achieve a common European executive and legislature – though he did not rule out such a development. Two years later he characterised 'the unity of Europe' as meaning 'the habit of working together to reach accepted goals'. Heath's understanding of the growth of the EC seems to have been quite consistent over time. In 1988 he wrote that the EC had 'developed *sui generis* and the final form of its political organisation will be *sui generis*. For this reason we are not using our time to the best purpose if we concentrate our argument around federalism. What we should concentrate on is making a success of the Community . . .'[11] He was not afraid of expanding EC institutions to

9. Interview with Sir Alec Douglas-Home, 1970s Archive; P. Whitehead, *The Writing on the Wall: Britain in the Seventies* (London, 1985), 52–4. And see: evidence of Lord Armstrong, 'The Heath Government' witness seminar, 188–219; D.C. Watt and J. Mayall, *Current British Foreign Policy, 1970* (London, 1971), 617–19 (speech by Heath at Chatham House, November 1970).

10. C.L. Sulzberger, *An Age of Mediocrity: Diaries 1963–72* (New York, 1973), 596.

11. E. Heath, *Old Worlds, New Horizons: Britain, the Common Market and the Atlantic Alliance* (London, 1970), 34, 56–7 and see 7; E. Heath, 'European integration over the next ten years', *International Affairs*, vol. 64, no. 2 (1988), 199.

advance mutual interests of member states, but he was confident that, once Britain had joined, it could control the pace and direction of EC common policies. Once inside, Britain would have its own representatives on Community bodies and ultimately could use its veto to prevent unwanted developments.[12]

It is important to note that, even in opposition under Alec Douglas-Home in 1964–65, the Conservative leaders remained deeply committed to EC entry. As noted above, Heath received a very 'pro-European' report from Lord Carrington's study group soon after becoming leader. Most work on the report had been done under Douglas-Home, whose shadow cabinet had decided in March 1965 that they must 'constantly (reiterate) our broad intention to seek entry' and must 'educate' their Party, the farming community and the Commonwealth about the need to pursue this course. Home's front bench expected that, by 1968, the EC would be a formidable political–economic grouping and that, to join it, Britain could not afford another detailed negotiation like that of 1961–63. Instead, the 'question would be one of joining an already fully existing organisation on its own terms', by accepting the Treaty of Rome. The 'possibility of turning to America' was discussed but rejected as likely to make Britain a 'backwater' of the US. Although some Conservative MPs continued to look at alternatives to EC membership,[13] Heath did not allow the Party's commitment to entry to be questioned in the late 1960s. He discovered in the 1966 general election that this course did not win popular support: at one point he warmly welcomed hints from the French that British entry to the EC might now be possible, only to have Harold Wilson accuse him of 'rolling on his back like a spaniel'. Wilson's insistence that Britain should only join the common market on *favourable* terms was popular with voters. Nonetheless, when Labour itself decided to seek membership in May 1967, Heath stuck to his principles and gave the government Conservative support, helping Wilson to secure a majority of over four hundred votes in favour.[14]

The Conservatives seemed far more united than Labour on the question of entry, although at the Party conference in 1969 there was some criticism of entry to the EC and Enoch Powell (who had sup-

12. See for example, interviews with Heath, 21 April 1970 and 30 June 1971, Hetherington papers, British Library of Political and Economic Science.

13. Leader's Consultative Committee, 30 March 1965, CPA LCC/65/37, and associated memoranda, and meetings of 24 February and 1 March 1965, LCC/65/24–5; on discussion of US links, see minutes of the Conservative Parliamentary Foreign Affairs Committee, 26 March 1968, CPA CRD/3/10/16.

14. J.W. Young, *Britain and European Unity, 1945–92* (London, 1993), 90–91 and 99–100.

ported entry under Macmillan) emerged as a critic on this, as on other issues. At first Powell concentrated most on the economic costs of entry which, it was widely accepted, would push up food prices and, initially at least, adversely affect Britain's balance of payments. Soon, however, Powell shifted the centre of his attack to the danger of compromising national sovereignty, which would be eroded as an EC member, even if the Community evolved only gradually.[15] Other MPs, not all of them Powellites, shared fears of higher prices, damage to the Commonwealth and loss of parliamentary authority. Even in 1970, most constituency parties were probably opposed to entry and a majority of Conservative voters certainly were.[16] Yet after winning the election, the new government – as when the Party was in opposition – never questioned *whether* Britain should enter the EC: Heath simply adopted Macmillan's decision of 1961 to seek entry.[17] Heath's Cabinet was carefully selected to support this aim. Peter Walker, the Minister of Housing, an opponent of Macmillan's application, had since been converted to the European future by Heath. Geoffrey Rippon later recalled that there 'was no dissent in the Cabinet of any kind' over EC membership.[18] Douglas-Home, the Foreign Secretary, though generally seen as an 'Atlanticist' – and certainly not outspokenly 'pro-European' – had long believed that there was no real alternative to EC membership if Britain was to remain a major power.[19] After 1970, Home chose to concentrate on foreign policy issues other than EC entry, but he chaired the Cabinet's European Policy Committee which also included, among others, the ministers responsible for trade (John Davies after July 1971) and agriculture (James Prior) as well as the new 'Mr Europe', Anthony Barber, who was charged with the actual entry negotiations.[20] Barber had specially pressed for this role.[21]

15. P. Cosgrave, *The Lives of Enoch Powell* (London, 1990), 265–9; R. Lewis, *Enoch Powell: Principle in Politics* (London, 1979), 145–51; D.E. Schoen, *Enoch Powell and the Powellites* (London, 1977), 74–9.

16. C. Lord, *British Entry to the European Community under the Heath Government, 1970–74* (Aldershot, 1993), 99–103.

17. Ibid., 9.

18. P. Walker, *Staying Power* (London, 1991), 53; interview with Rippon, 1970s Archive.

19. See, for example, remarks he made in December 1963, recorded in C.L. Sulzberger, *The Last of the Giants: Diaries 1954–63* (London, 1970), 1036.

20. The committee also included Lord Hailsham, Lord Carrington and William Whitelaw: U. Kitzinger, *Diplomacy and Persuasion: how Britain joined the Common Market* (London, 1973), 87.

21. Interview with Barber, 1970s Archive.

PROSPECTS FOR ENTRY IN 1970

Britain seemed in a stronger position to apply for EC entry in 1970 than had been the case in 1961 or 1967. In contrast to the attitudes of the Macmillan period, it was accepted by Heath that Britain could not renegotiate the Treaty of Rome or expect the six original members of the Community to alter their existing policies, such as the Common Agricultural Policy (CAP). Also in contrast to 1961, the National Farmers Union, an important body of opinion in rural constituencies, now saw gains for many of its participants from EC membership. Although MPs were reluctant to 'sell out' the Commonwealth, a Conservative study group in 1967 had advised that 'Britain must not be deterred by fears of offending some of . . . the Commonwealth from following policies which she believes to be . . . in her own interest'.[22] Fears of a loss of British sovereignty to the EC had been tempered in 1966 when de Gaulle secured the 'Luxembourg Compromise', which recognised that members could veto measures which threatened important national interests. The situation had also improved in several ways since Wilson's failed application: Britain's balance of payments and the position of Sterling were stronger and Heath's personal commitment to the EC, in contrast to Wilson's, was not in doubt. In a lecture at Harvard University in 1967, Heath had advocated Franco-British nuclear cooperation and he was ready to play down the significance of the 'special relationship' with Washington, attitudes which might appeal to Gaullist opinion in France.[23] Furthermore, during the 1970 election campaign, all three main political parties in Britain declared themselves favourable to entry on appropriate terms. Another important development was that Charles de Gaulle, the author of the 1961 and 1967 vetoes, had resigned as French President in 1969. At that time Heath had had no intention of making a third application if the likely result was another veto. He wished to apply for membership only if all members of the EC appeared to want it.[24] By June 1970, however, he could be more confident that this was the case.

Arguably the most important change in the prospects of British EC

22. 'Conservative Commonwealth and Overseas Council, Report of a Study Group on Policy for the Commonwealth', chaired by Lord Selkirk, April 1967, ACP(67)35.

23. Heath, *Old World, New Horizons*, 72–3 and see 4–5. But French foreign ministry officials still felt Britain was too close to the US: H. Alphand, *L'Étonnement d'Être* (Paris, 1977), 537.

24. Leader's Consultative Committee, 7 July 1969, LCC/69/314, and associated memoranda from the Conservative Research Department, 'European policy', 27 June 1969, 'Balance of Payments costs of entering the Common Market – changes since 1967', 13 May 1969, LCC/69/244–5; and see Heath, *Old Worlds, New Horizons*, 6–7.

membership, between the 1967 application and the Treaty of Accession in 1972, was not anything Britain did, but what happened in Paris. All the other five EC members wanted Britain to join. The departure of de Gaulle was obviously a turning point. British exclusion from the Community in the 1960s had much to do with the General's view of the world and particularly his fear that Britain would be a 'trojan horse' for US influence in Europe. Then again, de Gaulle had never ruled out British membership absolutely and in February 1969 he had made an extraordinary suggestion to the British Ambassador – a former Conservative minister – Christopher Soames, that Britain and France could work towards a new form of unity in Europe which abandoned the 'supranational' elements of the EC. For de Gaulle feared the threat of the EC to French independence as much as he feared US power.[25] The 'Soames affair' led to a crisis in Franco-British relations, after the Foreign Office (FO) revealed the President's ideas to the other EC members. But Soames and his Embassy staff recognised it as a sign that de Gaulle *was* ready to cooperate with Britain on Europe's future.[26] De Gaulle's attempted shift in policy may have been influenced by currency instability and increased fear of Germany, after a meeting of central bankers in November 1968, the franc had been left under severe pressure partly because the Germans refused to revalue the Deutschmark.[27] These factors continued to push de Gaulle's successor, Pompidou, in the direction of a revived *entente cordiale* to balance German power. Although Pompidou maintained the Franco-German alliance, he never enthused over it, was keen to match German industrial might and was cautious about German attempts to establish better relations with the Eastern bloc, especially after Willy Brandt became Chancellor in 1969.[28] Despite the 'Soames affair', one member of the Paris Embassy noted that both the British and the French soon 'started mending fences and by the time of de Gaulle's resignation . . our relations were already getting better.'[29] Pompidou's government included a number of Gaullists who were sceptical about British entry, but the new foreign minister Maurice Schumann was well disposed to Britain, and Centrist ministers, led by the finance minister, Giscard d'Estaing, were keen to revitalise

25. On the 'affair' see especially, B. Ledwidge, *De Gaulle* (London, 1982), chapter 22; J. Haines, *The Politics of Power* (London, 1977), 74–81; and J. Dickie, *Inside the Foreign Office* (London, 1992), 166–7.

26. Interview with Soames, 1970s Archive; A. Campbell, *Colleagues and Friends* (Salisbury, 1986), 74.

27. See F. Castigliola, *France and the United States: the Cold Alliance since World War II* (New York, 1992), 162–3.

28. F. Abadie and J.-P. Corcelette, *Georges Pompidou* (Paris, 1994), 338.

29. Campbell, *Colleagues and Friends*, 73.

the Community via British membership. Even some Gaullists saw one good reason to embrace British entry Michel Debré, a former Prime Minister, adopted the logic of de Gaulle's approach to Soames and argued that the British would be a valuable ally against greater supra-nationalism from Brussels. Any residual danger that de Gaulle himself might condemn British entry ended with his death in November 1970. Another powerful reason for which Pompidou might change French policy was that, at the Hague Summit in December 1969, EC leaders agreed to settle the future financing of the CAP which was particularly beneficial for French farmers. The British would have to accept the CAP as a pre-condition of entry and could expect, under the new financial arrangements, to have to contribute a substantial amount to its costs. As a condition of settling the CAP, the other five EC leaders at the Hague insisted on opening membership talks with Britain, Eire, Denmark and Norway. Even before these entry talks started, Pompidou told one newspaper owner 'I am working on the hypothesis that Britain will come in', and in May 1970, when Heath visited Paris as opposition leader, the President conceded that no progress would be possible on greater political integration in Europe until Britain was a member.[30]

THE NEGOTIATIONS BEGIN

An account of the Heath government's policy towards the EC after 1970 falls naturally into three sections: the entry negotiations down to June 1971, the battle in Parliament which followed, down to July 1972, and the year in which Heath led Britain as an EC member. The first phase actually began on 30 June 1970, a mere twelve days after polling day, when Barber and Douglas-Home travelled to Luxembourg for ministerial talks with the Six. The way was smoothed enormously by preparations made under the Wilson government in the months following the Hague Summit. Barber even used a statement which had been drafted for Labour's 'Mr Europe', George Thomson; this not only allowed Heath to move quickly, it also put pressure on Labour to support whatever terms the Conservatives achieved. The statement accepted existing EC policies and expressed support for future developments which might benefit Britain (including foreign policy cooperation and a European regional aid programme), but asked for a

30. Sulzberger, *Age of Mediocrity*, 606; I am grateful to Mr D.R. Thorpe of Charterhouse School for information on the Heath–Pompidou meeting; and to Professor Maurice Vaisse, of the Institut de France, for sending me sections of a forthcoming volume, *Georges Pompidou et l'Europe* (Paris, 1996).

'transitional' period before Britain fully opened its markets to other EC states, requested special arrangements for Commonwealth trade and expressed concern about Britain's likely financial contribution.[31]

As an industrial state, Britain could expect little money from the CAP, which represented the bulk of the EC budget, but would have to pay a large amount in: the EC took one per cent of members' receipts of Value Added Tax (VAT was introduced in Britain under Heath's government) and *all* tariffs on external trade, which in Britain's case was a vast amount, since the country was a major world commercial power. The original EC members insisted these payments were the Community's 'own resources' which states surrendered to the centre and could not negotiate back. CAP was a double problem because it worked by a form of intervention in the agricultural markets (leading to 'butter mountains' and 'wine lakes') to keep prices stable and guarantee farmers' incomes, and it used external tariffs to deter members from buying food outside the EC. The best estimates in 1970 suggested that the 'net cost' of British entry would be between £550 million and £750 million, and might force the government to deflate the economy to restore the balance of payments. Labour politicians were particularly concerned about the dangers of unemployment this might bring, as well as by higher food prices, and Wilson was soon critical of Heath, not on the general principle of membership but on the subject of the actual terms of entry he might obtain. The Treasury was determined, because of the potential implications for economic growth, to get the lowest possible financial contribution to the EC, and Treasury officials were recognised as the most serious doubters about entry in Whitehall. The Permanent Secretary, Douglas Allen, *was* favourable to entry but, like Wilson, saw the actual entry terms as vital and feared that British industry might not stand the strain of EC competition.[32]

It is possible to take three views of the negotiations of 1970–71. One is that they were 'doomed to succeed' thanks to Heath's determination to secure membership and Pompidou's readiness to let Britain in; any toughness shown by either side in the talks was for public consumption. A second view is that there were serious differences, that French policy was uncertain and failure a real possibility. The truth probably lies somewhere in between: agreement was always the most likely outcome but there were real gains and losses involved and the haggling over terms was a meaningful exercise.[33] Although all three

31. On the Luxembourg talks see S.Z. Young, *Terms of Entry: Britain's negotiations with the European Community, 1970–72* (London, 1973), 1–21.

32. Lord, *British Entry*, 63–4 and 88.

33. Ibid., 78.

major British parties said, during the election, that they favoured entry on appropriate terms, public opinion polls at the time were heavily opposed to membership. Heath may have believed that the dynamic gains of membership would outweigh any short-term economic costs, and John Campbell judges that the Prime Minister was ready to enter 'at almost any price' he could sell to parliament.[34] However, the Prime Minister could not ignore public opinion and could not therefore be seen to concede too much to achieve entry.

To reach an acceptable settlement required complicated and arduous discussion. Although ministerial conferences between the Six and the four applicants made the most important decisions in 1970–71, detailed solutions were slowly thrashed out in working parties meeting in Brussels. These were put to work after another ministerial conference on 21 July. By then Barber had moved to become Chancellor of the Exchequer, following the sudden death of Iain Macleod. The new 'Mr Europe' was Geoffrey Rippon, who was given a free hand by Douglas-Home to pursue the entry talks. Rippon was advised by a special interdepartmental group, led by two FO officials, Con O'Neill and John Robinson, who had been involved in earlier entry bids and were now well-versed in the ways of the Community. The personnel involved in the talks remained quite stable throughout, but frequent delays were caused by the need of the Six to agree on a common position, even when they had a single spokesman in the President of the Council of Ministers. It was always clear that, however much the Six tried to achieve a single outlook, it was the French, with a coherent policy driven from Paris, who would be most vital to the outcome.[35] The French often took an independent line from that of their partners, and Heath – who 'took a close interest without interfering too much' – wisely judged that, if the talks were to succeed, Britain must concentrate on winning over Paris.[36] This was in contrast to FO policy in the preceding few years which had relied on constant pressure, and support from the so-called 'friendly five', to force France to concede British entry.[37]

The 'fact-finding' stage of the membership negotiations lasted until

34. Campbell, *Edward Heath*, 336.

35. The organisation of the talks is fully described in Kitzinger, *Diplomacy*, 78–88.

36. This was evidently Heath's personal decision: Lord, *British Entry*, 66; quote from Campbell, *Edward Heath*, 354.

37. It is not true; however, as Hurd and Campbell assert, that in 1967 Harold Wilson had failed to see the importance of going through Paris: D. Hurd, *An End to Promises: Sketch of a Government, 1970–1974* (London, 1979), 58–9; Campbell, *Edward Heath*, 353–4. In the first half of 1967 Wilson made two attempts to win de Gaulle over: Young, *Britain and European Unity*, 89–90, 97–8, 100.

late October 1970 when officials were able to highlight points of agreement and disagreement. Even Con O'Neill, the leading British official, found it a 'boring' business. Dullest of all was the need to look over all previous EC legislation stretching back to the 1950s. 'There was not much room for negotiation', given British acceptance of past EC policies, O'Neill noted, 'and we all knew that . . . in advance.'[38] At another ministerial conference in Brussels, the negotiators were quickly able to resolve such issues as the market arrangements for milk, bacon and eggs and the association of British overseas dependencies with the EC.[39] Two months later, in December, there was general agreement on the period of gradual transition for British agriculture and industry to the rigours of the common market; Britain had originally wanted six and three years respectively, but Rippon settled for a uniform five years.[40] Both Rippon and Heath were determined not to get bogged down in detail, but to concentrate on certain key issues. As Ambassador Soames explained to the editor of *The Guardian*, Britain could not afford to 'go through the whole performance of everything from Kangaroo meat to Pakistani tennis rackets', as had happened with Macmillan's 1961 application.[41]

Rippon hoped to have a Treaty of Accession signed in January 1972,[42] however, two sets of complications now arose to threaten this hope. One was the insistence of the Six on continuing to develop EC policies ahead of the widening of the Community. There were three important developments following the Hague Summit of the previous year. Least divisive was the decision to begin 'European Political Co-operation' in foreign policy. This was something Heath favoured, and the British were allowed to join the consultations about it which began in November 1970. Of potentially great importance was the Werner report, finalised the previous month, which concerned Economic and Monetary Union (EMU) and (like the Delors Report of the late 1980s) eventually foresaw a common currency and banking system for the EC. Douglas Hurd, Heath's Political Secretary, was surprised to find that Downing Street staff had no knowledge of the Werner report when it appeared: he advised them that they should study it in earnest.[43] There

38. Interview with O'Neill, 1970s Archive.

39. *HC Debs.*, 5th ser., vol. 805, cols 439–54, 29 October 1970. It was possible to settle some issues, such as the number of British Commissioners, automatically.

40. Kitzinger, *Diplomacy*, 96.

41. Interview with Rippon, 1970s Archive; Lord, *British Entry*, 63; interview with Soames, 28 April 1970, Hetherington papers.

42. Conservative Parliamentary Foreign Affairs Committee, 19 January 1971, CRD/3/10/17.

43. Interview with Hurd, 28 October 1970, Hetherington papers.

was some annoyance in London that Britain and the other applicants were excluded from talks on this subject. In the short term, however, the Werner report did not plan any dramatic steps and the British government was confident that it would be inside the EC, with an influence over developments, before real steps were taken towards EMU. The real, complicating development was the decision of the Six to establish a Common Fisheries Policy. This seemed particularly unfair since the four applicant powers had more extensive fishing grounds than the Six, and Rippon later recalled it as being the 'most difficult issue' to arise in the negotiations.[44] Fisheries absorbed a considerable amount of time in the later stages of the talks, and did much to influence Norway's eventual rejection of membership in a referendum.

THE NEGOTIATIONS IN CRISIS

It was the second set of complications which specifically called British membership into question over the next six months, however. Simply because the negotiators had settled the easier problems by December 1970, differences on other, more important issues were bound to arise. These included special arrangements for Commonwealth trade and the vital issue of the transition period for Britain's financial contribution to the EC. Rippon proposed that this should rise, over a five-year period, from three per cent to fifteen per cent of total contributions, with a proviso that there should be a review of arrangements if they proved too burdensome. The French, however, adopted the extreme position, that Britain should pay its full contribution on entry, at about a fifth of total payments.[45] Pompidou met Brandt in Paris soon afterwards and declared that the talks had reached their 'humorous' stage: the British financial offer was quite preposterous. But Brandt countered that the French position too was unreasonable.[46] It threatened to doom the British economy to a heavy burden immediately after entry. Pompidou, however, evidently considered that he could push the British hard. Heath still argued publicly that he might reject entry if the terms were not right, but the French President believed that this was bluff, and that the London government was 'not only firm about wanting to get in but is a prisoner of its own statements' on the necessity of entry.[47] In early 1971 the French also demanded reassurances about the gradual

44. Interview with Rippon, 1970s Archive.
45. *HC Debs.*, 5th ser., vol. 808, cols 1354–70, 16 December 1960.
46. W. Brandt, *People and Policies* (London, 1978), 253–5.
47. Sulzberger, *Last of the Giants*, 690–91.

end of Sterling's role as a reserve currency. Rippon was already on record as saying that Sterling was not an issue in the talks,[48] but the French argued that Sterling's global importance and the need to defend its value would prevent Britain from adapting to market conditions in the EC. British officials began to grow despondent as the entry talks failed, for three months, to make progress. Did the French wish the negotiations to fail, were they seeking certain concessions or were they simply testing Britain's resolve? Soames considered French toughness a performance – a 'bore' – but was nonetheless concerned that a long delay could lead the talks to lose all momentum, while opposition mounted at home.[49] Brandt made it clear to Heath, when they met in Bonn in April, that Germany would not attempt to force France's agreement to British membership. (Consistently in fact, since the founding of the EC, the Germans had refused to fall out with the French over British entry). Yet Brandt believed that Pompidou *did* want Britain in and that the time had now come for a Heath–Pompidou Summit, which many had long believed would be necessary.[50]

The path to the Summit was paved by highly secret talks during early 1971 between Soames and the Secretary-General of the Elysée Palace, Michel Jobert. Pompidou (who sometimes had his own talks with Soames on British terms of entry[51]) seems to have been most insistent on the need for secrecy, not even consulting the French foreign ministry or Prime Minister's office. In London, knowledge of the talks was restricted to a small number of officials and ministers – Heath, Home and Rippon among them – to whom Soames made frequent visits. Great care was certainly needed, for neither side wished to hold a Summit which broke down in acrimony. Shortly before the Summit the entry negotiators made their most important agreements for months, when Britain accepted EC trade preferences in agriculture and the Six promised to help West Indian sugar producers. Prospects for Franco-British success may also have been aided by a German decision on 5 May, taken without consulting Paris, to 'float' the Deutschmark.[52] This was a dramatic reaction to the growing instability of world currency markets; it highlighted Germany's growing independence and led Pompidou to fear the collapse of the CAP. The President welcomed

48. Information Sheet 4 on 'Europe', recording press conference, November, 1970, CRD/3/10/13.

49. Interviews with Roger Jacklin, 17 March 1971, and Soames, 20 January 1971, Hetherington papers; C. King, *The Cecil King Diary, 1970–74* (London, 1975), 96.

50. Brandt, *People and Policies*, 249–50.

51. Interview with Soames, 20 January 1971, Hetherington papers.

52. Kitzinger, *Diplomacy*, 113–18.

Heath to Paris on 20–21 May. Much relied on the personal reaction of Pompidou to the frequently cold and unsociable Prime Minister; for Pompidou was determined to make decisions on British entry himself, and inform his officials of them later.[53] They had only met, briefly, once before and both needed an interpreter; but both 'had done their homework' and they 'got on very well' with one another. Although senior members of the British negotiating team from Brussels were on hand to give advice, Heath had prepared so thoroughly that he did not need them.[54] Eleven hours of head-to-head talks took place and the Prime Minister was forced to miss a race on his yacht, *Morning Cloud*.[55] At the end, however, he had his reward. Pompidou was convinced of the Englishman's sincere commitment to a European future and their ability to cooperate on an approach which played down the significance of supranationalism. Pompidou said that the interests of developing states in the Commonwealth must be safeguarded and he accepted rather vague undertakings that Britain would run down the reserve role of Sterling.[56] Building on proposals he had first put forward in 1967, Heath had also come to the Summit ready to offer Pompidou greater nuclear cooperation in future,[57] despite doubts from Lord Carrington, the Minister of Defence, about the practicalities of this.[58] Previously de Gaulle had shown great interest in this subject, but Franco-British cooperation had been blocked earlier by British undertakings to the US not to share nuclear secrets with third parties. Heath apparently won the agreement of America's Richard Nixon to alter this policy.[59] By 1971, however, the British and French nuclear deterrents had developed in different directions, France had its own successful system and Pompidou himself wanted to preserve his country's nuclear independence.[60] (Besides, within a few years, the Americans – without

53. Alphand, *L'Étonnement d'Être*, 554–5.

54. Interviews with O'Neill and Soames, 1970s Archive.

55. E. Heath, *Sailing* (London, 1975), 181.

56. Joint communiqué, *The Times*, 22 May 1971; *HC Debs.*, 5th ser., vol. 818, cols 31–49, 24 May 1971; and in general see Kitzinger, *Diplomacy*, 120–21.

57. Heath, 'European integration', 207. On British expectations of closer nuclear co-operation with France, see Conservative Parliamentary Foreign Affairs Committee, 19 January 1971, CRD/3/10/17; interview with Soames, 20 January 1971, Hetherington papers. In opposition, the shadow cabinet had considered a 'European Defence Organisation' under NATO which would include nuclear and conventional forces: Leader's Consultative Committee, 21 June 1965, LCC/65/55, and memo by Soames, 'European defence', 17 June 1965, LCC/65/37.

58. Lord Carrington, *Reflect on Things Past* (London, 1988), 221–2; Sulzberger, *Age of Mediocrity*, 648–9.

59. Heath, 'European integration' 203.

60. Ibid., 207; Sulzberger, *Age of Mediocrity*, 691, 788, 799–800.

informing London – began to provide France directly with technical advice on nuclear weapons.[61]) Ironically, therefore, after all the controversy under de Gaulle, Heath's readiness to move towards greater Franco-British cooperation in the nuclear sphere fell on deaf ears in Paris, and concessions in this area were not needed in order to achieve success.

After the Paris conference, Soames considered the remaining entry talks 'a formality', though for O'Neill and his team they still required a lot of detailed work.[62] By 23 June, Rippon had finalised the arrangements for British entry, with measures to protect New Zealand dairy produce for several years and a financial settlement by which Britain's contribution would rise gradually from about 9 per cent of total EC contributions on entry, to about 19 per cent in 1977.[63] The concessions on Commonwealth trade were vital to many Conservative backbenchers and showed that the EC was open to world trade, not a 'closed' trading bloc. Yet O'Neill complained that the arguments over Commonwealth interests, even if much less significant than those of 1961–63, made it more difficult for Britain to win concessions in other vital areas.[64] Most vital of all was the financial settlement which worried the Treasury because it would become so costly by the end of the decade. Added to worries over the balance of payments, this provoked real concern about whether the dynamic gains of membership would be enough to offset the direct costs. Heath was helped by the fact that, in 1971, world food prices rose so much that CAP prices seemed quite tolerable. He also argued that, once inside the EC, Britain could press for policies – most importantly a regional aid fund – which would benefit Britain financially. Furthermore, Rippon was clear that if the financial costs of entry became too great, there could be talks with Britain's EC partners to resolve the problem: June 1971 was not intended as a 'final' solution.[65] Given later problems over Britain's net contribution, during the renegotiation of 1974–75 and the era of the 'British Budgetary Question' in the early 1980s, it is still worth asking whether Rippon could have achieved a better deal. In particular, could France's desire to have Britain help pay for the CAP not have been exploited to squeeze out a lower financial contribution? Against this it has to be said that, as a supplicant, with two previous applications behind it,

61. R.H. Ullman, 'The covert French connection', *Foreign Policy*, 75 (Summer 1989), especially 8–11 and 32.

62. Interviews with Soames and O'Neill, 1970s Archive.

63. *HC Debs.*, 5th series, vol. 819, cols 1603–28, 24 June 1971.

64. Whitehead, *Writing on the Wall*, 59–60.

65. Evidence of Lord Croham, 'The Heath Government' witness seminar, 188–219; Lord, *British Entry*, 80–81, 93; interview with Rippon, 1970s Archive.

Britain was not strongly placed to ask for more and the French ensured, right down to the Paris Summit, that the possibility of failure in the talks *appeared* high. Besides, it would be wrong to suggest that the terms represented anything like a 'sell-out' by Heath. At the time they seemed reasonable enough, and the hope of achieving changes from the inside was a fair one. Arguably the real problems came *after* entry, when a poor world economic situation helped to dash the Conservatives' hopes of rapid, sustainable growth.

PASSING THE BILL

With Britain's entry terms basically settled, the government published a White Paper on 7 July which presented a lot of statistics on past EC performance but was thin on the future impact of entry on the British economy because the likely gains were actually difficult to quantify: how far the country seized the opportunity for growth depended upon the performance of its businessmen in investment, marketing and pricing. Food prices would rise, Commonwealth trade would continue to decline, but Britain would be part of a large commercial bloc, with a say in future EC developments (such as EMU and aid to developing countries) and a stronger voice in the world as part of a European whole. The paper did talk of 'a sharing and an enlarging of individual national sovereignties' in the EC, and thereby reflected Heath's belief that a narrow definition of sovereignty (as the ability of a country to have a 'final' say over its own future) was impossible in an increasingly interdependent world. Yet the tone of the document was hardly idealistic, for simultaneously it argued that, with the power of the veto in each member's hand, there would be no 'erosion of essential national sovereignty'. Another feature of the paper was the pointed reference to Harold Wilson's arguments in favour of entry in 1967, which were resuscitated in order to neutralise the Labour opposition.[66] Overall this document had the weaknesses of other major declarations by ministers on the EC at the time. It did not explain *exactly* how the EC would improve Britain's economic prospects, it fudged the issue of greater supranationalism in the Community in future and, while trying in some ways to present membership as a great opportunity and a visionary step, it blurred the impact of this by arguing that Britain would not be forced to change past policies.[67] Yet the government had to minimise

66. *The UK and the European Communities* (Cmd. 8715).

67. See for example Rippon's speech to the Conservative Party conference in October 1970 Watt and Mayall (eds), *British Foreign Policy 1970*, 498–503.

the possible adverse impacts in order to win over public opinion. At the start of 1971 polls suggested that only a quarter of Britons favoured entry, with particular fears over food prices. Historically, however, polls on membership had been very volatile and the government was right to predict that a successful outcome to the membership talks would improve the situation, especially by inducing Conservative voters to move in favour of entry. There was never a clear majority of the electorate who supported entry under Heath, but by the end of the year 'pros' and 'antis' were roughly even.[68] Actually, the government had begun a pro-European publicity campaign in early 1971, when Rippon was worried about the depth of opposition to membership in Britain because this could have an adverse effect on the governments of the Six: Heath's government had been reluctant to appear too deeply committed to entry in late 1970, for fear of weakening their negotiating position in Brussels, but there had to be a change of tack when the public's 'anti' majority was cited in France as evidence that Britain was unprepared for a European future.[69] Pro-European propaganda in the country at large was carried out by the government and the well-financed European Movement.

Heath's main immediate problem was not public opinion but parliamentary arithmetic, for Enoch Powell and about sixty other Conservative MPs still opposed entry, and Harold Wilson had continued to take the line that, while EC membership should not be ruled out, Heath had not won sufficiently good terms. Wilson's position, attacked at the time as unprincipled, seems to have been designed simply to hold Labour together. On the right of the party, a strong group of social democrats, most notably Roy Jenkins, were pro-market but many other Labour MPs, party activists and trade unions were opposed. Some simply wished to bring down the government; some believed that Heath's terms could damage the Commonwealth, push up food prices and lead to deflationary policies; others were opposed to membership, on any terms, of an undemocratic, capitalist 'club' which damaged working-class interests and harmed the trade of developing states (by preventing those states from selling agricultural produce in Europe). By 1971, Tony Benn had taken up the idea of a referendum on entry while James Callaghan, a potential rival to Wilson for the leadership, advocated the *renegotiation* of Heath's terms. By concentrating on the issue of the exact terms of entry, Wilson could hope to satisfy those

68. See the table in Lord, *British Entry*, 118.

69. The debate can be gleaned from Conservative Parliamentary Foreign Affairs Committee, 12 November 1970, CRD/3/10/16, and Advisory Committee on Policy, 21 January 1971, ACP(71)110.

who wished to attack the government; by refusing to rule out membership, he kept the loyalty of the social democratic wing in the party.[70] The danger of a defeat by a combination of Labour and anti-market Conservatives led Heath to delay a vote on the issue until after the summer recess. Conservative anti-marketeers argued that their stance was not contradictory to the 1970 Party manifesto, because the manifesto had only committed the government to *negotiate* entry, 'no more, no less' and Heath himself had famously declared that membership should only occur with the 'full-hearted consent' of Parliament and people, which arguably suggested a popular vote was needed. There was real concern in Paris that the Commons would vote against entry. Over the summer, pressure was put on Conservative 'anti' MPs to fall into line and the Conservative Group for Europe launched what has been called 'the largest internal education campaign . . . ever . . . undertaken inside the Conservative Party'.[71] Some MPs did change their view, influenced by a desire to stand up to Labour, by the shift in opinion polls and by the fact that this was a vital piece of government policy whose defeat could lead to a general election. Only two members of the government resigned over the idea of entry; one was a junior minister, Teddy Taylor, the other a member of the whip's office, Jasper Moore. Nonetheless, when the Conservative Party conference voted overwhelmingly in favour of entry in October, the Chief Whip, Francis Pym, was still concerned about the number of anti-marketeers in Parliament. In several meetings with senior ministers, Pym urged that Conservative MPs should be allowed a 'free vote'. His thinking was that the remaining Conservative 'antis' would vote against entry even if a three-line whip were used; whereas a free vote would put the pressure on Labour to do the same, and so allow Jenkins's social democrats to vote for entry. Pym won the influential support of William Whitelaw, but Douglas-Home, Carrington and Reginald Maudling argued that a 'free vote' would send the wrong message to France and the Six: all Conservative MPs should be expected to vote for such a vital measure. Heath too was 'awfully resistant' to Pym's pleading and only accepted his arguments on 18 October – three days before the Commons debate began.[72] In fact Wilson did not allow his own MPs a free vote, but Pym's gamble nonetheless succeeded. After six days of

70. For a fuller discussion see Young, *Britain and European Unity*, 114–15.

71. N. Ashford, 'The European Economic Community', in Z. Layton-Henry (ed.), *Conservative Party Politics* (London, 1980), 104.

72. Evidence of Lord Pym, 'The Heath Government' witness seminar, 188–219; interview with Pym, Seventies Archive; King, *Diary*, 143–4; W. Whitelaw, *The Whitelaw Memoirs* (London, 1989), 73–4.

intense debate, the longest since the war, 39 Conservatives voted against entry, but 69 Labour MPs were emboldened to vote in favour, and the winning margin, of 356 to 244, was much greater than expected. Returning to his Downing Street flat, Heath began his celebrations by sitting at the keyboard to play Bach's 'The Well-Tempered Clavier'.[73]

Although the vote of 28 October was a major triumph, it was not the end the parliamentary battle. Following Heath's signature of the Treaty of Accession in Brussels on 22 January 1972, a European Communities Bill on entry had to be voted into law. Anti-marketeers had hoped for a long and complex piece of legislation which could be attacked clause by clause, paralysing the Commons timetable. Instead the Bill, drawn up in the office of Sir Geoffrey Howe, the Solicitor-General, had only twelve clauses, which simply accepted the Treaty of Rome, existing EC regulations and the terms of entry. Despite this simplification of the legislative process the Bill took over three hundred hours of debate, it hindered the passage of other measures and it dominated the life of Pym and the whips' office for several months. Pym considered it 'the centrepiece of the whole parliament'.[74] Labour social democrats decided that, after October's successful vote in principle on entry, they would return to their party loyalty and this gave Conservative anti-marketeers new hope of preventing membership. Before the Bill's second reading on 17 February, Heath called potential rebels to a meeting and warned them that defeat would lead to a general election, but fifteen still voted against him and his majority fell to eight. Labour 'antis' complained that the government was only saved by the Liberals (who had been strongly pro-entry for more than a decade) and by social democrats who 'colluded' with Heath to ensure that, however low his majority fell, he never actually lost a vote. Pym himself later denied playing a 'numbers game' with the opposition and certainly took no chances with the Bill, forcing sick MPs on his own side to vote. But the Speaker, Selwyn Lloyd, 'had the impression that the Labour pro-marketeers were . . . determined to have enough abstentions to let the Bill through'; one Labour MP, Christopher Mayhew (who defected to the Liberals in 1974) later admitted to organising pro-marketeers in his party to ensure that the Bill passed its second reading; and, after April 1972, the Jenkinsite MP John Roper was in contact with the newest Conservative whip, Kenneth Clarke, to help ensure a

73. Evidence of Lord Armstrong, 'The Heath Government' witness seminar, 188–219.

74. Evidence of Lord Pym, ibid. Howe gives the credit for the ingeniously short Bill to his senior parliamentary counsel, Sir John Fiennes: Geoffrey Howe, *Conflict of Loyalty* (London, 1994), 67–9.

majority in all votes.[75] In early May the debates were cut short by the use of guillotines, which anti-marketeers claimed made further mockery of the complex questions involved in entry. Nonetheless, the Third Reading was not passed until 13 July, by which time there had been more than a hundred votes in all, one of which was won by a majority of only four. It was difficult to deny that EC membership had been fully debated even if it had required extraordinary measures to push it through. William Whitelaw considered that Pym's contribution to EC entry ranked alongside that of Heath and Rippon.[76]

HEATH IN THE COMMUNITY

The European Communities Act received royal assent on 17 October 1972 and British membership took effect on 1 January 1973. Only two days after the royal assent, however, Heath went to an EC summit called by Pompidou, to which the other new entrants, Denmark and Ireland, were also invited. (Norway had rejected membership after a referendum.) There was general hope at this summit of giving a new impetus to growth in the Community by supplementing the widening of membership with new measures to improve common decision-making, to extend the activities of the EC and to develop the member economies. As in later extensions of the Community, therefore, a *deepening* as well as a widening was envisaged. Yet the first nine-power Summit, despite all its hopes and initiatives, also proved that the differing interests of member states could make common action impossible. Heath's major aim was to establish a European Regional Development Fund (ERDF) which would benefit poor industrial areas in the EC, of which Britain was now one. He saw this as an industrial equivalent of the CAP.[77] It has been argued that the ERDF exposed Heath's 'federalist' tendencies, in that it showed him ready to create stronger institutions at the centre of the EC, even when his primary purpose was to achieve a British *national* aim. Unwilling to challenge the idea that the EC had its 'own resources', Heath sought to reduce Britain's net contribution to the EC by establishing a new common policy.[78]

75. Interview with Pym, 1970s Archive; D.R. Thorpe, *Selwyn Lloyd* (London, 1989), 423–4; C. Mayhew, *Time to Explain* (London, 1987), 190–91; M. Balen, *Kenneth Clarke* (London, 1994), 80–81.

76. Whitelaw, *Memoirs*, 75.

77. Interview with Heath, 14 June 1972, Hetherington papers.

78. Margaret Thatcher can be said to have been consistently anti-federal after 1979 by seeking to reduce Britain's net contribution through a rebate system. E. Dell, 'Britain and the origins of the European Monetary System', *Contemporary European History*, vol. 3, no. 1 (1994), 12–13.

The other members agreed to set up the ERDF by December 1973 as a way to tackle structural unemployment and economic imbalances in the EC, but the size of the fund remained to be decided and the Germans were privately sceptical about it, partly because it would distort the operation of market forces and partly because they would be the main contributor to it (as they were to the CAP). There were also differences on institutional reform, with Britain and France opposed to proposals from Italy and the Benelux states for a stronger Commission, a directly elected European Parliament[79] and majority voting. Heath believed that decision-making could simply be improved under existing institutions. When the summit closed on 20 October, its decisions looked dramatic and Heath considered the communiqué to be 'the finest . . . of modern times'. As well as the promise of an ERDF, there was talk of common action on the environment, of an EC social policy to improve working conditions (about which Heath was not enthusiastic), of removing barriers to internal trade (which he did support), even of creating a 'European Union' and EMU by 1980. Indeed, the debate in Paris can be seen, in retrospect, to have been very similar to the general lines of debate surrounding the Single European Act and Maastricht Treaty of many years later. The fact was, however, that in the 1970s none of the lofty hopes of the Paris summit were realised. EC institutions were not equipped to fulfil the ambitious aims, and differences between the member states ran too deep. Over the following eighteen months, deadlines which had been set for progress in Paris passed without action. There would be no 'European Union' for two decades.[80]

The most obvious failure after Paris was that of EMU, which the Six had first established as their aim at the Hague in December 1969. The intention of EMU was to secure monetary stability in Europe, give greater certainty to businesses trading across Community borders, maximise the volume of trade and deepen economic integration. A European Monetary Cooperation Fund *was* established in April 1973, but attempts to move further on the agenda for EMU completely failed. The aim of achieving EMU by 1980 was soon abandoned although attempts were made to tie EC currencies together (within a certain percentage of each other's value) in the so-called 'snake', which had come into operation in April 1972. One problem facing efforts

79. Until 1979 the European Parliament was made up of representatives from national parliaments.

80. On the Summit see especially Lord, *British Entry*, 148, 152, 156–7; S. George, *An Awkward Partner* (London, 1990), 56–60. Heath quoted from 'European integration', 200.

aimed at achieving EMU was the different intentions of members supporting monetary stability. Thus, the French wanted Europe to match the power of the US dollar, had little desire for a central supranational monetary institution and hoped to see Germany bear the burden of supporting the value of other European currencies; the Germans, in contrast, favoured a strong *Bundesbank*-style central institution which would force other European countries to accept deflationary discipline as a way to control rising prices, and which would not be a drain on German resources.

Britain, with its weak currency and inflationary habits, could not have faced the rigours of EMU on the German model; and, unlike the French, Britain did not see the power of the dollar as any kind of threat or feel the same need to place a brake on German power. Apart from these differences in national priorities, efforts at currency alignment also faced a daunting international economic scene, characterised by greater inflation, lower growth and greater currency instability than had been the case in the 1950s and early 1960s. In this environment even the attempt at a loose, flexible system like the snake failed to prosper. Britain entered the snake in May 1972 but left after only six weeks and never rejoined. The Treasury had little faith in European efforts at currency alignment, wished to preserve its own freedom of manoeuvre and, in any case, lacked sufficient reserves to maintain Sterling's value. On 23 June 1972 – as with the *Deutschmark* before it – Sterling was floated against other currencies without any attempt to co-ordinate action with the rest of the EC. In March 1973, when Heath visited Bonn for the first time as political leader of an EC member, Brandt did seem ready to support Sterling as part of a 'joint float' of EC currencies (at a time when the value of the dollar was falling rapidly). But the German Economic and Finance Ministries were sceptical about this, given the likely costs of the scheme to Germany, the weakness of the pound and their preference for reliance on market forces. Heath for his part apparently raised the radical suggestion of a rapid move to a central bank with a joint pooling of EC reserves, but his own officials pointed out that Britain had no reserves to offer such a system![81] Britain was not the only country to experience difficulties with the snake. After the October 1973 Middle East War, when oil prices quadrupled, even the French found it difficult to keep their

81. The currency crisis overshadowed other issues which Heath had wanted to discuss in Bonn, most notably the European Regional Development Fund. Brandt, *People and Policies*, 251–2; Heath, 'European integration', 203; N. Henderson, *Mandarin* (London, 1994), 58.

currency in step with the *Deutschmark*, being forced out of the snake in January 1974. It increasingly became a German-dominated group.

Even if the Treasury avoided the costly discipline of the snake, EC membership still proved a burden to Britain's economy after 1972, and not only because of the higher food prices under CAP, the loss of earnings from external tariffs and the greater openness to EC competition which membership brought. The ill-fated budget for domestic expansion, which Barber announced in March 1972, was partly designed to prepare Britain to take advantage of the common market and to compensate for the lack of investment by British companies ahead of the cold douche of European competition. (Heath's increasing readiness to intervene in the economy at this time reflected, in part, the same desire.) The 'Barber boom' of course resulted in inflation and a trade deficit, and in 1973 EC membership became associated with the country's deepening economic malaise.

If Heath could not reverse the country's economic weaknesses through membership, neither could he alter popular attitudes to the European adventure. Opinion polls showed that British people, especially in older age-groups, were less willing than those in the original Six to accept common EC policies and greater powers to EC institutions. The British took a pragmatic view of Europe, as of so many subjects, and looked for material gains; when such gains failed to emerge, the sense of disappointment was all the worse. In Parliament and government too there was little idealism about Europe. The debates among MPs in 1971–72 had, of course, revolved around self-interest, party-political arguments and a tendency among supporters to play down the changes EC membership would bring. In 1973 the all-party Ways and Means Committee of the Commons devoted its attention to ensuring that there would be effective parliamentary control over new EC legislation and there was grave concern when this proved difficult to achieve. Meanwhile, among civil servants there was a growing sense of frustration that so much effort had been devoted to securing membership for little reward. The Treasury was determined not to accept further commitments in the Community unless Britain received back at least as much as it contributed.[82] As early as February 1973 the Ambassador to France, Nicholas Henderson, took part in a meeting of the interdepartmental 'European Unit' and 'found that the top civil servants in Whitehall were hardly enthusiastic about Europe'.[83]

Heath himself apparently became disappointed with the indecision

82. On the attitudes of populace, Parliament and government see Lord, *British Entry*, 132–44, 165–6, 169.

83. Henderson, *Mandarin*, 51.

of Community institutions during 1973. Before entry he had privately told one newspaper editor that achieving agreement in the Council of Ministers 'couldn't be worse . . . than getting Margaret Thatcher to agree with some of her colleagues'.[84] But the Council of Ministers (representing the member states) did indeed prove cumbersome so that, by July 1973, the British government favoured regular summits of European leaders to break through the differences and push cooperation forward. Heath discussed this idea with Brandt in October.[85] Yet when European leaders did meet in Copenhagen in mid-December, there was still division and deadlock. The summit was meant to review work done under the Paris programme of 1972 but there was little success to report. Instead, the Copenhagen meeting was overshadowed by the oil crisis and by pressure from Brandt for Britain to share its North Sea oil wealth (due to come on tap in the following few years) with the rest of the Community. Heath, facing a coalminers' strike and deepening dissatisfaction over the EC at home, rejected this proposal but still expected the Germans to agree to set up an ERDF of £1,250m. In response Brandt would only offer a paltry £250m. To the British it seemed that the EC was unwilling to help a new member in trouble; to the Germans ERDF was another potential burden on their own well-disciplined, low-inflation economy. At one meeting in early 1974, Anglo-German differences apparently became so heated that references were made to the Second World War![86] Heath's failure to cooperate with the Germans has been blamed by some on a preference (first seen during the entry talks) to concentrate on building up a close relationship with Paris. Actually, however, Heath seems to have hoped for a triangular London–Paris–Bonn relationship which had failed to emerge because of differences between all three.[87] Certainly Pompidou was as disappointed as anyone with Britain's performance during its first year of EC membership.[88]

84. Alastair Hetherington's summary of an interview with Heath, 30 June 1971, Hetherington papers.

85. Regular Summits of the 'European Council' were eventually inaugurated in 1975. See remarks by John Davies, Advisory Committee on Policy, 18 July 1973, ACP(73) 125; Brandt, *People and Policies*, 252.

86. Brandt, *People and Policies*, 276; Heath, 'European integration', 200–201; Lord, *British Entry*, 166.

87. Lord, *British Entry*, 170–71.

88. Abadie and Corcelette, *Pompidou*, 342.

CONCLUSION

Problems over the EC dogged Heath's premiership to the very end. In the closing days of the February 1974 election campaign, Enoch Powell urged Conservative anti-marketeers to vote Labour, because Wilson's party at least promised renegotiation and a popular vote on continued membership. Given the narrowness of the election result, Powell's advice may have been a fatal development for Heath.[89] It is difficult to deny that entry to the EC was a great success for the Prime Minister and the most important step for Britain taken by his government. He and Rippon seemed to win reasonable terms for British membership and the issue was debated at great length. Yet, membership did have serious economic costs and, once Britain was inside the EC, its policy could hardly be described as successful. One writer has argued that this was because the Prime Minister himself was not, actually, more 'pro-European' than other postwar British premiers, the evidence being that his government criticised the workings of CAP, did little to support EMU and maintained the country's world trading role.[90] But this line of criticism is misdirected. All member nations try to secure national ambitions within the EC. The essential fact about Heath, unlike for other British leaders, was that he was *communautaire* in behaviour, committed to the European ideal, ready to extend the competency of EC institutions and believing, as one policy document put it, that 'As a member of a powerful Community . . . we should have more not less control of our destiny.'[91] He offered all his ministers the chance of free tuition in another EC language,[92] and the Conservative Party machine was urged to 'think European' in devising new policy proposals.[93] One flaw in the government's approach, however, may have been the desire to develop the EC on an evolutionary, pragmatic basis and ultimately preserve Britain's control over its own destiny. Heath of course wanted the Community to develop *sui generis*; as one Conservative policy

89. D. Butler and D. Kavanagh, *The British General Election of February 1974* (London, 1975), 55–6, 89–91, 103–5.

90. S. George, *Britain and European Integration since 1945* (London, 1991), 50–53.

91. Conservative Research Department memo, 'The Policy Implications of Community Membership', 13 July 1973, ACP(73)79.

92. Evidence of Christopher Chataway, 'The Heath Government' witness seminar, 188–219; and see Henderson, *Mandarin*, 59.

93. Memo, 'Thinking European', 4 February 1972, CRD/3/10/14. Conservative Research Department documents in 1971 show a readiness to accept 'sovereignity in common', the development of EC activities outside the Treaty of Rome, democratisation of Community institutions, and common monetary and foreign policies: 'Towards a Programme for the Ten', not dated, and 'The Development of Britain's European Policy', 16 April 1971, CRD/3/10/13.

document argued, 'It is only through a careful process of growing together, and not through the establishment of theoretical blueprints, that we shall advance . . .'[94] Yet ministers, when they committed the country to a European future, probably underestimated the need for both a radical change in national outlook and a strengthening of EC decision-making. They took the easy course of 'selling' Europe to the British people as a pragmatic step, and did little to overcome the persistent lack of eagerness among Parliament and people for the European 'adventure'. Neither did they succeed in the practical step of preparing the economy adequately for the blast of European competition.[95] Besides, Heath himself 'failed to communicate' his own vision of Britain in Europe, partly because of a personal inability to generate enthusiasm in an audience,[96] but also because the scale of such a task was a formidable one in 1970s Britain: his 'Fanfare for Europe' festival of January 1973 was received with depressing indifference. It would be wrong, however, to blame Heath's government alone for the failures of the EC after the 1972 Paris Summit. Targets set in Paris were overambitious, EC members faced different national problems and priorities, and certainly Pompidou was no keener than the British to make a significant shift in decision-making towards the centre. Finally, it must be conceded that Heath faced the worse possible circumstances in 1973 for exploiting EC membership. He had had little more than a year as an EC leader; the West as a whole was entering an era of stagnant growth; his government was beset at home by inflation, unemployment and strikes. With several more years as premier, Heath might have been able to tackle the country's indifference towards the Community. As it was, the popularity of membership fell in opinion polls alongside his own. When he lost office, the EC was at the start of a period of stagnation and Britain was set on the course of renegotiating the entry terms he had obtained, a depressing saga which would not properly end until Margaret Thatcher won a new deal on Britain's budgetary contribution a full decade later.[97]

94. 'The Policy Implications of Community Membership'.

95. See the general thesis of Lord, *British Entry*.

96. Campbell, *Edward Heath*, xvii.

97. I am grateful to the following for commenting on an earlier draft of this chapter: Dr Philip Lynch of Leicester University; Mr D.R. Thorpe of Charterhouse School (especially for comments on the role of Douglas-Home of whom Mr Thorpe is the official biographer); Dr John Barnes of the London School of Economics.

CHAPTER TWELVE

The foreign policy of the Heath government

Christopher Hill and Christopher Lord

THE IMPACT OF EC ENTRY ON WORLD POLICY

In terms of domestic politics, the Heath government is variously regarded as an interlude between the Labour governments of 1964–70 and 1974–9, a precursor to the Thatcher experiment, or as an administration that destroyed any claim to an identity of its own through its policy reversals. By contrast, the successful conclusion of Britain's entry to the European Community (EC) is seen as giving the external policy of the Heath government a clear and enduring importance; indeed, to mark it out as a turning point in Britain's international position, bringing to an end a period of semi-detachment from West Europe and initiating a process of absorption into the European Community that would be continued with the Single European Act (1986) and the Maastricht Treaty (1991).

This chapter must, therefore, begin where John Young's leaves off, for the central foreign policy question for any UK government in the early 1970s was one of how the wider canvass of Britain's external relations would be related to its imminent membership of the EC. What is of great interest and importance is that two quite different assumptions about this problem emerged at the heart of the Heath government. The first saw EC entry as being as much about the shoring up of Britain's traditional relations with the Commonwealth and the US as it was concerned with West Europe itself; as a minor rebalancing of Britain's foreign policy made necessary by the way in which its absence from the European Community had attenuated its influence elsewhere; and as likely to produce a much-needed transfusion of economic resources for a flagging *national* diplomacy. The second and more radical view presupposed that Britain would owe its new partners the duty of prior consultation, even if it continued to have important attachments beyond the Community. This seemed to be the inescapable implication of the argument that Britain should join the Six in a more co-ordinated approach to foreign policy, in order to combat the relative under-representation of western Europe in the international system. Where the first view might crudely be characterised as an attempt to join the EC in order to make Britain great again, the second suggested that the future management of external problems would be apportioned between national and European frameworks and that efforts to improve the latter, and direct them towards the handling of a collaborative foreign policy, would be as important as the status of Britain's own national diplomacy.

This difference did not amount to anything as tidy as a Heath–Home split, though it will be seen that there was one occasion in which it almost manifested itself in this form. It is more revealingly located in a contrast between the early Heath and the later Heath. In his first speech to the Conservative Party conference, Heath promised a 'new era in British diplomacy which would leave behind the years of retreat'.[1] At that time, he seems to have assumed that Britain's diminished position in the world was purely the product of mismanagement by the Wilson government and that the Conservatives, returning to office after six years, could pick up many of the UK's foreign policy roles where they had been left in 1964.[2] Presupposing the diplomacy of manoeuvre associated with the conventional view of what EC entry would mean for Britain's foreign policy beyond Europe – rather than the diplomacy of commitment implied by the more radical perspective – he argued that British policy would henceforth be based on the sole criterion of *national* interest and a determination to view others as neither permanent friends nor permanent allies.[3] He was also quite as vociferous as his predecessors in rejecting the notion that Britain was merely a regional power, confined in its roles to its own corner of the world.

By the time of the crucial second reading of the European Communities Bill in February 1972, Heath acknowledged that a shift had taken place in his own reading of Britain's international position. He told the House of Commons, 'I believed until recently that we could carry on fairly well outside' the EC.[4] With a more pessimistic view of the constraints on a purely national diplomacy, Heath became increasingly interested in the practicalities of forging a collective diplomacy within the EC.[5] Between 1972 and 1974, he made various suggestions

1. J. Campbell, *Edward Heath* (London, 1993), 310.
2. *Financial Times*, 20 December 1970.
3. E. Heath, 'Realism in Foreign Policy', *Foreign Affairs*, 1 (1969), 39–51.
4. *House of Commons Debates*, 9 February 1972.
5. C. Lord, *British Entry to the European Community Under the Heath Government of 1970–4* (Aldershot, 1993), 44–6.

that were both distant from the centre of political gravity in his own government and, in some ways, even beyond anything that has ever been achieved to date in European foreign policy and security co-operation. He was eager that European policy processes should develop their own integrity, free from excessive outside penetration. He thus aligned with Pompidou to reject a German proposal that the US should have formalised rights of consultation with the EC. He was also keen that the EC countries should be able to deploy some concrete foreign policy instruments of their own, and to that end, he tended to disagree with Pompidou's preference for a rigid separation between the European Economic Community and new processes of diplomatic concertation.

The question of whether the Heath government represented a clean break from the past, or an untidy one that contained the seeds of future confusion, has been flagged in the literature on Britain's postwar foreign policy. F.S. Northedge has argued that it was at this point that British governments found that there really was 'nowhere else to go except into the Europe of the six'.[6] Joseph Frankel continued this theme. For three decades, the perceptions of British governments of their power and status had lagged behind the changing realities of their international situation, and much substance had been dissipated on nostalgic attempts to rediscover great power status. Now, UK foreign policy was at last taking a form more appropriate to a middle-ranking state, whose interests were concentrated on its own immediate region of West Europe and whose domestic economy needed a supportive external policy, rather than the other way round.[7]

However, more recent authors have suggested that the reformation in British foreign policy attitudes in the early 1970s proceeded at different speeds, replacing the relatively tight foreign policy consensus of the early 1950s and 1960s with two contrasting schools of thought. On the one hand, a traditionalist school saw no reason why national decline should translate into changes in foreign policy behaviour beyond the need to be more modest in matching international responsibilities to national capabilities. On the other hand, a transformationalist school suggested that Britain's external condition was not merely declining, it was also changing in character. A growth of interdependence meant that even if the British state remained a central foreign policy actor, it would have to behave in very different ways. There would have to be a shift from unilateral to multilateral policy-making, a blurring between the management of Britain's internal and external affairs, and a new

6. F.S. Northedge, *Descent from Power: British Foreign Policy, 1945–73* (London, 1974), 328.

7. J. Frankel, *British Foreign Policy: 1945–73* (London, 1975), 310–37.

agenda that gave more weight to the transnational dimension of economic and social issues and a little less weight to the cultivation of military power capabilities. In all, it would mean giving more attention in foreign policy to the politics of pleasing non-state actors, such as domestic political constituencies, global markets and international organizations.[8]

At the time of the Heath government, some took this transformationalist position to be one of the messages of the large-scale review of British foreign policy that had recently been carried out in the Duncan report of 1969, itself a follow-up to the retrenchment of British overseas policy announced in January 1968 with the withdrawal from East of Suez. Thus one of the authors of the report wrote: 'Britain has become convinced of the need to act collectively with neighbours on matters which were previously considered purely domestic concerns.'[9] Before returning at the end of this chapter to crucial debates such as these, our analysis needs to acknowledge the two-way flow between broad concepts of foreign policy direction and the daily grind of meeting or ignoring political promises, negotiating deals, managing crises, honing the institutions of foreign policy-making and cultivating particular relationships. It should also be remembered that the culture of British foreign policy-making tends to eschew conceptualisation and to emphasise empirical adjustment (which some call 'muddling through' and others 'pragmatism'). Even at a time of movement represented by the early 1970s, therefore, big ideas and theoretical choices did not always get the attention they deserved, a point not lost on Keith Joseph and Margaret Thatcher in the context of domestic policy.

EAST OF SUEZ

As part of its commitment to restore a sense of determination to UK foreign policy, the Heath government had made more specific promises on international questions than is common in the election manifestos of British political parties. Some means would be found to maintain Britain's security roles in Singapore, Malaysia and the Persian Gulf; arms sales would be resumed to South Africa; and one last effort would be made to secure a settlement with the rebel regime in Rhodesia.

It is possible to view these commitments as owing more to domestic

8. M. Smith, S. Smith and B. White (eds), *British Foreign Policy* (London, 1988), 3–25.

9. A. Shonfield, 'The Duncan Report and its Critics', *International Affairs*, 2 (1970), 247–68.

political competition than to international realities. By promising to reverse the withdrawals from East of Suez, the Conservatives were able to distinguish themselves from Labour in foreign policy. Since Labour's conversion to EC entry removed any difference on what was probably the main external issue of the day, Heath sought to establish a distinction on a secondary issue; and, at the same time, to suggest a general difference of attitude between Conservatives who were prepared to face up to Britain's international obligations, and a Labour government that was irresponsible in its handling of foreign affairs. Such positioning was arguably encouraged by Wilson's decision to make governing credibility a major factor in party competition by claiming for Labour what had previously been one of the Conservatives strong suits – the claim to be the natural party of government. On the other hand, all these pledges to maintain an active role in Africa and Asia related to the legacy of Empire, and were more likely to appeal to floating Conservative voters than to progressives. They were essential to maintain a balancing act within the Conservative Party itself and to assuage a body of opinion that feared the excessive Europeanisation of foreign policy under Heath's leadership. East of Suez can be seen as occupying the same place in the party politics of opposition as the pledge to hold a referendum on EC entry held for Wilson between 1972 and 1974 – it postponed foreign policy differences to a time when they could be managed with the disciplines of government available to the party leadership.

Much of the first half of the Heath government was, indeed, taken up with managing a graceful retreat from its early promises in matters of foreign policy and there was some speculation that this presented a bigger problem than had been anticipated, for the promises may have been made in the belief that there would be no election until 1971, by which time the withdrawals from East of Suez would have conveniently passed a point of no return.[10] Nonetheless, it would be a mistake to conclude that they lacked any vestige of sincerity. To see why, it is necessary to set the plans which Heath inherited for the rationalisation of Britain's international commitments away from the Middle and Far East in the context of the decline of the containment doctrine, according to which the west had aimed to maintain capabilities to meet an 'aggression' at *any point* along the lengthy Eurasian perimeter of the Communist world. Given that Britain was still very much a power in the Middle and Far East in the 1950s, containment outside Europe had been largely an Anglo-American joint enterprise. However, the geostrategic scope of the doctrine meant that it encouraged an over-

10. *Financial Times*, 26 June 1970.

stretch of resources, a problem that British governments encountered in the need to withdraw from East of Suez under the pressure of currency crises in the late 1960s.

It was, however, hard to abandon the containment mind-set. The incoming Heath administration, therefore, found it difficult to conceive of a complete withdrawal from Britain's responsibilities in the Gulf and Far East without conjuring up the image of a power vacuum into which unwelcome forces would rush on Britain's departure. The Gulf was ridden with conflicting territorial claims and seemed by some misfortune to have developed one of the least stable of possible state structures. Small oil-rich states nestled between three large rivals who were rapidly developing their military capacity. The withdrawal of British protection from some of the smaller sheikhdoms seemed likely to lead to the competitive development of client–patron relations in the area, if not physical aggression from some of the larger neighbours. In both cases – Singapore and Malaysia and the Gulf – Heath and Home were much preoccupied with the build-up of the Soviet navy. As Henry Kissinger was to point out, this represented a significant change in the whole nature of Russian power. The 'Soviet threat' now seemed to have a mobile and ubiquitous presence, where previously the USSR's ability to project conventional force had been limited to the use of land armies from fixed positions along the edges of the Warsaw Pact.

However, a simple contradiction pervaded the attempt of the Heath government to remain in the Middle and Far East, for the policy was based on the hope that a security guarantee could be constructed without cost or risk: that commitments of British power could be made credible enough to deter aggressors, even while the new Heath government continued the work of its predecessor in minimising the financial cost of security roles and limiting Britain's liability to pour further troops into non-European arenas in the event of an emergency. By early 1971, it was clear that withdrawals from the Gulf would continue much as planned by the Wilson government and although the Defence Secretary, Lord Carrington, succeeded in arranging a continued British presence in Singapore and Malaysia, it was on an entirely different basis to that which had existed up to 1968. The Anglo-Malaysian Defence Agreement was revoked, leaving Britain free of any *automatic* commitment to defend the area. The permanent presence was reduced to just 10,000 troops and most of these were garrisoned in Singapore, rather than in Malaysia where they would have been more useful – but also more exposed to real dangers, such as spill-over conflicts from Indochina. Above all, Britain only remained in the area as a facilitator of a Five-Power Defence Pact which the

Heath government negotiated with Singapore, Malaysia, Australia and New Zealand. Ten years earlier it had on its own been the main provider of security for the region, but now many suspected that even its membership of the five-power pact was provisional and unlikely to last much beyond the mid-1970s.[11]

The continuation of a penny-packet commitment to Singapore and Malaysia was only made possible because of major differences between this region and the Gulf, the most obvious of which was that a continued British presence enjoyed the consent and cooperation of local states in the first case but not in the second. The policy was not really sustainable beyond the first few weeks of the Heath government when Iran, Iraq, Saudi Arabia and even Kuwait confirmed that Britain would only remain in the Gulf in the face of the active hostility of the larger players in the region, any one of which would have been able to overwhelm the token forces that would probably be the limit of any British commitment. Even the smaller states that were supposedly in need of UK protection were unwilling to lose the rationale for their own rearmanent programmes afforded by the prospect of British withdrawal. Some were also concerned that their regimes would be delegitimised if seen to be propped up by British force at a time of rising radicalism in the Arab world. In any case, it was unlikely that British guarantees, already devalued in their credibility by the fact that they had been unilaterally withdrawn once before by a UK government in financial trouble, would ever amount to very much and certainly not enough to make it worthwhile to remain in a security relationship unacceptable to Iran. It was also hard to see how Britain could reconfigure its role in the Gulf to new realities without increasing costs and risks to itself. The few military capabilities it still had in the region were geared to the defence of Kuwait against an invasion from Iraq, and not to the new role that the Heath government envisaged of protecting the twelve smaller Gulf states. Indeed, these all had idiosyncratic defence needs, so the continuation of a credible British defence role in the region would have been a complex and probably expensive exercise in security planning.

By the end of July 1970, the British government seemed to acknowledge the limitations of its Gulf policy by changing its intended role from security provider to external federator. A retired diplomat, Sir William Lane, was sent out to explore the possibilities for at least pulling the small Gulf States together into some kind of political entity

11. M. Leifer, 'Retreat and Reappraisal in South East Asia' in M. Leifer (ed.), *Constraints and Adjustments in British Foreign Policy* (London, 1971), 86–103.

that would be collectively more defensible with or without Britain. However, Conservative promises to reverse withdrawals had already delayed the 'federating process' and, in the meantime, Bahrain – a key state – had gone its separate way by signing a security pact with Iran. The prospect of a meaningful political union of the small states rapidly lost 'critical mass' as Dubai saw little point in joining without Bahrain, and Britain was left with the prospect of sponsoring an association of some of the shakier and least reputable of the local regimes.

A further difference between the Middle and Far East was that the United States, which had originally been deeply concerned about UK withdrawals from the Gulf, was already tilting towards an alternative to continued British involvement. Nixon and Kissinger increasingly saw Iran in the role of reliable regional hegemon, and this left the Heath Government with little choice but to go with the flow by accepting that any future military involvement in the Gulf might have to take the form of British access to Iranian security infrastructures, a possibility that the Shah refused even to discuss until Britain had completed its withdrawals of permanent forces from the area. By contrast, the US was willing to support the Heath government's plans to remain in Singapore and Malaysia. Having failed to get Wilson to contribute British troops to Vietnam, Britain's presence in a 'counter-insurgency' role in another part of South East Asia was the nearest thing to getting an ally alongside.

SOUTHERN AFRICA

The promise to resume arms sales to South Africa partly reflected the commercial frustration that other countries, unconstrained by membership of the British Commonwealth, were picking up contracts that might otherwise have gone to the UK. However, strategic concerns were also of importance and these, once again, centred on the development of Soviet naval power. Home looked back to his own government's negotiation of the Simonstown Agreement in 1964 to reach the conclusion that South Africa was a pivotal point in the defence of the South Atlantic and Indian oceans; and to argue that Britain was obliged to supply South Africa with naval hardware to defend sea lanes around the Cape.

Arms to South Africa, and a suspicion that it was preparing the way for a soft settlement in Rhodesia, pitched the Heath government into public and acrimonious conflict with the Commonwealth. To a degree, Heath used this for his own purposes, exploiting issues on which many African and Asian countries had succeeded in infuriating the Conservative Party, to declare Britain's own relative independence from the Commonwealth and to downgrade it as a forum for the UK's external involvements. However, it is hard to avoid the conclusion that the Commonwealth remained a significant constraint even for the 1970–74 government. Heath and Home seem to have been genuinely suprised by the extent of Commonwealth opposition to their policies in Southern Africa, with none of the 47 members – except for the maverick Malawi regime, whose support almost added to Heath's embarrassment – supporting the original plans to resume sales. The extent to which even Heath felt a continuing relationship with the Commonwealth was necessary was suggested by the repeated postponement of a definite announcement on arms sales between June 1970 and February 1971 to allow prior discussion of the problem by a full Commonwealth conference in Singapore in January 1971; and by the eventual limitation of the hardware supplied to a few spare parts and some helicopters. Even this was probably only a token gesture which saved the government's *amour propre* after all it had done to insist that it would not be pushed around by the Commonwealth. Indeed, it was the minimum that the law officers claimed that the UK needed to supply to South Africa under the letter of the Simonstown Agreement of 1964,[12] and it is also significant that, when the South African government sought to test Heath's willingness to go further by offering to place a lucrative contract for frigates with British shipyards, the temptation was studiously ignored.[13]

At least three countries – Tanzania, Uganda and Zambia – threatened to resign from the Commonwealth if the Heath government sold arms to South Africa. Although there was some speculation that Heath might even welcome a rationalised Commonwealth, stripped of those members he felt were too eager to 'put Britain in the dock', he ultimately chose to avoid a crisis. There was no way of telling precisely where a wave of resignations might stop; a Commonwealth polarised between its black and white members would also have been personally distasteful to Heath; and the government could not put the whole Commonwealth at risk just as it was trying to secure EC entry against the opposition of a substantial section of its own Party.

All of this meant going along with a majority opinion that was unconvinced by the claims of the British government that it could sell arms to South Africa that would bolster its defence of sea lanes around

12. *Financial Times*, 23 February 1971.
13. *Financial Times*, 16 April 1971.

the Cape, without also contributing to its capacity for internal repression or the projection of force against its black neighbours. Even those who accepted the feasibility of this distinction felt that it was beside the point, for any resumption of sales would be used by South Africa to claim some external legitimation of apartheid and to assuage domestic anxieties about the long-term sustainability of that system in the face of international opprobrium. The more skilful opponents of arms sales carefully undercut the claim that South Africa was strategically significant to the defence of the non-communist world as a whole. At the Singapore Commonwealth conference in January 1971 a compromise was suggested in which the joint UK–US base on the Maldives would be reinforced, as a substitute for Simonstown, and a working party would be appointed to look into the whole problem of security in the Indian Ocean. From outside the Commonwealth, the US also inclined to the thesis that the southern seas could be best defended from a string of bases in islands and micro-states, untouched by the complications of Southern African politics. Stripped of a clear security rationale, Heath's policy appeared increasingly commercial in intention, and commercially unwise at that, for UK trade was evenly divided between South Africa and other African countries which threatened reprisals against British economic interests.

At first sight the promise to make one more attempt to reach a settlement with Rhodesia was one that could have been easily satisfied by going through the rituals of negotiations, however hopeless. Yet, of all the foreign policy involvements of the Heath years, this was one in which it was hardest to calculate the balance of bargaining strengths, or the political effects, domestic and international, of the various options open to the British government.

Taking the whole period of the 'Rhodesian rebellion' from 1965 to 1980, the early 1970s seem to have been among the least propitious years for a settlement. The British government had long since scaled down the military capabilities which it would have needed to intervene with force.[14] By 1970, sanctions had been in operation for five years without effecting any perceptible interruption to the steady growth of the Rhodesian economy at a rate of 4–5 per cent per year. The Smith regime showed growing confidence that the British government would simply allow sanctions to fall into desuetude. They were costly to enforce, worked against Britain's own commercial interest and created friction between the government and its own backbenchers. The British government also seemed to have every incentive to get Rhodesia off

14. B. Castle, *The Castle Diaries 1964–70* (London, 1984), 191.

the political agenda as part of a rationalisation of its external involvements and a new concentration on Western Europe. Indeed, Carrington would later write of Rhodesia that 'its importance was as an irritant – with the Commonwealth, with our European partners and with the United States'.[15]

In reopening talks with Smith, Heath and Home also faced a problem of maintaining control over such negotiating leverage as they had and of preventing others from undermining their bargaining position in advance. A constant stream of British right-wing visitors fed Rhodesian delusions that the new Conservative government was ready to settle on any terms. The resumption of arms sales to South Africa reinforced this impression by suggesting a general attitude of friendliness to white Africa. And the US boosted Rhodesian confidence that they were under no economic pressure to settle by choosing to renew chrome imports at a sensitive moment in February 1972.

It was also clear to everyone – the Smith regime included – that the timing of the Heath government's moves was more closely linked to the need to avoid the annual embarrassment of a Conservative back-bench rebellion on sanctions than it was to choosing the optimal moment to press the Rhodesians into a settlement. Although it was by no means clear that there was any basis for a settlement, Home agreed in November 1971 to fly to Salisbury to open talks because the government had every reason to fear that without some initiative it would suffer a major back-bench rebellion at the very moment that it needed to show that it still had control of its majority if it was to continue with the enabling legislation necessary for entry to the European Community.

On the other hand, there were factors working towards a settlement even in the early 1970s. High economic growth in Rhodesia was only enough to match a population explosion among the black majority. This meant that personal living standards were stagnant, expectations were disappointed, and political and racial domination went untempered by material advance. The white population, already outnumbered 250,000 to 5 million, responded to a growing sense of internal insecurity by attempting to introduce a South African-style system of apartheid with the passage of a Land Tenure Act. Although this meant that London and Salisbury were even further apart in 1972 than had been the case when Wilson had last negotiated with Smith on HMS *Fearless* in 1968, the shift towards entrenchment of racial discrimination only worked to highlight the long-term unsustainability of white Rhodesia.

15. Lord Carrington, *Reflect on Things Past* (London, 1988), 287.

The project of racial separation required infrastructural investment well beyond the colony's capital surplus and, if carried through, would have created the very economic dislocation that sanctions had singularly failed to inflict. The Smith regime also had to reckon with the mortality of the Heath government and the likelihood that a Labour successor would insist on a tougher set of terms. By a paradox that shows the subtle interplay of strengths and weaknesses in negotiation, two of the factors which might have allowed a settlement at the time were the domestic unpopularity of the Heath Government and a perception on the Rhodesian side that it could be wise to quit while the going was relatively good.

Although Home apparently considered Wilson's position of 'no independence before majority rule' to be a 'terrible mistake' which took 'control of Rhodesian affairs out of Britain's hands', he knew that he would probably have to work within the five principles for a new Rhodesian constitution that he had himself laid down in 1963.[16] These five points required that any constitution should allow for the possibility of unimpeded progress towards majority rule, even if it was not to be granted immediately; that there should be some mechanism to entrench a settlement and render it incapable of amendment without the consent of the black community; that there should be some immediate improvement in the political status of the black population; that there should be an end to racial discrimination, and that the terms of any agreement should be acceptable to the population as a whole. In the event, the Heath government felt that it was able to accept a complex agreement negotiated with Smith as lying within the five principles. However, it deftly shifted the onus of final decision by appointing a commission under Lord Pearce to take evidence on the acceptability of the settlement to all sections of the Rhodesian population.

At first, the Pearce commission was suspected as a device for fabricating a phoney consent for the settlement. However, it eventually emerged as an effective mechanism for registering black rejection. Few black leaders were willing to accept a settlement in which they had had no opportunity for participation as full negotiating partners. There was also little confidence that there really would be unimpeded progress to majority rule so long as a government of the white Rhodesian front remained in place. The Smith–Home agreement envisaged an ever wider black franchise as more members of the majority satisfied a set of educational, occupational and wealth qualifications. However, the Smith regime would, in the meantime, have considerable scope to

16. K. Young, *Sir Alec Douglas-Home* (London, 1970), 246.

manipulate access to educational and material advance. Estimates of how long it would take to reach majority rule under the agreement thus varied from 10 to 100 years.[17] In any case, there was room to doubt the security of the constitutional clauses which were meant to entrench the new franchise so long as there was any prospect of black MPs being intimidated or bought by the Smith regime.

Even though Heath and Home failed to solve the Rhodesian problem, their effort can be seen as indirectly contributing towards the eventual solution in 1979–80. The Pearce commission had the effect of mobilizing black opinion and greatly adding to its coherence. The lesson of 1972 was that there could be no further talks which did not involve the majority leaders as direct interlocutors. And the fact that a Conservative government – under a Foreign Secretary largely trusted by the right – had done its best to bring about a settlement had the effect of calming and containing the pro-Rhodesian faction in Westminster.[18]

MALTA AND ICELAND

Negotiations to renew Britain's use of its naval base on Malta provided one of the main foreign policy 'media events' of the Heath government. Indeed, the talks may have been more of a 'comic side-show' than a serious political problem. As a consequence of withdrawals from East of Suez, a partial run-down of the Malta base was already under way when Heath assumed office. This severely dislocated the island's economy and brought about the election of Dom Mintoff's Labour party with a commitment to use Malta's strategic importance to demand extra payments for the use of its facilities. NATO shipping throughout the east Mediterranean and into the Black Sea made use of Malta, as did air traffic control of airspace as far south as the Sudan. However, important though these roles were, it was less than clear that NATO's only option was to have access to Malta.

This was not the only weakness in Mintoff's negotiating position. Financial desperation – with the Maltese government running short of cash to pay its own civil servants – provided a powerful incentive to settle. Nor was Mintoff quite able to sort out whether his main objective was to extract more money from the UK or to pursue his instincts for an independent and non-aligned Malta by insisting that Britain could

17. *Financial Times*, 31 December 1971.
18. Campbell, *Edward Heath*, 339.

only stay so long as it did not perform any NATO roles from the island. A further problem was that many islanders, members of Mintoff's own cabinet included, were worried about the Soviet build-up in the Mediterranean and feared that any mishandling of the crisis could deliver up the island to Soviet dependency. The result was that Mintoff was reduced to not very plausible flirtations with the likes of Libya and Romania, in order to maximise what little negotiating leverage he had with the UK. In view of all this, Lord Carrington, who was in charge of the negotiations with Malta, was probably right to calculate that Mintoff's bluff could be called. The British government simply allowed the withdrawals from Malta to proceed and they were well under way before Mintoff agreed to sign a new agreement with the UK after all. In the meantime, an offer was made to increase the payment to Malta from £5m to £13.5m. Although this was short of the £20m Mintoff demanded, it did mean that he faced the loss not just of Malta's set earnings – but the prospects of receiving more – by allowing UK withdrawals to continue.

From 1972, the Heath government also had to deal with the 'cod war' with Iceland. There were some parallels here with the Malta issue. Both involved the problem of what to do when complex international agreements threaten small and relatively marginal countries with intolerable levels of economic instability. Both saw newly elected left-wing governments seeking to escape this dilemma by claiming a more independent path of internal development; and, in both cases, Britain was the focus of their attempts to renegotiate their deal with the outside world. In both cases, threats were made to close down NATO facilities, so the responses of the Heath government had to be sensitive to the concerns of the broader Atlantic Alliance and not just to Britain's own interests.[19] However, some of the foreign policy was farcical, with Iceland evidently the only country to have considered a formal declaration of war against the United Kingdom during the period of the Heath government.[20] The core of the problem was the fact that 80 per cent of Iceland's exports and 20 per cent of its GNP were accounted for by the fish industry and, by the early 1970s, an international regime that preserved only the first twelve miles for local fishing was quite inadequate to its needs. The twelve-mile zone faced depletion of its stock and could not, in any case, be managed separately from the wider continental shelf to which outsiders had access. The precarious nature of Iceland's economic existence had been visible in 1967–68 when

19. W. Wallace, *The Foreign Policy Process in Britain* (London, 1975), 234.
20. H. Kissinger, *Years of Upheaval* (London, 1982), 172–3.

GNP had declined by 15 per cent, just as a result of a poor herring catch. Yet the British government could not easily accept Iceland's unilateral extension of limits to 50 miles. This would have completely excluded the UK from waters that employed 20 per cent of its own fleet. It was also calculated that the British industry would be an overall loser from a general move by all countries to 50-mile limits. The negotiating strategy of the British government in this instance seems to have been to take Iceland to the international court in the Hague, while offering a 'settlement out of court' in the form of an agreement that would have confined the 12–50-mile zone to just a few countries that had traditionally fished in the area.[21] In the end, Heath agreed to reduce the British catch by 27 per cent within the 50-mile zone, but this was not to prevent a fourth cod war breaking out in 1975–76.

THE MIDDLE EAST

Throughout Heath's premiership, the Middle East teetered on the edge of war. The hijacking of five aircraft by Palestinian terrorists in September 1970 provided the 1970–74 government with its first international crisis. The outbreak of full hostilities in the Middle East with the Yom Kippur War of October 1973 destabilised the domestic policy of the Heath government and contributed to its eventual demise.

In the hijacking crisis of September 1970, the British government found itself having to deal with the one terrorist who had been unsuccessful in capturing her plane. Leila Khaled was taken into custody after the aircraft landed in London. The Fedayeen promptly added her to a list of prisoners from various countries they wanted released in exchange for the hostages from two of the planes that had ended up in the Jordanian desert. To put more pressure on the British government, they also captured a further plane, this time a BOAC jet with several UK citizens on board.

This was one of the first acts in the modern wave of international terrorism, and governments lacked the experience they were later to acquire in dealing with the problem. At one level was the moral dilemma: was it right to risk, and possibly sacrifice, existing hostages in order to assert the principle of no compromise with terrorism and to protect future, unknown individuals who might fall victim to a belief that hijacking was a cost-free method of making political demands? At another level, there were problems of international co-ordination and

21. *House of Lords Debates*, 5th series, vol. 328, cols 1257–63, 2 March 1972.

constructing new international processes for dealing with terrorism. In all, there were five governments – Israel, Switzerland, West Germany, the United Kingdom and the United States – who would have to be brought into any deal with the terrorists. One danger was that there could be a 'race to the door' to settle unilaterally, with individual governments saving their own citizens at the cost of leaving the rest to face the terrorists down on their own. A converse problem was that one government might be unwilling to settle when the rest were prepared to do so. The five governments, accordingly, formed themselves into the 'Basle group' and succeeded in holding to the principle that not one Palestinian prisoner would be released until all hostages were freed. Heath's eventual consent to the release of Khaled has coloured retrospective perceptions of his approach to foreign policy. To right-wing critics it was an interference in due legal process and an act of appeasement that encouraged a wave of international terrorism that would last for the next twenty years. However, Heath himself claims that he called the Palestinians' bluff. Khaled was retained as a bargaining chip, even though her crime had not been committed in British jurisdiction and there was no basis for prosecution in the UK.[22]

To a degree which has not been commonly recognized, the hostage problem was but a part of a major strategic crisis in the Middle East during September 1970, and this inevitably constrained the Heath government's reactions to it. Over the previous months, King Hussein's government had been steadily losing control of Jordan to Palestinians displaced from the West Bank. The decision to land two of the hijacked aircraft in Jordan was an overt challenge to the King's authority which precipitated the final showdown between the Hussein regime and Palestinian radicals. Iraqi and Syrian troops moved into Jordan to back the PLO radicals. However, Jordan was a buffer state essential to the stability of the region as a whole. Neither Israel nor the United States could allow it to fall to the cause of Arab radicalism. While Israel pinned the Syrians down by threatening to outflank them from the Golan heights and the US held the Iraqis in check by signalling its preparedness to intervene, the outcome of the crisis depended on whether the Jordanian army would carry out Hussein's orders to expel the Palestinians from Jordan. For three weeks, the British government had little choice but to do nothing that might inflame opinion in the Jordanian army, previously on the verge of mutinying in favour of the Palestinians, and hope that Hussein would eventually be successful. This was the real context in which the fate of the hostages was decided.

22. Campbell, *Edward Heath*, 307–8.

Throughout the next three years, the Middle East filled Heath with foreboding. Brandt recalls that, as early as 1971, Heath expected the Arab states to cut off oil supplies to the West in the event of a further Arab–Israeli war.[23] As West Europe was more dependent than the United States on imported oil, London became increasingly impatient with what it saw as US foot-dragging on a Middle Eastern settlement. The Heath government thought that there was a basis for progress in the UN resolutions that had been passed after the 1967 war and the four-power talks process between the US, USSR, Britain and France, which had traditionally been invoked to deal with the problems of the region. Heath and Home worked closely with their French counterparts on the problem and it is no coincidence that the Middle East formed one of the first topics for the new EC-based process of European Political Cooperation. However, the US administration was divided. While the State Department was prepared to proceed on the lines preferred by Heath and Home, Kissinger, as National Security Adviser in the White House, was eager to draw matters out, so that a settlement could not be taken as a reward for Arab radicalism or Soviet influence, both of which were strong in the Middle East in the early 1970s. He wanted to avoid any multilateral deal that would give a veto to the most extreme powers in the region and encourage Arab states to settle one by one with Israel under American auspices.[24] As this meant bypassing the 4-power process, Britain and France had to be frozen out, as well as the Soviet Union.

With the outbreak of war in October 1973, Britain joined the rest of NATO Europe in requesting that the US should neither use UK bases, nor over-fly its air space, in order to resupply Israel. To many, this was craven proof that Arab oil threats worked, but Heath insisted that Britain's wish to avoid taking sides arose from a genuine belief that the blame was evenly proportioned and that Israel and the US had put everyone else in danger by showing little interest in a settlement over the previous three years. Heath's relations with Washington reached an all-time low at the end of October when the White House, sensing an imminent Soviet move to deploy troops in the Middle East, put its troops in West Europe on what was called 'Def Con III' red alert. This was decided without consultation, even though the allies would have been put at physical risk in any escalation of threat and counter-threat between the superpowers.

Heath was, however, unable to save his government from Arab use

23. W. Brandt, *People and Politics: 1960–75* (London, 1978), 466–7.
24. H. Kissinger, *The White House Years* (London, 1979), 575–82.

of the oil weapon. Although Britain and France were considered to have shown sufficient impartiality during the war not to be embargoed after December 1973, their economies could be insulated neither from a general shortage of oil in the world economy, nor from the quintupling in oil prices that followed. Among EC countries, Britain led, rather than restrained, a competitive, nationalistic scramble for supplies.[25] Bilateral deals were concluded with particular oil producers, a block was put on the re-export of oil in flat contravention of the Treaty of Rome and, at one stage, Heath allegedly even attempted to order all British petroleum tankers laden with oil supplies to divert to the nearest UK port.[26] The solidarity of the new Community of nine was severely compromised and one of the last acts of the Heath government was to lend support to a way of tackling the energy crisis under US auspices. At the energy conference held in Washington in February 1974, among the European foreign ministers Home was particularly supportive of follow-up action that was eventually to result in the formation of an International Energy Agency after Heath had left office.[27] Perhaps more than at any time since the Second World War, or at least since the economic problems of 1947, the foreign policy of a British government consisted of desperate, ad hoc measures to cope with the immediate exigencies of political survival, for the oil crisis transformed the bargaining power of Britain's miners. If Bevin had exaggerated when he said in 1947 that he would be able to negotiate from strength with a few more million tons of coal, by 1974 the rising price of coal and oil undermined both Britain's foreign policy and the government of the day.

THE SPECIAL RELATIONSHIP AND DÉTENTE

In the eyes of contemporaries, the early 1970s was a period of change in the general character of international relationships, not just of the particular orientations of the British state. A period of détente seemed to promise a more multipolar world in which relationships between the two great alliance systems would be loosened, leaving more room for West Europe, Japan and China to take their place as regional centres of growing independence of the superpowers. A complex interdependence of trade, money and communications was thought likely to change the agenda as well as the structure of international power,

25. R. Keohane, *After Hegemony* (New Jersey, 1984), 223.
26. Senior Foreign Office official, interview with Christopher Lord, January 1989.
27. Kissinger, *Years of Upheaval*, 906–20.

shifting the subject matter of diplomacy from defence to economics and creating a series of hierarchies in which states important in one type of dealing were less significant in another.[28] Although these changes would in many ways be postponed between 1974 and 1985, they seemed to be real enough in the early 1970s to provide the contexts in which the Heath government had to consider the future of NATO, the continued significance of its relationship with the US, its own role in any détente with East Europe, bilateral West European relationships outside and inside the EC and, once again, the future of the British Commonwealth.

Several factors combined in the early 1970s to suggest that the US might reduce its troop commitments to West Europe and that this could, in turn, require reconsideration of the basic structures of the Atlantic alliance. These factors included the rising wealth and increased political cohesion of the Europeans, who increasingly appeared as free-loaders in the view of US opinion; fatigue with external commitments induced by Vietnam; and deficits on US public and external accounts. In spite of amendments introduced to Congress each year by Senator Mansfield, no one quite believed that the US would withdraw its troops from West Europe altogether. However, it was generally acknowledged that the best way to avoid such an outcome was for the Europeans to indicate their willingness to do more. A guide to what might be required seemed to be contained in Nixon's 'state of the world' message for 1971–72, in which the President argued that the US should be able to maintain troops in Europe without any greater balance of payments costs than would be entailed in keeping the same forces in the US.

All of this presented the Heath government with awkward dilemmas. Carrington sensed that influence over any reshaping of NATO would probably be proportionate to extra contributions to the common defence, and that it was unlikely that the European allies would reach a consensus on doing more unless all were prepared to put more into the kitty.[29] Clearly, it would be hard to maintain the presence East of Suez, spend more on European defence, and devote more resources to Heath's principal ambition of reversing domestic economic decline. It was, in a sense, unfortunate that 90 per cent of Britain's defence budget had already and involuntarily been concentrated on West Europe as a result of the 1967–68 currency crises and that, at 5.7 per cent of GNP, Britain's defence expenditure represented a greater overhead on economic competitiveness than any carried by other European partners.

28. A. Buchan, *The End of the Postwar Era* (London, 1974).
29. Carrington, *Reflect*, 288.

This meant that the Heath government had little more to offer and that it accordingly risked appearing to be an awkward partner in spite of the very high base line of its contributions. Reflecting the foreign policy constraints of a still delicate balance of payments, the government opened with the position that Britain's commitment to an enhanced defence should be limited to the physical transfer of more capabilities to mainland Europe, and that the UK should otherwise be exempted from extra cash payments. But it was unclear whether it was even in a position to deliver on this offer, for the gathering crisis in Northern Ireland absorbed six battalions of troops where the previous government had expected only to have to commit two battalions.

The Heath government looked to various devices to ease the resource pressures of maintaining an ambitious military capacity. Yet each of these proved problematic. Agreement in 1971 to hold East–West talks on mutual balanced forced reductions (MBFR) offered the possibility that US troops in Europe could be reduced without matching increases in West European contributions. In fact, most of the European allies had mixed feelings about a process which they suspected could lead to some of their own defence forces being negotiated away by the superpowers, perhaps with the British and French nuclear deterrents being included in proposals for an MBFR deal. The UK government also looked to West Germany to provide some 'offset' payments to cover some of the costs of the British Army on the Rhine. However, it was hard to see how these could take the form of West German purchases of UK armaments, as the Federal Republic was already absorbing as much American matériel as it needed in an effort to meet American demands for burden sharing. On the other hand, the British government rejected the alternative of cash payments on the grounds that this would give UK forces the status of mercenary soldiers.[30]

Meanwhile, it was becoming increasingly difficult to create a positive relationship between high military spending and civilian economic development. By the early 1970s, the UK lacked critical mass for many high-technology projects, in terms both of small domestic markets and of limited public purchasing power. Yet the lesson of the Heath government was that attempts to forge international partnerships or sell technology on to other countries would draw UK governments into complex patterns of foreign policy-making in which decisions crucial to key sectors of British manufacture would be taken in extra-territorial political processes. The struggle to sustain Rolls-Royce and therewith Britain's continued presence in the aero-engine industry, the attempt

30. *Financial Times*, 4 January 1971.

to secure sufficient landing rights and air routes to make Concorde viable, and the question of whether the UK should take an enhanced role in the Airbus consortium, all involved the Heath government in lobbying congressional committees, estimating the viability of US corporations and combating alliances between environmental and protectionist interest groups in other countries. They also raised, not for the last time, the problem of whether Britain should forge European or Atlantic partnerships in technologies, a question in which large issues of economic development could not be easily separated from different predispositions to develop the UK's diplomacy in Atlanticist or Europeanist directions.

Heath is often seen as having made a determined effort to direct Britain away from pretensions to a 'special relationship' with the US and to begin the work of constructing a common European foreign policy. The 1970–74 government was indeed a period of unusual fractiousness in UK–US relations, with rows over the decline of the Bretton Woods fixed-currency system, the India-Pakistan War of 1972, Kissinger's Year of Europe initiative and, above all, the Middle Eastern crisis of October 1973. Meanwhile, Heath attempted to reduce expectations on both sides of the Atlantic of the maximum possible gains from UK–US relations by talking of a 'natural' rather than a 'special' relationship. By this he seems to have meant that personal affinities, made possible by common language, should not be confused with political realities by which the UK was physically located in West Europe and intimately entangled in its economic and military subsystems. As part of his bid for a 'quiet revolution' in attitudes, he allegedly enjoined all Whitehall departments in early 1972 to consider how they could best adapt their activities to the new context of EC membership.[31]

Heath's instincts for a reorientation of British foreign policy from America to Europe can be seen in his personal dealings with Nixon and Pompidou. According to Henry Kissinger, Nixon's immediate response to the Conservatives' victory on 19 June 1970 was to offer Heath the opportunity of continuous and unlimited contact with the Oval office by telephone. No other foreign leader would enjoy this privilege, and it also represented just the kind of personal access to the thinking and decisions of the US Presidency by which Heath's predecessors in Downing Street had sought to give substance to the 'special relationship'. Yet, as Kissinger recalls, Heath would come close over

31. *Financial Times*, 24 January 1972.

the next three-and-a-half years to 'insisting on receiving no preferential treatment'.[32]

The need to renounce claims to a special relationship with the US was obviously linked to Britain's bid to enter the European Community. As the minister who had been responsible for the first round of negotiations between 1961 and 1963, Heath was well aware of De Gaulle's objection that Britain would be a 'Trojan Horse' for the United States, providing a surrogate veto for any US Administration over European attempts to develop external policies of their own. Sensitivity to this charge was not without cause, for when Heath went to see Pompidou in May 1971 for what was the decisive meeting in Britain's successful bid for EC entry, the French President insisted on reassurances that Britain would not compromise European cohesion by giving priority to its American relationship. In the exchange that followed, Heath seems to have offered three such reassurances.[33] He argued that British governments had always sought membership of some other international organisation to the Atlantic alliance, in order to protect themselves from the inherent inequalities of the UK–US relationship. From this it followed that Britain could be expected to throw itself into making West Europe the core sphere of its external involvements with the same enthusiasm as it had once pursued this objective in relation to the Commonwealth. Heath then went on to meet Pompidou's concern that the pound and the dollar were linked in a way that would prevent West Europe functioning as a bloc in international monetary negotiations by, in effect, agreeing to liquidate sterling's role as the second international currency after the dollar. Most strikingly of all, Heath expressed an interest in Anglo-French nuclear cooperation. This would, of course, have effected a major change in relations between the two powers, coupling them in the physical production of their defence of last resort and substituting France for the United States in one vital dimension of Britain's external attachments. Since the Godkin lectures in 1967, Heath had envisaged that the two countries should work together in the future development of their deterrents and that these might eventually be 'held in trust' for the EC as a whole, with other members being consulted on deployments and strategic doctrines.[34] In a manner that may have simplified the position somewhat, Heath would

32. Kissinger, *White House Years*, 932–4.

33. Information about the Heath–Pompidou conversation is based on Heath's interview with Christopher Lord in November 1988. Some useful reflections are also to be found in E. Heath, 'European Integration over the next ten years: from Community to Union', *International Affairs*, vol. 64, no. 2 (1988).

34. E. Heath, *Old World, New Horizons: The Godkin Lectures 1967* (London, 1970).

later claim that Nixon had already agreed in advance of the Paris summit that Britain could share with the French any technical nuclear information it received from 'American sources'.[35]

The argument that the Heath government represented a consistent and well-thought-out effort to wean British foreign policy away from the 'special relationship' with the US can, however, be taken too far. The same is also true of the charge that Heath was motivated by an instinctive scepticism of the reliability of American friendship, dating back to the Suez crisis of 1956. In fact, during his first visit to the United States after the 1970 election, Heath looked forward to UK–US relations recovering to the same level of intimacy as in 1964 and early bilateral contacts reveal a determination to play the classic British foreign policy role of staunch and supportive ally. Heath thus cautioned against an early withdrawal from Vietnam and showed concern about Soviet military build-ups in Eastern Europe and on the high seas. In 1972, the government deferred to American concepts of Indian Ocean defence by switching away from attempts to build up South Africa's role and granting what David Sanders has described as a 'virtual carte blanche' to the US to fortify and enhance the facilities of the Diego Garcia base as it wished'.[36] Heath showed no desire to rock the Anglo-American boat, except on his own priority of the construction of Europe.

Above all, frictions in UK–US relations in the early 1970s had their origins in Washington as much as in London. The foreign policy of the Nixon administration provided a far more hostile environment for Britain's merger with the EC than would probably have been the case with its Democrat predecessor of the 1960s. Of all postwar US administrations, Nixon's was probably least willing to accept short-term costs in the hope of ultimately benefiting from European integration; and most aware that American relations with a unifying Europe would be conflictual, as well as collaborative. Just before entering office, Heath had accepted the Kennedy–Johnson formula by which the enlargement of the European Community to include Britain could be made most attractive to the US by using this as an opportunity to relieve the United States of some of the economic and security burdens that it carried on behalf of the western world as a whole.[37] However, the idea of joint US–EC management of international economic questions was less attractive to an administration that believed that these

35. Heath, 'European integration', 207.

36. D. Sanders, *Losing an Empire, Finding a Role: An Introduction to British Foreign Policy since 1945*, (London, 1989), 123.

37. Heath, *Old World*, 14.

problems had either been over-managed, or that the US might, from time to time, be better off determining its trade and monetary policies unilaterally. In August 1971, Nixon shocked the western world by announcing a 10 per cent import surcharge on all good and services entering the United States and suspending the dollar convertibility which had lain at the centre of the Bretton Woods system of fixed currencies.

Meanwhile, changes in American relations with the Soviet Union meant even if the United States retained an interest in greater European political cohesion, it was eager that this should be limited by the demands of superpower détente. This would cause a spat between Heath and Kissinger in 1973 and, to understand why, it is necessary to go back to the decision taken at the Hague in 1969 to develop a limited process of foreign policy co-ordination between members of the EC. By 1973, what was to be known as European Political Co-operation was beginning to take shape and Kissinger was eager to find out how it would cohere with Atlantic Alliance policy. Accordingly, he launched a Year of Europe in which he proposed to use NATO's coming twenty-fifth birthday to occasion a review of Alliance relations.

Heath was furious, later suggesting that this was an impertinence on a level with a British Prime Minister standing up in Trafalgar Square to announce a Year of America.[38] On a more serious level, he came to regard the Year of Europe initiative as an attempt to 'capture' European foreign policy for an ambitious conception of US–Soviet relations that would impel the US to seek to control the external affairs of other western powers if it was to have the degree of leverage over future Soviet behaviour that Kissinger required. His suspicions seem to have been sharpened when his Private Secretary, Robert Armstrong, discovered from a conversation with French Foreign Minister Michel Jobert that Kissinger seemed to be selling both Britain and France the same deal – an opportunity to assume the foreign policy leadership of Europe in exchange for advancing US priorities.[39] Heath, accordingly, responded with a reinforcement of the ideas which he had already been developing in interviews and private meetings as to how Britain might contribute to the development of a more independent European policy. Not only was he eager that EC countries, Britain now included, should concert their positions before any one of their number dealt with the United States, but also he now told Nixon that no information should be given to anyone in London unless Washington was willing that this

38. Edward Heath, interview with Christopher Lord, November 1988.
39. Ibid.

should be passed on to other European partners. From now on, all foreign policy advantages would be pooled and EC members would eschew a temptation to compete for privileged relations with outsiders that would prevent their realising a common front among themselves.[40]

Among other relationships, that with the Commonwealth recovered after the argument about arms to South Africa. The 1973 conference in Ottawa was comparatively harmonious. One aspect of the UK's foreign policy that remained strangely under-developed in the early 1970s was, however, relations with the Soviet Union. This was curious from both historical and contemporary perspectives. Heath differed from at least three other postwar Conservative Prime Ministers – Churchill, Macmillan and Thatcher – in not attempting at some stage to open a dialogue with the USSR. Nor did he respond, as Pompidou did, to Brandt's Ostpolitik by looking to develop his own détente with East Europe. On the contrary, the only major event in UK–USSR relations was the expulsion of 105 Soviet diplomats in 1971, apparently on suspicion of industrial espionage related to Russian interest in Concorde! One possibility is that Heath, involved as he was in the delicacies of British entry to the EC, did not want to repeat Macmillan's mistake of seeming to discuss issues such as Berlin over the head of the West German government; another possibility is that a British role in the thawing of superpower relations was precluded by Heath's attempts to renounce a 'special relationship' with the US and the comparatively healthy state of direct US–USSR contacts. For certain, Heath is known to have shared Kissinger's analysis that unless relations with the USSR were handled through multilateral frameworks there was a risk of a competitive détente with western allies attempting to out-bid one another in the concessions they were prepared to make to the Soviet Union.[41] Heath and Home thus fully supported the idea that West European governments should respond to the potentially divisive East–West Conference on Security Cooperation in Europe (CSCE) by developing a common negotiating position in European Political Cooperation and bargaining as a group. If the Heath government lagged behind its partners in European détente, a perhaps unexpected compensation was that this allowed it to be second only to the United States in the opening to China, which was determined to reward Heath's 'soundness' towards the Soviet Union.

40. Kissinger, *Years of Upheaval*, 189.
41. Kissinger, *The White House Years*, 938.

THE MAKING OF FOREIGN POLICY

As has been seen, European Political Cooperation was still in the cradle, and Heath's ideas for it were advanced even by continental standards. His Foreign Secretary seems to have been less prepared to sustain EC solidarity at all costs and more willing to contemplate circumstances in which the American and European poles of British diplomacy would continue to be traded off to the advantage of the former. Kissinger recalls that 'Home and the Foreign Office' continued to follow 'more established habits of collaboration' and that, without Heath's knowledge, the Cabinet Secretary (Sir Burke Trend until 1973, Sir John Hunt thereafter) sought bi-monthly meetings with the State Department, in order to keep US–UK relations on an unchanged basis.[42] This view is, of course, only part of the story. Increasingly, Foreign and Commonwealth Office officials like Michael Palliser were sympathetic to Heath's approach, and in any case most officials and politicians were far more concerned to reconcile the European and US relationships than to polarise them.

Nonetheless, Kissinger's observation does raise the important question of decision-making – can we assume that the foreign policy of the Heath government was made in a fairly coherent and unified fashion, or did significant elements of bureaucratic politics come into play, such as the possible divergence between Number 10 and the FCO?

In personal terms the Heath–Home relationship was cordial and effective, unlike that of George Brown and Harold Wilson only a few years before, and the Chamberlain–Eden pairing which Home had seen from the inside and was determined not to repeat. Although the reversal of seniority which had taken place from the Macmillan years was potentially awkward, in some ways it was immensely helpful for Heath to have an experienced, respected elder statesman holding together the traditional strands of British diplomacy (and reassuring conservative opinion both at home and abroad) while he pushed on with the transformational initiative of Europe. On the other hand, the two men represented both different generations and opposite wings of the Conservative Party. Their differences (e.g. on arms to South Africa or policy towards India) could be concealed without undue effort for most of the time; they briefly surfaced, however, and insignificant though this may have been in terms of the conduct of British foreign policy, they were symbolic of the strains which membership of the EC were to impose on traditional British policies, even in the external realm.

42. Kissinger, *Years of Upheaval*, 143.

During the prolonged period of tension which followed the outbreak of the Yom Kippur War on 6 October 1973, policy was inevitably being made for the most part on the hoof. Given the rapidly evident difference of view which emerged – between the United States and a French-led Western Europe – over the conduct of the war and the response to the oil embargo imposed by the Organisation of Petroleum-Exporing Countries (OPEC), Britain found itself inevitably being pulled in opposing directions. Heath quickly came to see the crisis both as requiring European strategies to protect distinctive European interests and as an opportunity for promoting European solidarity. Home was not convinced on either point, and was certainly not willing to endanger the vital hinge of his diplomacy, the relationship with Washington. Their differences of view came to a head over Heath's close consultations with Jobert and his refusal to keep Kissinger closely informed, in contrast to Home's determination to keep open the channel across the Atlantic. Had the government not fallen in February 1974, it is conceivable that this incipient rift between Prime Minister and Foreign Secretary could have widened to the point of embarrassment.

Given the relatively stable leadership provided by Heath and Home, the role of the permanent bureaucracy in foreign policy at this time was unexceptionable. Although officials like O'Neill and Palliser were of crucial importance in shaping Britain's commitment to the EC, they were able to do so because of Heath's enthusiasm and Home's support. In general, the FCO was in the middle of a period of internal change and uncertainty, engendered by the merger with the Commonwealth Relations Office in 1968 (which led to an unwieldy official body and sharply reduced the number of ministers to supervise it), by the absorption on 12 November 1970 of the Overseas Development Ministry (after its creation and separate existence – with a Cabinet seat until 1967 – under the first Wilson government) and by the Duncan report of 1969 (which had recommended more concentration on economic matters and – ironically, given the move from 'FO' to 'FCO' – on Atlantic and European affairs at the expense of a global role). Duncan's recommendations were estimated to involve expenditure savings of 5 per cent by the mid-1970s.[43]

In 1970 the FCO was therefore entering the period of about twenty years when it was to become everyone's favourite scapegoat for the confusions and deficiencies which accompanied Britain's abandonment of its world role and failure to fasten enthusiastically on the European

43. Wallace, *Foreign Policy Process*, 60.

alternative. There were to be some institutional compensations once the office settled into co-ordinating Whitehall's dealings with Brussels, but these were hardly evident during Heath's time as Prime Minister. Fortunately, relations with the other parts of the external policy-making process, notably Lord Carrington's Ministry of Defence, proceeded without excessive conflict. It was William Wallace's view that Carrington became something of 'a second Foreign Secretary, discussing topics which ranged far beyond his strictly departmental responsibilities with, for instance, the Greek, Nigerian, and Kenyan governments'.[44] Fortunately, the 'mutual confidence' of the personal relations between Sir Alec Douglas-Home and Lord Carrington prevented friction.

In the wider political environment as well, consensus was largely the order of the day. Perhaps because the issue of EC entry loomed so large, took up so much political energy, and cut across the usual party lines to such devastating effect, the rest of British foreign policy continued more or less unhampered. As we have seen, Heath and Home were hemmed in on both right and left in their opinions over a Rhodesian settlement, but the East of Suez question aroused little general interest, while the first shoots of détente made it possible for opposition and government to converge on East–West relations. The increasing signs of US disengagement in Vietnam meant, ironically, that Heath was rather less likely to be accused of guilt by association than his Labour predecessor had been.

CONCLUSIONS

Foreign policy under the Heath government can reasonably be seen as a *mare tranquillitatis* by comparison to the domestic troubles which finally engulfed it, with such traumas as there were being externally generated and affecting Britain for the most part indirectly. Heath and Home presided over a relatively smooth period, absorbing most of the defence cutbacks made by the preceding Labour government and benefiting from an improved climate in superpower relations.

However, this favourable view is less than half the whole picture. It skates over the fundamental choice about Britain's position in the world which arguably faced the Heath Cabinet. The upheavals of 1967–69, which produced the Duncan report after the devaluation of the pound and the withdrawals from East of Suez, were followed under Heath by the 'Nixon shocks' in both economic policy and the turn towards

44. Wallace, *Foreign Policy Process*, 127.

China. These were reinforced by the increasing tendency of Moscow and Washington to talk exclusively to each other about strategic arms policy. In this context there seems to be a *prima facie* case for arguing that Heath should have gone for a thorough-going refurbishment of British foreign policy, involving a further scaling-down of commitments and aspirations.

Edward Heath might well argue that this is precisely what he did with the move towards Europe, and the consequent distancing from the USA which made him (apart perhaps from Eden) the least comfortable partner for the White House of all postwar British prime ministers. Certainly Heath, despite the presence of Home, did not attempt to turn the clock back to the days when his Conservative predecessors Macmillan, Eden and Churchill behaved as if Britain were one of the 'big three' great Powers. Yet nor was he in fact able to carry through substantial changes in foreign policy. The initiative over Rhodesia came to nothing, given that the Smith regime was not yet under enough internal pressure to reach a deal. The tentative contacts with France over nuclear cooperation – immensely radical in their potential – also (predictably) fizzled out. Even the tendency to differentiate British positions from those of the United States eventually lost its impetus. By the end of his administration, Heath was agreeing to cooperate with the US-sponsored International Energy Agency, despite France's virulent opposition to the institution, and he had begun the modernisation of the Polaris deterrent. US power, together with the strong lobby for the special relationship within the UK government, was difficult to overlook.

Moreover it was inherently difficult even for a forward-looking prime minister like Heath to refashion British foreign policy at this time, when the very concept of foreign policy was coming under challenge. Classical foreign policy was being squeezed into an ever-smaller space by developments on two sides. First, other states and actors were beginning to use different kinds of pressures. Hostage-taking and oil embargoes found most western governments conceptually and practically unprepared, and foreign ministries were not always the best equipped parts of the machine to mobilise a response. Second, domestic politics was less easily demarcated from the outside world than it had been during the cold war, and increasing numbers of linkages were made between internal and external factors which bypassed governments. It was one such linkage, that between discontented coal miners and a destabilised international energy market, which was to bring down Heath. Yet this hardly constituted a conventional 'foreign policy' problem which Home and Heath could tackle, and the confusing of the old boundaries was epitomised by the uneasy appointment of Carrington to head the new Department of Energy in January 1974 – a foreign policy specialist in the Lords running a ministry whose major responsibilities were in the areas of economic and industrial policy. 'I went without enthusiasm'.[45]

With hindsight, it can be seen that the early 1970s were a time of considerable flux in the international system and in the nature of international politics. It was difficult to see this clearly at the time, let alone to fashion the new concepts and modalities needed to impose a shape on events. Entry into the European Community was an understandable (if over-simplified) way of trying to cope with change and confusion, and Heath has to be credited for attempting to anticipate further change by fostering European foreign policy cooperation, accepting the limits of the US alliance, and even dabbling in Anglo-French defence cooperation. But international organisations, even of the stature of the EC, are not panaceas, and they tend to resist all efforts to move too fast. It is not surprising, therefore, that when the storm of international crisis and domestic discontent burst over the Heath government in 1973–74, the new protective wall provided by the Prime Minister's turn towards Europe should prove incapable of containing it. The longer term may prove Edward Heath right in his international orientation; in the short run, he was forced to watch an incoming Labour government return the country to the comfortable routines of Atlanticism.

45. Carrington, *Reflect*, 262.

CHAPTER THIRTEEN

The Conservative Party and the Heath government

Stuart Ball

The Heath government was a troubled period for the Conservative Party.[1] In 1970 victory was attained when defeat had been widely expected; this gave satisfaction, but no great sense of confidence. The fifteen years from 1964 to 1979 were the one period during which to many people Labour seemed to be the natural party of government: 'history', 'progress' and social change were thought to be working in its favour, while Conservative initiatives were assumed to be anachronistic and doomed to failure. This cultural atmosphere was not confined to an intellectual elite, but was widely diffused through all social classes. Conservative supporters were by no means immune, and this explains much of the confusion and uncertainty which characterised their response to the perplexing problems of 1970–74. Compounding this sense of swimming against the tide was the rapidity with which the Conservative government became unpopular and beleaguered. The Conservative Party found itself on the defensive, buffeted by unforeseen events. Together with the pragmatic changes of direction into which its leaders were drawn, this slowly but surely led to demoralisation and defeat.

1. This chapter is based upon the records of the Conservative Party Archive (CPA), Bodleian Library; of the National Union (seen at Central Office, subsequently deposited at CPA); of the 1922 Committee (at CPA); of the regional Areas (at CPA); and of *c.* 70 local constituency Associations (from material collected by John Ramsden and Chris Stevens – held in the care of the former at Queen Mary & Westfield College, University of London – during a survey funded by the Economic and Social Research Council). I am most grateful to the Chairman of the Party, the Secretary of the National Union, the Chairman and Executive of the 1922 Committee, and John Ramsden respectively for granting access to these documents; the latter also kindly allowed me to read the manuscript of his volume in the Longman 'History of the Conservative Party' series: *The Winds of Change: Macmillan to Heath, 1957–1975* (London, 1996).

EUROPE, INDUSTRIAL RELATIONS, AND INFLATION: 1970–71

Victory in 1970 was a personal triumph for Edward Heath. After a difficult period as Leader of the Opposition, he alone seemed to have kept his nerve and spirits during the campaign. The result settled the question of leadership, gave him a fund of authority on which to draw, and reinforced his insular self-confidence. In the first key area of policy – the application to join the European Economic Community – this was an asset, but later it was to become a serious flaw. Entry into Europe was the great undertaking of the Heath government. At the outset it had the lukewarm support of the majority of the Party, but a significant minority were anxious about the impact on trade in other markets, unhappy about loosening links with the former Dominions, and suspicious over the potential erosion of sovereignty.[2] In 1970 pro-entry MPs formed the 'Conservative Group for Europe', chaired by Sir Tufton Beamish, a Vice-Chairman of the 1922 Committee, and this steadily gained adherents. The situation remained fluid while the terms of entry were under negotiation and the attitude of the Labour Party was unclear. In early 1971 the whips estimated that 194 Conservative MPs were in favour of entry, 70 were uncertain, and as many as 62 were hostile.[3] There was a similar balance when the 1922 Committee discussed the issue on 6 May: eleven of those who spoke were in favour, seven were doubtful, and six were against.[4]

The decisive shift in party opinion took place during the spring and early summer of 1971, before any legislation came before Parliament. None of the fourteen resolutions on Europe sent in for the Central Council meeting of April 1971 was openly hostile, and in May the Scottish party conference voted in favour of entry by 'a margin of 600 to 50'.[5] Between April and July most of the undecided MPs swung behind the party leadership, isolating the minority of 'anti-Marketeers'. The Conservative Group for Europe began an active campaign to win over the doubters, while the success of the Heath-Pompidou summit of 20–21 May increased expectations of a positive outcome. This took

2. 'The Queen's Speech', C[onservative] P[olitical] C[entre] contact programme, September 1970, CCO/4/10/81; Middlesborough C[onservative] A[association], Exec., 1 June 1971; 1922 Ctte., 6 May 1971.

3. P. Norton, *Conservative Dissidents: Dissent within the Parliamentary Conservative Party 1970–1974* (London, 1978), 67.

4. 'Summary of discussion on Britain's application to join the Common Market, 1922 Committee, 6 May 1971', 1922 Ctte. corres. 1969–72.

5. Tactical Ctte., 18 May 1971, CCO/20/7/12; N[ational] U[union] Central Council agenda, 2–3 April 1971.

shape in a White Paper, published on 7 July 1971, which was followed by a publicity campaign from both the government and Conservative Central Office.[6] In the first half of 1971 opinion polls recorded rising support for entry among the public in general and Conservatives in particular, with 68 per cent of the latter in favour by July. The stance adopted by the Sevenoaks constituency association in May 1971 was typical, loyally endorsing the negotiations while asking the government to spell out the advantages which entry would bring.[7] Heath met this need on 14 July at the special Central Council meeting on Europe, and his strong performance had an impact on the leading constituency officers who were present.[8] Crucially, the Labour Party moved to oppose the terms negotiated, thereby putting the question on a partisan basis. The natural consequence was a marked increase in Conservative support for their leaders, due more to loyalty than to enthusiasm for Europe.[9] This movement continued throughout the summer and autumn months, and in October 1971 it was estimated that joining was favoured by 90 per cent of those present at the annual general meeting of one safe London seat.[10] Opinion was even more pronounced in the prosperous farming areas, with a vote of 69 to 1 for a resolution of full support in the Dorset West constituency.[11] By the time of the party conference in October 1971, the message was unequivocal: 69 of the resolutions sent in on Europe were for entry and only 4 were definitely against. The party leadership underlined this by the unusual step of holding a ballot after the debate, which they won by the handsome margin of 2,474 to 324. A discussion of entry by local Conservative Political Centre groups in September and October demonstrated 'the tremendous extent to which loyalist sentiment in the party had swung round to support the Market', although the underlying attitude was a reluctant acceptance that there was no viable alternative.[12]

6. Tactical Ctte. and Ctte. on Europe, joint meeting, 6 July 1971, CCO/20/7/12; Party Chairman's circular to constituencies, 14 July 1971, CCO/20/6/6.

7. Sevenoaks CA res., 10 May 1971, CCO/20/70/4.

8. Burton CA, Council, 9 September 1971.

9. 'Current political situation and outlook', 2 September 1971, OG/71/85; Advisory Committee on Policy, 21 July 1971, ACP(71)113; Northern Area res., NU Exec. agenda, 4 December 1970; Hemel Hempstead CA, Exec., 16 July 1971; comments of MP, Sheffield Hallam CA, Exec., 3 August 1971; The Wrekin CA res., 17 September 1971, CCO/20/70/4.

10. Titchener-Barrett to Thomas, 29 October 1971, CCO/20/3/11.

11. Dorset West CA, Exec. council, 20 April 1971.

12. Advisory Committee on Policy, 26 January 1972, ACP(72)116; of the 576 groups to report back, 491 were in favour of entry, 55 were divided or abstained, and only 23 were clearly against, 'The Common Market', CPC contact programme, September–October 1971, CCO/4/10/81.

On the advice of William Whitelaw and Francis Pym, the former and current Chief Whips, the Commons vote on the principle of entry had been postponed until after the 1971 summer recess, so that the increasing support of the party grass-roots could percolate through to the backbenches. The delay enabled pro-entry MPs to soften the sceptics in their constituency parties, while loyal associations influenced MPs who were doubtful but wavering. Pressure exerted on anti-Market MPs from their constituency parties came of its own volition. The Conservative tradition of the independence of the MP remained strong, and the associations of most dissenting MPs only drew a line if their actions put the existence of the government in danger.[13] Even then, their reaction was tempered by the desire to avoid a confrontation which would split the local ranks or provoke an inconvenient by-election. Dissident MPs were constantly suspicious, but there is little evidence that Central Office sought to manipulate local opinion against them, while the Chief Whip actually discouraged some constituency executives from taking action against prominent rebels.[14] Local pressure may not have restrained the hard-core anti-Marketeers, but it limited their numbers and was one of the elements which kept dissent within survivable limits. Even so, the Conservative whips were uncertain of the outcome if a straight party vote was held. On 18 October, only three days before the debate was to open, Pym finally persuaded a reluctant Heath to give Conservative MPs a free vote. This was the key to success, and when the division was taken on 28 October there was a majority of 112 for entry; the 39 Conservative MPs who voted against had been more than outweighed by the Labour MPs who defied their own whip by voting in favour or abstaining.

After this, the number of Conservative rebels dwindled. Several had given undertakings to their local associations to accept the verdict of the House, while others decided not to pursue their opposition beyond the vote on second reading on 17 February 1972. The interviews which Heath held shortly before this with a number of anti-Marketeers thought to be open to persuasion or to appeals to their loyalty helped to limit the rebellion, while the partisan tone of the Labour leader, Harold Wilson, in the debate swayed many more. Even

13. Burton CA, Council, 9 September 1971; Twickenham CA, special Exec., 19 July 1971; A. Seldon and S. Ball (eds.), *Conservative Century: the Conservative Party since 1900* (Oxford, 1994), 266–8; Norton, *Conservative Dissidents*, 179–91, 197–200.

14. Central Office and the whips monitored developments, but do not seem to have instigated them: Denisson (Chairman, Thirsk and Malton CA) to Party Chairman, 22 November 1971, Pym to Thomas, 30 November 1971, Webster to Pym, 8 November 1971, and memo 'EEC vote: Parliamentary Redistribution', 1 November 1971, CCO/20/3/11.

so, fifteen Conservative MPs took the unprecedented step of going into the lobby against their own Party on a vote of confidence. The government nearly fell, scraping home by only 309 to 301. However, this was to be the last serious alarm. Only a small group of Conservative MPs doggedly fought the legislation through its remaining stages, and in July 1972 the third reading was carried by 301 to 284; sixteen Conservatives voted against and four abstained. Passage had been secured, but the controversy had exhausted the party. There was little enthusiasm after entry took effect on 1 January 1973. The benefits to the economy were not readily apparent and the introduction of VAT was a further negative factor, with pressure to ensure that various emotive commodities were given a zero rating.

In its first eighteen months the government made progress in implementing three key aspects of the 1970 manifesto: entry into Europe, reductions in taxation, and a statutory framework to regulate industrial relations. The cuts in income and corporation tax announced in the 'mini-budget' of 23 October 1970 were widely welcomed.[15] Anthony Barber's 1971 budget was described by the chairman of the National Union executive as 'both a Party and a personal triumph' which 'had had a tonic effect'.[16] Whatever the antipathy it aroused among the trade union leaders, the Industrial Relations Bill was popular with the general public, especially in late 1970. This support faded a little during 1971, but the legislation was 'far more supported in the electorate as a whole than opposed.'[17] As late as September 1971 it was still regarded as 'one of the strongest political plus marks from the government's performance'.[18] Such high hopes made for the greater disappointment when the Act failed to contain industrial strife and seemed to become part of the problem which it had been intended to solve. Party demands for a firm stand against a series of strikes by key groups of workers, especially in public utilities, were impossible to satisfy. Tactical weaknesses and the vagaries of public opinion meant that the government would be the loser in any lengthy dispute, but the apparent setbacks which it suffered along the way steadily diminished its prestige.

The handling of industrial relations was hampered by the problems

15. 1922 Ctte., 19 November 1970; Wessex Area, Harrow West CA res., NU Exec. agenda, 5 November 1970.

16. Advisory Committee on Policy, 21 April 1971, ACP(71)111; Steering Committee, 16 June 1971, SC/71/4.

17. 'Current political situation and outlook', 26 April 1971 (misdated as 1970), OG/71/80; 'Industrial Relations', CPC contact programme, December 1970–January 1971, CCO/4/10/81.

18. 'Current political situation and outlook', memo by 'J.H.', 2 September 1971, OG/71/85.

of the domestic economy. The unprecedented combination of rising unemployment and rising prices produced a perplexing and alarming situation. There was no honeymoon: within six months of the Party taking office, concern was being expressed by the chairman of the 1922 Committee 'that our policy was right, but time was running out'.[19] Results were needed which could be demonstrated quickly, rather than in the long term. An 'economic breakthrough was essential' on political grounds, for 'without economic growth we could help the relatively small numbers of people at either end of the income scale but could do very little for the people in the middle, where most of the votes were'.[20] The issue which caused most concern within the Party was inflation. While the Chancellor of the Exchequer admitted privately that the government was following an implicit incomes policy, compulsory powers were ruled out as incompatible with Conservative principles.[21] Nevertheless, the Party was being propelled in the direction of pragmatic intervention and statutory regulation for, with voluntary restraint clearly failing, there was a growing expectation that the government would have to take action.

At the same time, Conservatives were sensitive to any further encroachment by the state. Support for intervention to deal with unemployment or for expansionist programmes in education and social services ran parallel to the desire to cut bureaucracy, limit the state sector, and reduce taxation.[22] The themes of self-reliance, 'freedom and responsibility' enunciated when the government took office were warmly endorsed by the rank and file, for whom the pledge not to support any more industrial lame ducks had a wider symbolism.[23] It was against this background that the first of the 'U-turns' took place: the nationalisation of Rolls-Royce and assistance to the Yarrow and Upper Clyde shipyards which were announced in February 1971. The provision of what was intended to be temporary help to Rolls-Royce was broadly acceptable to most Conservatives. The company bore a famous name with a reputation for excellence which was a source of national pride, while the maintenance of an independent defence industry was a matter of national security. Shop-floor militancy had not been a factor, and instead there was a loyal and skilled workforce who were

19. Advisory Committee on Policy, 25 November 1970, ACP(70)109.

20. Steering Committee, 16 June 1971, SC/71/4.

21. Advisory Committee on Policy, 21 April 1971, ACP(71)111.

22. Western Area res., 24 April 1971, South East Area res., 22 November 1971, CCO/20/70/4; NU Central Council agenda, 24–25 March 1972; for uncertainty over action to reduce unemployment, see Ruislip Northwood CA, Exec., 28 September 1971.

23. West Midlands Area res., NU Exec. agenda, 5 November 1970.

seen as the victims of incompetent management. The later rescue of Upper Clyde Shipbuilders was a very different matter, and regarded as such by the parliamentary Party; there was little natural Tory sympathy for either the region or the industry, and it appeared to be a surrender to illegal and militant action in which there was a prominent Communist involvement.

From the autumn of 1970 the government lost popularity, although there was consolation in the thought that the most difficult measures were being dealt with early in the Parliament.[24] Conservative activists approved the start which had been made in implementing the pledges in the manifesto, but regretted that this was not understood or appreciated by the public.[25] The feeling grew that the leadership were failing to get their message across, largely by default. Ministers had been too occupied with their departments and legislation to do much in the way of old-fashioned platform speaking, and had been reluctant to appear on television. Opportunities had been lost during the receptive period of the government's first year. As Heath's Political Secretary, Douglas Hurd, noted in his diary, 'there are always excellent reasons for missing boats, and we are getting good at it.'[26] The Prime Minister's desire to underline the contrast in style with the Wilson era by severely restricting his own media appearances was welcomed at first, but gave rise to concern when Conservative popularity started to slide. Confidence was shaken by the poor local election results of May 1971, with even the Tory heartlands of the south-east reporting 'substantial losses'.[27] The Party's private polling confirmed that the Conservatives were seen as remote from ordinary people, unrepresentative and uncaring.[28] One Area warned with 'great emphasis' of 'the need for the Party not only to care for people, as it does, but also and especially in the climate of present public opinion, to be seen to care'.[29] Some of the government's successes were two-edged swords: taxes were cut and the overall tax

24. Advisory Committee on Policy, 21 July 1971, ACP(71)113.

25. NU Exec., 6 March 1971; Wessex Area res., NU Exec. agenda, 10 June 1971; Tavistock CA res., NU Central Council agenda, 2–3 April 1971.

26. Diary entry quoted in D. Hurd, *An End to Promises: Sketch of a Government 1970–1974* (London, 1979), 79; Party Chairman to all cabinet ministers, 15 March 1971, Douglas to Party Chairman, 5 March 1971, CCO/20/1/19; Tactical Ctte., 5 January, 23 February, 27 April 1971, CCO/20/7/11; East Midlands Area, Exec., 1 March 1971.

27. South East Area, Council, half-yearly report, November 1971.

28. 'Re-examination of Party Communication Methods', memo by Thompson, 29 October 1970, CCO/20/7/10; 'Public Attitudes to the Conservative Party', circular from Carrington, 1 May 1972, CCO/20/1/19; Advisory Committee on Policy, 9 June 1971, ACP(71)112.

29. Wessex Area res., NU Exec. agenda, 6 November 1971.

burden fell, but there was a perception that the better-off had gained the most. While Conservatives are not egalitarian, a belief in natural fairness has always been at the core of their outlook. This was recognised by the leadership: 'so far as the impact on our own supporters was concerned, the government must be seen to be looking after the defenceless'.[30] Conservative strategists were aware that social services, and in particular the National Health Service, also benefited the middle class.[31] Other problems included the ending of free school milk, the continuing closure of grammar schools, and the introduction of museum admission charges. Symbolic of the extent to which the aims of 1970 were drifting out of sight was the failure to cut the size of the civil service, for at first numbers actually rose.[32]

During 1971, many MPs and local parties were preoccupied by the consequences of the first major redistribution of constituency boundaries since 1949. In many places there were time-consuming details resulting from the closure or merger of constituency associations, with the inevitable attendant clashes of ego and squabbles over shares of local funds. There were some undignified scrambles between sitting MPs, and an embarrassing clash developed between Heath himself and his neighbour, Dame Patricia Hornsby-Smith, over the new Sidcup division. Two of the bitterest struggles occurred between John Peel and Tom Boardman over Leicester South, and Patrick Cormack and Fergus Montgomery over South-West Staffordshire, but there were distracting and unsettling lesser upheavals in many other places. These disputes were over personal and not political matters, a fact graphically demonstrated when the inaugural meeting of the reluctantly merged North and South Kensington associations elected 'a Monday Club chairman, and a Bow Group deputy'.[33] Despite the problems which the new boundaries caused in some places, as a whole the redistribution was to the Conservatives' advantage – it was for this reason that the Labour government had postponed it before the 1970 election.

By the end of 1971 there had been difficulties and disappointments, but these were balanced by some successes. This was an active government, passing 76 bills in its first session and carrying out many of its manifesto pledges. The position was bleaker in the vital areas of dom-

30. Advisory Committee on Policy, 25 November 1970, ACP(70)109.

31. Advisory Committee on Policy, 9 June 1971, ACP(71)112.

32. Chief Agent, West Leicester CA, to Thomas, 18 June 1971; Jellicoe to Thomas, 25 June 1971, CCO/20/1/19; Wales and Monmouthshire Area res., 27 November 1971, CCO/20/70/4; Advisory Committee on Policy, 1 December 1971; ACP(71)115; Morrison to Thomas, 7 October 1971, CCO/20/4/6; Hampstead CA, Exec., 19 July 1971.

33. Titchener-Barrett to Thomas, 29 October 1971, CCO/20/3/11.

estic policy and, as the chairman of the National Union executive stressed, 'at the end of the day the Party would be judged on its handling of unemployment and prices'.[34] However, there were grounds for optimism in some of the economic indicators. The Conservatives were not too far behind Labour in the opinion polls, and could feel that they still had plenty of time to play with.[35] Party morale was bruised but still intact, with a successful annual conference in October 1971. The critical year for Conservative fortunes was 1972, in which the Party was shaken by the humiliating surrender to the miners and disoriented by the U-turns in policy. However, the damage which these caused only partly accounts for the Conservative traumas of the early 1970s; the rest of the explanation is to be found in the broader economic and social changes which were disturbing the daily lives of the Party's supporters.

THE CLIMATE OF OPINION

The early 1970s were a difficult time for those of Conservative values and temperament. A remarkable conjunction of changes affected much that was familiar, and the complex responses of the Conservative Party during the Heath government can only be fully understood when set against this troubled background. The 'permissive society' is popularly associated with the 1960s, but its impact on suburban and provincial Britain was apparent only at the end of that decade and in the early 1970s. Changes in morality and behaviour spread rapidly in this period: divorce, abortion, and a youth culture which in dress, behaviour and music took a much more unsettling form than ever before. This was the period of the *Oz* obscenity trial, of the giant rock festivals, and of a growing drugs problem in the major cities. The more extreme fashions emerged after 1968, especially in length of hair and 'hippie' psychedelia in clothes; the emphasis upon ethnic styles appeared to older Conservatives to embrace barbarism and primitivism. Student protest was especially unpopular, and it was a source of resentment to the lower middle-class constituency stalwarts that it was being subsidised by grants from the taxpayers' pockets.[36] There was much talk of the alienation

34. Advisory Committee on Policy, 26 January 1972, ACP(72)116; see also 'Current political situation and outlook', memo by Fraser, 7 May 1971, SC/71/3.

35. 'Current political situation and outlook', memo by Fraser, 7 May 1971, SC/71/3, pp. 7–8; 'Public opinion', memo by Fraser, 13 September 1971, SC/71/5.

36. Maldon CA res., NU Exec. agenda, 6 March 1971; Beckenham CA, Holborn and St Pancras South CA res., NU Exec. agenda, 20 April 1972.

of youth and the 'generation gap'. Popular music enlarged on this, with the appearance of still more alarming and bizarre social and sexual images. Through the medium of *Top of the Pops* such incomprehensible figures as David Bowie and Alice Cooper (complete with snake) were beamed into the living rooms of middle-class parents on a weekly basis, and few of them appreciated it.

Unpleasantness of every kind seemed to be on the increase: a sudden apparent spread of obscenity and pornography, together with rising crime, violence, hooliganism and juvenile delinquency. Law and order issues were neither new nor unique to this period, but they were now being linked to a lack of discipline and loss of respect for authority; the Party grass-roots were 'gravely concerned at the continued increase of lawlessness and vandalism'.[37] On top of this was added the new and frightening phenomenon of terrorism: the 'Angry Brigade' bomb attack on the home of cabinet minister Robert Carr, aircraft hijackings by the Palestinians, and a vicious downwards spiral of violence in Northern Ireland. At a deeper level, many Conservatives mourned the continued decline of the old social structures and institutions, especially in rural areas. There was a sense that selfishness and greed were becoming paramount, affirmed by the activities of speculators in the City, the Lonrho and Slater–Walker affairs, and the squalid details of the Lucan murder and Lambton sex scandal. At the other end of the social pyramid, the fear and loathing which had built up over the issue of coloured immigration during the 1960s was given a sharp stimulus by the sudden influx of the Ugandan Asians. Although the extensive media coverage of the vicious nature of the Amin regime eased tensions and evoked sympathy, this further wave of entrants touched a raw nerve among the Conservative rank and file, especially in the influx areas.[38] Political extremism was more visible than had been the case since the 1930s, causing alarm in the Party about the spread of 'seditious elements'.[39] This was not only a matter of the National Front's exploitation of racial antagonism, but also of Communist and far left shop stewards and union leaders, such as Mick McGahey of the NUM, and the Trotskyist factions active in demonstrations in London and the universities. Finally, the disintegration of mainland Britain became a

37. Carlisle CA res., NU Central Council agenda, 23–24 March 1973; 'Combating Crime', CPC contact programme, February 1972 CCO/4/10/81; West Midlands Area res., 23 October 1971, CCO/20/70/4.

38. Southwark Peckham CA, Exec., 20 September 1972; NU Central Council agendas, 2–3 April 1971, 23–24 March 1973; NU Exec. agendas, 11 November 1972, 6 December 1973; NU annual conference, 12 October 1972.

39. Horncastle CA, Exec., 16 July 1974.

real possibility for the first time, due to the rise of the Welsh and Scottish nationalist movements.

There were also profound changes in the conduct of ordinary life. The decimalisation of the currency which took effect on 15 February 1971 was a matter of daily stress for older citizens in particular – many of whom were Conservative supporters. In the minds of many people it became entangled with the effects of inflation, making comparisons with past prices difficult or misleading. There were also unfounded fears about the imminent imposition of metrication.[40] The latter was linked to the larger change of entry into the EEC, which may have offered a great opportunity but also represented a break with the past. In fact, the impact of joining never matched the stirring rhetoric of either its advocates or its opponents. The reorganisation of local government impinged on more people, and proved to be more of an upheaval. There seemed to be more losers than gainers, and Conservative rural districts feared absorption into or domination by nearby Labour metropolitan areas. The dislocation was controversial within Conservative circles, leading to apathy and a lack of empathy with some of the new bodies – the elimination of the historic Yorkshire ridings was particularly unpopular. Any gain in efficiency was at the price of adding to the impression of remote and faceless government.[41] Even where the new boundaries did not cause controversy, party workers were horrified at the demands which the introduction of annual elections for district councils would place upon them. During these years the physical environment became a matter of concern across the political spectrum. The property boom of the early 1970s caused a wave of redevelopments in traditional town centres which contributed to middle-class alienation, while new towns and high-rise council blocks continued to uproot established working-class communities. The sense of how much things had changed was emphasised by the increasing number of local party resolutions which focused on the problems of pollution and industrial waste.

Feelings of economic insecurity were even more widespread. Retail prices increased by one-third between June 1970 and December 1973 and house prices rose by nearly three-quarters in just two years, while in September 1973 interest rates reached an unprecedented 11 per cent.

40. 'Notes on metrication', memo for Tactical Ctte. by Douglas and Wolff, 30 April 1971, CCO/20/7/12; South East Area, Exec., 17 July 1972; Worthing CA res., NU Exec. agenda, 10 November 1973.

41. Advisory Committee on Policy, 16 May 1973, ACP(72)123; Ripon CA, Exec., 16 December 1971; Monmouth CA res., 29 June 1971, CCO/20/70/4; Odey to Carrington, 7 August 1973, CCO/20/54/6.

Bitterness focused upon the much misunderstood Conservative pledge to reduce the rise in prices 'at a stroke', a phrase which was to haunt the Heath government. The effects of inflation pressed heavily upon white-collar workers, middle managers, shopkeepers, small businessmen, and those such as pensioners who lived upon savings or fixed incomes; in short, upon the heartlands of Conservative support.[42] The professional and self-employed middle class felt most exposed, lacking the protection apparently provided by corporate big business or militant organised labour: 'their whole confidence had been undermined'.[43] During the previous decade the public had been confronted by a bewildering variety of economic problems and terminology – balance of payments, cost-push inflation, productivity, invisible earnings, and so on – which many people barely understood. As soon as one aspect improved, two new problems appeared in its place. There was confusion, helplessness, and a growing belief that those in authority were out of their depth.[44]

The combined effect of all these factors was an atmosphere of inexorable flux and change, in which powerful economic and institutional forces were grinding down individuality and tradition. It appeared that even a strong government could not contain the challenge of sectional groups or prevent them from holding society to ransom, and that popular support for the authority of the government and even of the ballot box was crumbling. When Heath posed the same constitutional question with which Baldwin had undermined the General Strike – who governs Britain? – the public response of 1974 was shockingly different to that of 1926. Party officials recognised that 'one reason for the present mood is that government is felt to be remote, difficult to influence and unconcerned with ordinary people'. A mood of disillusion and cynicism about politics was spreading rapidly, especially among the young. Public faith in the ability of governments to control events and of politicians to deliver on their pledges was eroded.[45] Basic values and historic foundations were under vague but alarming threat,

42. South East Area, Exec., 22 May 1972; for party concern, see Thomas to Barber, 9 Februaury 1971, CCO/20/1/19.

43. Official Group, 21 December 1972, OG/73/113; Steering Committee, 28 February 1973, SC/73/19; Hazel Grove CA res., NU Exec. agenda, 6 December 1973; Advisory Committe on Policy, 8 May and 12 June 1974, ACP(74)129–130; Smith (Deputy Chairman, Pudsey CA Women's Advisory ctte.) to Morrison (Party Vice-chairman), 9 June 1973, circulated at Fraser's request to Official Group, 21 June 1973, OG/73/125.

44. 'Current Political Scene', memo by Douglas, 22 October 1973, OG/73/131.

45. 'The next manifesto – policy', memo by Newton and Douglas, 17 March 1972, SC/72/11; Advisory Committee on Policy, 26 January 1972, 16 May 1973, ACP(72) 116, 123.

and no remedies seemed to be at hand. The mixture of economic pressures, social malaise and fear of anarchy produced a sense of dislocation, in which incomprehension was mingled with powerlessness. In 1973 the Party's Advisory Committee on Policy noted 'a general fear about the state of our society, the feeling that we are not in control'.[46] The early 1970s were suffused by a sense of alienation and frustration: thus began a decade marked by despair about the 'British disease' – economic decline, industrial strife, political ungovernability, and the breakdown of social unity. It was against this background that the Heath government was tested and found wanting: its natural supporters sensed instinctively that it was not achieving the ends which they desired, but the lack of any other means plunged them into despair rather than revolt.

STRESSES AND STRAINS: 1972–73

Despite all the problems which the government had faced since taking office, at the start of 1972 the rank and file were still wedded to the 'true Conservative principles and policies' of the 1970 manifesto; 'any wavering will cause great dissatisfaction'.[47] Their mood was one of increasing frustration, for the leadership had done little to meet the heartfelt wishes of the party activists on issues such as immigration, corporal and capital punishment, or the denial of social security benefits to strikers' families. Approaching mid-term, the government had already disappointed many of its supporters. One association frankly declared itself 'greatly concerned with the lack of strength currently being shown by the present Conservative administration', and demanded 'more firmness in dealing with the disruptive elements within our society'.[48] By the summer of 1972 the feeling was growing that the government was drifting, without any idea of how to control inflation. The chairman of the National Union executive considered that 'the problem was more than a mid-term malaise, and had to do with the fact that there seemed to be a change of mind on many fronts and that some policies seemed to be failing'.[49]

During the last two years of the Heath government political con-

46. Advisory Committee on Policy, 14 March 1973, ACP(72)122.

47. Official Group, 3 August 1972, OG/72/109; Swindon CA, Exec., 20 September 1972; Croydon Central CA, Harrow West CA res., NU Exec. agenda, 11 November 1972.

48. Ravensbourne CA res., NU Exec. agenda, 11 November 1972.

49. Advisory Committee on Policy, 19 July 1972, ACP(72)119.

fusion merged into national chaos. The turning point was the surrender to the miners in February 1972. This traumatic event did deep and lasting damage to Conservative morale, provoking 'a terrible beating from our own supporters'.[50] The Party rank and file were insistent that the government had to stand firm against unreasonable wage demands, 'believing that failure to do so would result in a loss of confidence and support from the majority of electors and Party members'.[51] However, by February 1972 the government's position had become untenable, as the balance of economic power was against it. The Party's own trade union wing was only the most vehement among the chorus of disapproval, 'angered and disillusioned by the refusal – even abdication – of the government to show itself willing to govern during the recent miners' strike'. In their view, 'the handling of the whole issue showed a serious lack of political judgement which is both dangerous and frightening to the future of the country and Party'.[52] The coal strike not only damaged the government's confidence and standing, but also forced it to embark upon a new path in economic and industrial strategy. Both the public and the Party were ill-prepared for this, and the impression of a series of U-turns was vividly impressed into the national consciousness. At a fundamental level, the actions of the government and the instincts of the Party were in conflict.

The reversals of policy for which the government is chiefly remembered occurred in five areas, all of which were central to its credibility. The first was the rescuing of 'lame duck' companies by taking them into public ownership; although this only happened twice, the decisions had a very high profile. The Rolls-Royce and UCS nationalisations seemed to show a government at the mercy of events despite all the planning which had taken place while the Party was in opposition between 1964 and 1970. The other four changes of direction were concentrated into the twelve months after the end of the coal strike, creating as they unfolded a logic and momentum of their own. The second reversal was the decision to adopt state-directed economic planning and regional development. In March 1972, an Industrial Development Executive was established which seemed depressingly similar to the Labour quangos so swiftly abolished in 1970. The most interventionist measure of all, the Industry Bill published in May 1972, followed from this and provoked deep Conservative unease. Hostility was expressed in

50. J. Prior, *A Balance of Power* (London, 1986), 77; *The Whitelaw Memoirs* (London, 1989), 124–5; Islington North CA res., NU Exec. agenda, 20 April 1972.

51. Wirral CA res., NU Exec. agenda, 15 June 1972; [Conservative] Trade Unionists N[ational] A[dvisory] C[ommittee] res., NU Exec. agenda, 25 January 1973.

52. Trade Unionists NAC res., NU Exec. agenda, 20 April 1972.

the back-bench Trade and Industry committee on 16 May, and the passage of the legislation was marked by the sporadic dissent of a handful of free-marketeers and the troubled reluctance of the mainstream. When the Trade and Industry Secretary, John Davies, introduced the bill his speech was met by cheers from the Labour benches and silence from the Conservative side of the House. Party feeling was vocalised by the chairman of the 1922 Committee, Sir Harry Legge-Bourke, who described the measure as 'obnoxious' and 'a Socialist bill by ethic and philosophy'.[53]

The impact of the miners strike was most immediately apparent in the third 'U-turn': the tacit abandonment of the industrial relations legislation and the quest for stability and growth through a tripartite consensus. The talks which commenced at Chequers on 26 September 1972 between the government, the TUC and the CBI marked the high tide of corporatist elitism. The nature of the process implied that political legitimacy was no longer defined by the constitution, but shared between powerful economic blocs; the senior member of the cabinet who gave the Party's Advisory Committee on Policy a report on the talks revealingly referred to the participants as 'the three partners'.[54] After the bitter struggles over the passage and utilisation of the Industrial Relations Act, this felt like another surrender to the unions. It was only too clear that the Cabinet were negotiating from a position of weakness, and not of strength. Lord Carrington, Chairman of the Party from April 1972, noted the growing complaint that 'we were too often running away' over economic policy and inflationary pay demands.[55]

The fourth 'U-turn' was still more startling: the adoption of a compulsory prices and incomes policy. The final collapse of the tripartite talks on 2 November 1972 left the government with no remaining voluntary options. Four days later Heath announced a statutory 90-day freeze of pay and prices, and on 8 November Barber moved the second reading of the Counter-Inflation (Temporary Provisions) Bill. While the freeze was in place, 'Phase II' of the programme was introduced in the main Counter-Inflation Bill in January 1973, with a 'Phase III' to take effect in the autumn. During this same period of late 1972 and early 1973 the government also embarked upon its fifth and final change of tack: a massive increase in public expenditure. The aim of encouraging growth was not in itself a change, but these methods and

53. *House of Commons Debates*, 5th series, vol 841, col. 2402, 28 July 1972; *The Times* 23 May 1972.

54. Advisory Committee on Policy, 8 November 1972, ACP(72)120.

55. Lord Carrington, *Reflect on Things Past* (London, 1988), 260–1.

their consequences ran counter to the tone and content of the 1970 manifesto. Anxiety about the rising level of state spending was expressed in the back-bench Finance committee on 30 January 1973 and taken up in debate on the White Paper on 7 February, where the critics included the new 1922 Committee chairman, Edward Du Cann. It was brushed aside by Barber in his budget in March, but only a few weeks later official statistics indicated that the economy was overheating, and in a further change of direction the programmes had to be slashed, first in May and again in December 1973. These cuts were generally welcomed by Conservative MPs, but they added to the confusion over party strategy and hardly improved confidence in its leadership. There was also back-bench concern over three expensive and unpopular projects which the Prime Minister reaffirmed in July: Concorde, the building of a third London airport at Maplin, and a Channel tunnel.

Pragmatism and inconsistency were the twin hallmarks of the rank-and-file response to the problems of industry and inflation, of intervention or non-intervention. There were some positive calls for action to restrain wages before the inflationary spiral worsened. Concern over the economic situation inspired calls for strong leadership, while the Conservative values of authority and responsibility shaped the recognition that government could not stand aside in such circumstances.[56] By November 1972 the bulk of the party accepted that voluntary restraint had failed and that action had to be taken, and there was even some relief that the government were reasserting their authority after the unhappy period of the tripartite talks. The pressure of events and improvisation, rather than plan or principle, led to the statutory policy. At the outset it was regarded as a temporary reaction to exceptional circumstances, and the overwhelming majority of Conservative MPs accepted the value of the initial 90-day freeze. The few ideological free-marketeers who dissented stood alone; only Enoch Powell voted against the third reading of the interim bill on 20 November, with John Biffen and Jock Bruce-Gardyne abstaining. A wider circle were troubled by the change of direction, but criticism of the main Counter-Inflation Bill in the back-bench Finance committee on 23 January 1973 was deflected by an able speech from Barber. Six days later the second reading was carried with a majority of 36, and in March 1973 the budget was given a 'loyal but muted welcome' by the Conservative benches.[57] However, this support was founded not upon confidence or enthusiasm, but upon the suppression of misgivings. Most of the Party

56. Cheltenham CA, Harrow West CA, Enfield North CA res., NU Exec. agenda, 11 November 1972; Weston-super-Mare CA res., NU Exec. agenda, 25 January 1973.
57. *The Times*, 7 March 1973.

chafed under the feeling that there was no workable alternative, although some rejected that assumption and called for a 'return to a system of free enterprise'.[58] A microcosm of the confusion in the ranks can be found in the opinions of the national committee of the Conservative trade unionists' organisation. Originally they had firmly rejected any statutory incomes policy, but under the pressure of events they endorsed Phases I and II, partly to safeguard the interests of the low paid; by March 1973 they were uneasily but implicitly accepting protectionism and state intervention as necessary features of the economy.[59] As the government settled into the groove of the statutory approach and moved on to more deliberate legislation, its followers trooped dispiritingly behind it displaying various degrees of loyalty, anxiety and reluctance.

One of the Conservative Party's greatest strengths is its instinctive cohesiveness when under external attack or in a hostile environment. At the nadir of February 1972 one observer noted that there was 'always great pressure within the Conservative Party to support a Tory government at all costs when it is in trouble'.[60] The rank and file remained supportive in public, while sending some remarkably crisp and frank reactions up through the confidential channels of communication within the party structure. In October 1972 the annual conference had its usual steadying effect, and party managers were 'generally agreed' that it had 'in the circumstances gone extremely well'.[61] Conservative supporters, perhaps more readily than the general public, were willing to acknowledge that the difficulties which the government faced were caused by forces beyond Britain's control, and to make allowances for this in their criticism. There was some admiration for the government's determination to attack the problems, whatever the means which they had to use.[62] At the same time, there was a perception that Heath and his team were willing to accept much upheaval in order to modernise the country, and this was not necessarily what Conservatives wanted. Heath presided over a government willing to take difficult decisions and eager to throw into relief the weakness and fudging of its Labour predecessor. Nettles were grasped, though sometimes with painful results. The Deputy Party Chairman, Sir Michael Fraser, observed that the Prime Minister's determined assault upon complacency tended to convey to the public an attitude of 'nasty medicine is good for you'.[63]

58. Tonbridge CA res., NU Exec. agenda, 24 May 1973.
59. Trade Unionists NAC res., NU Exec. agenda, 15 June 1972, 24 May 1973.
60. *Financial Times*, 14 February 1972; Norton, *Conservative Dissidents*, 73.
61. Tactical Ctte., 17 October 1972, CCO/20/7/16.
62. Bolton East CA res., NU Exec. agenda, 25 April 1974.
63. Official Group, 4 November 1971, OG/71/95.

Loyalty and deference are the ties that bind the Conservative Party, but they can fray or snap if put under too great a strain. Principles and objectives may be set aside in a crisis, but not for ever. In February 1973 Fraser warned the Steering Committee that while the grass-roots 'generally had readily accepted' the statutory counter-inflation policy, 'there could be increasing problems if government involvement on this scale looked like becoming permanent'.[64] Many who had accepted Phases I and II urged that Phase III 'should begin a gradual return to a freer economy'.[65] When constituency association Conservative Political Centre groups discussed the statutory incomes policy in October 1973, hardly any thought that it had been a complete failure but only 20 per cent of replies rated it a 'considerable success'.[66] As time passed and statutory regulation became an increasingly familiar part of the landscape, the question inevitably arose whether it was to be permanent. By late 1973 questions were being raised as to how long it could go on, and what would follow after Phase III – return to pay-claim anarchy or a 'Phase IV'? In the event, criticism was partly muted by some encouraging signs that the new policy was working, as unemployment began to fall in 1972–73.[67] There were grounds for optimism in the summer of 1973, with the pay policy appearing to hold with both employers and unions, while Conservative opinion poll ratings improved in the spring. The Party leadership began to look towards an election in late 1974 or the spring of 1975 with more confidence, and hence to trumpet their better record on economic growth.[68] However, at the individual level there was no 'feel good' factor, for any improvements seemed minor when set against the insecurities of rising prices, high mortgage rates, and apparently endless industrial strife.

Remaining loyal to the leadership in such circumstances was made all the more difficult by having to eat the words of the recent past. South East Area, for example, had unambiguously dismissed a wages and prices freeze as 'fundamentally wrong' in 1971; a sentiment which was hard to square with the counter-inflation policy of 1973.[69] Antagonism to state control remained strong: the Young Conservatives described Phase II as 'contrary to Conservative philosophy' – a voluntary prices and incomes policy being 'infinitely more

64. Steering Committee, 28 February 1973, SC/73/19.

65. Wessex Area res., NU Exec. agenda, 14 June 1973.

66. 'Phase III and after', CPC contact programme, October 1973. CCO/4/10/81.

67. Advisory Committee on Policy, 14 March 1973, ACP(72)122.

68. 'Future Policy', Research Dept. memo, 15 January 1973, OG/73/114; Hurd, *An End to Promises*, 108.

69. South East Area, Exec., 8 February 1971.

preferable'.[70] Economic liberalism was stronger in the Party at an instinctive level than might appear from the handful of visible and intellectually coherent free-marketeers. There was a fear that dangerous precedents were being established which a Socialist government could later use. The short-term expedients of the battle against inflation were 'being allowed to obscure the grave constitutional dangers inherent in any long-term governmental interference in the market economy of this country'.[71] There was no revolt, but the price of loyalty was tension and a corroding sense of doubt and unhappiness at all levels, together with rumbling discontent in the parliamentary party over the U-turns and publicity failures.[72] When a party is following a course which conflicts with its customs and ethos, the passage of time only increases the itch beneath the saddle. In November 1972, Birmingham Conservatives expressed their 'grave disquiet at the present state of affairs in the United Kingdom', and demanded that the government should 'act in a more firm and decisive manner, especially with regard to their electoral promises'.[73] In February 1973 there was talk in the press of a party crisis; by the middle of that year, one Area Agent reported, 'few associations do not contain a substantial minority of members who openly criticise the government and the Prime Minister'.[74] More dangerously, the resilience of the majority had also been sapped.

From the end of 1971 the Party frequently had to cope with crises which occurred with bewildering speed and on several simultaneous fronts, and their nerves were becoming increasingly frayed. The Conservative grass-roots and backbenches were uncomfortably aware of having become passengers, at the mercy of events. They felt themselves to be distanced from their leaders, and placed much of the blame for their predicament on the government's failure to put its case across. In the difficult early months of 1972 one constituency agent warned Central Office that 'few electors have the remotest idea of what the government is seeking to achieve', an ignorance which had produced 'a credibility gap of huge proportions'.[75] A few weeks after the surrender to the miners, the Conservative students' conference despaired of 'the

70. Y[oung] C[onservatives] NAC res., NU Central Council agenda, 23–24 March 1973.

71. Trade Unionists NAC res., NU Exec. agenda, 6 December 1973.

72. Patten to Party Chairman, 'Meeting with the Executive of 1922 Committee', 1 May 1973, CCO/20/59/2.

73. Birmingham CA res., NU Exec. agenda, 7 December 1972.

74. Henderson (Deputy CO Agent, Greater London Area) to Morrison, 21 June 1973, CCO/20/2/5; Carrington, *Reflect on Things Past*, 261.

75. Dockerill (Agent, Arundel CA) to Webster, 8 February 1972, circulated to Tactical Ctte., CCO/20/7/13.

apparent inability of the party at all levels to explain clearly and simply Conservative policies to the general public'.[76] There was no improvement, and by the autumn of 1973 denunciations of the failure of the government's public relations were being heard from all quarters.[77] Most of these should be taken at their face value, for political activists tend to equate unpopularity with ignorance of their party's true aims and achievements. In some cases, however, it became the code for a more direct attack upon policy.[78] On the whole, it was easier to direct the blame outwards to the media. Conservatives believed that BBC news and current affairs programmes were not 'put over factually' but slanted by reporters whose views were 'often left-wing, anti-establishment, ill-considered and immature'.[79] They complained of the 'continuing erosion of moral standards and the subversive presentation of news and views as expressed by the BBC', which was regarded as a far worse offender than commercial television.[80] In fact the problem was within rather than without: the Cabinet were preoccupied with the demands of administration, and lost touch with the Party. In 1971 Heath's Political Secretary, Douglas Hurd, noted that the government seemed to be less politically aware than previous Conservative ministries.[81]

The alienation of the middle class was a source of deep concern in the Party. The budget changes and welfare reforms 'had all tended to redistribute away from the middle, where most of our votes come from, towards the extremes of the very poor and the very rich'.[82] Many Conservative voters were not wealthy enough to gain much from the tax cuts, but not poor enough to qualify for the increased benefits. At the same time, they were being 'ground between the cost of living on the one hand and a more or less fixed income on the other'.[83] The disillusion of those earning between £30 and £50 per week was like

76. Federation of Conservative Students annual conference res., NU Exec. agenda, 20 April 1972; Croydon Central CA, Harrow West CA res., NU Exec. agenda, 11 November 1972; Oxford CA res., NU Exec. agenda, 7 December 1972.

77. Aylesbury CA, F&GP ctte., 12 September 1973; 'Phase III and after', CPC contact programme, October 1973, CCO/4/10/81; Young Conservatives NAC res., NU Exec. agenda, 10 November 1973.

78. Cambridgeshire CA, Exec., 25 April 1974; Carrington, *Reflect on Things Past*, 261.

79. Abingdon CA res., NU Central Council agenda, 24–25 March 1972.

80. Chislehurst CA res., NU Exec. agenda, 4 December 1970; 'Broadcasting', CPC contact programme, February–March 1971, CCO/4/10/81; Isle of Wight CA res., NU Exec. agenda, 25 April 1974; Tactical Ctte., 5 January 1971, CCO/20/7/11; Womens NAC res., 22 April 1971, CCO/20/70/4.

81. 'The Party as auxiliary to Government', Hurd to Heath, August 1971, in Hurd, *An End to Promises*, 94–5.

82. Advisory Committee on Policy, 9 June 1971, ACP(71)112.

83. Advisory Committee on Policy, 26 January 1972, ACP(72)116.

a stake through the Party's heart. The bedrock of Conservative support – 'honest middle-class people, good citizens, people with principles and standards to maintain' – now felt themselves cast adrift, 'in a vacuum'.[84] Not surprisingly, local associations in middle-class areas responded with alarm. Worthing blamed the government's U-turns and criticised it for 'an undue lack of appreciation of the aspirations and desires of those who would normally be expected to vote for the Conservative candidate' – a remarkable complaint given the increasing middle-class element in the parliamentary Party and Cabinet, headed by the first lower-middle class party leader.[85] From the centre of the prosperous Surrey stockbroker belt, the Dorking executive committee told the leadership 'that in many matters the Government appears to be high-handed and not sufficiently responsive to local opinion'.[86]

The Labour Party gained relatively little from the alienation of the middle class in suburban and rural districts, but it provided fertile ground for the Liberals. These years saw further dealignment from both the main parties: their ties to social class continued to loosen and their roots among younger generations became shallower. They both lost credibility in office, and there was a general atmosphere of 'a plague on both houses'. As the Deputy Central Office Agent for Greater London reported in June 1973, 'frankly, the electorate is bored and disillusioned with the two main parties'.[87] The reorganisation of local government provided the Liberals with fresh opportunities, for in many districts council elections had not previously been fought under national party labels. Both at ward level and in parliamentary by-elections, the Liberals were adept at exploiting parochial issues. They were often able to field young and energetic candidates who made a striking contrast with their Tory opponents. During 1972 and 1973 opinion poll ratings, by-election defeats and local election losses all indicated the drift of Conservative voters to the Liberals. In the council elections of spring 1973 the Liberals won control of Liverpool and made gains in other cities. By the summer they were viewed as a 'growing threat' which was especially dangerous in safe seats and throughout southern England.[88]

84. Smith (Deputy Chairman, Pudsey CA Women's Advisory ctte) to Morrison (Party Vice-chairman), 9 June 1973, circulated at Fraser's request to Official Group, 21 June 1973, OG/73/125.

85. Worthing CA res., NU Central Council agenda, 23–24 March 1973.

86. Dorking CA res., NU Exec. agenda, 6 December 1973.

87. Henderson (Deputy CO Agent, Greater London Area) to Morrison, 21 June 1973, CCO/20/2/5.

88. Tactical Ctte., 17 July 1973, CCO/20/7/18; meetings on 'The Liberals', 15 May and 25 September 1973, CCO/20/2/5, 'By-elections meeting', 12 November 1973, CCO/20/7/19; Dorking CA res., NU Exec. agenda, 6 December 1973; Truro CA, Finance and General Purposes committee, 14 November 1973.

Party officials were aware of 'the underlying and probably increasing volatility of the electorate', which caused both concern and some optimism about the chances of recovery.[89] Although Liberal by-election victories were unsettling, Conservative anxiety would have been much greater if the Labour Party had been making gains. On the same day that Sutton and Cheam fell to the Liberals, Labour failed to take the more marginal Conservatives seat of Uxbridge. The Labour Party gained little from the problems which the government was facing. The shift to the left in Labour policy during 1970–74 made switching an unattractive option for disgruntled Conservative voters, and Wilson lost much public credibility by his manoeuvres on Europe. While there was some concern in Central Office about the length of time during which the Conservatives were lagging behind in the opinion polls, there was also complacency that the opposition lead did not match the levels which had been recorded for lengthy periods during the Macmillan and Wilson governments.[90] Labour's advantage was consistent enough to encourage Conservative unity and perseverance, but never large enough to cause despair. The Conservatives fell behind in early 1971, and Labour were briefly ahead by 18–22 per cent in June, July and September 1971. After this the position improved: during 1972 and 1973 the Conservatives were normally trailing by around 9 per cent and sometimes considerably less. However, the narrowing of the gap with Labour in the final few months of the Heath government reflected gains by the Liberals rather than any real increase in Conservative strength. Liberal support rose from November 1972, peaking at 28 per cent in August 1973 and remaining above 20 per cent until December. This proved to be critical for Conservative fortunes when the election came in February 1974.

PROBLEMS IN THE PARTY ORGANISATION

The combined effects of social change and political unpopularity further exposed weaknesses in the party organisation which had been apparent since the early 1960s. During the period of the Heath government there were several modernising initiatives, most of which foundered. In 1970 the Party had failed to recover lost ground in the cities, winning only 22 of the 122 constituencies here. The weakness was partly social and partly organisational: in the words of the chairman of

89. Steering Committee, 16 June 1971, SC/71/4.

90. 'The Strategic–Tactical Situation in 1973', memo by Fraser, 14 Febuary 1973, SC/73/17; Advisory Committee on Policy, 5 December 1973, ACP(72)127.

the National Union executive, 'the city organisations had developed into small private empires largely officered by absentee landlords'.[91] They held aloof from their regional Areas, and concentrated too exclusively upon municipal politics. The problem had been tackled after the 1964 defeat, when an enquiry under Sir Henry Brooke recommended full integration into the Area structure. This proved to be a slow process of siege warfare, but between 1966 and 1976 the resistance of most of the cities crumbled as their finances and organisation deteriorated. The decision of the Central Council meeting of March 1972 to remove the right of the overall city federations to any separate representation within the party – effectively abolishing them – was a symbolic but bitterly resisted step along the way. Analysis after the 1970 election also pointed to a worrying lack of support among younger voters.[92] Opinion research conducted in 1971 revealed trends which Heath considered to be deeply disturbing.[93] Initiatives after 1970 placed much emphasis upon securing the votes of young people, and the recently elected MP John Gummer was appointed as a Vice-Chairman of the Party to co-ordinate this effort in 1972. He worked closely with Sara Morrison who, during her service as a Vice-Chairman from 1970 to 1975, played an energetic and pivotal part in the drive for modernisation.

Attempts were also made to tackle deficiencies at local level, by shifting the focus from organisational work to political activity. This was also the aim behind the fundamental reappraisal which had been set in motion by the National Union immediately following the election victory. In July 1970 a Review Committee was set up with the ambitious mandate of seeking ways in which 'the Conservative Party in all its aspects outside Parliament might be made more democratic'. Chaired by Lord Chelmer, its work stirred up a hornet's nest of suspicion and ill-feeling, especially on the part of the parliamentary Party.[94] While the constituencies were favourable to the interim report on candidate selection procedures, reactions to the committee's final report

91. Advisory Committee on Policy, 25 November 1970, ACP(70)109.

92. Varley, circular to all local agents, 10 December 1970, CCO/20/3/10; 'Re-examination of Party Communication Methods', memo by Thompson, 29 October 1970, CCO/20/7/10; Advisory Committee on Policy, 25 November 1970, ACP(70)109.

93. Steering Committee, 8 December 1971, SC/71/10, discussing memo 'Survey on the politics of young people', 1 December 1971, SC/71/9; 'New voters', memo by J. Douglas, 13 September 1971, SC/71/6; Official Group, 4 November 1971, OG/71/95.

94. Du Cann to Taylor, 23 February, 16 July 1973, and memos in 1922 Ctte. corres. files 1969–72, 1973–74; P. Seyd, 'Democracy within the Conservative Party?', *Government and Opposition*, 10 (1975), 219–40; Z. Layton-Henry, *Reorganisation in the Conservative Party: an analysis of the Chelmer Inquiry* (Dept. of Politics, Warwick University, 1975).

of September 1972 were mixed. It divided the Party rather than united it, and support diminished over the following year: by the autumn of 1973 a majority of the executive of the powerful South East Area were definitely opposed to its proposals.[95] Central Office sought to keep the report 'at a very distant arms length', and were happy to let it lapse.[96] In October 1973 the report was debated at a special meeting of the Central Council, but no consensus emerged. Although it was formally accepted, implementation was postponed until after the next election. In fact the Chelmer report simply faded away, and most of the problems which it had been intended to address were left unresolved. The need to make constituency associations more outward-looking and effective had been a principal stimulus behind the Chelmer inquiry. Analysis of the key marginals revealed that only about £150 of a typical annual income of £5,000 was being spent on propaganda and publicity – and this included advertising meetings and socials.[97] The habits and priorities of local parties were a long-standing problem, but efforts to widen their horizons had little effect.

Money and membership have been the perennial concerns of local Conservatism, but during this period social change, inflation and unpopularity combined to create even greater pressures. Membership was being steadily eroded by long-term changes in family and work structures, especially affecting middle-class women, and in leisure, especially drawing away the younger members. The total had halved since the 1950s, and was now estimated to be between 1.25 and 1.5 million. In 1971 it was decided to initiate the first centrally encouraged membership drive for more than a decade, and thus 1972 was designated 'Support the Conservatives Year'. However, constituencies were left to decide the timing of their efforts, which would depend largely on their own resources.[98] Even without the cooling of the political atmosphere in 1972, this inevitably led to a patchy effort in which little was done in most of the weaker seats. The benefits were mainly felt in the stronger seats, which reported 'a favourable response where the effort is made to go out and collect new and lapsed subscriptions', and one

95. South East Area, Exec., 7 February 1972, 11 December 1972, 24 September 1973.

96. Patten to Party Chairman, 'Meeting with the Executive of 1922 Committee', 1 May 1973, CCO/20/59/2.

97. 'The Conservative Party – Communications', memo by Morrison, 15 November 1971, CCO/20/7/13.

98. Varley (Deputy Director of Organisation) to Area Agents, 12 August 1971, to Heads of Departments at Central Office, 22 October 1971, CCO/4/10/213; NU GP ctte., 1 December 1971; Party Chairman's circular to constituencies, 30 December 1971, CCO/20/6/6.

consequence of the campaign was to widen further the gap between strong and weak constituencies.[99] Even where it was successful, the effects proved to be only temporary. The Brighton Kemptown association was far from alone in registering a 'considerable' decline in membership between 1970 and late 1973, and there was particular erosion among the Young Conservatives during the early 1970s.[100] Middle-class alienation sapped the fund-raising and dining clubs which were a vital element in involving professionals and businessmen and securing effective local leaders.[101] The rapid inflation required associations to raise what appeared to be even greater sums just to maintain the existing level of activity; at Lichfield and Tamworth, expenditure rose from £3,483 in 1968 to £7,540 in 1974. In May 1972 the Area Agent for Yorkshire candidly admitted that all the associations in the region were in serious financial difficulties.[102] Even in the party's strongholds in central and southern England, it became increasingly difficult to meet local needs and make the 'quota scheme' target payment to Central Office.[103] Inevitably there was pressure upon the largest single charge on most constituency balance sheets, the salary of a professional full-time agent, and the consequent redundancies continued the decline which had been in progress since the early 1960s. In 1968 there had been 409 qualified local agents, but by 1974 the total had slipped to 375.[104] Recruitment tailed off, while the wastage rate increased. The number of newly qualified agents was only seven less than the number of departures in 1971 but the gap widened to 33 in 1973 and, by the end of that year, concern about the lack of experienced agents was being voiced at regional level.[105]

In the cabinet reshuffle of April 1972 Peter Thomas relinquished the Party Chairmanship to the Defence Secretary, Lord Carrington. Despite a heavy departmental burden, Carrington energetically tackled the

99. South East Area, Exec., Area Agent's report, 17 July 1972; Varley to Area Agents, 11 April 1972, CCO/4/10/287; Working Party minutes, 29 March, 18 May 1972, CCO/500/11/16.

100. Brighton Kemptown CA, Finance and GP ctte., 19 November 1973; Burton CA, Council, 29 September 1972; Sheffield Hallam CA, Exec., 21 February 1972; Aylesbury CA, Exec., 3 November 1973, F and GP ctte., 13 December 1973.

101. Twickenham CA, Exec., 5 February 1973; Sheffield Hallam CA, F and GP ctte., 8 February 1972; Swindon CA, Exec., 21 March 1973.

102. Sheffield Hallam CA, Finance and General Purposes ctte., 25 May 1972.

103. Area Treasurer's remarks, East Midlands Area, Exec., 10 July 1973; Wessex Area res., NU Exec. agenda, 14 June 1973.

104. 'Agents (and others) employment state', 26 January 1968, CCO/500/2/13; 'Agent situation report as at 28 August 1974', CCO/500/2/24.

105. '1973: Review of Agents, Women Organisers, and Cadet Agents', May 1974, CCO/500/2/24; South East Area, Exec., 10 December 1973.

problems of preparing to fight the next election. He had four immediate priorities: to review what was being done, to improve party publicity, to tackle the alienation of young voters, and to strengthen the organisation in the key marginals.[106] A committee to review the work of Central Office was established, the Publicity Department was reorganised, and regional publicity liaison officers were appointed. In August 1973 a Youth Department was formed, with a Youth Development Officer in each of the party's eleven Areas. The critical seats were given more help with publicity, and were the focus of a campaign overseen by another cabinet minister brought in to be a second Deputy Chairman, James Prior. The problem of directing resources to the marginals led Carrington logically to the final major initiative of the 1970–74 period: a scheme for the central employment of local party agents. This had been proposed from time to time since the Second World War, but never proceeded with because of rank-and-file hostility to any encroachments upon local autonomy. After the 1970 election, the idea was actively promoted by a prominent member of the National Union executive, Sir Arnold Silverstone, but once again it failed to arouse enthusiasm. The decisive impetus was given by the appointment of Carrington as Party Chairman in 1972, for he seized upon the proposal as a means of strengthening the machine before the next election. However, when the scheme was introduced in 1973 it lacked widespread support on either the professional or the voluntary side of the Party. Although there had been some general discussion beforehand, Carrington only advised the National Union executive of his decision two days before the public announcement on 21 July 1973. While this peremptory treatment offended some, many others were sensitive about the implications for the cherished tradition of local autonomy.[107] The scheme took effect on 1 January 1974, initially in 60 seats, but it was swamped by the two poor election results of 1974 and undermined by inflation and practical problems of raising the necessary funds. Costs rose, there were complaints of lack of contact between the Central Board and local associations, and after Carrington's departure the scheme was slowly wound down. However, while it came too late to have much impact on the February election, taken together with the targeting of other resources on a more restricted group of key marginals it may have significantly helped to limit Labour gains in October, with crucial results for the history of the 1974–79 government. Carrington's

106. Patten to Party Chairman, 'Office Meeting', 5 April 1973, CCO/20/3/13.

107. NU Exec., 19 July 1973; Bury St Edmunds CA, Exec., 3 December 1972; Barry CA, AGM, 5 April 1974; Lichfield and Tamworth CA, Management ctte., 19 November 1973; see corres. in CCO/20/54/6; Seldon and Ball, *Conservative Century*, 284.

Chairmanship was a microcosm of the Heath government as a whole. He tried to do too much too quickly, assumed that efficiency and logic would triumph over custom and self-interest, and failed to communicate with those whose consent was needed; the aims were clear and sincere, but more problems were created than resolved. New initiatives are difficult to launch during periods of unpopularity. The changes of 1972–73 met 'resistance and backbiting' from traditionalists at Smith Square and stone-walling negativism in the constituencies, and were mostly overtaken and undermined by the defeats of 1974.[108]

THE MAINTENANCE OF UNITY

In view of the catalogue of internal and external problems which it faced, the most striking feature of the Conservative Party during 1970–74 was the extent to which unity was preserved. The Conservative Party is not a perfectly disciplined force: real unrest cannot be contained by the whips, the National Union executive, or even by local association pressure. Dissent by MPs is expressed when it is felt strongly, and the rank and file cannot be prevented from signalling criticism if they wish, whatever the formal powers of the platform at party gatherings. During the Heath government there was widespread back-bench grumbling and more rebellions than were comfortable for a ministry with a fairly small Commons majority. However, most of the public dissent related either to Europe or to local interests affected by a particular measure. Although remaining at historically high levels, dissent did not increase as the Parliament progressed. The peak occurred in the 1971–72 session, mainly due to Europe: opposition to entry accounted for 88 of the 128 divisions where one or more Conservative MPs voted against the official whip.[109] Europe was the only issue throughout the entire 1970–74 Parliament upon which the number who entered the rebel lobby was larger than the government's majority of 30. It could be argued that the depth of feeling on Europe was underlined by the fact that this dangerous level was reached on fourteen occasions. However, despite some nervous moments for the whips, the government was never in real danger, because of the near certainty that the Conservative rebels would be cancelled out by Labour pro-entry votes and abstentions – and there were some suspicions that the rebels calculated the effects of their actions accordingly. Although such exercises in brinkmanship could always go awry, the apparently spectacular

108. Carrington, *Reflect on Things Past*, 261.
109. Norton, *Conservative Dissidents*, 40, 201–10.

rifts over Europe were largely gesture politics. Indeed, by providing a vent for the emotions of the anti-Marketeers, they actually increased the long-term stability of the parliamentary party.

Apart from those on Europe, dissenting votes rarely involved more than two or three MPs. The government suffered defeat on only six occasions, and all of these were on fairly minor matters. There was certainly back-bench resentment towards Heath over the defeat by the miners and the reversal of economic policy in 1972, and a feeling that the Prime Minister was not paying much attention to the views of his Party. The parliamentary defeat over the immigration rules in November 1972 was motivated as much by resentment of Heath's tendency 'to ride roughshod over his backbenchers' as it was by the merits of the case. Back-bench unrest over Heath's remote and authoritarian style of leadership also found expression in the election of known critics to key posts in the parliamentary party.[110] Edward Du Cann, dismissed by Heath as Party Chairman in 1967 and left out of the government in 1970, was elected Chairman of the 1922 Committee on 16 November 1972. In the same month John Biffen became chairman of the industry committee, and Nicholas Ridley chairman and Jock Bruce-Gardyne vice-chairman of the finance committee.

The radical nature of the government's legislation and its departure from its manifesto policies were one factor in promoting dissent. Doubts were turned into grievances not only by the content of measures but also by the manner of their passage. Too often an unheralded somersault on policy was followed by lack of consultation on the legislation, unresponsiveness to back-bench opinion, and grudgingly few concessions to objections raised in debate. Heath's dominance of the Cabinet and its cohesion meant that a distance opened up between the leadership and the Party as a whole. As early as May 1971, the Director of Organisation at Central Office warned that 'there was some danger of front and back bench members "drifting apart".'[111] There was a feeling that members of the Cabinet were out of touch, and after Macleod's death there was a lack of ministers who were good communicators or who could dominate the House. All of this became bound up with complaints over Heath's personal style as leader: criticism focused upon his abrasiveness, aloofness, and stubbornness. Problems were exacerbated by the refusal to use the lubrication of patronage on the expected scale, the infrequency of reshuffles and promotions, the lack of regard for the views of supporters, and the confrontational response to parliamentary

110. *The Times*, 24 November 1972; Norton, *Conservative Dissidents*, 240; E. Du Cann, *Two Lives: The Political and Business Careers of Edward Du Cann* (Malvern 1995), 194.
Tactical Ctte., 11 May 1971, CCO/20/7/12.

dissent.[112] Even so, under strong attack from without and in difficult circumstances, the Party remained loyal. The paradox is not that there was so much unrest, but that it was so little and so late.

Parliamentary dissent was inhibited by three forces. In this Parliament the whips under Francis Pym were almost too effective at containing and concealing the scale of dissatisfaction.[113] However, it is important not to exaggerate their power or misunderstand their methods. Pym continued the less autocratic and more approachable style which had been introduced in 1964 by his predecessor, William Whitelaw. The authority of the whips was a matter of consent as much as command, and they maintained control by reason and politeness rather than by intimidation. Communication was more effective than confrontation: forbearance and tact limited dissent and, where that proved to be impossible, mitigated ill-feeling. A second and more powerful force for unity was the disapproval of the constituency associations for actions which damaged the government and therefore aided the enemy. The third force was the least visible, but the strongest and most pervasive of them all. Due to their personal convictions and feelings of obligation to their supporters and colleagues as much as to their leaders, Conservative MPs do not normally need to have their arms twisted to support the party line. There is an assumption of common purpose, and cohesion is the instinctive option. In the ethos of the Conservative Party, loyalty is valued over individual expression, and team spirit rather than deference explains the cohesion and resilience of the Conservatives at Westminster and in the constituencies. After the unusually long interval of six years in opposition, there was a heartfelt desire to make the Conservative government work and to stick by it in time of trouble.

Several other factors also played a part in containing any dissent, both in the parliamentary party and at the grass-roots. First was the unity and confidence of the leadership: the Party as a whole is always responsive to directness and certainty. Heath was a determined leader; his authoritative tone and sense of direction were not shaken by the changes of course, and remained impressive.[114] The Prime Minister had no close equal due to the death of Iain Macleod, the passivity and then departure of Reginald Maudling, and the concentration on external policy of the Foreign Secretary, Sir Alec Douglas-Home. The Cabinet was remarkably cohesive over policy and in its personal relations.[115]

112. R. Maudling, *Memoirs* (London, 1978), 207.

113. Hurd, *An End to Promises*, 107; Norton, *Conservative Dissidents*, 95, 163–73.

114. Advisory Committee on Policy, 17 October 1973, ACP(73)126.

115. P. Walker, *Staying Power: An Autobiography* (London, 1991), 111, 123–4; Hurd, *An End to Promises*, 107.

Furthermore, through all the changes Heath's strategy retained the support of the Conservative press. There was no point at which a more attractive alternative appeared credible to any large or influential number of Conservatives. Some cabinet ministers had their doubts, but each move seemed to be unavoidable and a logical response to the circumstances. There were no cabinet resignations on policy, and no effective leadership for dissent in the parliamentary party. Enoch Powell was thought to be too embittered and controversial, while the small group of persistent back-bench critics were regarded as cranky, negative and backward-looking, and far from being the prophets of future policy. Equally significant was the Conservative grass-roots contempt for and detestation of Harold Wilson. Most Conservatives believed that the previous government had cheapened the reputation of the country at home and abroad. The sharp move to the left by the Labour Party after 1970 encouraged Conservative cohesion, while the feeling that the opposition were providing easy targets eased concern about the current state of the opinion polls.[116] The final factor was the seriousness and complexity of the problems. It was not difficult to make a case in the government's defence, and loyalty in a crisis was the Party's natural instinct. The rank and file endorsed the government's aims, and broadly supported its methods. Most Conservatives saw no alternative to the course which the government had taken: it retained most of their loyalty, while enthusiasm ebbed steadily away.

THE ROAD TO DEFEAT: 1973–74

Even though unrest and divisions within the Party were kept below the surface, morale was low by the end of 1973. This was clearly apparent in the early stages of the Hove by-election in September, when the normally efficient arrangements for 'mutual aid' from the surrounding safe seats produced only a quarter of the help expected.[117] The annual conference as usual steadied the nerves, and delegates 'left in a better mood than that in which they had arrived.[118] However, the effect was artificial and short-lived and, when they returned to their constituencies, the confidence which had been raised soon ebbed away.

116. Harker to Deslandes, 22 October 1971, memo for Tactical Ctte., by Thompson, 11 November 1971, CCO/20/7/13; Advisory Committee on Policy, 19 July 1972, ACP(72)119.

117. South East Area, Exec., 24 September 1973; there had been similar problems in July at Ripon and the Isle of Ely, see Hurd, *An End to Promises*, 109, 115–16.

118. Tactical Ctte., 16 October 1973, CCO/20/7/19.

The South East Area executive were warned on 10 December that 'subscriptions were not being collected and contact was being lost with professional people'.[119] The critical mood in the parliamentary ranks was manifest at the 1922 Committee meeting on 18 October 1973. Back-bench morale was dealt a further heavy blow by the £298 million monthly trade deficit announced on 13 November, which pushed interest rates to their highest level ever of 13 per cent. Later in the same week the failure of the counter-inflation policy was underlined by statistics which showed that food prices had risen by almost 19 per cent in the previous year. Against this gloomy background, the Chancellor was pressed to attend the 1922 Committee meeting of 15 November, where his critical reception reflected the loss of confidence. From this low point, matters slightly improved. The further large cuts in public expenditure which Barber announced on 17 December were given an ovation at the back-bench finance committee; most of the parliamentary party saw this as a move in the right direction, and felt that all that was possible was being done. The four by-elections held on 8 November saw the loss of Berwick to the Liberals, but Hove was retained despite a 21 per cent fall in the Conservative vote. The Party also held Edinburgh North fairly easily against Labour, while the latter lost Govan to the Scottish Nationalists. In early December, some opinion polls began to record a Conservative lead, while the Liberal figure fell below 20 per cent for the first time in nearly six months.

It was against this background that the government grappled with its deepest crisis. In early November the mineworkers began an overtime ban in support of a pay claim which, if conceded, would breach Phase III of the pay policy and undermine all that had been painfully achieved in wage restraint. Heath and the Cabinet nevertheless sought to avoid another bruising confrontation with the NUM, and weeks were consumed in a fruitless exploration of possible solutions with the miners' leaders and the TUC. Persuasion and negotiation failed to secure agreement and, after the humiliation of 1972, a second surrender to the NUM was out of the question. The only option left was to create a fresh situation by reaffirming the government's mandate, and support mounted within the Party for the calling of a general election. The feeling that a favourable opportunity might exist was the least factor, for the indicators were far too variable. Exhaustion played a larger part than confidence, but strongest of all was a growing recognition that a showdown was inevitable and that going to the country was the only card which the government had left to play. Conservatives had no

119. South East Area, Exec., 10 December 1973.

doubt that they were facing a national crisis, and assumed that the country would share this view and support them. A crisis 'appeal to the nation' drafted at Central Office by Nigel Lawson in early December caught the mood of the Party, declaring that 'the very fabric of our society is at risk' and concluding apocalyptically 'this is the moment of truth for the British people'.[120] The introduction of the three-day week deepened the sense of national emergency and created an atmosphere of unprecedented chaos. The Conservative rank and file shared their leaders' analysis of the gravity of the situation and rallied to support the government. There was bitter resentment of the NUM, and widespread belief that far left and Communist elements within its leadership and executive were seeking as much the destruction of the government as a higher rate of pay.[121]

Even so, there was much hesitation and anxiety over the decision to go to the country. In early December 1973 the professional Deputy Chairman, Sir Michael Fraser, sounded an optimistic note, although other leading figures were more cautious.[122] Pressure for a swift appeal was voiced at the Conservative Research Department's weekend seminar at Cumberland Lodge on 6 January. Next day, Carrington found that three-quarters of the Area Chairmen favoured a quick dissolution, while the meeting of the professional Area Agents in London on 10 January was unanimous for an early election.[123] This apparently bullish mood belied the underlying confusion and uncertainty, which was particularly apparent in the parliamentary party. Only four of the twenty MPs who spoke at the 1922 Committee on 10 January favoured dissolving Parliament, although the proportion rose to 18 out of the 30 backbenchers consulted in a newspaper random survey published on 16 January.[124] During the following few days, a poll by NOP gave a Conservative lead of 4 per cent. Heath's talks with the TUC at Downing Street finally foundered, and the industrial picture worsened with the addition of rail strikes. Opinion moved in favour of a showdown, and at the next meeting of the 1922 Committee there was a clear majority

120. 'An Appeal to the Nation', draft of 'alternative manifesto', by Lawson, 7 December 1973, OG/73/136. Lawson worked as a temporary special adviser at Central Office in late 1973; the tone of his text shocked some of the more cautious elements in the party machine, and a less hawkish and alarmist approach was adopted for the actual manifesto.

121. East Midlands Area, Exec., 8 January 1974; Cambridgeshire CA, Exec., 24 January 1974; NU Exec., 24 January 1974; Whitelaw, *Memoirs*, 126; Walker, *Staying Power*, 125.

122. Advisory Committee on Policy, 5 December 1973, ACP(72)127.

123. D. Butler and D. Kavanagh, *The British General Election of February 1974* (London, 1974), 34–5.

124. *The Times*, 14 and 16 January 1974.

for an early election. Since the closing days of 1973 the Party Chairman and his other deputy, the cabinet minister James Prior, had been urging a tough approach to the strike and pressing for an election. Their advice was certainly 'in tune with the Party's sentiments at the time' – but it was founded upon weakness rather than strength. Both men were convinced that 'we couldn't face another humiliating climb-down with the miners, the Party was only just recovering from the 1972 debacle'.[125] There was no over-confidence, and those around Heath were aware of the risks. The advocates of an election were concerned that the situation would only worsen and that the chance of victory was slipping out of reach. After the meeting of the Steering Committee at Chequers on 13 January failed to come to a clear decision, Douglas Hurd noted in his diary 'we are in a desperate plight'.[126]

The missed opportunity of calling the election for early in February lost vital momentum and sacrificed much of the emotive value of a crisis appeal. This public hesitancy left the Party puzzled and confused, and when the dissolution was finally announced on 7 February – the date originally favoured for the actual poll – many local associations were caught unprepared.[127] More surprisingly, despite all the delay and debates, the national party organisation was not poised for an election either. Completion of the manifesto was rushed and confused, and it was not ready until some time after Labour's; the official *Campaign Guide* had not been finalised, and party political broadcasts had to be improvised. Since the First World War the Conservative Party had consistently benefited from an underlying public belief in their governing competence, but by February 1974 that image had been badly dented. The main cause of defeat lay in the erosion of Conservative support throughout the life of the Heath government, but the events of the campaign did nothing to encourage their return to the fold. Negativity and disarray were exacerbated by announcements of workers being laid-off, the appearance of poor economic statistics, an apparent repudiation of the Industrial Relations Act by the Director of the CBI, and the release of some inopportunely bountiful profits for the banks and oil companies. Worst of all, a week before the poll the interim results of the Pay Board's investigation of miners' wages threw the basis of the dispute into doubt. It made the government look foolish and inept, and the crisis – with its aggravating impact on daily life in the bitter winter months – seem unnecessary. There was a fundamental

125. Prior, *Balance of Power*, 90–91; Carrington, *Reflect on Things Past*, 263.
126. Hurd, *An End to Promises*, 127.
127. High Peak CA, F and GP ctte., 18 and 28 January 1974; New Forest CA res., Wessex Area Council, 18 May 1974.

ambivalence in Conservative strategy during the election. The Party was torn between the need to emphasise the starkness of the crisis, while at the same avoiding a confrontational tone which would alienate moderate feeling in all classes and working-class supporters in particular. In fact, the Party fared worst with the middle class, and it was the movement of votes to the Liberals rather than to Labour which proved to be crucial in the February 1974 defeat. Compared to their position in 1970, Conservative support fell by 16.1 per cent in the most affluent social categories A and B, but only by 8.2 per cent in the lower middle-class (C1) and 8.6 per cent in the skilled working-class (C2).[128] In the wake of defeat, the Party concluded that it had lost touch with its natural constituency – the middle income, middle-aged. The Yorkshire Area believed that lower-paid workers and pensioners had been retained but that housing and mortgage policies had lost the 'young marrieds', who had shifted to the Liberals.[129]

Defeat was a more bitter blow than the tally of seats lost or votes won would suggest. It was not just that the Conservative Party hates to lose; failure on these issues, when so much seemed to be at stake, was deeply unsettling and frustrating. Afterwards, everything about the previous four years was called into question in a way which had not been the case before losing office: images, organisation, policies – and, ultimately, leadership.[130] There was no immediate challenge to Heath, especially with another election likely to be called within the next few weeks or months. However, he had lost much ground and was in the precarious position of being maintained less by any positive feeling than by the lack of an alternative.[131] The temperature of party opinion in the wake of defeat was typified by two discussions which took place in April 1974. The Eastern Area formally pledged its continued confidence in Heath and simultaneously criticised the failure to communicate with the public; an amendment that the leadership 'should change its negative approach' was rejected by only 57 votes to 53.[132] At the executive committee of the Hemel Hempstead association a few days later, a resolution demanding the abandonment of statutory incomes policies was carried by one vote.[133] By the spring of 1974 the Conserva-

128. M. Wilson and K. Phillips, 'The Conservative Party: from Macmillan to Thatcher', in N. Nugent and R. King, (eds), *The British Right: Conservative and Right Wing Politics in Britain* (Farnborough), 1977, 31–2.

129. Yorkshire Area, Exec., 27 April 1974; Tynemouth CA. Exec., 29 March 1974.

130. 'Policy Suggestions Box', CPC contact programme, April 1974, CCO/4/10/81.

131. Swindon CA, Exec., 20 November 1974; York CA, F and GP ctte., 20 January 1975.

132. Eastern Area Council, 27 April 1974; NU GP ctte., 16 October 1974.

133. Hemel Hempstead CA, Exec., 23 April 1974.

tive Party had found from bitter experience which paths led to failure – but they were far from sure which would lead to success.

CONCLUSION

The impact of the Conservative Party on the Heath government is not easy to measure. Conservative attitudes and aspirations shaped the policies devised in opposition before 1970 and the course which the government sought to follow; for that reason, the problems encountered were damaging to the morale and credibility not just of the leadership but of the Party as a whole. During the 1970–74 government, the Cabinet were aware of the concerns of the rank and file but found it impossible to respond adequately to them. Lines of communication certainly existed, most immediately from Conservative MPs through the whips and in encounters with ministers in the Party back-bench committees or in the lobbies, bars and smoking room of the House. Constituency opinion could also make itself felt by the same channel, or through the Area Agents, the Party Chairman, the Advisory Committee on Policy and the various levels of the National Union.[134] The problem was that these messages did not seem to be reaching receptive ears. From the outset of the government Thomas, the Party Chairman, and Hurd, Heath's Political Secretary, complained of the reluctance of ministers to pay sufficient attention to the presentation of their actions and to the needs of the Party. Although it would be wrong to blame Heath entirely for this atrophying of political sensitivity, all governments tend to absorb the tone and style of the Prime Minister. Heath had always found purely partisan considerations to be uncongenial, and his preference for administration and managerialism became more pronounced within the isolating cocoon of Downing Street, surrounded by civil service advisors and piles of red boxes. Incisive and determined in executive decisions, Heath was often slower to form a judgement and less confident in his touch in political matters, a trait exemplified by an apparent reluctance to focus upon them. Over the question of a free vote on Europe in 1971 this nearly led to disaster, while over the timing of the February 1974 election many believed that it made the difference between victory and defeat.

The early 1970s were not a particularly distinctive period for the Conservative Party in organisational terms, and in this area Heath's impact on the Conservative Party was relatively small. Party manage-

134. Seldon and Ball, *Conservative Century*, 214–20.

ment was never one of his main interests, and it was left in the hands of capable and trusted lieutenant: Whitelaw, and later Pym, as Chief Whips; Barber, and later Carrington, as Party Chairmen, assisted by Fraser, Morrison, and later Prior at Central Office. The Heath government saw the continuation of trends within the Conservative Party which had begun in the late 1950s and which have continued to the present day. The first of these was the changing social composition of the parliamentary party, with an increasing proportion of MPs coming from relatively unprivileged middle-class backgrounds; among those who entered the House during the Heath government were the three Normans – Tebbit, Fowler and Lamont. Second was the problem of a dwindling membership, concentrated in the older generation.[135] Although a number of initiatives and reorganisations were embarked upon, none had a significant effect upon the long-term decline.

In other respcts, the impact of the Heath government on the Conservative Party is much more visible: policy failure, parliamentary disunity, public disillusion, and two electoral defeats. By the end of the government, many in the Party felt that it had abandoned true Conservative principles and lost touch with its natural supporters. The resentment of MPs over Heath's autocratic and aloof style of party management combined with this, and led directly to his downfall. At all levels, the Party experienced a wounded puzzlement similar to that with which Admiral Beatty had regarded his battlecruisers in the First World War: impressive on paper, but fatally flawed when put to the test. To paraphrase Beatty, there was a widespread conclusion that 'there's something wrong with our bloody policies today'. At first, and for much of the rank and file, feeling remained at this inarticulate level; but this sentiment was to legitimise Thatcher's bid for the leadership and shape the change of direction after 1975. Even so, the traumas of the Heath government had scarred the Party so deeply that recovering office in 1979 was not enough on its own to restore confidence. Memories of 1970–74 did not lose their sting until the events of 1982–85 – the Falklands War, the 1983 election landslide and, most of all, the humbling of trade union power so aptly symbolised by the defeat of the miners' strike of 1984–85.

135. Seldon and Ball, *Conservative Century*, 159–67, 290–93.

CHAPTER FOURTEEN

*The fatal choice: the calling of the February 1974 election**

Dennis Kavanagh

In many respects the crisis election of February 1974 may serve as an epitaph for Edward Heath's government, for he called it with a heavy heart. Far from choosing the election date freely and at a time of maximum advantage, he felt pushed into it. The election campaign was held in inauspicious circumstances, during deep winter, a three-day week, petrol rationing and a coal miners' strike. The election is a case study in the limitations of one of the so-called levers of prime ministerial power – the right to dissolve Parliament.

The election campaign itself was full of surprises, most of which were unhelpful to the Conservative Party. These included Enoch Powell's dramatic intervention in which he called on Conservative supporters to vote Labour, the Relativities Board's press briefing about the miners' pay which seemed to call into question the basis on which the election was held, and the surge in support for the Liberals. The biggest surprise, however, viewed from the perspective of 1970, was the Conservative election manifesto, *Firm Action for a Fair Britain.* It stressed the need for a statutory prices and incomes policy in the fight against inflation, and the need to prepare for tough times ahead. These claims flew in the face of the prospectus on which the Party had fought and won an election three-and-a-half years earlier: then, the central claims were that government should stand aside from wage negotiations, which should be left to employers and trade unions, and that ministers would pursue a policy of economic expansion.

The consequences of the election were far-reaching. The election was called in part to contain trade union power, but the outcome ensured that the miners and other unions were the short-term winners and able to dictate policy to the next Labour government. The outcome marked a turning point in Heath's career and in the character of the

* The author is indebted to James Douglas and Peter Morris for their comments on an earlier version of this chapter.

Conservative Party. If Heath's leadership had been strengthened by the Conservatives' winning the 1970 general election, then he and his style of Conservatism were major casualties of the 1974 election defeat. The path was open for Margaret Thatcher and Sir Keith Joseph to argue for a new kind of Conservatism. The result, in conjunction with that of the October election later that year, induced something of an electoral crisis in the Conservative Party; the Party's lowest share of the vote in elections since 1945 was followed by the lowest gained in the course of the twentieth century. The decline in the Conservative share of the vote between 1970 and February 1974 (8.6 per cent) is still the largest suffered by any government party since 1945.

The assumption of most discussions of the timing of elections is that a government calls one only after it has prepared the ground, through tax give-aways and pump-priming to induce a 'feel good' mood among voters, and is reassured by a run of favourable opinion polls. Heath's government had no such comfortable background. Other Prime Ministers had called 'early' elections – for example, Clement Attlee in 1951 because he had a majority of only six, and Harold Wilson in 1966 one of only four. James Callaghan was forced to call an election after his government lost a vote of confidence in the House of Commons in 1979. But his government was already in a minority and the Parliament was near the end of its life. None of these excuses or explanations are available for Heath in 1974. The only parallel case this century of a government feeling itself forced into calling an election and with a clear majority and a good part of its mandate still to run was in 1923.

The decision to call an election was highly political and largely confined to ministers and party advisers. It was made free from the advice of civil servants, pressure groups or international organisations. But, in contrast to most other decisions about election timing, it was closely tied in with major political issues of the day. It is, therefore, worth exploring how the decision was made.

BACKGROUND

Any European government was bound to be in difficulty in the 1970s because of international economic pressures. In October 1973, Arab oil-producers had quadrupled their prices and cut back oil supplies to Western states in the wake of the Yom Kippur War between Arab states and Israel. This move came on top of large rises in the prices of many raw materials and foodstuffs. Few realised at the time that the war and the oil shocks that followed were a turning point in postwar economic history in the industrialised countries. It would help to destroy the postwar Keynesian consensus and the political stability which accompanied it. Living standards would have to fall. How would societies adjust?

For reasons analysed in chapter 7, the Heath government was by the time of the Yom Kippur War operating a statutory prices and incomes policy. In February 1972, a miners' strike had destroyed the government's policy of free collective bargaining combined with gradual reductions of the level of wage settlements in the public sector. The strike was only settled by the recommendations of a committee led by Lord Wilberforce for a wage increase of 27 per cent; the National Union of Mineworkers (NUM) executive then further humiliated the government by visiting Downing Street to demand, and get, even more. Conservative backbenchers were furious, and they and ministers agreed that it was politically 'unthinkable' for the government to endure another such reverse.[1]

The government then embarked on its experiment with 'tripartism', trying to get the agreement of the TUC and CBI to a joint approach to economic problems, including voluntary restraint over wages and prices. After further industrial disputes and failure to reach agreement with the TUC, the government announced in November 1972 statutory controls on prices and incomes. The policy worked well, and by October 1973 it was in Stage III. This had been drawn up in the summer to accommodate the likely demands of the NUM whose leader, Joe Gormley, held secret talks with Heath and Sir William Armstrong, the Cabinet Secretary. These were so secret that officials in the Department of Employment and the National Coal Board were unaware of them.[2] At the end of September, the main hazard for ministers was whether a powerful union would challenge and break Stage III. Ministers did not want another confrontation with the miners and expected that the pay policy would hold.

But the decision of the Arab oil-producers greatly strengthened the bargaining position of the miners and brought into question the viability of Stage III, which had been drawn up before the oil cutback. Events then moved swiftly. On 2 November, the government announced plans for cutting oil consumption. On 8 November, the NUM executive rejected the Coal Board's opening pay offer and voted for an overtime ban which began four days later. A State of Emergency was announced

1. Interview with Michael Wolff, May 1974.

2. Sir Dennis Barnes, in 'Symposium: The Trade Unions and Fall of the Heath Government', Institute of Contemporary British History witness seminar, *Contemporary Record*, vol. 2, no. 1, (1988), 44.

the next day, 13 November, and eight days later the NUM executive rejected the Coal Board's offer of a 13 per cent wage increase. A week later Heath called the miners' executive to Downing Street and appealed to them, in the national interest, to end the overtime ban. The appeal fell on deaf ears. The miners were determined to use the changed energy situation, to improve their position in the wages 'league'. Heath, however, seemed unwilling to acknowledge that the actions of the Arab oil-producers had transformed their hand.

For much of the postwar period, British governments have struggled to cope with the country's long-standing relative economic decline, exacerbated by troubled industrial relations, declining competitiveness, poor investment and, now, accelerating inflation and a worsening balance of payments. The Heath government, like governments before and after, was caught up in this cycle of economic decline. But it also seemed to be presiding over a new intensity of industrial conflict. Between 1920 and 1970, governments declared a total of seven States of Emergency; in the next three-and-a-half years of the Heath government five were declared, often to cope with disruptions caused by the withdrawal of labour by key groups of workers. In 1972, largely as a consequence of union opposition to the 1971 Industrial Relations Act, Britain lost more working days as a result of strikes than in any year since 1926, the year of the General Strike.

Not surprisingly, perhaps, this was also a period of popular discontent with the governing parties. From the mid-1960s voters at by-elections were becoming increasingly volatile and more likely to vote against the government of the day. On 26 July 1973, the government lost two of the Party's safest seats – the Isle of Ely and Ripon – to the Liberals in by-elections. Within four months of winning the 1970 election, the Conservative opinion poll lead in Gallup had disappeared; it was not regained until January 1974, and then only by the tiny margin of two per cent. Support for the government fell as low as 26 per cent in July 1971, and during 1973 only once exceeded 33 per cent (34 per cent in June).

The years 1973–74 were also the heyday of the Liberal revival. Having gained only 7.5 per cent in the 1970 general election, the party's support in the polls remained at that level until 1973, when it rose to and remained in double figures, at one point reaching 20 per cent. The haul of by-election gains (4 from Conservatives, 1 from Labour) resulted in the near doubling of the number of Liberal MPs from six to eleven during the lifetime of the Parliament. In by-elections in 1973 the votes for Liberal candidates exceeded those for either Labour or Tory candidates.

AN EARLY ELECTION

Conservative Central Office and Research Department staff have to think about election dates and strategies, not least because much of the burden of preparing and fighting the campaign falls upon them. By summer 1973 a draft manifesto existed, together with a tentative list of possible election dates. The first date pencilled in was spring 1974, although party officials and ministers were thinking more in terms of autumn 1974 or spring 1975 as likely election dates. In early February 1973, a Research Department paper reviewed different types of general election appeals. One was a 'snap' election, which it did not welcome because it was likely to be brought about by a crisis and likely to concentrate on one issue. It warned that 'however much a Government . . . may wish to fight an election on one issue there is no guarantee that the electorate or significant parts of it will not decide to vote about something else, with possibly disturbing results.'[3]

After the summer recess some officials began, in the now fashionable phrase, to 'think the unthinkable'. The Director of the Conservative Research Department, James Douglas, argued in a paper in early November that the rise in world commodity prices and the Middle East War had drastically changed the country's economic prospects.[4] The dash for growth would have to be abandoned, and ministers would need a fresh mandate to take the necessary tough measures to deal with inflationary pressure and balance of payments deficits in the next few years. He recommended an election in early December. The idea found little support in the Research Department or Central Office, and when it was conveyed to Michael Wolff, an adviser to Heath, he doubted that it could be sold to the Party and the country.[5] After all, the government was trailing in the polls and few neutral observers thought that the Conservatives would actually improve their position in an election.

Another person was also making the case for an early election. John Ramsden's study of the Conservative Research Department reveals that in October 1973 ' . . . a Conservative journalist was recruited to the Conservative Research Department'[6] and the Nuffield study of the election comments that 'a Conservative adviser submitted to Mr Heath a reasoned argument for a much earlier election' (i.e. earlier than spring

3. 'The Strategic/Tactical Situation in 1973', memo by Fraser, 14 February 1973, CPA SC/73/17.

4. Interview with James Douglas, 9 April 1974.

5. Interview with Michael Wolff.

6. J. Ramsden, *The Making of Conservative Party Policy* (London, 1980), 301.

1974).[7] The journalist was Nigel Lawson, and his title was 'Special Political Adviser Attached to Conservative Party Headquarters'. He understood that his remit was to provide bite for the Party's political communications, including the manifesto, and that his job would end when the election was announced. He thought that the lengthy draft manifesto, celebrating economic success, was quite inappropriate. Its optimism was '1959ish', said one who had been involved with its composition. Lawson thought that the economic prospects were poor and that people should be warned of the tough times ahead. The political prospects were also unpromising. The Sunningdale arrangements in Northern Ireland had upset the Unionists and made them shaky allies for the government. This, and further by-election losses, would threaten the government's majority in the Commons. Some Party officials now argued that a strong government was needed to cope with difficulties and that the Party should 'actually campaign on the extreme nature of the crisis', following the cutback in oil supplies.[8] Lawson's case, like Douglas's, rested on the threatening politico-economic prospects, *not* possible future difficulties with the NUM or the trade unions.[9]

Lawson's memo was shown to Wolff, who again stressed the need to search for a politically acceptable reason for calling an election. It was sent on to Heath on 9 November (the day after the NUM Executive had voted for an overtime ban). There was no reaction from Heath but it was understood by those around him that he would not welcome an election fought against the miners. On 13 November, another State of Emergency was proclaimed and measures to save electricity, including reductions in street lighting and television programmes, were announced. On 2 December, William Whitelaw was recalled from Ulster to be Secretary of State for Employment, a move that encouraged some commentators to anticipate that his 'trouble shooter' skills would find a face-saving solution.

On 5 December, Lawson lunched at the Garrick with Douglas Hurd, Heath's political secretary from 1968 to 1974, and argued the merits of his memo. Hurd had earlier expressed his concern to Party officials about the 'expansionist' thrust of ministers' speeches and the draft manifesto.[10] Lawson must have had some effect, for on the following

7. D. Butler and D. Kavanagh, *The British General Election of February 1974* (London, 1974), 28.

8. Ramsden, *Conservative Party Policy*, 301.

9. Material in the next two paragraphs is based on an interview with Nigel Lawson, 4 April 1974.

10. 'An Appeal to the Nation', draft of 'alternative manifesto', by Lawson, 7 Dec. 1973, CPA OG/73/136.

day the political advisers met informally with Hurd and drafted a paper for the Prime Minister which pressed the case for an election early in 1974. It emphasised that the important economic indicators were unlikely to improve in the following year or two, that Labour was in political difficulties, and that the authority of government would gradually diminish during 1974 as the natural end of the Parliament approached. In a covering note, Hurd echoed Lawson's argument for a change of strategy:

> There is therefore, in our view, a strong argument for a change of approach over the next 7/8 days. The Government should seek to *emphasise* the gravity of the situation, drawing together the various threads. Next week is particularly important because of the NUM meeting on the 13th, and the possible start of action on the railways which would gravely inconvenience individuals and give a further serious twist to the energy situation.[11]

Hurd acknowledged that ministers would have to explain the change from the optimistic statements about the economy which they had been making.[12] On 14 December, Lawson had a lengthy meeting with Lord Carrington, the Party Chairman, and his special assistant Chris Patten, and again pressed for an early election. Although Carrington played the role of devil's advocate, he was becoming convinced of the case.[13]

Preparing for an election involves writing a manifesto and thinking about the case which the party leaders will make to the voters. In late November, Sir Michael Fraser, who combined the posts of Deputy Chairman of the Party and Chairman of the Research Department, suggested to Lawson that since he, Lawson, had been thinking about a crisis election, he should draft a contingency part one of the manifesto, and address the crisis conditions in which an election was likely to be held. At this time, a Conservative manifesto was largely the work of a Steering Group, of the leader and senior politicians, and an Official Group, of senior party officials, drawn from Central Office and the Research Department. The Lawson manifesto draft was discussed by the Official Group on 12 December. It was given a critical reception, particularly for its strongly worded defence of Stage III against the miners' claim for special treatment. Douglas suggested that voters would be more likely to turn to Labour to save them from the unions and

11. D. Hurd, *An End to Promises: Sketch of a Government 1970–1974* (London, 1979), 120.

12. Ibid, 119.

13. Interview with Lord Carrington, 11 March 1974

extremists. According to the minutes: 'He felt we should fight on the grounds of dealing with the external threat presented by the Arabs and the Middle East situation'. Tony Newton, the group secretary, expressed his unease that the document might 'stoke up a class warfare situation'.[14]

The draft was then sent to members of the Steering Committee which met on 20 December.[15] This was the Committee's first meeting for over six months, and it was now faced with Lawson's draft (*An Appeal to the Nation*) which differed greatly in tone from the original. The draft warned of the dangers posed by union extremists and asked for 'A mandate to take whatever measures are necessary'. According to the minutes of the meeting, Carrington '. . . felt that the general tone was rather hard and anti-union', and called for something less divisive and 'more One-Nation'. He was supported by Anthony Barber, Robert Carr and Sir Alec Douglas-Home. Heath wanted it to be made clear that inflation – not the NUM – was the enemy.[16]

Discussions about an election were taking place among Heath's political advisers, and staff at Central Office and the Research Department. Most advisers linked the miners' overtime ban with the case for an election; they doubted that a settlement could be made and therefore supported calling an election. Heath and Whitelaw, however, still concentrated their energies on trying to persuade the NUM to settle within the Stage III guidelines. At the meeting on 20 December Heath gave no signal of his thinking, and few of those present declared themselves for an early election. Most ministers, like Heath himself, felt that calling one was a risk and that there had been no credible build-up to it.[17]

But the pressures for an election continued. Lawson went away to rewrite the entire manifesto over Christmas and the New Year. Surveys by the Party's private polling agency, Opinion Research Centre (ORC), indicated that the Party was likely to win an election if one were called quickly in defence of Stage III. The unions were unpopular and the public supported the incomes policy, although there was sympathy with the miners' case and the government was blamed for rising prices.

14. Official Group, 12 December 1973, OG/73/138.

15. The Steering Committee consisted of Heath, Sir Alec Douglas Home, Anthony Barber, Lord Carrington, James Prior, Robert Carr, William Whitelaw and the Chief Whip. In addition to Sir Michael Fraser (Secretary), James Douglas and Tony Newton from the Research Department usually attended, as did Douglas Hurd and Michael Wolff from Number 10; Nigel Lawson attended all meetings from 20 December onwards.

16. Steering Committee, 20 December 1973, SC/73/25.

17. Hurd, *An End to Promises*, 126, 129.

ORC warned that, if the government delayed calling an election, the ground could shift and public opinion turn against it.

It would be understandable if ministers were feeling the effects of their gruelling spell in office. The battles over prices and incomes policies, handling industrial relations disputes, imposing direct rule in Northern Ireland and carrying British entry into the European Community through Parliament had imposed a heavy toll on their energy and perhaps affected their ability to concentrate and exercise good judgement. Heath appeared to colleagues at this time to be particularly uncertain and unhappy[18] and may have been suffering from the effects of a thyroid deficiency which was diagnosed 18 months later.[19] Hurd, who had a ringside view of the pressures on ministers, noted that 'they do not notice the onset of fatigue. But if they allow themselves no respite, their pace slows, they increasingly miss their strokes, they begin, without realising it, to move through a fog of tiredness'.[20] In the second week of December 1973, for example, when discussion about an election was developing, Heath entertained visiting heads of state from Italy and Zaire, presided over the Sunningdale Conference on the future of Northern Ireland and attended a European summit at Copenhagen. As Hurd notes of the schedule, 'They all involved talks, travel, long meals, extensive briefing beforehand; yet none of them had anything to do with the crisis which was swallowing us up.'[21] Whitelaw, recalled from Northern Ireland to take over as Secretary at the Department of Employment, only realised how exhausted he was after the election.[22] Lord Hunt of Tanworth, who took over as Cabinet Secretary in late 1973, recalled the strains imposed on ministers at the time: ' . . . they were all very tired men and they were not taking decisions in the most sensible way'.[23] Ministers and party officials were engaged in endless meetings – (in Downing Street, Chequers, Central Office and the Research Department – and none was very productive.[24] Sir William Armstrong, sometimes called deputy Prime Minister because of his closeness to Heath, suffered a nervous breakdown on 1 February 1974 and left the service soon afterwards.

On the night of 12 January, Heath invited members of his Communications Group to Chequers. These were people drawn from media and

18. Interview with Michael Wolff.
19. J. Campbell, *Edward Heath: A Biography* (London, 1981), 576.
20. Hurd, *An End to Promises*, 113.
21. Ibid., 121.
22. S. Fay and H. Young, *The Fall of Heath* (London, 1976).
23. In witness seminar, *Contemporary Record*, vol. 2, no. 1 (1988), 44.
24. James Douglas, letter to author, 17 March 1995.

public relations backgrounds who had helped him before and during the election campaign of 1970.[25] They included Geoffrey Tucker, Jim Garrett, Ronald Millar, Barry Day and Dick Clements. After dinner they were asked for their views about the timing of an election and their unanimous (though apparently unco-ordinated) advice was to dissolve immediately or not at all. Heath listened in silence and gave no reaction.[26]

Anthony King comments that between the beginning of January and the first week in February a strange consensus emerged: not that an early election was desirable, but that for some reason it was inevitable.[27] Carrington and Prior, his Deputy Chairman at Central Office, were already persuaded of the case for a 7 February election. They were convinced that the NUM would not settle on anything like reasonable terms and told the Prime Minister and the Cabinet that the Party's grass-roots supporters would not accept a settlement that went much beyond Stage III: 'We could not get away with another Wilberforce.'[28] Party officials continued to make election preparations, drafting a manifesto, establishing various campaign committees and consulting with different groups in the Party. Carrington's meetings of the Area Chairman and Area Agents found large majority support for holding an election on 7 February. The Executive of the 1922 Committee was more evenly divided. Cabinet ministers also visited Heath, individually or in small groups, to give their views. For many, it was a finely balanced decision. Few expressed strong views, no doubt trying to guess what Heath's long, brooding silences portended. Some, notably Whitelaw and Francis Pym (who was concerned about establishing the newly created power-sharing executive in Northern Ireland), were opposed.[29]

Meanwhile, the work of government continued. On 8 January Heath announced a limited Cabinet reshuffle, involving the creation of a new Energy Department, and Carrington moved from Defence to head it. On 9 January Parliament resumed work after the Christmas recess. But the attentions of senior ministers and officials were still directed to finding a way to persuade the NUM to settle under Stage III. The threat of a miners' strike was now clearly inter-linked with the oil crisis

25. D. Butler and M. Pinto-Duschinsky, *The British General Election of 1970* (London, 1971).

26. R. Millar, *A View from the Wings* (London, 1993), 221.

27. A. King, 'The Election that Everyone Lost', in H. Pennimann (ed.), *Britain at the Polls* (Washington DC, 1974), 23.

28. Interview with Lord Carrington.

29. Butler and Kavanagh, *General Election of February 1974*, 35.

and pressures for an early election. On 9 January, the TUC representatives at the monthly meeting of NEDC offered what they thought was a solution: they promised to use their good offices to ensure that no union would use a settlement with the NUM in excess of Stage III to support its own case. Ministers were suspicious of this sudden announcement, and pointed out that the TUC had no power to commit member unions and most union executives had no power to commit their memberships. Talks continued but made no progress. Union leaders and civil servants gathered at a seminar fourteen years after the event still regarded this as a missed opportunity. Len Murray, the TUC leader, reflected that Heath could have put the TUC to the test: if it failed to hold back other unions then the government could still have called an election and the unions would be in the dock.[30]

Further meetings of the Steering Committee and party officials were held at Chequers. The meetings encouraged further press speculation that an election would be called for 7 February and the opinion polls were still, on balance, encouraging. Most party officials attending Chequers expected to be told to prepare for an election and departed in some frustration when they were not given any lead. At the end of the day, Cabinet ministers convened to discuss the political situation without any advisers present. The discussion was inconclusive. Heath did not rule out the idea, but his lack of interest and evident unhappiness about having an election was evident to all. In this he was joined by Whitelaw.[31]

Ministers were having to guess Heath's thinking. Complaints about his long periods of silence, alleged lack of political 'feel' and preference for working with permanent secretaries in government are now commonplace.[32] This uncertainty may, however, be part of a more general problem for political cabinets when the civil servants withdraw and Cabinet ministers are left alone to talk about party and political matters. The formality, sense of hierarchy and pressure to come to a decision, normal in Cabinet discussions, are less obvious. One Conservative insider comments: 'Political cabinets are a shambles, because Cabinet ministers (were) used to addressing a problem, with papers on it, and then taking a decision. But when talking about election strategy, every minister has his own views, speaks from a different viewpoint and the meeting is too large anyway.'[33]

30. In witness seminar, *Contemporary Record*, vol. 2, no. 1 (1988).
31. W. Whitelaw, *The Whitelaw Memoirs* (London, 1989), 169.
32. Campbell, *Edward Heath*, 490.
33. Cited in D. Kavanagh, *Election Campaigning: The New Politics of Marketing* (London, 1995).

Yet if the government was to call an election for 7 February, it had to decide by 17 January. The officials used that deadline to demand last-minute corrections to the manifesto from ministers by 14 January. 17 January passed without an election announcement. Conservative-supporting newspapers complained of government indecision, and local constituency leaders of having been marched up the hill. Ministers and Number 10 staff defended the speculation on the grounds that it might force Labour to bring pressure on the NUM to settle: at the time, few Labour leaders wanted a 'Who Governs?' election.[34]

Hurd regretted the decision not to call an election on 7 February. He thought that the issues were becoming blurred and the opposition parties had gained time to prepare themselves. On 15 January, when it was clear that the option of 7 February had already passed, he wrote a note to Heath arguing for an election on 14 February. The options which the government had for putting pressure on the NUM included: sitting through the strike; threatening a more stringent Stage IV (to provide an incentive to settle under Stage III); and calling an immediate election. If the Conservatives won the election a new situation would result, ' . . . both because the miners would face a government armed with fresh authority and because the government would have a much freer hand'. He concluded: 'A decision to reject 14 February would in practice involve a decision that in autumn 1974 or spring 1975 we would be better placed. Given the economic situation, and the political consequences of a coal settlement substantially outside Stage III, this is not easy to sustain'.[35] Carrington was concerned that as a result of the miners' strike there would be no stocks of coal by the beginning of March: 'There were only two alternatives, an election or a cave-in. Though the date of the election is important, those who were opposed to any election had not taken on board this rather important issue'.[36]

Another lengthy meeting between the miners' leaders and government was held in Downing Street on 24 January. This provided no way forward, and the NUM executive immediately called for a strike ballot – not to decide on the NCB offer but to seek support for the executive. On the same day, the Relativities Report of the Pay Board was published and suggested methods for dealing with anomalous cases under the pay policy. Heath in the next few days indicated that the miners' case could be referred to the Relativities Board if the miners resumed normal working.

On Monday 4 February, it was revealed that 81 per cent of miners

34. Interviews with Douglas Hurd, 18 March 1974, and James Prior, 14 March 1974.
35. Hurd, *An End to Promises*, 128–9.
36. Letter to author from Lord Carrington, 16 March 1995.

had voted to support the Executive's call for a strike. The TUC and the government met yet again in Downing Street but made no progress. Although Heath said nothing directly, he seemed to his staff to be reconciled to an election. He told them that, if there were an election, it should be fought on the oil crisis and the serious problems this created for the country.[37] Preparations were speeded up. Two days later, Sir Michael Fraser reported to Heath on the findings of the private and public opinion polls about the state of public opinion. The Steering Committee met again that afternoon to work on the manifesto. The next day, 7 February, it was announced that a general election would be held on 28 February. A Steering Committee met that morning and again that afternoon to do further work on the manifesto, now entitled 'Firm but Fair'.

There was no sense in Number 10 that the government was in control as another confrontation with the miners, and this one for higher stakes, loomed.[38] Heath and his advisers felt boxed in – between pressure from backbenchers who would not countenance another sell-out to the miners, and pressure to be seen to be doing something. In his broadcast on 7 February, Heath claimed that an election would allow people to say to powerful groups: 'Times are hard, we are all in the same boat, and if you sink us now we will all drown.' He continued, '. . . the Government you elect will be in a far stronger position to reach a settlement with the miners which safeguards your interests as well as theirs.' The manifesto promised that 'A Conservative Government with a new mandate and five years of certain authority ahead of it would be in a good position to reach . . . a settlement.' What the settlement would involve was not elaborated.

DECISION

What of Heath himself, the man who would have to make the final decision? Asking the monarch to grant a dissolution has clearly been a prime ministerial prerogative since Lloyd George took the initiative unilaterally in 1918. It is a lonely and taxing decision: the Prime Minister has all to lose and little to gain. If his party wins, he carries on in government and ministers as a whole get credit. If his party loses, he gets the blame and almost inevitably his leadership will come under challenge and perhaps even be terminated, as Douglas-Home had found

37. Interview with Douglas Hurd, 18 March 1974.
38. Hurd, *An End to Promises*, 132.

out when he led his party to election defeat ten years before, and Callaghan was to find out five years later. Heath liked to receive dispassionate analyses and recommendations from his permanent secretaries; having listened to the pros and cons, he would slowly come to a decision. He enjoyed reading policy briefing papers and believed that through analysis and discussion a rational or, in a favoured word, a 'reasonable' decision would emerge.

But choosing an election date is a highly political and personal decision, never more so than in the circumstances of January 1974. The Heath style of decision-making was not best suited to handling the highly political issue of the miners' pay claim. The Cabinet Secretary at the time, Sir John Hunt, was present at many of the key meetings on the claim, and reflects that too often officials and ministers were 'really ignoring the politics to it'.[39] The pros and cons of an election were highly speculative, and many of the alleged political advantages of a victory (e.g. demonstrating to the unions and the NUM how unpopular they were, or discrediting 'moderates' in the Labour Party, or holding an election on an old register which would enable the Tories to exploit their superior postal vote organisation) were not to Heath's liking. There seemed to be no obvious reasonable course of action, beyond making a settlement; but the terms that the NUM would insist on seemed politically impossible to sell to Conservative MPs. As they argued before Heath, colleagues found it difficult to read his mind. What could be deduced throughout was his unhappiness at what seemed the inevitable election; one spoke of his 'long periods of brooding and introspection'. He did not want to fight anything resembling a 'Who Governs?' election.

Heath had after all worked hard to reach some kind of long-term agreement with the trade unions. A bitter general election, even if it were won by his party, would set back the prospects of cooperation with the unions. If the Conservative Party were returned with a bigger majority (and anything less would be a rebuff), it was not clear how this would influence the miners or weaken their bargaining position. And if he called an election, he was warned by Central Office officials that he could not guarantee the ground on which it would be fought. Voters might prove to be more resentful of rising prices and more expensive mortgages than of inconvenience caused by NUM strikes; they might also be unwilling to heed Heath's appeal for sacrifice in the tough times ahead; the outcome might be indeterminate or Labour might win the election. The case for calling an election was to appear

39. Contribution to 'The Trade Unions and the Fall of Heath', 44.

to be taking action. By 4 February, when the NUM voted for an all out strike, there was clearly no point in hoping for further negotiations. This effectively forced Heath's hand.

Heath's delay in coming to a decision could be defended on a number of grounds. The first is that the initial case for an election had developed too suddenly. Time was needed to prepare the Party, the public, the media and, above all, Heath himself. In early January, cabinet ministers were still divided over calling an election for 7 February. A month later there was no dissent about calling one for 28 February. The expression used at the time by Carrington was that delay allowed the 'pie to be baked', for all ministers to agree on an election.[40]

A second defence for delay is that nobody could doubt that Heath had strived mightily to avoid an election. Delay gave an opportunity for the negotiations to continue, for the TUC to try to use its good offices and for the government to show that it was acting responsibly. Going to the country was not Heath's initiative; in some ways, it was not even his decision. But even if he had implicated virtually all levels of the Party in the decision, he would bear the ultimate responsibility if things went wrong.

Finally, delay allowed Heath to define in his own mind and the minds of those around him what he regarded as the key issue – the need to prepare for tough times ahead. But that is not how all sections of the Party or the supporting press viewed the election. For them, it was a case of a trade union challenging the elected government and the election would be about trade union power and 'Who Governs?' Given that the political ground and intellectual case made by the Conservative Party had changed from those in June 1970, how would ministers answer the question – what would the election do to provide a solution to the miners' strike? What would ministers say to impress the electorate with the seriousness of the situation, and the relevance of an election to its solution? Could one invoke the spectre of a crisis and simultaneously call for moderation and defence of Stage III, was the question posed by Douglas – 'Can Oedipus ever be a moderate?'[41] It is not clear that party leaders developed a plausible answer.

MYTHS AND CONCLUSION

The election of 28 February did not produce a decisive result. Compared to that at dissolution, the number of Conservative MPs fell from

40. Interview with Lord Carrington.
41. Douglas to Lawson, 10 December 1973, OG/73/136.

322 to 297 and the number of Labour's MPs increased from 287 to 301, 17 short of a majority. The Conservatives had lost, but Labour had not won. The Conservatives had gained 200,000 votes more than Labour, but ended up with four seats fewer. Heath's offer to the Liberals of coalition was refused, although the two parties would still have lacked an overall majority. He resigned and Wilson formed a minority Labour government.

The gainers from the election were the minor parties. The number of Liberal MPs increased from 11 in the outgoing Parliament to 14, while MPs for 'other' parties increased from 8 to 23. The election was a significant step to multi-partyism in British elections. In general elections between 1950 and 1970 inclusive, an average of only 10 MPs were not connected to either the Conservative or Labour Parties. In 1974 the figure increased to 37.

The election was also a turning point in the postwar history of the two-party system. The substantial falls from 1970 in the vote share for the two main parties (Conservatives 8.6 per cent and Labour 5.8 per cent) were the biggest postwar reductions for each party. Labour's only consolation was that it did less badly than the Conservatives. The performance of the other parties reflected the electoral disillusionment with the two main parties. The Liberals increased their share of the vote from 7.5 per cent to 19.3 per cent or 6 million votes. In Scotland, the Nationalists increased their vote share from 11.4 per cent to 21.9 per cent. The two-party system has never recovered its former hold on the electorate. In general elections between 1945 and 1970, the average aggregate vote for the two main parties was 90 per cent. In 1974 it fell to 75.4 per cent, and has remained near that figure in subsequent general elections. Only the disproportionate effects of the first-past-the-post electoral system has preserved the dominance of the two main parties in the House of Commons.

The election did not produce strong government. All parties immediately began making preparations for the general election which would inevitably follow. A week after the election, the NUM executive and coal board agreed a new wage offer, on the basis of a report from the Relativities Board. The miners accepted the offer and returned to full working on 11 March.

The election of February 1974 rapidly became overlaid with myth. One myth, the staple of Labour Party communications for the rest of the decade, was that Heath was set on a confrontation with the miners. That confrontation was to be contrasted with Labour's social contract with the unions. The vision of the dark nights and the three-day week in the last weeks of the Heath administration became part of election folklore, just as the Conservatives have used the 'Winter of Discontent' to remind voters of life under the 1974–79 Labour government. It seems fated to go down in history as a 'Who Governs?' election. This grossly distorts Heath's position, but may be a measure of his failure in terms of communication.

A second myth was that no government could govern without the consent of the trade unions. The 'Winter of Discontent' five years later showed that a government could not necessarily govern with them either, largely because of the lack of union leaders' effective control over their members. Sir Keith Joseph and Margaret Thatcher realised that the Conservatives could never compete with Labour on social contracts and the Party turned its back on incomes policies, full employment and tripartism. Viewed from the 1990s, the 1974 elections seem to represent a different world. The panoply of pay boards, price commissions, relativities boards, wage 'norms', tripartite bargaining at NEDC along with meetings in Downing Street between the Prime Minister and union leaders is over. Statutory incomes policies inevitably called into question the authority of Parliament and government if a powerful group challenged or broke the laws. Heath's critics on the free-market wing of the Party complained that the government should never have got into this dilemma.

This relates to the third myth: that Heath, having started out on a proto-Thatcherite agenda, betrayed his mandate at the first whiff of grapeshot. Out of office, Thatcher and Joseph were convinced of the need for the Conservative Party to adopt a coherent set of policies based on convictions. What was needed was more resolute leadership, an end to U-turns; Heath was a negative model for Thatcher. It is true that the 1970 Conservative manifesto repudiated incomes policies, and promised to encourage competition and strengthen anti-monopoly policy. But Heath was also a pragmatist, and if new policies were required in response to changing circumstances and the demonstrable power of the unions, then what could be more Tory? Hence the U-turn. By background, he was a One-Nation Tory, in the line of Churchill, Eden and Macmillan, and believed in an active role for the state, not least in the provision of welfare and in promoting economic growth.

A final myth is that the election was inevitable, because the miners would not settle and Conservative MPs would not tolerate a 'sell out'. But until mid-January there were other possibilities open to creative politicians. The many meetings of politicians, civil servants, party officials and advisers did not seem to cover fully all available options. In October or November 1973 ministers could have accepted that the

Arab–Israeli War created a totally new situation and acknowledged the miners' special claims. Some, notably Lawson, argued that calling an early election might have prevented a strike:

> . . . if Heath had announced a General Election, and the NUM had responded by calling a strike ballot, it would have been easy to portray it as an intolerable interference with the democratic process; an attempt at intimidation which would surely have backfired. The big mistake was to allow the NUM to call their ballot first.[42]

Alternatively, ministers could have settled outside Stage IV and tested the TUC offer on 9 January or taken action immediately on 24 January, when the Relativities Board presented its report. The Stage III guidelines contained a clause which allowed ministers to break the code where they thought it in the public interest to do so. Ironically, Heath referred the claim to the Board on 7 February, but at the same time as announcing an election. For some of his advisers this not only undermined Stage III but weakened the idea that the election was necessary to force the miners to settle.[43]

It is difficult not to conclude that political skill was lacking. The idea of calling an early election rather than settling with the miners on terms beyond Stage III had become a mantra for many in the party, particularly those around Heath. It is a good example of the phenomenon of group think, the drive for consensus and the premature closure or inadequate appraisal of alternatives among members of a cohesive group, particularly at a time of great stress.[44] Talks continued with the miners but only within the Stage III guidelines, which the miners were determined to break. It was a dialogue of the deaf.

As Prime Minister, Heath had a problem with communication. His communication advisers had battled hard while in opposition before 1970 to project a new Heath.[45] They are unanimous in saying that he and his fellow ministers spurned public relations when in office and neglected the importance of communicating with the public. This is a familiar complaint about most governments. Central Office staff and Tory party publicists regularly complain about their lack of access to government ministers who allegedly think governmentally not politically, and spend too much time in the company of civil servants. The party machine often has to compete with many other claimants for the

42. Lord Lawson, letter to author, 22 March 1995.

43. Interview with Brendon Sewill, 21 March 1974.

44. On the phenomenon of 'group think', see I. Janis, *Victims of Group Think* (Boston, 1972).

45. See Butler and Pinto-Duschinsky, *The British General Election of 1970*, and Kavanagh, *Election Campaigning*.

time of ministers, but the complaints were expressed particularly strongly about the Heath government. Ramsden writes that, as early as 1971, Douglas Hurd was warning Heath of the widespread impression within the Party that his government '. . . is in fact less politically conscious than its Conservative predecessor'[46]. Hurd's memoir is eloquent in conveying his sense that ministers had forgotten the lessons about communications. He complained that, 'Instead of speaking to people, Heath would too often speak at them' and that the leader's liking for jargon meant that 'much of his matter was incomprehensible to the television audience'.[47]

Heath periodically invited Tucker, Day and Garrett to Downing Street and Chequers to receive their ideas for election broadcasts and major interviews. But Day recalls 'We were always aware that Ted was now surrounded by the civil service machine and he was thinking like it. The Party communicated to get into office but did not do this as an ongoing process.'[48] When it came to preparing broadcasts for the February election, they were very disappointed to find how little film of the work of Conservative ministers had been preserved and of how little interested ministers were in thinking about election communications. Tucker recalled

> It is a very difficult task to deal with a party in government. Heath enjoyed being a Prime Minister and statesman more than he enjoyed being a party man and a television personality. He slipped back, he became more attached to the civil service than to the party and his television appearances showed this . . . the warmth and the contact died. Public relations in all its aspect took a back seat. When he called a snap election in February 1974 we were all unprepared.'[49]

We return to a British Prime Minister's power to decide the election date. The elections of 1970 and February 1974 came as something of a 'surprise' to ministers, commentators and the public. Most elections, notably those in 1950, 1951, 1959, 1964, 1983, 1987 and 1992, had been widely anticipated, either because of the government's lack of a working majority or because Parliament was near its end. Deciding to call an election, as argued above, differs from other political decisions a Prime Minister makes. He can dissolve only once in a Parliament and if he gets it wrong he is out of office. That is rarely the case with other decisions. Even when Thatcher held so many advantages in 1983

46. Ramsden, *Conservative Party Policy*, 41.
47. Hurd, *An End to Promises*, 73.
48. Cited in Kavanagh, *Election Campaigning*, 54.
49. Ibid., 167.

and 1987, her decisions to call an election were preceded by elaborate analysis of opinion poll data and local election results, a decisive lead in the opinion polls which had lasted for several months, favourable economic statistics, and a build-up of media comment. Yet even then she found the decision a difficult one.

Twenty-one years later, it is still not clear what major advantages the Heath government could have gained from calling an election. If the election result had produced a similar outcome to that of 1970, the hands of the government and the NUM would have been unchanged. If the Conservatives had won by a large majority, it was not clear that this would have induced the miners to settle. There would still have been a severe shortage of oil and a shortage of miners, and to extract more coal it would have been necessary to pay the miners above what was envisaged in Stage III of the incomes policy. A clear election victory might have given the government freedom to make a settlement which broke the guidelines but, paradoxically, it had called the election in defence of Stage III, and being 'fair' to the four million workers who had already settled under it. Apologists for Heath say that he was unlucky, that the government suffered from bad timing (i.e. not dissolving earlier) and the vagaries of the electoral system – the Conservatives won 200,000 more votes than Labour but ended up with four fewer seats. Perhaps, but there still remains the question: what would an election victory have done that would get the miners back to work and still uphold Stage III? The election still appears to have been called because the government wanted to be seen to be doing something. At the time and in retrospect, Heath could be forgiven for doubting that his right to choose the election date was a 'power'. It could be argued that if the 'opt out' of an election had not existed, then ministers might have been more creative in exploring other paths to a settlement. A few days after the election, senior colleagues tried to comfort a depressed Heath, urging him not to blame himself for the outcome. He replied: 'It was my fault for taking your advice.'[50]

50. William Waldegrave, letter to author, 9 March 1995.

CHAPTER FIFTEEN

The fall of Heath and the end of the postwar settlement

Vernon Bogdanor

I

'Who governs Britain?' That was the question which Edward Heath put to the voters on 28 February 1974. The voters, however, failed to return an unequivocal answer. The result of the general election, as compared with that of 1970, was as follows:

TABLE 15.1 *General Election Results*

	1970		*February 1974*	
	Seats	*% Votes*	*Seats*	*% Votes*
Conservatives	330	46.4	297	37.9
Labour	287	43.0	301	37.1
Liberals	6	7.5	14	19.3
SNP	1	1.1	7	2.0
Plaid Cymru	0	0.6	2	0.6
Irish Unity	2	0.4	–	
Republican Labour Party (Northern Ireland)	1	0.3	–	
Protestant Unionist	1	0.3	–	
United Ulster Unionist Council	–	–	11	1.8
SDLP	–	–	1	0.9
Others	2	0.4	2	0.4
Total	630	100.0	635	100.0

The election yielded an outcome that was quite unexpected, a hung Parliament, Britain's first since 1929. The Conservatives remained the largest party in terms of votes, but Labour had won more seats. Labour, however, was 17 seats short of an overall majority. The Liberals with nearly one-fifth of the vote won just over 2 per cent of the seats, and only three seats more than the United Ulster Unionist Council, which had gained less than one-tenth of the Liberal vote.

None of the minor parties on its own held the balance of power. Even if one of the major parties could have secured an alliance with the largest of the minor parties, the Liberals, this would still not have been sufficient. The support of at least two of the minor parties would have been necessary for an overall majority.

Heath did not resign immediately, but instead, on the Saturday following the election, invited Jeremy Thorpe, the Liberal leader, to Downing Street and offered him full Liberal participation in a coalition government. Heath claimed that the two parties could agree upon policy, since the Liberals supported the Conservatives but disagreed with Labour both on Europe and on incomes policy. Thorpe agreed to consult his party, but indicated that for Liberals a basic precondition of coalition must be a commitment to proportional representation.

Aware that an agreement with the Liberals would be insufficient for a majority, Heath made a parallel approach to the MPs from Ulster, offering the Conservative whip to the seven Ulster Unionist members of the United Ulster Unionist Council.

Until 1972, the Ulster Unionist MPs had taken the Conservative whip in the Commons. With the abolition of Stormont they broke with the Conservatives. The United Ulster Unionist Council had been formed in January 1974 to resist the Sunningdale agreement which provided for a power-sharing executive in Northern Ireland and a Council of Ireland where representatives of Northern Ireland and of the Republic of Ireland would discuss matters of common interest for the whole island. The Council comprised three parties, the Ulster Unionists, Rev. Ian Paisley's Democratic Unionist Party and William Craig's Vanguard Unionist Progressive Party. The reply of the Unionists to Heath was that either all eleven of the Council's MPs should be offered the Conservative whip or none of them would accept it. Heath, however, could not offer the Conservative whip to Paisley or Craig, for that would mean explicitly repudiating the power-sharing executive in Northern Ireland which had come into existence in January.

Meanwhile, Thorpe was consulting his party. There are indications that he was attracted by Heath's coalition offer. But there was never any chance that he would be able to persuade his party to look favourably upon it. Of the 14 Liberals returned, all but two had won their seats from Conservatives, while 'of the 100 unsuccessful Liberals with the highest percentages, 98 lost to Conservatives and only 2 to Labour'.[1] Thorpe therefore told Heath that the Liberals would join a

1. D. Butler and D. Kavanagh, *The British General Election of February 1974* (London, 1974), 259.

coalition only if he could guarantee proportional representation. If that were not possible, however, he proposed a parliamentary pact similar to that later to be agreed by Steel and Callaghan in 1977. This would provide for Liberal support for a minority government based on a mutually agreed programme.

On the Monday after the general election, Heath held a Cabinet meeting to discuss the Liberals' terms. When he mentioned proportional representation, it appears that only two or three ministers were prepared to consider it. Margaret Thatcher, hitherto one of the more silent members of his Cabinet, is said to have burst out, 'Oh, no we couldn't. Think how many seats we would lose.' It was at this point, according to one observer, that her hostility to Heath as a traitor to Conservatism crystallised. For in her view, Heath was prepared to sacrifice any chance of the Conservatives ever again achieving an overall majority on their own for a mere temporary renewal of power.[2]

Having failed to secure a coalition, Heath resigned, to be succeeded by Harold Wilson as Prime Minister of a minority Labour government. Wilson sought no deals with any of the minority parties, but, at his best in a complex tactical situation, held on until October, when, following a further general election, he managed to secure an overall majority of 3.

II

At first sight, the general election of February 1974 seemed a victory for consensus politics, since the voters had rejected both 'confrontation' under Heath and the radical alternative offered by Labour. In reality, however, the election destroyed consensus politics for nearly two decades in every part of the United Kingdom. Indeed, it destroyed consensus at two levels, that of the political system itself and that of social relationships.

Instead of answering the question 'Who governs?', the election posed a quite different question: 'How was Britain to be governed?' But there was also the hint of a more dangerous question lurking in the background, the question of whether Britain was in fact governable at all.

The administration formed by Harold Wilson in March 1974 would have to confront two threats to the governability of Britain. The first was a revolt from the non-English parts of the United Kingdom, a revolt which put the unity of the kingdom itself at risk.

2. Private information.

The success of the United Ulster Unionist Council in returning 11 out of the 12 MPs from Northern Ireland, albeit on only 51 per cent of the Northern Ireland vote, effectively doomed the power-sharing executive. Indeed, one reason why William Whitelaw had been so opposed to a general election in February 1974 was his fear that it would undermine the settlement in Northern Ireland which had been so painstakingly constructed over the preceding months. In January 1974, the Ulster Unionists had rejected the Sunningdale agreement and forced the resignation of the Party's leader, Brian Faulkner. The general election took place before the Faulknerites were able to regroup into a new party which could take the case for Sunningdale to Unionist voters. The election result in Northern Ireland showed that the power-sharing executive was rejected by Unionist voters and that the new arrangements agreed at Sunningdale lacked democratic legitimacy.

Edward Heath had called the February 1974 general election to meet the threat of trade union power. The outcome, however, not only strengthened the trade unions on the mainland; it also gave a fillip to the Protestant trade unions in Northern Ireland which, organised as the Ulster Workers' Council, were to call a general strike against the executive in May 1974. By restricting electricity and fuel supplies, the Council brought life in Northern Ireland to a halt and the power-sharing executive came to a rapid end – the only example of successful direct action by the working class in British politics since 1945.

It seems, then, that the outcome of the February 1974 general election gave the Unionists of Northern Ireland a veto over constitutional change in the province. That veto has proved effective in preventing the introduction of stable local institutions in Northern Ireland from that day to this. It was not until 1985 that the Unionists' ace was trumped, for it was in that year that the Anglo-Irish Agreement provided for a form of joint consultation between Britain and the Republic of Ireland over the domestic affairs of Northern Ireland which did not rely upon Unionist consent.

In Scotland, the advance of the SNP destroyed the consensus on the Union. In the October general election, the SNP gained 30 per cent of the Scottish vote, the highest vote secured by any 'ethnic' party in Western Europe since the war. The SNP was now the second largest party in Scotland in terms of percentage of the vote. It won 11 of the 71 Scottish seats and was second in a further 42, including 35 of Labour's 41 Scottish seats; a swing of five per cent to the SNP from the sitting incumbent would give it a further 16 seats, destroying Labour's electoral base in Scotland, and threatening Labour's chances of ever governing Britain on its own again. Labour responded to this threat with a hasty and ill-considered scheme of devolution which, when put to referendum in 1979, gained the support of only 33 per cent of the Scottish electorate, while 31 per cent opposed it. Parliament refused to allow the government to legislate for devolution on so narrow a majority, and the Scottish issue died away only to be resurrected again in the 1990s.

III

The second challenge to the authority of the state came from the trade unions, for the election posed in its starkest form the problem of how a government could govern against the wishes of the trade union movement. Britain, as Keith Middlemas has shown, had been the first industrial society to answer the question of how the working class could be incorporated into the political system of an industrial society without alienating other classes.[3] During the immediate postwar years, Britain seemed indeed to have succeeded in conciliating class conflict more successfully than any other industrial democracy. The destruction of the Heath government, however, posed the question of whether the postwar dispensation could survive except at ruinous cost.

It was under the wartime coalition led by Churchill that the trade union movement had first been brought into a constructive relationship with government. In the 1930s, Churchill had appreciated that rearmament depended upon the cooperation of the unions; unlike Chamberlain, he believed that this cooperation would be forthcoming, the unions being as committed to national defence as were the Conservatives. For Churchill, those who had helped to save the country could not be denied the right to rule it. The year 1945 was merely the confirmation of that right.[4]

Under the postwar consensus, the maintenance of economic stability – full employment together with stable prices – depended crucially upon the restraint of organised labour; and this required governments, whether of left or right, to enter into bargaining relationships with the trade unions. Whether governments sought to moderate wage claims

3. See K. Middlemas, *Politics in Industrial Society: The Experience of the British System Since 1911* (London, 1979); and the magnificent trilogy by Middlemas, *Power, Competition and the State, vol. 1. Britain in Search of Balance, 1940–61* (London, 1986); *vol. 2. Threats to the Postwar Settlement, Britain 1961–74* (London, 1990); *vol. 3. The End of the Post-War Era: Britain Since 1974* (London, 1991).

4. M. Gilbert, *Winston Churchill, vol. VI. Finest Hour, 1939–41* (London, 1983), *passim.* The best account of the construction of the postwar consensus remains P. Addison, *The Road to 1945* (London, 1975).

through 'incomes policies' – either statutory or voluntary – or through other methods, they needed to secure the consent both of union leaders and of the rank-and-file membership if economic management were to be successful.

Until the advent of Margaret Thatcher's government in 1979, the challenge to the settlement had seemed to come from the left and not from the right. It was the Bevanites in the 1950s and the Bennites in the 1970s who appeared to offer the greatest threat to the postwar equilibrium. The economic liberals of the right, by contrast, seemed fustian and absurd – rather like men in frock coats who had failed to notice that sartorial styles were changing. For the policies that they were advocating – the abdication of government from the wage-bargaining process and the regulation of the economy through monetary means – would cause mass unemployment and prove electorally disastrous.

Edward Heath, in the second phase of his premiership, had gone further than any other Prime Minister in offering the trade unions partnership in the making of economic decisions. He sought a powerful and more centralised trade union movement which, together with a strong management and a strong government, could set firm priorities in industrial relations and economic policy. The Heath government was 'the last loyal signatory' of the 1944 pact by which governments promised to secure objectives such as full employment in return for wage restraint.[5] Yet, by the end of the Heath government, in the words of the *National Institute Economic Review,* Britain found herself 'confronted with the possibility of a simultaneous failure to achieve all four main policy objectives: of adequate economic growth, full employment, a satisfactory balance of payments, and reasonably stable prices'.[6] The experience of the Heath government thus put an end to the possibility that Britain could find her economic salvation along German and Scandinavian lines through power-sharing between government, industry and trade unions.

The very effort which Heath had put into achieving agreement with the unions, and the increase in state power which it involved, was difficult for Conservatives to accept. Most Conservative MPs were instinctively repelled by the extent of central direction which Heath's policies required. Whether or not the economy could be regulated in a corporatist way, such a method of economic management was not,

5. Middlemas, *Power, Competition and the State*, vol. 2, 390.

6. *National Institute Economic Review* (National Institute for Economic and Social Research, February 1974), quoted in Middlemas, *Power, Competition and the State*, vol. 3, 21.

surely, one that a Conservative government ought to have any truck with. On this view, corporatism was a profoundly un-Conservative nostrum since Conservatives believed in minimising, not extending, the role of the state.

It was natural, moreover, for Conservatives to reach the conclusion that, whether or not there were a case for an incomes policy, Conservative governments could not and ought not to seek to operate one, since Labour, through its links with the trade unions, would always be able to outbid them in Britain's adversarial political system. If corporatism were to be resuscitated, therefore, it could not be from the right. Therefore, some alternative method of managing the economy which did not rely upon trade union consent would have to be found. That alternative method was monetarism, championed by Margaret Thatcher, who was to wrest the Conservative leadership from Heath just one year after the February 1974 general election.

In retrospect, therefore, Edward Heath's corporatist period 1972–74, like Harold Macmillan's interventionism from 1961 to 1963, appears as an aberration in the twentieth-century history of the Conservative Party rather than, as Macmillan had hoped, a new 'middle way' abjuring the ideological extremes of capitalism and socialism. With the threat of economic instability, the Conservatives returned, as they had done in the 1930s, to their traditional nostrums of cutting public expenditure and distancing government from the economy.[7] Indeed, economic liberalism had remained an important if subterranean force in the postwar Conservative Party, coming out into the open only on rare occasions – in 1957 when the Treasury team led by Peter Thorneycroft had resigned in protest at the failure to cut public expenditure; and in the speeches of the economic Powellites – Enoch Powell, John Biffen and Nicholas Ridley.

From this standpoint, then, 'Thatcherism' was not a new departure in Conservative history, but a reversion by the Party to the primitive idols which it had worshipped before the Second World War. It was not that Conservatives were converted to doctrines such as monetarism, but rather that their adherence to Keynesian economics was comparatively superficial, a product as much perhaps of Conservative guilt at the mass unemployment of the interwar years as of any ideological conversion to Keynesianism. That guilty feeling would have eroded as the generation whose formative experience lay in the 1930s was coming to be replaced by a new generation whose experience was gleaned in

7. Compare S. Ball, *Baldwin and the Conservative Party: The Crisis of 1929–1931* (New Haven and London, 1988), 218–19.

the postwar era when inflation and relative economic decline seemed the central problems. 'Thatcherism', therefore, was perhaps more a *consequence* of profound social and generational changes than a *cause* of change, but the collapse of the Heath government accelerated the speed with which it was able to capture the Conservative Party. Under new leadership, the Conservatives were able to become, in the 1980s, once again the natural governing party of the country as they had been in the 1930s and the 1950s.

Margaret Thatcher, however, sought to solve Britain's economic and social problems outside the constraints which the postwar settlement had imposed. The commitment to full employment was implicitly abandoned and incomes policies were to come to an end, with prices and wages being returned to the determination of the market. Government was to become a framework-setter rather than an active participant in industrial policy: an important part of the Conservative programme for restoring authority was to minimise the role of the state so that it concentrated on those things which it could do well – national defence, law and order, and the establishment of a sound monetary framework. Government could not of itself promote growth; all it could do was to encourage attitudes conducive to it, attitudes such as self-help and the acceptance of personal responsibility. Thus, while Heath had striven to preserve the postwar settlement, Margaret Thatcher sought to break away from it. Conservative electoral success was to be secured not by resurrecting Heath's legacy but by repudiating it.

By contrast with the Conservatives, Labour, in triumphal mood, utterly failed to comprehend the message which the voters were sending. Claiming to have 'won' the election, Labour failed to notice that it had lost over one-eighth of its vote since 1970, when it had been ejected from government. This was the largest loss of votes from the main opposition party between one general election and the next until Michael Foot's disastrous 1983 campaign.

Misinterpreting the electoral signals, Labour proceeded to pass a series of measures increasing trade union influence, although all the evidence from opinion surveys indicated that the public believed the unions to be too strong, not too weak. Labour, however, held that its links with the unions would enable it to implement a 'social contract', a final *rassemblement* around the idea of the postwar settlement.[8] The social contract, however, proved one-sided since the TUC lacked the power – and possibly also the will – to reciprocate, proving perhaps

8. K. Middlemas, 'Power, Competition and the State', *Contemporary Record*, vol. 5, no. 3 (1991), 521.

that Heath had been right not to trust the TUC's promise to police Stage III in 1974. Labour continued, nevertheless, to believe that its links with the unions made it electorally impregnable, since any party which sought to govern against the wishes of the unions would be charged, as Heath's had been, with 'confrontation'. The trade union leaders happily cooperated in this masquerade until their hubris led them into the public sector strikes of the 'Winter of Discontent' of 1978–79, which paved the way for the Conservatives' return to power. The trade unions had become, in the words of Paul Johnson, a left-wing convert to Conservatism in the 1970s, a brotherhood of national misery. 'There is no question', claims Bernard Donoughue, Head of the Policy Unit under Wilson and Callaghan, 'that the public sector unions elected Mrs Thatcher in 1979; indeed, she subsequently said thank you to them in her own individual way.'[9]

After 1979, the trade union card became one for the Conservatives to play, since images of rats in the street, of the unburied dead and of cancer patients being turned away from hospitals by union pickets entered into the folk history of the British people, to prove a potent source of propaganda not only for Margaret Thatcher but even for John Major in the general election of 1992. Labour was thus to pay a high price in the 1980s for its misunderstanding of the significance of the February 1974 election result, and its association with an unpopular trade union movement which was seemingly out of control. 'The trade unionist', Aneurin Bevan had declared after Labour had lost the 1959 general election, 'votes at the polls against the consequences of his own anarchy'.[10] It was an aphorism whose truth was to be brought painfully home to Bevan's disciples Michael Foot and Neil Kinnock in the 1980s.

In fact, Labour was to be brought down in 1978–79 by the very same forces that had brought down Heath. These were forces not of militant collectivism, as was thought at the time, but of a new individualism 'Think nationally', Heath exhorted the unions when explaining his Stage III proposals, 'Think of the nation as a whole. Think of these proposals as members of a society that can only beat rising prices if it acts together as one nation.'[11] Such an exhortation might have been treated with respect in the days of Churchill and Attlee. By the 1970s, however, freed from the constraints of privation and unemployment and with wartime solidarity a dim memory, trade unionists were no

9. B. Donoughue, *Prime Minister: The Conduct of Policy under Harold Wilson and James Callaghan* (London, 1987), 187.

10. Middlemas, *Power, Competition and the State*, vol. 2, 236.

11. J. Campbell, *Edward Heath: A Biography* (London, 1973), 472–3.

longer prepared to accept restraint where it seemed to conflict with their own short-term interests.

Moreover, the trade unions had never seen their purpose, except perhaps in wartime, as being to assist governments in securing national aims. Instead, their prime *raison d'être* had become the avoidance of government encroachment upon their own domain. Indeed, the Labour Party first gained the enthusiasm of the organised working class after the Taff Vale decision of 1901, since it promised to restore the *status quo ante*, one in which the trade unions remained at a distance from both government and the law. The trade unions were dedicated not so much to collectivism as to 'collective laissez-faire', to securing by collective means their freedom from government interference. The main characteristics of the trade union movement were, in the words of one authority, 'its aversion to legislative intervention, its disinclination to rely on legal sanctions, its almost passionate belief in the autonomy of industrial forces'.[12]

Thus governments, whether Conservative or Labour, in asking the unions to police incomes policies for them, were asking them to take on functions for which they were not equipped. The social solidarity and self-discipline which could alone have sustained such policies was being undermined by the very prosperity and affluence which governments, both Conservative and Labour, had championed and which were themselves a product of the postwar settlement.

The consequence of the close involvement with the trade unions of Conservative and Labour governments in the 1970s was to undermine rather than strengthen that settlement. For, instead of providing the means to more rapid economic growth, it served to weaken the state upon whose efficacy the settlement relied. The failure of governments to succeed with incomes policies or successfully to regulate the trade unions cast doubt on the whole ideology of planning and on the leadership qualities of those who claimed to be able to deliver economic growth without tears. 'The more society tends to the corporate', Ghiţa Ionescu has noticed, 'the less authoritative is the state.'[13] So it was that the central task facing Harold Wilson in 1974 and Margaret Thatcher in 1979 was to restore the authority of the state.

The prime threat to the state lay in the demands of organised labour. From 1969, when Harold Wilson had been forced to drop his 'In Place of Strife' proposals, the threat of the trade union veto cast its baleful shadow over British politics. It affected not only economic policy and

12. O. Kahn-Freund, 'Labour Law', in M. Ginsberg (ed.), *Law and Opinion in the 20th Century* (London, 1959), 224. The phrase 'collective laissez-faire' is Kahn-Freund's.
13. Cited in Middlemas, *Politics in Industrial Society*, 496.

industrial relations, but the public services as a whole. For governments felt unable to risk proposing reforms in health or education which might alienate the public sector trade unions. It was not until the defeat of Arthur Scargill's miners in 1985, so reversing the verdict of 1974, that the trade union veto was removed, and it was achieved by a government which believed in distancing the state from society and the economy. The restoration of the authority of the state was a precondition not only of Thatcherism, but also of any resurrection of social democracy. For social democrats also could only hope to secure the public interest if the state were strong enough to control powerful private interests.

The February 1974 general election marginalised social democracy as a force in the Labour Party. Following its defeat in 1970, Labour had swung to the left, repudiating policies such as incomes policy and pro-Europeanism which it had supported in office. In 1972, Labour's leading social democrat, Roy Jenkins, resigned from the Shadow Cabinet. His reason for resigning was Labour's commitment to a referendum on Europe; his deeper reason perhaps was a distaste for the tacking and weaving which characterised the Wilson regime, and which Jenkins saw as destructive of any settled strategy at all. Following his resignation, Jenkins made a series of speeches, published in 1973, staking out his position as an alternative leader of the Labour Party were Wilson to stumble.[14] Jenkins was well placed to challenge Wilson after what was widely expected to be a further Labour election defeat. Wilson's unexpected victory, therefore, was as much a defeat for Jenkins – who, in 1976, left British politics to become President of the Commission of the European Community – as it was for Heath.

For the left of the Labour Party, by contrast, the outcome of the February 1974 election was a stimulus to further effort, since the Party's swing to the left since the 1970s had not prevented it from being victorious. The left, therefore, intensified its attempt to reform the Party's constitution so that the party activists could wield more power. Their efforts culminated in the Labour Party conference of 1980 when the Party adopted an electoral college for leadership elections and instituted mandatory re-selection of MPs. At the same time, conference committed the Party to unilateral nuclear disarmament, abolition of the House of Lords and withdrawal from the European Community without a referendum. Henceforth, so it seemed, social democrats would have to find a home outside the Labour Party as indeed many of them did when the SDP was formed in 1981.

14. R. Jenkins, *What Matters Now* (London, 1973).

The roots of Labour's troubles in the 1980s lay in their misunderstanding of what the electorate had been signalling in 1974. Power, Labour believed, would eventually fall into its lap if only it remained united and kept its nerve. The Conservatives were, Labour thought, ill-equipped to run a modern industrial society which depended crucially upon the acquiescence of organised labour; and a government, like that of Margaret Thatcher's, which sought to govern without the support of organised labour would inevitably, so the canons of the postwar settlement held, destroy itself. But the Labour left overestimated the radicalism of the organised working class which was likely to become militant only when under direct attack from government, as in the years between 1918 and 1921 and as it felt itself to be in 1974. Margaret Thatcher defused militancy through curbing trade union power by a series of incremental legislative measures rather than by a single all-embracing measure such as the Industrial Relations Act had been; nor would it be possible to persuade trade unionists that their fate was bound up with that of an extreme and unpopular trade union as Arthur Scargill's mineworkers seemed to be in 1984.

IV

In February 1974, for the first time since the Second World War, the electorate showed its dissatisfaction with both major parties. Labour and Conservatives together secured just 75 per cent of the popular vote – as compared with 97 per cent in the heyday of two-party politics in 1951. Betwen 1945 and February 1974, the two parties averaged 91 per cent of the popular vote in general elections. Since 1974, the figure has been just under 75 per cent.

The February 1974 general election thus revealed a deep-seated frustration with both of the major parties, and with the elites that had led them since the war. Not only were trade unionists more militant than they had been in the past, but workers on the shop floor were refusing any longer to follow the advice of trade union leaders, while voters were refusing to follow the advice of their political leaders. Voters were coming to be alienated from a political establishment that was seeking, with increasing desperation, to manage the postwar settlement so that its gains could be maintained. The outcome of the February election revealed a degree of alienation that took many by surprise. Yet this alienation from government was by no means a sudden or new arrival on the British political scene. Its earliest manifestations had been seen in the widespread enthusiasm for Enoch Powell in the late 1960s, an early and slightly unexpected indication that popular discontent would undermine the consensus from the right rather from the left. Events of 1968 showed that Enoch Powell, the John the Baptist of Thatcherism, was a far more potent harbinger of discontent than the fashionable student radicals of that year which foolish commentators had believed to represent the wave of the future. Enoch Powell, not Tariq Ali, was the real revolutionary of the 1960s.

In 1974, however, popular frustration found its outlet not on the Right but through supporting Jeremy Thorpe's Liberals. As a result, the February general election brought back on to the political agenda, for the first time since the war, constitutional issues, issues which had been banished from British politics since the Irish settlement of 1921 and the overthrow of the Lloyd George coalition a year later. The Liberals alone had continued to insist upon the need for constitutional reform, but they had been a marginal political force since 1924, except during the years 1931 and 1932. Devolution, which both of the major parties came to believe was essential in the 1970s, was a long-held Liberal nostrum; while the outcome of the February general election and the second general election in October created a powerful constituency for electoral reform.

Writing to a supporter in November 1974, Jeremy Thorpe claimed that:

> The hopeful thing is that we have (except for Ted, who is going anyway) convinced some Tories (e.g. Du Cann and Whitelaw) that we are here for good, and may accept (a) that the Labour Party will never and has never polled 50% or more of the votes but (b) under the present electoral system 39% of the vote can and has given one party a majority – in October we proved that there was a 3 party system linked to a 2 party electoral system. All of this has to be achieved before the Tories recover and start to think they can win without us! I think we can do it.[15]

With the Conservatives and Labour no longer trusted as purveyors of consensus, it seemed that there might be a gap in the political market which the Liberals could exploit. The Liberal Party dedicated itself accordingly to the ending of adversary politics through a whole raft of constitutional reforms which would begin with electoral reform. Proportional representation would entrench the position of the Liberals in the political system and make them a key partner in future coalition governments.

The Liberal call for an end to adversary politics was to be taken up

15. Jeremy Thorpe to Jack Hayward, 28 November 1974, quoted in L. Chester, M. Linklater and D. May, *Jeremy Thorpe: A Secret Life* (London, 1979), 201–2.

by the Conservatives. In the October 1974 general election campaign, Edward Heath was to make an explicit appeal for a government of national unity which

> would seek to put aside party bickering and concentrate on mobilising the full resources of a nation united to beat the crisis. The crisis of authority in our democratic system represents a problem for any government. To tackle it, we need a broadly based government to call on the support of the whole community and protect the public interest. The strength of such a government lies in the national unity that backs it.[16]

In his Dimbleby Lecture of 1976, Lord Hailsham was to coin the slogan 'elective dictatorship' to describe the activities of the Labour government, and he called for constitutional reform to combat it.

Neither Heath nor Hailsham favoured proportional representation, but there were grounds in 1974 for believing that the Conservatives might become converted to it. For the basic Conservative defence of the first-past-the-post electoral system had been that it yielded, if not mathematical accuracy, a rough and ready correspondence between seats and votes. It was difficult to argue that any longer. Not only had the 'wrong' party won in February 1974, but the Liberal tally of just over 2 per cent of the seats for 19 per cent of the votes seemed to affront basic notions of fairness. Moreover, many Conservatives became deeply disturbed that, with the support of only 37 per cent of the voters in February and 39 per cent in October, the Wilson government nevertheless proceeded to implement its programme as if it enjoyed majority support in the country. Faced with such policies as the nationalisation of the aerospace and shipbuilding industries and the docks, the imposition of comprehensive education upon local authorities and the phasing out of pay beds in the National Health Service, Conservatives began to ask themselves whether it was right that a radical government enjoying office through the support of a minority of the voters, should be able to impose seemingly irreversible changes upon the country. Many business supporters of the Conservative Party agreed, holding that the 'adversary politics' of the 1960s and 1970s was damaging Britain's prospects of economic success by making it difficult for industrialists to draw up long-term investment plans with any degree of confidence. In 1979, the report of a Hansard Society commission *Politics and Industry: The Great Mismatch* – chaired by Sir Richard Marsh, the chairman of British Rail – concluded that adversary politics, though 'deeply embedded in British constitutional convention . . . is now pro-

16. Message to candidates, October 1974, cited in T. Russel, *The Tory Party: Its Policies, Divisions and Future* (Harmondsworth, 1978), 144.

ducing increasingly pernicious effects so far as industry is concerned'. The commission declared that there was a need for a modicum of consensus on industrial policy between the parties, and that if electoral reform could help to create this 'by tending to produce governments of the centre rather than either political extreme', then 'we would support the view that it deserves serious consideration'.[17]

The nature of the argument for proportional representation changed after the 1974 general election. The argument in the past had concentrated on the unfairness of the first-past-the-post system. Opponents of proportional representation had often been prepared to concede that it might be fairer than first-past-the-post, but they argued that it was impractical and would lead to bad government. Now, the argument was that not only was proportional representation fairer, but also that it would lead to better government; and that coalition, hitherto derided as a Continental expedient of dubious worth, had positive virtues if it helped to produce consensus. In 1975, S. E. Finer, Gladstone Professor of Government and Public Administration at Oxford, edited a volume entitled *Adversary Politics and Electoral Reform* which proved an influential expositor of what was becoming a new orthodoxy.[18] Proportional representation was becoming an establishment cause and was rapidly losing the taint of crankiness which had clung to it since the 1920s.

Yet, unfortunately for Jeremy Thorpe and the Liberals, Heath was replaced as Conservative leader not by a support of electoral reform but by one of its most dedicated opponents, Margaret Thatcher. Her opposition was based in part on her belief that, if coalition was needed, the Liberals would generally side not with the Conservatives, but with Labour, as they had done in 1924, 1929 and 1974 and were to do again in 1977–78. Thus proportional representation would condemn the Conservatives to permanent minority status.

There was, however, a deeper reason for the failure of Liberal hopes after 1974. For the frustrations of the mid-1970s were anything but liberal in their nature. They were motivated less by worries about the constitution than by alienation from that very postwar settlement which the Liberals were seeking to entrench through proportional representation. The mood of the 1970s, therefore, was hardly liberal but fearful both of inflation and of social dislocation. It had little in common with the consensual agenda being championed by the Liberal Party. Yet the frustrations of the 1970s were not to be given full expression until the 1980s when they were to find their outlet in 'Thatcherism'.

17. Hansard Society, *Politics and Industry: The Great Mismatch* (1979), 56, 57.
18. S.E. Finer (ed.), *Adversary Politics and Electoral Reform* (London, 1975).

Thatcherism was the manifestation of a social mood which owed as much to the folk image of the thrifty shopkeeper as it did to the economic doctrines of Friedman and von Hayek. Survey evidence has shown that support for the Conservative Party from 1964 came primarily not from the managerial, professional or administrative elite, from those who had managed the postwar settlement, but from the petty bourgeoisie, small employers and the self-employed.[19] The Party appealed not so much to the rich as to those with little or no capital of their own, and who, therefore, were frightened of losing what little they had. It was the small employers and the self-employed such as the small shopkeepers who saw themselves as the prime victims of Edward Heath's economic policies; and it was this section of society which felt most frightened by the seeming triumph of the trade unions in 1974 and by the *grande peur* of the 1978–79 'Winter of Discontent'. Not belonging to one of the great estates of the realm which the postwar settlement had legitimised, the petty bourgeoisie seemed bereft of any organisation by which to defend its interests. Only a Conservative Party purged of its corporatist heresies could undertake that role.

Furthermore, natural Conservative supporters did not perhaps share the internationalism of their political leaders, an internationalism which was manifested most strikingly in Heath's commitment to the European Community. Hitherto the Conservative Party had seemed to stand for British nationhood, not for merging Britain's identity with a Continental grouping. During the 1970s, the very economic difficulties and sense of social dislocation experienced by many Conservative supporters tended to heighten national solidarity at the same time as these phenomena were weakening the *social* solidarity upon which parties of the left depend. In Britain, economic decline weakened the force of altruism, and as voters narrowed their concerns so also they would come to lessen their expectations of what the state could do.[20] The response to decline came to be a withdrawal from wider social ties, a privatisation of life, a drawing inwards, an attachment rather to Burke's 'little platoons – the first principle (the germ as it were) of public affections'. It was to these familial virtues of self-discipline, responsibility and care for one's own, that Margaret Thatcher's brand of Conservatism would appeal.

It was the forgotten people under the Heath regime, the petty bourgeoisie, who formed the backbone of so many local Conservative

19. A. Heath, *et al.*, *Understanding Political Change: The British Voter 1964–1987* (Oxford, 1991), 68–9.

20. J. Alt, *The Politics of Economic Decline: Economic Management and Political Behaviour in Britain since 1964* (Cambridge, 1979), *passim*.

associations who transformed both the Conservative Party and then the state itself. In his novel, *Coningsby*, Disraeli's hero spoke of a party which

> without any embarrassing promulgation of principles, wish to keep things as they find them as long as they can, and then will manage them as they find them as well as they can . . . Whenever public opinion, which this party never attempts to form, to educate, or to lead, falls into some violent perplexity, passion, or caprice, this party yields without a struggle to the impulse, and, when the storm has passed, attempts to obstruct and obviate the logical and, ultimately, the inevitable results of the very measures they have themselves originated, or to which they have consented. This is the Conservative Party. (Book VII, Ch. II).

Previous Conservative administrations – those of Stanley Baldwin and Harold Macmillan – had acted in an essentially accommodationist and defensive spirit, seeking to preserve a society whose values they saw as supportive of Conservatism. Heath too sought to preserve society, but, aware of Britain's economic problems, appreciated that it could only be preserved through a radical dynamism more characteristic of a Roosevelt or a de Gaulle than a British Conservative leader. There was, claimed Douglas Hurd, Heath's Political Secretary between 1970 and 1974,

> a real chance . . . that Mr Heath and his colleagues would break out of inherited attitudes and make possible a sharply higher level of achievement by the British people. In short, there was a chance that they could do for Britain what Adenauer and Erhard had done for Germany and de Gaulle for France.[21]

The Heath government nevertheless still appealed to a mood that was recognisably conservative.

The difficulty was, however, that the central symbols of Conservatism – the nation, religion and social order – seemed in decline in a Britain that was becoming a secularised and seemingly rootless mass society whose only principle appeared to be that of material gratification. Both Macmillan in his later years and also Heath sought to come to terms with the social changes of the postwar years by establishing the Conservative Party as the party of efficient management and economic growth. Margaret Thatcher, however, symbolised more radical frustrations. She represented a quite distinct brand of Conservatism, no longer accommodationist and defensive, but radical and populist, pre-

21. D. Hurd, *An End to Promises: Sketch of a Government 1970–74* (London, 1979), 138–9. This book remains, together with John Campbell's biography, by far the best account of the Heath government.

pared to react against the statism of the postwar consensus and against a society whose morality had been undermined by the permissive culture of the 1960s. In this, she was also reacting no doubt against her predecessors; but she was to become, almost uniquely amongst Conservative leaders, in tune with the party in the country. She was, claims Nigel Lawson,

> unusual, for a Tory leader, in actually warming to the Conservative Party – that is to say, the party in the country, rather than its Members of Parliament. Certainly that had not occurred for many years. Harold Macmillan had a contempt for the party, Alec Home tolerated it, Ted Heath loathed it. Margaret genuinely liked it. She felt a communion with it, one which later expanded to embrace the silent majority of the British people as a whole.[22]

Margaret Thatcher, far from accepting the social changes which she inherited, appreciated that the social changes of the 1960s were anathema to her brand of Conservatism. She sought to create an ordered and responsible society, but this could only be achieved through the reassertion of market disciplines. The return to such disciplines, however, would be inhibited by the great established institutions – the civil service, the trade unions, local government – which the postwar settlement had legitimised. So it was that Margaret Thatcher's brand of Conservatism was to be hostile to the *status quo*, not supportive of it. Its enemies lay at the very heart of the establishment which had endorsed previous Conservative leaders, and she was to lead a more powerful attack against it than anything that the left has ever been able to mount. For the mood which Margaret Thatcher was to exploit was far from being a *conservative* mood in the traditional sense of that term; it was a mood which could be exploited only by a political leader willing to move beyond Conservatism as it had been understood in Britain since 1945. This was to involve the transformation of a party which had hitherto been at the very least sceptical of popular majorities – indeed its resistance to the tyranny of the majority had been the feature which John Stuart Mill had most admired about it – into an explicitly populist party. It was to become once again a party believing that the nation was fundamentally sound, but that its heartbeat was being muffled by an establishment that had become insensitive to, and remote from, the popular mood.

22. N. Lawson, *The View from No. 11: Memoirs of a Tory Radical* (London, 1992), 14.

V

The central paradox of twentieth-century politics is the coexistence of economic weakness with political stability. Britain's economic decline has led neither to 'crisis' of the kind so confidently predicted by Marxists, nor to 'renewal' of the kind hoped for by Joseph Chamberlain and his successors, who included both Edward Heath and Margaret Thatcher and believed that the British would have to become a more efficient people if they wanted to compete successfully in the modern world. Edward Heath lay squarely in the Chamberlain tradition. His biographer compares his approach to leading the British people with that of the conductor of an orchestra. Heath tried to elicit a certain sort of performance from the nation just as, from the rostrum, he would try to elicit a certain sort of performance from the orchestra.[23] Yet, as a Conservative leader greater than Heath had noticed nearly a hundred years before, 'It is a very difficult country to move . . . a very difficult country indeed, and one in which there is more disappointment to be looked for than success'.[24] The general election of February 1974 showed yet again the truth of Disraeli's dictum. The British people have listened politely to the sermons which their leaders have prepared for them, but they have consistently refused all offers of salvation and remained what they have always been – inhabitants of a peaceable if rather run-down civic kingdom – ostriches for the most part rather than lions.[25] Even so determined a politician as Edward Heath could do little to change such deep-rooted attitudes. Instead, by straining the postwar settlement to its limits, he snapped it in twain; and we are still living in the shadow of its demise.

23. Campbell, *Edward Heath*, 497.

24. R. Blake, *Disraeli* (London, 1966), 764.

25. A. Koestler, *The Lion and the Ostrich*, Eighth Annual Lecture under the 'Thank-Offering to Britain Fund' (Oxford, 1973).

CHAPTER SIXTEEN

A chronology of the Heath government

Stuart Ball

1970

9 Apr.	Greater London Council elections show modest swing to Labour: the Conservatives keep control but lose 16 seats and control of Inner London Education Authority.
14 Apr.	Roy Jenkins introduces a restrained budget despite having a record £2,444 million revenue surplus.
7 May	Borough elections suggest considerable swing back to Labour, who make a net gain of 443 seats while the Conservatives lose 327.
13 May	Gallup poll in the *Daily Telegraph* indicates 7.5 per cent Labour lead.
18 May	Harold Wilson announces the election (prorogation on 29 May).
26 May	Publication of the Conservative manifesto, which pledges tax and government spending cuts, introduction of greater competition, and targeting of social welfare spending.
15 June	Publication of trade figures for May show sudden increased deficit of £31 million.
18 June	*Polling day*: election returns 330 Conservatives, 288 Labour, 6 Liberals, and 6 others; Conservative overall majority of 30.
19 June	Edward Heath accepts the Royal Commission to form a government, and becomes Prime Minister.
20 June	Announcement of Cabinet posts.
23 June	First meeting of the new Cabinet, faced with threat of a dock strike.
30 June	Sir Alec Douglas-Home and Anthony Barber visit Brussels and Luxemburg and revive the British application to join the European Community (EC).

2 July	Queen's Speech opens new session of Parliament: principal measures outlined are an industrial relations Bill, the reduction of immigration, and the curbing of inflation; there is a renewed commitment to full employment and a regional policy.
7 July	In his only statement to the House as Chancellor, Iain Macleod gives an unexpectedly cautious indication of his future policy.
15 July	Dock members of the Transport and General Workers' Union (TGWU) vote to reject the port employers' offer, and the existing unofficial strike is extended and becomes official.
16 July	State of Emergency declared due to the dock strike.
17 July	Lord Justice Pearson appointed to conduct an enquiry into the dock dispute.
20 July	Sudden death of the Chancellor of the Exchequer, Iain Macleod.
23 July	National Union Executive set up a Review Committee, chaired by Lord Chelmer, to investigate the democratisation of the Conservative Party.
29 July	Pearson's recommendation of a 7 per cent pay award to the dockers is accepted by Employment Secretary Robert Carr.
6 Aug.	Carr meets chairmen of nationalised industries and urges the need for wage restraint in the public sector.
1 Sep.	Heath returns to Downing Street from holiday.
6 Sep.	Arrest of Leila Khaled at Heathrow begins the Palestinian hijack and hostage crisis.
29 Sep.	After negotiation, the hostages are released; next day Khaled is flown to Cairo.
10 Oct.	Heath's speech at the Party Conference, Blackpool, closes with the theme of the 'quiet revolution'.
13 Oct.	Carr meets the Trades Union Congress (TUC) General Council but makes clear that the main features of the Industrial Relations Bill are not negotiable.
15 Oct.	Publication of White Paper on reorganisation of government departments, creating two large units of the Department of Trade and Industry (DTI) and Department of the Environment (DoE).
27 Oct.	Barber's 'mini-budget' takes 6d. off income tax and cuts corporation tax by 25 per cent, balanced by removal of subsidies, increased prescription charges, end of free

	school milk for children aged 8–11, and introduction of museum admission charges.
28 Oct.	Publication of the Family Income Supplements Bill, and of the Defence White Paper which reaffirmed an 'east of Suez' commitment.
29 Oct.	Talks on the EC application open formally in Brussels; the appointment of Lord Rothschild to head the new Central Policy Review Staff announced.
2 Nov.	Abolition of the Prices and Incomes Board announced.
5 Nov.	5-week strike by local authority dustmen and sewage workers ends after the independent arbitrator, Sir Jack Scamp, awards £2. 10s. of the claimed £2. 15s., justified due to the level of inflation.
9 Nov.	23 Conservative MPs vote against the government motion to renew sanctions against Rhodesia.
11 Nov.	Decision to make a government loan of £42 million to Rolls-Royce aero-engines, to avoid bankruptcy over the RB211 engine contract.
3 Dec.	Publication of the Industrial Relations Bill.
7 Dec.	Power station workers begin a work-to-rule; power cuts follow.
12 Dec.	State of Emergency declared, rota of power cuts established.
14 Dec.	Work-to-rule called off and agreement reached on the appointment of a court of inquiry under a High Court Judge, Lord Wilberforce.
15 Dec.	Industrial Relations Bill passes 2nd reading by 324 votes to 280.

1971

1 Jan.	Heath's first honours list contains no hereditary titles, and no political honours.
12 Jan.	'Angry Brigade' bomb attack on the home of Robert Carr.
14–22 Jan.	Commonwealth Prime Ministers' conference, Singapore, at which there is further criticism of the resumption of arms sales to South Africa.
20 Jan.	Post Office workers' strike in pursuit of a 15–20 per cent increase begins.
1 Feb.	Strike begins at Ford plants following rejection of a 10 per cent offer, becoming an official strike on 5 Feb.

4 Feb.	Announcement of decision to nationalise Rolls-Royce aero-engines.
5 Feb.	The first death of a British soldier on service in Northern Ireland.
8 Feb.	Emergency motion in the House of Commons over assistance to Rolls-Royce; Enoch Powell speaks against government and abstains in the division.
10 Feb.	Lord Wilberforce's enquiry into power station workers' pay recommends an award worth at least 15 per cent (though less than the 25 per cent which had been claimed).
11 Feb.	Rolls-Royce (Purchase) Bill receives unopposed second reading.
15 Feb.	Decimal currency comes into effect.
16 Feb.	White Paper on local government reform proposals published.
24 Feb.	Immigration Bill published, receives second reading on 8 Mar.
(Feb.)	Labour recover their opinion-poll lead, which they do not lose again until after the end of the government.
1 Mar.	One-day protest stoppage against the Industrial Relations Bill affects 1.75 million engineering workers and closes newspapers.
8 Mar.	Post Office workers' strike is called off on the basis of acceptance of the original offer plus a committee of inquiry.
10 Mar.	Murder in Belfast of three off-duty soldiers.
15 Mar.	Henry Ford II, President of Ford, lunches with Heath and points to the possibility of the company diverting investment elsewhere.
20 Mar.	Major James Chichester-Clark resigns as Prime Minister of Northern Ireland; succeeded on 23 Mar. by Brian Faulkner.
30 Mar.	Barber's first full budget cuts taxation by £546 million (halving Selective Employment Tax and reducing corporation tax and surtax) and increases pensions and benefits by an estimated £560 million (of which £467 million to be raised from increased National Insurance contributions); Ford workers vote to accept 33 per cent pay award over two years together with a no-strike deal.
19 Apr.	Unemployment figure published for March shows rise to 814,149.

5 May	Report of inquiry into the postal dispute chaired by Sir Henry Hardman recommends only a 9 per cent award and is critical of both sides.
10–15 May	Conservatives lose 1,943 seats in the local elections, and lose control of 71 borough councils and the GLC.
20–21 May	Heath's successful summit meeting with President Pompidou in Paris resolves the main problems in the path of EC entry.
27 May	Labour win the Bromsgrove by-election, overturning a Conservative majority of 10,874.
23 June	Conclusion of the EC entry negotiations.
25 June	Margaret Thatcher announces a building programme of £132 million for primary schools in 1973–76.
7 July	Publication of the White Paper announcing the terms for EC entry.
14 July	Heath argues the case for EC entry at a special meeting of the Central Council of the National Union, declaring that the Commons will decide (but not on a free vote).
19 July	Further measures from Barber intended to increase demand: purchase tax cut by 18 per cent, restrictions on Hire Purchase lifted, removal of rent controls.
29 July	A 'work-in' to resist closure begins at Upper Clyde Shipbuilders.
6 Aug.	Industrial Relations Act receives the Royal Assent.
9 Aug.	Introduction of internment in Northern Ireland, together with a ban on Orange marches and parades; 342 persons arrested.
20 Aug.	First auction of North Sea oil drilling concessions.
23 Aug.	Partial flotation of the £.
24 Sep.	Expulsion of 105 Russian diplomats for espionage activities.
13 Oct.	Annual Conference of the Conservative Party, at Brighton, votes in favour of the government's terms for EC entry by 2,474 to 324.
18 Oct.	Heath announces that Conservative MPs will be allowed a free vote on the bill for EC entry.
21 Oct.	Parliamentary debate on EC entry begins.
28 Oct.	Vote on terms negotiated for EC entry: government carried with majority of 112 (356–244) due to Labour cross-votes and abstentions; 39 Conservative MPs vote against entry and 2 abstain.
2 Nov.	Queen's Speech opening the new session declares that the government's 'first care will be to increase employment'.

5 Nov.	Thatcher announces increase from £32 to £62 per pupil of state supply for places at direct-grant schools.
15 Nov.	Sir Keith Joseph drops plan for cost-related prescription charges.
17 Nov.	Decision to retain the state-owned banking system, Giro.
23 Nov.	Barber announces £160 million increase in infrastructure projects.
24 Nov.	Home reaches agreement with Rhodesian leader Ian Smith on a proposed constitutional settlement.
16 Dec.	Unemployment figure published for November is 966,802.
20–21 Dec.	Heath meets US President Nixon at Bermuda.

1972

9 Jan.	Miners begin a strike in pursuit of a 47 per cent pay claim.
20 Jan.	Official unemployment total rises above 1 million for the first time in 25 years, to 1,023,583.
22 Jan.	Heath signs the Treaty of Accession, formally joining the EC.
26 Jan.	Publication of the unexpectedly short European Communities Bill.
30 Jan.	Troops fire on crowd in Londonderry, killing 13 – 'Bloody Sunday'.
9 Feb.	State of Emergency declared as a result of the coal strike.
10 Feb.	Pickets directed by Arthur Scargill force the closure of the Saltley Gate cokeworks, Birmingham; Carr announces a Court of Enquiry into the dispute, to be chaired by Lord Wilberforce.
17 Feb.	Second reading of the European Communities Bill treated as a vote of confidence, but government only survive by a majority of 8 (309–301), 15 Conservative MPs voting against and 4 abstaining.
18 Feb.	Wilberforce reports that the miners had 'a just case for special treatment' and recommends increases of up to £6 per week; terms initially rejected by National Union of Mineworkers (NUM) leaders and only accepted after further concessions directly negotiated by Heath in Downing Street.
1 Mar.	National Industrial Relations Court (NIRC) 'code of good practice' becomes law.

9 Mar.	Talks on the state of the economy between senior ministers and the TUC General Council held at the government's invitation.
13 Mar.	Trade deficit of £32 million for February reported: sterling falls by 25 points in the New York exchange.
16 Mar.	Similar talks held with the Confederation of British Industry (CBI).
21 Mar.	Barber's budget cuts taxes by £1.2 billion but allows public expenditure to rise.
22 Mar.	Minister for Industrial Development appointed, and publication of White Paper *Industrial and Regional Development* which announces establishment of an Industrial Development Executive to plan injection of £315 million new investment in 1973–75: leads to legislation in the Industry Act.
24 Mar.	Suspension of the Stormont Parliament and imposition of direct rule over Northern Ireland announced, internment to be phased out, and William Whitelaw appointed to new office of Secretary of State for Northern Ireland.
28 Mar.	Northern Ireland (Temporary Provisions) Bill passes second reading, becoming law on 30 Mar.
29 Mar.	NIRC imposes the first fines on trade unions.
17 Apr.	British Rail work-to-rule begins (lasting to 12 June).
1 May	Industry Bill published.
2 May	Government guillotine resolution on the European Communities Bill carried by 302–293, a government majority of only 11.
6 May	Widespread Labour gains in local elections.
22 May	Speech by Davies introducing the Industry Bill in the House of Commons is received with silence on the Conservative backbenches and cheers from Labour MPs.
23 May	Pearce Commission reports that native Rhodesian opinion is strongly opposed to the proposed settlement, which then lapses.
31 May	Publication of results of ballot of railway workers (ordered by the NIRC on 13 May) shows 6-to-1 majority in favour of the action.
12 June	Railway dispute settled by concession of additional £2.2 million.
14 June	NIRC orders arrest of three TGWU members for contempt of court; dock strike in sympathy spreads to most ports by 16 June. House of Commons votes on the

	crucial clause 2 of the European Communities Bill, which integrates past and future EC law into British law: carried by only 8 votes, with 15 Conservative MPs voting against and 8 abstaining.
16 June	After intervention by the Official Solicitor, the Appeal Court quashes NIRC contempt order; heavy selling of sterling begins.
22 June	1 per cent rise in Bank Rate.
23 June	The £ allowed to float freely.
13 July	European Communities Bill passes third reading by 301 to 284, but 16 Conservative MPs vote against and 4 abstain.
18 July	Resignation of Reginald Maudling as Home Secretary, in connection with the Poulson scandal.
21 July	NIRC gaols five dockers for contempt after their refusal to follow a court order on 7 July; unofficial dock strike begins.
26 July	Intervention of the Official Solicitor on behalf of the imprisoned dockers leads to NIRC ordering their release.
27 July	TGWU special delegate conference rejects the Aldington-Jones report proposals; official national dock strike begins next day.
1 Aug.	White Paper on reorganisation of the National Health Service.
3 Aug.	State of Emergency declared to empower government to move essential goods held up by the dock strike.
4 Aug.	Expulsion of Asian population from Uganda begins.
16 Aug.	Dock strike called off after further proposals by the Aldington-Jones committee.
4 Sep.	TUC resolves to suspend any union which registers under the Industrial Relations Act.
18 Sep.	Main influx of Ugandan Asians: 15,000 refugees admitted between 18 Sep. and 15 Oct.
26 Sep.	Tripartite talks at Chequers with the TUC and CBI begin: the government proposes a prices and incomes policy.
12 Oct.	Heated debate at Conservative Party conference on admission of Ugandan Asians: motion congratulating government on facing its obligations carried by 1,721 to 736.
16 Oct.	First tripartite meeting at Chequers settles general principles of a voluntary prices and incomes policy.

17 Oct.	European Communities Bill receives Royal Assent.
26 Oct.	Liberals win Rochdale by-election from Labour.
30 Oct.	Publication of Green Paper proposals on the future government of Northern Ireland.
2 Nov.	Talks between government, CBI and TUC (in almost continuous progress since 26 Oct.) break up without reaching agreement on repeal of the Industrial Relations Act and control of prices.
5 Nov.	Cabinet reshuffle in which Peter Walker becomes Secretary of State for Trade and Industry and Sir Geoffrey Howe becomes Minister for Trade and Consumer Affairs.
6 Nov.	Government announces a 90-day freeze on wages, prices, rents and dividends; the interval to be used to work out a long-term policy.
8 Nov.	Barber moves second reading of Counter-Inflation (Temporary Provisions) Bill, carried with a majority of 35; no Conservatives vote against, but Powell, Biffen and Bruce-Gardyne abstain.
9 Nov.	Sanctions orders against Rhodesia renewed by 266 votes to 29.
20 Nov.	Third Reading of Counter-Inflation (Temporary Provisions) Bill carried: Powell only Conservative to vote against, Biffen and Bruce-Gardyne abstain.
22 Nov.	Government defeated on proposed immigration rules by 275 to 240 after 7 Conservative MPs vote against and 49 abstain.
6 Dec.	Margaret Thatcher publishes White Paper *Education: A Framework for Expansion* projecting a £1 billion increase in expenditure by 1981, mainly on nursery and higher education.
7 Dec.	Liberal gain safe Conservative seat of Sutton and Cheam with a majority of 7,417.
11 Dec.	Walker announces decision to reverse contraction of coal industry with a package worth up to £1 billion up to March 1976, writing off debt and subsidising the use of coal in power-generation.
18 Dec.	One-day strike by the Amalgamated Union of Engineering Workers in protest at NIRC fine of £50,000 imposed on 8 Dec. for contempt.
21 Dec.	Walker announces 10-year rationalisation and development plan for the steel industry, costing £3 billion.

1973

1 Jan.	Britain formally becomes part of the European Economic Community.
4 Jan.	Announcement of the main features of Phase Two, to take effect on 1 Apr., and of statutory bodies to be set up to oversee this.
16 Jan.	First British delegation of MEPs take their seats in Strasbourg.
17 Jan.	White Paper *The Programme for Controlling Inflation: The Second Stage* published.
23 Jan.	Criticism of economic policy at Conservative back-bench Finance Committee countered by successful speech by Barber.
29 Jan.	Second reading of Counter-Inflation Bill carried with majority of 36; Powell votes against, but no other Conservative MPs rebel or abstain.
31 Jan.	Heath and Home meet with President Nixon in Washington for two days of talks, concluding on 1 Feb.
7 Feb.	Protest strikes in Northern Ireland after the first internment of suspected Protestant terrorists on 5 Feb.
13 Feb.	Civil servants vote for token strikes against Phase Two.
14 Feb.	Gasworkers begin an overtime ban.
20 Feb.	Government defeat in Commons on Local Government (Scotland) Bill, due to 5 Conservatives voting against, leads to survival of Fife as a region.
1 Mar.	Appointments announced of Sir Arthur Cockfield as Chairman of the Price Commission, and Sir Frank Figgures as Chairman of the Pay Board; strike of hospital ancillary workers begins.
6 Mar.	Barber presents a 'neutral' budget containing counter-inflation measures but refusing to cut back public expenditure; Value Added Tax introduced at 10 per cent, but certain items zero-rated.
8 Mar.	Referendum in Northern Ireland on the continuation of partition provides massive majority in favour, by 591,820 to 6,463.
20 Mar.	White Paper *Constitutional Proposals for Northern Ireland* published, proposing 'power-sharing' Assembly with 80 seats, elected by proportional representation.
23 Mar.	Gasworkers end their 'go slow'.
1 Apr.	Phase Two of the prices and incomes freeze comes into

	force, limiting pay rises to £1 per week plus 4 per cent, maximum of £250 p.a.
2 Apr.	Publication of the Northern Ireland (Emergency Provisions) Bill.
4 Apr.	Mortgage rate rises to record 9.5 per cent; government provides £15 million subsidy to prevent further rises for three months.
10 Apr.	Heath at the Guildhall declares union militants are losing support and Phase Two is being accepted as 'a victory for common sense'; Northern Ireland Assembly Bill published.
11 Apr.	On a free vote, restoration of the death penalty defeated by 142.
12 Apr.	Elections for new local government units: Labour win control of the Greater London Council plus 6 of the new metropolitan councils and 11 of other counties.
14 Apr.	£30 million pay offer ends hospital ancillary workers' strike.
16 Apr.	Northern Ireland Assembly Bill given unopposed second reading; Lord Goodman appointed Chairman of both new Housing Corporation and National Building Agency.
1 May	Day of 'national protest and stoppage' called by TUC against prices and incomes policy, but only 1.6 million workers strike.
15 May	Heath comments that the Lonrho remuneration case reveals 'the unpleasant and unacceptable face of capitalism'. Government statistics published indicate boom conditions with industrial production at 9 per cent annual growth rate; next day trade figures show return to surplus on current account after several months in the red.
21 May	Barber announces expenditure cuts of £100 million in current year, rising to £500 million in 1974–75; welcomed by much of Conservative parliamentary party.
22 May	Resignation of Anthony Lambton, Defence Under-Secretary for the Royal Air Force, over 'call girl' scandal.
24 May	Resignation of Lord Jellicoe, Lord Privy Seal, for same reason.
30 May	Local government elections in Northern Ireland.
(May)	Unemployment total falls below the 600,000 level inherited from Labour when the government was elected.
28 June	Elections for the Northern Ireland Assembly.

12 July	Security Commission report on the 'call girl' affair declares that there has been no breach of security.
19 July	Announcement of tax credit scheme to give mothers £2 per week per child, together with tax changes intended to help poorer families.
25 July	White Paper heralding changes in company law to be introduced next session, partly in response to the Lonrho incident.
26 July	Conservatives lose the Ripon and Isle of Ely by-elections to the Liberals.
31 July	Northern Ireland Assembly meets and elects a 'presiding officer', with some Unionist hostility, then adjourns for a month.
31 Aug.	First session of Northern Ireland Assembly ends in uproar after seizure of the floor by Ian Paisley and hardline Unionists.
5 Sep.	TUC conference at Blackpool rejects, by a large majority, motion to boycott the Pay Board and the Downing Street talks on Phase Three.
7 Sep.	Heath affirms the 'national necessity' of containing pay rises.
13 Sep.	Pay Board special report calls for a rigorous ceiling on pay claims aimed at recovering ground lost in Phase One; the Prices Commission approves increased electricity and telephone charges.
14 Sep.	Mortgage rate rises from 10 per cent to new record of 11 per cent.
17 Sep.	Heath pays first visit to Eire of a serving Prime Minister, to meet Irish PM Liam Cosgrave for nine hours of talks near Dublin.
18 Sep.	Heath and senior ministers meet leading figures in the CBI.
24 Sep.	Lord Rothschild strikes a pessimistic note in a public speech, leading to public and private rebukes from Heath.
6 Oct.	Outbreak in Middle East of Arab–Israeli 'Yom Kippur' War (to 22 Oct.).
8 Oct.	Publication of the consultative document on Phase Three of the counter-inflation policy.
11 Oct.	At the Conservative annual conference, a motion for restoring the death penalty is carried against the wishes of the platform.

16 Oct. Home announces embargo on supply of weapons or military equipment to both sides in Arab–Israeli War; criticised as being pro-Arab in effect.

22 Oct. Amalgamated Union of Engineering Workers fined £75,000 for contempt of court by NIRC.

23 Oct. Maplin Development Bill authorising £1 billion to construct the third London airport passed after much controversy.

30 Oct. Heath announces the content of Phase Three.

31 Oct. Report of Royal Commission on the Constitution, chaired by Lord Kilbrandon.

1 Nov. Phase Three comes into effect for prices.

7 Nov. Phase Three for wages limits rises to £2.25 per week, or 7 per cent.

8 Nov. Rhodesia sanctions order renewed without serious dissent by 133–26; Liberals win the Berwick-upon-Tweed by-election, Scottish National Party gain Govan from Labour.

12 Nov. Miners' overtime ban begins.

13 Nov. State of Emergency declared due to energy crisis: restrictions on heat and lighting, television broadcasts to end at 10.30 p.m. Publication of monthly balance of payments figure reveals worst-ever trade gap of £298 million; Barber announces emergency credit squeeze, Bank rate rises to 13 per cent.

16 Nov. Figures show that in Oct. food prices rose by 3.3 per cent, the largest monthly rise for 18 years, putting the annual rate at almost 10 per cent.

19 Nov. Censure debate on the economic crisis, Conservative dissidents press for substantial expenditure cuts; Walker announces 10 per cent cut in fuel and petrol supplies due to the Arab–Israeli War.

20 Nov. Walker introduces the Fuel and Electricity (Control) Bill to extend government powers of control; government majority falls to 6 on introduction of admission charges for national museums.

21 Nov. NUM national executive rejects a revised pay offer from the National Coal Board.

22 Nov. Heath publicly warns the miners that the government cannot surrender to their demands; after complex negotiations, Whitelaw announces a power-sharing Northern Ireland Executive Council to consist of 6 Unionist rep-

	resentatives, 4 Social Democratic and Labour Party and 1 Alliance.
26 Nov.	Walker announces issuing of petrol rationing books will begin by post on 29 Nov., in case they are needed.
28 Nov.	Railways programme worth £900 million over 5 years announced; Heath and NUM leaders meet at Downing Street, without agreement, and miners decide to go ahead with an overtime ban.
2 Dec.	Cabinet reshuffle: Whitelaw moved to Employment, Pym to Northern Ireland.
3 Dec.	Railway drivers' union ASLEF rejects British Railways offer of 12 per cent as inadequate, starts overtime ban from 12 Dec.
6 Dec.	*Financial Times* share index shows a record fall in one morning of 19.7 points; *Times*/ITN poll gives Conservatives 40 per cent, Labour 35 per cent, Liberals 23 per cent.
6–9 Dec.	Tripartite talks at the Civil Service College, Sunningdale, between British and Irish governments and Northern Ireland party leaders, reach agreement on the formation of an overall Council of Ireland.
11 Dec.	First cuts in electricity supplies.
12 Dec.	Renewal of the State of Emergency.
13 Dec.	Heath announces the 'three-day week' to take effect from 31 Dec.; businesses permitted to open on only 5 of the days between 17 and 31 Dec.
14–15 Dec.	EC heads of state summit, Copenhagen.
17 Dec.	Barber 'mini-budget' cuts expenditure plans by £1,200 million by 1974–75.
19 Dec.	Publication of the Companies Bill.
28 Dec.	Settlement of the power workers' dispute.

1974

1 Jan.	The 'three-day week' takes effect; Brian Faulkner takes up office as Chief Executive of new Northern Ireland power-sharing executive.
8 Jan.	Lord Carrington moved to head a new Department of Energy.
9 Jan.	Parliament reconvened for an emergency debate on the crisis. TUC leaders offer at National Economic Develop-

ment Council meeting not to use any miners' settlement as a precedent for other claims.

10 Jan. ASLEF leaders decide to begin strikes of one day each week.

14 Jan. Talks between Heath and TUC leaders at Downing Street fail to find a means of settling the miners' dispute.

15 Jan. Gordon Richardson, Governor of the Bank of England, forecasts that 'years of economic austerity' lie ahead; first one-day stoppage by train drivers.

21 Jan. TUC leaders offer not to regard a generous settlement of the miners' dispute as a precedent for claims by other unions.

24 Jan. Publication of government-appointed Pay Board's general report on relativities, which some argue could provide a means to resolve the miners' pay claim.

4 Feb. Final breakdown of efforts to settle the coal dispute.

5 Feb. NUM executive call all-out strike to begin on 9 Feb.

7 Feb. Heath announces dissolution of Parliament; party strength at dissolution is 322 Conservative MPs (including 7 remaining Ulster Unionists), 297 Labour, 11 Liberals, 2 Scottish National Party, 8 others.

15 Feb. Retail price index shows rise in food prices of 20 per cent during previous year.

23 Feb. Enoch Powell speaking at Birmingham strongly attacks Heath.

25 Feb. Trade figures for January show record deficit of £383 million gap in visible trade.

26 Feb. Campbell Adamson, CBI director-general, calls for repeal of the Industrial Relations Act.

28 Feb. *Polling day*: 297 Conservatives elected, 301 Labour, 14 Liberals, 9 Welsh and Scottish Nationalists, and 14 others (12 from Ulster); note: new Parliament consists of 635 MPs rather than previous 630.

2 Mar. Heath meets Thorpe and invites Liberals to join in a coalition.

3 Mar. Thorpe consults other leading Liberals, and returns to tell Heath shortly before midnight that the proposal has been rejected; Heath offers an inquiry into forms of proportional representation.

4 Mar. Meeting of Liberal MPs rejects offer of coalition; Heath resigns as Prime Minister that evening and Harold Wilson accepts office.

APPENDIX

The Heath cabinet 1970–74

The Prime Minister took office on 19 June 1970 and resigned on 4 March 1974. The members of the Cabinet during this period were:

Office or Department	*Name*	*Appointed*
Prime Minister	Edward Heath	19 June 1970
Chancellor of the Exchequer	Iain Macleod Anthony Barber	20 June 1970 25 July 1970
Foreign Secretary	Sir Alec Douglas-Home	20 June 1970
Home Secretary	Reginald Maudling Robert Carr	20 June 1970 18 July 1972
Lord President of the Council	William Whitelaw Robert Carr James Prior	20 June 1970 7 April 1972 5 November 1972
Lord Chancellor	Lord Hailsham	20 June 1970
Lord Privy Seal	Earl Jellicoe Lord Windlesham	20 June 1970 5 June 1973
Agriculture, Fisheries and Food	James Prior Joseph Godber	20 June 1970 5 November 1972
Defence	Lord Carrington Ian Gilmour	20 June 1970 8 January 1974
Duchy of Lancaster	Anthony Barber Geoffrey Rippon John Davies	20 June 1970 28 July 1970 5 November 1972
Education and Science	Margaret Thatcher	20 June 1970

Employment (and Productivity, until 12 November 1970)	Robert Carr Maurice Macmillan William Whitelaw	20 June 1970 7 April 1972 2 December 1973
Energy	Lord Carrington	8 January 1974
Environment	Peter Walker Geoffrey Rippon	15 October 1970 5 November 1972
Health and Social Security	Sir Keith Joseph	20 June 1970
Housing and Local Government (absorbed into new Department of the Environment, 15 October 1970)	Peter Walker	20 June 1970
Northern Ireland	William Whitelaw Francis Pym	24 March 1972 2 December 1973
Paymaster-General (office previously not in cabinet)	Maurice Macmillan	2 December 1973
Scotland	Gordon Campbell	20 June 1970
Technology (absorbed into new Department of Trade and Industry, 15 October 1970)	Geoffrey Rippon John Davies	20 June 1970 28 July 1970
Trade (absorbed into new Department of Trade and Industry, 15 October 1970)	Michael Noble	20 June 1970
Trade and Industry	John Davies Peter Walker	15 October 1970 5 November 1972
Trade and Consumer Affairs	Sir Geoffrey Howe	5 November 1972
Wales	Peter Thomas	20 June 1970

Other Government and Party offices of importance were held as follows (in some cases, these were combined with cabinet positions listed above):

Office	*Name*	*Appointed*
Attorney-General	Sir Peter Rawlinson	23 June 1970
Solicitor-General	Sir Geoffrey Howe	23 June 1970
	Sir Michael Havers	5 November 1972
Chief Whip	Francis Pym	20 June 1970
	Humphrey Atkins	2 December 1973
Chairman of the Conservative Party	Anthony Barber	11 September 1967
	Peter Thomas	31 July 1970
	Lord Carrington	7 April 1972
	William Whitelaw	11 June 1974
Leader of the Party in the Lords	Earl Jellicoe	20 June 1970
	Lord Windlesham	5 June 1973
	Lord Carrington	28 October 1974

INDEX